Diplomacy by Design

Asad Ullah

Diplomacy by Design

China's Belt and Road Initiative and the Reordering of the Middle East

palgrave
macmillan

Asad Ullah
Shandong University
Qingdao, China

ISBN 978-981-95-7875-7 ISBN 978-981-95-7876-4 (eBook)
https://doi.org/10.1007/978-981-95-7876-4

This Palgrave Macmillan imprint is published by the registered company Springer Nature Singapore Pte Ltd.
The registered company address is: 152 Beach Road, #21-01/04 Gateway East, Singapore 189721, Singapore

The supreme art of war is to subdue the enemy without fighting.

—Sun Tzu, The Art of War

To my mom and dad—my first teachers, my constant inspiration, and the quiet strength behind every page of this book.

Preface

Researching and teaching international politics in the twenty-first century means confronting a world that is itself unsettled and in transition. Living and working in China, while engaging closely with colleagues and interlocutors from across the Middle East, has given me a vantage point that is both proximate and comparative. I have not walked the streets of Riyadh or Tehran, nor sat in the ministries of Cairo or Abu Dhabi, but I have spent countless hours in dialogue with scholars, researchers, and practitioners from those places. These conversations, sometimes formal, often informal, have been as revealing as any field visit. They have shown me how the region sees itself, how it interprets China's growing presence, and how it imagines its future.

The Middle East is often described as a region of crises, but what struck me in these exchanges was not only the persistence of conflict but the intensity of future-building. Scholars from Saudi Arabia spoke of NEOM not merely as a megacity but as a symbol of transformation, a deliberate attempt to leapfrog into a post-oil era. Iranian colleagues emphasized resilience, the capacity to endure sanctions and isolation while still seeking external partnerships. Emirati and Egyptian interlocutors highlighted logistics, ports, and digital platforms as the new arteries of relevance in a global economy. These were not abstract discussions. They were grounded in the lived realities of scholars who, while working within their own national contexts, were acutely aware of the structural shifts reshaping the region.

From my position in China, these conversations resonated with what I was observing around me. The Belt and Road Initiative was not a distant slogan; it was a lived reality, visible in policy documents, academic debates, and the physical infrastructures being built across Asia. Chinese colleagues spoke of connectivity not as a metaphor but as a strategy. They described ports, railways, and digital corridors as instruments of engagement, designed to embed China into the economic and logistical foundations of partner states. The language was technical, but the implications were unmistakably strategic.

It was in the intersection of these two vantage points: China's outward gaze and the Middle East's inward recalibration, that the idea for this book took shape. I began to see that what was unfolding was not simply a story of investment or development. It was a story of design: of how infrastructures are deliberately placed, sequenced, and embedded to create durable interdependencies. It was also a story of ambiguity: of how China managed to engage adversarial states simultaneously, embedding itself in both sides of rivalries without demanding exclusivity or provoking resistance.

The concept I developed here: Designed Strategic Interdependence (DSI), is my attempt to capture this logic. It is not a theory of harmony, nor a celebration of connectivity. It is a framework for understanding how influence is constructed in subtle, infrastructural ways. DSI suggests that power today is less about commanding from above than about designing the environments within which others must act. It is about creating dependencies that are not easily undone, embedding presence in ways that outlast political cycles, and sequencing engagement so that each step deepens the next.

Although many books have been written about the Belt and Road Initiative, most either treat it as a sweeping narrative of Chinese grand strategy or as a catalogue of infrastructure projects scattered across continents. What is often missing is a sustained analysis of how the BRI operates in regions of entrenched rivalry, where influence cannot be secured through alliances or coercion. The Middle East provides precisely such a test case. This book, therefore, takes the region as a whole—tracing China's engagements from the Gulf to the Levant and North Africa—but its primary focus rests on Saudi Arabia and Iran. These two states, locked in a rivalry that has long defined the regional order, are also the sites where China's infrastructural diplomacy is most visible and most consequential. By examining how Beijing embeds itself simultaneously in both

Riyadh's future-building projects and Tehran's resilience strategies, the book shows why the BRI in the Middle East is not simply additive to existing dynamics but transformative of them.

This book is therefore both analytical and personal. It is analytical in that it seeks to provide a rigorous framework for understanding China's role in the Middle East, grounded in comparative insights and informed by international relations theory. But it is also personal in that it reflects my own journey as a scholar: the challenge of navigating Chinese academic institutions, the privilege of engaging with Middle Eastern colleagues, and the intellectual excitement of trying to make sense of a world in motion.

Teaching has been central to this journey. In the classroom, I encountered students who were grappling with the same puzzles that animated my research. They asked why China was investing in Saudi Arabia's futuristic projects while simultaneously deepening ties with Iran. They wondered how digital platforms could become instruments of diplomacy, or how renewable energy could be leveraged as a tool of strategic influence. Their questions pushed me to clarify my arguments, to translate abstract concepts into accessible language, and to connect theory with practice. In many ways, this book is an extension of those classroom conversations, written not only for specialists but for anyone seeking to understand how power is being redefined.

The process of writing was shaped by dialogue. Workshops with colleagues in China forced me to situate my arguments within broader debates about global order and multipolarity. Conversations with Middle Eastern scholars reminded me that infrastructure is never neutral—it is always political, always contested. Exchanges with international peers highlighted the need to move beyond simplistic binaries of "development" versus "geopolitics," and to recognize how the two are intertwined. These interactions were not always easy. They often revealed tensions, disagreements, and blind spots. But they were essential in sharpening the book's arguments and ensuring that it speaks across disciplines and regions.

This book is not the final word on China's Belt and Road Initiative in the Middle East. The infrastructures I describe are still being built, the alignments I analyze are still in flux, and the theories I propose will no doubt be tested by events yet to come. But I hope it offers a framework that is useful not only for understanding China's role in the Middle East, but for thinking more broadly about the future of diplomacy in a world where influence is embedded, designed, and quietly transformative.

I am deeply grateful to the scholars from across the Middle East who shared their insights with me, often generously and candidly. Their perspectives enriched this book immeasurably, even if they do not always agree with my interpretations. I am equally indebted to my colleagues in China, whose debates and critiques pushed me to refine my arguments. And I am thankful to my students, whose curiosity and skepticism reminded me that the purpose of scholarship is not only to explain the world but to inspire others to see it differently.

This book is offered in that spirit: as a contribution to an ongoing conversation about power, diplomacy, and the infrastructures that shape our collective future.

Qingdao, China Asad Ullah

Acknowledgments This book emerged from years of dialogue, debate, and intellectual exchange across institutions, regions, and disciplines. I am grateful to everyone who contributed to its development, though I alone bear responsibility for its arguments and any shortcomings.

At Shandong University, I have been fortunate to work within a department that values rigorous inquiry and encourages interdisciplinary engagement. My colleagues in the Department of Political Science and Public Administration provided the intellectual environment within which this project took shape. Their questions sharpened my thinking, their critiques forced me to strengthen weak arguments, and their encouragement sustained me through the inevitable challenges of long-term research.

This book has been profoundly shaped by conversations with scholars from across the Middle East. Colleagues from Saudi Arabia, Iran, the UAE, Egypt, and elsewhere generously shared their perspectives on regional transformations, from energy transitions to digital infrastructures to geopolitical realignments. These exchanges, conducted over conferences, workshops, and countless informal discussions, provided insights that no document or dataset could replicate. Their willingness to engage candidly with my arguments, even when skeptical of my conclusions, enriched the analysis immeasurably. I hope this book honors their expertise, even where we disagree.

I owe special thanks to Ms. Fengzhu, whose intellectual partnership has been invaluable throughout this project. She read multiple drafts with extraordinary care, challenged my assumptions with precision, and pushed me to clarify ideas that remained muddled in early versions. I am also deeply grateful to Mr. Rachid Adamou Sirifo and Mr. Ahmad Nurcholis, who read early drafts of individual chapters and offered incisive feedback that improved both the theoretical framing and empirical substance.

Workshops and conferences provided crucial opportunities to test the book's core claims. Colleagues working on international security, infrastructure politics, energy geopolitics, and Chinese foreign policy offered constructive criticism that pushed me to refine the framework of Designed Strategic Interdependence and situate it within broader debates about power, influence, and regional order. These exchanges reminded me that scholarship advances through dialogue and contestation, not through isolated research.

Finally, I wish to thank my family. To my parents, whose sacrifices made my education possible and whose unwavering belief in me sustained this long journey, I owe more than words can express. Their love and encouragement gave me the strength to see this project through.

All errors, omissions, and misinterpretations remain entirely my own.

Competing Interests The author has no competing interests to declare that are relevant to the content of this manuscript.

Contents

List of Figures

List of Tables

Chapter 7

CHAPTER 1

From Periphery to Pivot: China's Diplomacy by Design in the Middle East

The Middle East stands at a decisive moment. For more than seven decades, the region has been the testing ground for competing visions of global order: American containment of Soviet influence during the Cold War, the unipolar moment of American dominance following 1991, and now the uncertain multipolarity of the twenty-first century. Yet conventional narratives about Middle Eastern geopolitics have obscured a fundamental transformation occurring beneath the constant churn of crises. The region is no longer simply an arena for great power competition defined by military bases, security alliances, and ideological confrontation. It is increasingly a space where influence operates through infrastructure corridors, energy supply chains, technological systems, and patient capital deployment. This shift is not incidental to the global order; it is constitutive of it.

For decades, analysts and policymakers approached the Middle East through a prism of American primacy. The question was not whether the United States would lead but how effectively it would exercise that leadership. The Soviet challenge during the Cold War was containable; regional actors could be managed through security guarantees and military aid; regional conflicts could be mediated through American diplomatic pressure backed by credible military might. This framework, while never perfectly accurate, organized how scholars and policymakers understood the region.

A. Ullah, *Diplomacy by Design*,
https://doi.org/10.1007/978-981-95-7876-4_1

This assumption is no longer tenable. Not because American power has disappeared, the United States remains the world's most powerful military force with bases dotting the region and security commitments anchoring regional alignments. But American preponderance no longer translates automatically into comprehensive influence. New forms of power have emerged that do not rely on military dominance. Economic centrality, infrastructure embedding, technological standards, and long-term financial commitments can generate influence as durable and consequential as military alliances. They operate through different mechanisms, create different constituencies, and embed themselves through different institutional channels.

China's rise in the Middle East exemplifies this transformation. It is neither a simple story of replacement, with Beijing displacing Washington through superior power, nor one of marginal addition, China as merely another commercial actor. It is instead a story of a different kind of power emerging, one that reshapes the regional landscape through mechanisms unfamiliar to analysts trained to focus on military capabilities and alliance commitments. To understand this transformation requires moving beyond traditional frameworks and developing new conceptual tools capable of capturing how influence actually operates in contemporary international relations.

The people living in the Middle East are not merely passive subjects of great power strategies. They are active agents making choices about which partnerships to cultivate, how to leverage great power competition for domestic purposes, and how to navigate between competing external pressures. Understanding China's rise in the region, therefore, requires not only analyzing Beijing's strategies but also examining how Middle Eastern actors shape outcomes. Saudi policymakers are not helpless victims of Chinese engagement but sophisticated actors managing multiple great power relationships simultaneously. Iranian leaders are not simply adapting to Chinese dominance but actively deploying the Chinese partnership to advance their own interests and resist American pressure. Egyptian officials are not passively receiving Chinese infrastructure but deliberately integrating it into development plans they have themselves designed. Regional agency matters enormously for how this story unfolds.

This broader context helps explain why the moment in March 2023, when Saudi and Iranian officials clasped hands in Beijing to restore diplomatic relations after 7 years of estrangement, carried significance well beyond the bilateral rift it formally addressed. The agreement, brokered quietly by Chinese diplomats over months of patient facilitation, did not simply resolve bilateral differences between two historical rivals. Rather, it signaled a fundamental shift in Middle Eastern geopolitics. China, long peripheral to the region's security architecture, had acquired sufficient diplomatic credibility and structural leverage to convene the two states most central to Gulf stability. For many observers, the handshake epitomized a deeper transformation—the movement of China from an outsider at the margins of Middle Eastern affairs into an indispensable diplomatic and economic actor capable of reshaping regional alignments.

Yet this moment was not an abrupt pivot but rather the culmination of decades of evolving engagement. From Maoist solidarity with anti-colonial struggles in the 1950s, through the energy-driven pragmatism of the 1980s and 1990s, to the sprawling infrastructure and trade initiatives of the Belt and Road era, China's presence in the region has grown quietly but relentlessly. What began as symbolic gestures of revolutionary solidarity has matured into complex webs of trade, investment, and institutional interdependence. The 2023 Saudi–Iran accords merely dramatized a trajectory that had been unfolding for decades, one constructed through deliberate architectural choices about how influence should be exercised and embedded.

This chapter makes three arguments. First, China's transformation from periphery to pivot represents neither opportunistic expansion nor the inevitable consequence of economic growth, but rather a systematically designed strategy of statecraft. Whether this design emerged from a master plan conceived in the 1990s or from institutional learning across state actors matters less than recognizing its coherence by the BRI era. By the 2010s, Chinese engagement exhibited clear patterns of coordination across ministries, state-owned enterprises, and policy banks patterns suggesting deliberate statecraft rather than accumulated accident.

Second, this strategy operates through a distinctive mechanism: Designed Strategic Interdependence (DSI). DSI functions across four dimensions—spatial, diplomatic, normative, and temporal—deploying three interlocking mechanisms: infrastructure-first engagement that embeds Chinese technical standards within host economies; energy interdependence that creates mutual vulnerabilities binding both parties together; and strategic patience that allows Beijing to cultivate relationships across regional rivalries without becoming entangled in zero-sum competitions. Taken together, these mechanisms make China difficult to dislodge from positions of influence once established, while creating legitimate benefits for all parties involved.

Third, this model reveals both possibilities and limits. DSI enables China to establish economic centrality without military dominance, but economic leverage does not automatically translate into political compliance. Regional states retain significant autonomy, and American military preponderance persists. The result is not Chinese hegemony replacing American dominance but rather a differentiated multipolarity in which economic and military power operate through distinct channels. Understanding this differentiation is essential for grasping how contemporary great power competition actually functions.

The chapter proceeds in four steps. Section 2 introduces the DSI framework, explaining its theoretical foundations and operational mechanisms. Section 3 traces China's historical evolution in the Middle East across five periods, showing how today's systematic engagement emerged from decades of accumulated learning. Section 4 previews the book's two central cases Saudi Arabia and Iran, demonstrating how DSI adapts to radically different political contexts. Section 5 examines the constraints limiting Chinese influence, situating achievements within persistent asymmetries. The conclusion synthesizes the argument and maps the book's analytical journey through subsequent chapters.

1 Diplomacy by Design: Analytical Framework

The Concept and its Logic

The framework advanced in this book conceptualizes China's engagement in the Middle East as ***diplomacy by design***: the deliberate construction of economic, technological, and financial interdependencies through which influence is embedded within the political economies of other states. This approach differs fundamentally from traditional models of great power influence, which emphasize military alliance-building, security guarantees, and coercive statecraft. Instead, it privileges the creation of mutual dependencies that make alternative arrangements progressively more costly and complicated for all parties involved, thereby constraining future choices while creating present benefits.

The question of intentionality—whether this represents conscious strategic planning or adaptive learning—requires careful handling. Chinese policy documents from the 1990s show no evidence of a master plan to dominate Middle Eastern infrastructure. Yet by the BRI era (2013 onward), the patterns are unmistakable: systematic coordination between the Ministry of Foreign Affairs, National Development and Reform Commission, state-owned enterprises, and policy banks; consistent deployment of similar instruments (infrastructure financing, technical standards, operational protocols) across diverse countries; and accumulated institutional knowledge about what works in different political contexts.

This book argues that whether design emerged from foresight or hindsight matters less than recognizing its systematic character by the 2010s. Even if Chinese engagement began opportunistically—filling gaps left by Western withdrawal, responding to energy scarcity—it evolved into something more deliberate. Institutions learned. Patterns solidified. Coordination improved. By the time Xi Jinping announced the BRI, Chinese statecraft exhibited sufficient coherence to warrant analysis as designed strategy rather than accumulated accident. The relevant distinction is not between "master plan" and "muddling through" but between random commercial activity and systematized statecraft. China's Middle East engagement clearly falls in.

Diplomacy by design draws on three theoretical foundations, though it integrates them in distinctive ways. First, it engages analyses of *structural power* in international political economy: the concept that influence operates not merely through direct coercion or negotiation but through the organization of systems themselves. When China constructs a port using Chinese specifications and deploys Chinese operating protocols, it does not dominate through threats. Rather, it embeds itself within the functioning of critical infrastructure. Over time, the path dependencies created by these technical choices constrain the alternatives available to host governments. The ongoing requirement for Chinese expertise, spare parts, and technical support creates persistent leverage that does not depend on active enforcement but rather on the logic of technological systems.

Second, the framework incorporates insights from *interdependence theory*, yet with important modifications. Classical dependency theory, developed to explain relationships between wealthy industrialized states and resource-dependent developing countries, emphasized asymmetrical relationships in which powerful states subordinate weaker ones through economic mechanisms. Yet China's approach is more sophisticated: it creates mutual vulnerabilities that bind both parties together. China depends on Middle Eastern energy supplies; Middle Eastern states depend on Chinese markets, financing, and technical expertise. This mutual vulnerability constrains coercive options for all parties and encourages long-term partnership over short-term extraction of maximum advantage.

What distinguishes DSI from conventional interdependence is its architectural character. Normal interdependence emerges organically from trade, investment, and exchange. DSI, by contrast, involves deliberate construction of dependencies through infrastructure choices, technical standards, and institutional frameworks that embed one party's presence within another's economy. A country trading oil for manufactured goods experiences interdependence. A country whose ports operate on Chinese software, whose railways use Chinese signaling systems, and whose power plants require Chinese maintenance experiences designed interdependence. The former can be redirected relatively easily; the latter creates switching costs and path dependencies that persist across decades.

Third, the framework highlights the workings of *soft power*, understood as the ability of a state to shape preferences, norms, and operational habits through attraction, influence, and the quiet pull of partnership. When Saudi Arabia adopts Chinese industrial standards, when Iran incorporates Chinese technology into vital infrastructure, or when the UAE designs its logistics systems around Chinese models, the effect is not merely technical alignment. It reflects the persuasive appeal of China's developmental approach and the subtle authority that accompanies it. Over time, such choices cultivate familiarity, confidence, and comfort with Chinese practices, making them the intuitive reference point even when other options remain available.

Diplomacy by design is not manipulation or coercion, though it can shade toward coercion under certain circumstances. It is the strategic orchestration of economic structures, technological systems, and financial mechanisms in ways that advantage the designer while creating legitimate benefits for other parties. It is power exercised not through domination but through the creation of mutually beneficial arrangements that, over time, increase the structural dependence of all participants on the system itself and on the actor who designed it.

Designed Strategic Interdependence: The Four Dimensions

DSI operates across four interrelated dimensions that together produce durable influence. These dimensions are not separate strategies but interlocking logics that reinforce one another.

Spatial Design refers to the physical embedding of infrastructure, technology, and operational systems within partner states. Chinese-built ports, railways, industrial zones, and telecommunications networks do not merely facilitate economic activity—they establish material dependencies. Ports designed for Chinese container specifications, railways operating on Chinese signaling systems, and telecommunications networks running Chinese software create technical lock-in. Maintenance requires Chinese expertise; upgrades require Chinese components; and expansion requires Chinese financing. These spatial dependencies accumulate over time, making alternative arrangements increasingly costly.

Diplomatic Design involves the construction of institutional frameworks that regularize engagement and create expectations of continuity. Bilateral agreements, joint commissions, working groups, and strategic partnerships establish routines of cooperation. The 25-year Comprehensive Strategic Partnership with Iran, for example, does not legally bind China to specific commitments, but it signals long-term engagement and creates institutional channels through which routine cooperation occurs. These frameworks reduce uncertainty, facilitate coordination, and embed expectations that relationships will endure despite political turbulence.

Normative Design shapes the principles and discourses legitimizing cooperation. By emphasizing sovereignty, non-interference, mutual benefit, and development-first engagement, China positions its partnerships as respectful alternatives to Western conditionality. This normative framing appeals to states weary of human rights scrutiny or governance reforms attached to Western aid. It also provides political cover for deepening economic ties with Beijing. Regional governments can defend Chinese partnerships domestically by invoking principles of sovereignty and autonomous development. These norms do not determine behavior, but they shape how partnerships are publicly justified and politically defended.

Temporal Design reflects strategic patience and sequential deployment of initiatives. Rather than demanding immediate political alignment, China builds relationships incrementally. Initial infrastructure projects demonstrate competence and reliability. Energy contracts create commercial interdependence. Technology transfer builds institutional familiarity. Over time, these layered commitments accumulate into comprehensive partnerships that prove difficult to unwind. Temporal design also allows China to wait out political crises without abandoning partners, reinforcing perceptions of reliability compared to Western powers that withdraw during instability Table 1.

These four dimensions interact dynamically. Spatial embedding (infrastructure) requires diplomatic frameworks (agreements) legitimized through normative discourse (sovereignty) and deployed sequentially (patience). DSI's power lies not in any single dimension but in their cumulative reinforcement. A country might exit one Chinese infrastructure project, but when dozens of projects span multiple sectors, when institutional frameworks regularize cooperation, when norms justify partnership, and when decades of sequential engagement have built trust, exit becomes progressively harder.

Three Mechanisms of DSI

This book identifies three principal mechanisms through which China constructs DSI in the Middle East. These mechanisms operationalize the four dimensions described above, translating abstract design principles into concrete practices.

Infrastructure-First Diplomacy represents the primary vector of Chinese influence and the most visible component of the BRI in the Middle East. Rather than leading with security guarantees or formal political alignment, Beijing deploys state-owned enterprises backed by policy banks to construct ports, railways, industrial zones, power plants, and telecommunication networks. These projects deliver immediate material benefits employment opportunities, prestige from visible development progress, and technological modernization, while simultaneously embedding Chinese firms, standards, and technologies into host economies.

What distinguishes infrastructure-first diplomacy from conventional infrastructure investment is its explicit integration with long-term strategic objectives. Chinese engineering specifications ensure compatibility with Chinese equipment; operational procedures require Chinese technical expertise; and maintenance and upgrades necessitate ongoing Chinese involvement. Over decades, these discrete projects coalesce into systemic integration that makes alternative arrangements increasingly

Table 1 The four dimensions of DSI

DSI dimension	*Mechanism*	*Observable indicators*	*Causal logic*	*Constraints*
Spatial	Infrastructure embedding	Host country adopts Chinese technical standards in >50% of major projects; Chinese firms hold long-term operation/ maintenance contracts	Technical lock-in creates switching costs; path dependency makes alternatives expensive	Requires partner willingness to cede technical sovereignty; vulnerable to political backlash if perceived as exploitative
Diplomatic	Institutional frameworks	Bilateral agreements establish joint commissions; regular high-level visits; strategic partnership declarations	Routinization reduces uncertainty; creates expectations of continuity	Frameworks lack enforcement mechanisms; can be suspended during crises
Normative	Principled engagement	Official discourse emphasizes sovereignty, non-interference, mutual benefit; minimal governance conditionality	Legitimizes partnerships domestically; provides political cover for deepening ties	Norms can ring hollow if practices contradict them; limited appeal where human rights matter domestically
Temporal	Strategic patience	China maintains engagement during partner's isolation (e.g., Iran under sanctions); incremental project deployment over decades	Reliability builds trust; sequential commitments accumulate into comprehensive partnerships	Patience requires tolerating partner behavior China dislikes; slow payoffs test domestic political support

costly. A government cannot simply switch to alternative suppliers without incurring enormous switching costs; technological dependencies create path lock-in that persists across political administrations and changing preferences.

Yet infrastructure-first diplomacy faces limits. It requires partner governments willing to accept Chinese technical standards and operational control, which can trigger nationalist backlash if perceived as neo-colonial. Projects concentrated in authoritarian regimes risk reputational damage if those regimes face legitimacy crises. Infrastructure also locks China into long-term commitments in volatile regions, if a railway becomes a target in civil conflict, or if a port loses commercial viability due to regional instability, Chinese investments become liabilities. Finally, infrastructure creates influence over economic decisions but rarely translates directly into political compliance on foreign policy issues unrelated to the projects themselves.

In Saudi Arabia, this approach has aligned seamlessly with Vision 2030 ambitions, with projects including industrial cities, renewable energy ventures, and metro systems functioning as integral components of Riyadh's broader transformation. The Riyadh Metro exemplifies these dynamics. It serves as more than urban transport, it embodies comprehensive transplantation of Chinese urban planning principles, integrating smart city technologies, unified payment systems, and data-driven management mechanisms that mirror Chinese models of urban governance. When Saudi officials visit Beijing or Shanghai to study best practices, they encounter systems that correspond directly with infrastructure being implemented domestically, generating feedback loops that perpetuate Chinese influence long after initial construction is completed.

In Iran, the same principle operates under entirely different conditions. Sanctions have constrained Western firms, leaving infrastructure gaps that Chinese entities are uniquely positioned to fill. Railways connecting industrial zones, energy pipelines, and urban development projects funded or constructed by Chinese firms offer Tehran lifelines during periods of isolation. The Tehran–Isfahan high-speed rail project links Iran's political center to its industrial heartland through Chinese technology, financing, and construction expertise. More significantly, the railway incorporates Chinese signaling systems, rolling stock, and maintenance protocols, thereby establishing long-term technological dependencies that will endure for generations.

Energy Interdependence constitutes the second pillar, yet extends far beyond simple buyer–seller relationships. China's transformation to a petroleum importer created a structural requirement for reliable Gulf supplies, but contemporary energy partnerships transcend conventional commodity exchange. Chinese national oil companies have evolved into fully integrated partners within Middle Eastern energy sectors, participating in upstream exploration, midstream processing, and downstream refining. This vertical integration generates multiple layers of connection and mutual exposure, making relationships increasingly difficult to disentangle.

The partnership between Saudi Aramco and Chinese energy enterprises exemplifies this transformation. Joint ventures in refining, petrochemicals, and renewable energy cultivate shared strategic interests extending far beyond commodity trade. Aramco's investments in Chinese refineries, most notably the large complex in Liaoning Province, represent long-term commitments to partnership. These facilities are designed specifically to refine Saudi crude, creating technical interdependencies that would be prohibitively costly and time-consuming to reproduce with alternative suppliers.

Energy interdependence, however, does not guarantee political alignment. Saudi Arabia's dependence on Chinese markets has not prevented Riyadh from maintaining close security ties with Washington or pursuing regional policies Beijing finds unhelpful. Iran's reliance on Chinese oil purchases has not stopped Tehran from regional interventions that complicate China's preference for stability. Energy creates leverage, but converting that leverage into political compliance requires credible threats to withdraw—threats China rarely makes because disrupting energy flows would harm its own interests. Mutual dependence constrains both parties, limiting coercive options even as it deepens interdependence.

In Iran, energy interdependence operates under the shadow of sanctions, creating asymmetries that complicate the relationship while making it indispensable for both sides. Tehran has relied heavily on China as a buyer of crude, often through discounted or opaque arrangements. Chinese purchases of Iranian oil during sanctions periods have provided Tehran with crucial revenue, estimated at billions of dollars annually. However, these transactions typically occur at significant discounts to market prices and often involve barter arrangements or payments in Chinese currency, limiting Iran's financial flexibility while enhancing China's leverage.

Chinese investments in Iran's energy sector add additional layers of complexity. Participation in the development of the South Pars gas field, investments in oil infrastructure, and technology transfer arrangements bind the two countries together across multiple dimensions. These relationships often involve Chinese companies taking equity stakes in Iranian projects, creating shared interests in the success of Iranian energy development while giving Beijing influence over strategic resource decisions.

Calibrated Political Engagement and Strategic Equidistance comprise the third pillar, representing perhaps the most sophisticated element of China's approach. Rather than attempting to replicate American patterns of alliance-building and security provision, Beijing has crafted a distinctive model of engagement that maximizes economic opportunities while minimizing political risks. This differentiated engagement maintains multiple partnerships while calibrating the intensity and focus of each relationship according to strategic priorities and practical constraints.

Beijing has cultivated a willingness to expand ties gradually, avoid military entanglement, and maintain relations across rivalries that would normally be considered mutually exclusive in traditional great power competition. In a region where alignment has historically been binary—either Western-aligned or Soviet/Russian-aligned—China has positioned itself as a partner to multiple sides simultaneously. It buys oil from Saudi Arabia while investing in Iran, signs technology deals with the UAE while deepening trade with Turkey, and courts both Egypt and Israel.

Strategic equidistance carries costs. By refusing to choose sides, China forgoes the deeper influence that comes from exclusive partnerships and security guarantees. Saudi Arabia values Chinese economic engagement but ultimately relies on American military protection, limiting how far Riyadh will align with Beijing. Iran accepts Chinese investment but resents Beijing's unwillingness to provide political backing against American pressure. Critics argue this reflects passivity rather than strategy, a reluctance to assume the burdens of great power responsibility. Yet equidistance also offers distinct advantages: it allowed China to mediate Saudi–Iran rapprochement precisely because Beijing had maintained credibility with both sides.

China's ability to mediate between Saudi Arabia and Iran in 2023 was a direct product of years spent cultivating credibility on both sides without overcommitting to either. The diplomatic breakthrough that restored relations between Riyadh and Tehran was possible precisely because Beijing had maintained equidistant relationships that allowed it to serve as an acceptable intermediary. The mediation itself revealed sophisticated diplomacy underpinning China's regional role. Rather than imposing solutions or offering guarantees, Chinese officials facilitated dialogue by providing neutral venues, managing logistics, and creating face-saving formulas allowing both sides to claim victory.

Together, these three mechanisms, infrastructure-first diplomacy, energy interdependence, and calibrated political engagement, operationalize the four dimensions of DSI. They translate spatial, diplomatic, normative, and temporal design into concrete practices that embed Chinese influence across the Middle East. Yet as the constraints discussed above make clear, DSI generates durable leverage without guaranteeing control. It shapes contexts more than dictates outcomes. Understanding both its power and its limits is essential for assessing China's regional transformation.

2 Historical Evolution: From Periphery to Pivot

To understand China's contemporary role, one must trace its evolution across five distinct periods, each building upon and transforming what came before. This trajectory reveals not a sudden pivot but an accumulation of engagement that, by the BRI era, exhibited sufficient systematization to warrant analysis as designed statecraft.

Cold War Marginality and Ideological Positioning (1949–1978)

For much of the early People's Republic, China occupied the periphery of Middle Eastern affairs, constrained by limited resources and preoccupied with domestic consolidation following the Civil War. The early regime projected its international identity through anti-colonial rhetoric and revolutionary solidarity. Mao Zedong's China presented itself as a champion of the dispossessed, standing apart from both Western imperialism and Soviet hegemony, a Third World power aligned with newly independent states skeptical of both superpowers (Westad, 2005).

The 1955 Bandung Conference crystallized this posture. Chinese representatives, led by Zhou Enlai, positioned their nation as a champion of the Third World and an ally of Arab nationalist movements (Lee, 2010). The principles of peaceful coexistence articulated at Bandung provided ideological cover for what was fundamentally a pragmatic effort to build solidarity with states that possessed little in common with communist China except their opposition to Western dominance.

Palestine and Algeria became emblematic causes through which Beijing accumulated political capital. Chinese officials vocally supported Palestinian liberation and condemned colonialism in North Africa, though their material capacity remained modest. Token arms shipments and training to select liberation movements could not compete with Soviet or American resources (Burton, 2022). Yet this disparity proved less disabling than might be expected. Middle Eastern leaders recognized in China a partner that articulated anti-imperialism without the baggage of great power dominance. Unlike the Americans, whose Cold War alliance system implied support for monarchical regimes, or the Soviets, whose revolutionary rhetoric masked imperial pretensions in Central Asia, China appeared as a distant friend offering solidarity without subordination.

This symbolic credibility proved surprisingly durable (Massad, 2018). Chinese leaders invested in relationships with liberation movements, hosted visiting delegations, and maintained diplomatic presence in regional capitals (Cordesman, 2020). When Chinese officials received Palestinian leaders or Algerian revolutionaries, they were not merely performing solidarity; they were constructing networks and establishing credibility that would prove invaluable when China's economic power eventually materialized.

Yet China's preoccupation with its own revolutionary consolidation and factional struggles within the Communist Party meant that official attention to the Middle East remained episodic rather than systematic. The foundation was being laid through patient cultivation of political relationships, but it remained invisible to most contemporary observers.

Pragmatic Reorientation and Energy Interdependence (1978–2001)

Deng Xiaoping's reforms initiated a profound reorientation. The shift from revolutionary fervor to economic modernization redirected Beijing's foreign policy toward pragmatic bilateral engagement and trade expansion. The famous dictum *seek truth from facts* signaled a new era in which ideology would serve economics rather than the reverse (Vogel, 2011). This was not merely tactical; it represented a fundamental reconceptualization of China's role in global affairs.

The Middle East entered Beijing's strategic calculations through structural necessity. China's industrializing economy demanded secure energy supplies, and the Gulf possessed unmatched reserves. As China's factories multiplied throughout the 1980s, energy consumption soared. Initial domestic oil production could not sustain this rapid industrial growth; Beijing therefore required reliable access to external supplies. The Middle East, with its vast proven reserves and established export infrastructure, became increasingly central to Chinese economic planning (Wu, 2014).

The critical inflection point arrived in the early 1990s when China transitioned to net petroleum importer status. This structural dependency fundamentally altered Beijing's calculus. Prior to this transition, China's engagement with the Middle East remained somewhat optional (Tang, 1995). The shift to net importation transformed energy security into a paramount concern. Chinese planners recognized that import dependency created strategic vulnerability: any disruption to Gulf supplies could throttle industrial growth and undermine the political legitimacy that the Communist Party had increasingly staked on economic performance.

The 1990–91 Gulf War vividly demonstrated this vulnerability. As Iraqi forces invaded Kuwait and oil markets seized with uncertainty, Chinese analysts studied American military capabilities with acute attention. The United States demonstrated capacity to project overwhelming force into a distant region and impose outcomes through military superiority (Ullah & Xinlei, 2024, pp. 282–288). Simultaneously, Chinese analysts recognized a critical truth: Beijing could never replicate such military capabilities in the Persian Gulf. The distances were too great, the technological gap too wide, and the regional presence too marginal (Alterman & Garver, 2008).

This recognition of asymmetry proved strategically productive. Rather than pursuing impossible military competition, Chinese strategists pursued an alternative model: deepening economic interdependence, securing long-term contracts with Gulf producers, and positioning themselves as non-threatening partners willing to engage in regions and sectors where Western firms hesitated. By becoming an indispensable customer for Gulf energy supplies, China could shape behavior and outcomes without deploying military force. Chinese energy demand continued to accelerate throughout the 1990s and 2000s, making China increasingly valuable to Gulf economies seeking to maximize revenues and ensure market stability (Haghirian & Zaccara, 2023).

During this period, Chinese state-owned enterprises began establishing themselves across the Middle East. Chinese construction companies won contracts for infrastructure projects; Chinese oil companies signed exploration and development agreements. Chinese workers appeared on construction sites; Chinese managers negotiated with regional authorities; and Chinese money flowed into regional economies. This transformation from symbolic to material presence proved decisive for later influence.

The 1990s also witnessed important diplomatic institutionalization. Beijing established or elevated diplomatic missions across the region, recruited specialists on Middle Eastern affairs, and began developing the bureaucratic infrastructure necessary for long-term engagement (Beaujard, 2019). Chinese diplomacy became more systematic and sophisticated, reflecting growing institutional investment in the region.

Integration and Expansion (2002–2013)

China's economic surge created insatiable energy demand, particularly following accession to the World Trade Organization in 2001. This integration into the global economy accelerated industrialization and urbanization, driving petroleum consumption to unprecedented levels. Energy demand that had seemed enormous in 1995 proved insufficient by 2005; Chinese planners projected further dramatic increases extending decades into the future (Yoncacı, 2023).

The 2003 Iraq invasion, while Western-led, inadvertently created significant commercial opportunities for Chinese firms comfortable with political risk and willing to operate in unstable environments. As American and European companies grappled with security challenges in occupied Iraq, Chinese firms stepped in. Construction companies undertook infrastructure projects, oil companies pursued contracts, and trading companies facilitated commerce with a state widely regarded as a pariah (Karsh, 2014). These activities proved consequential, demonstrating that Chinese firms possessed competitive advantages in operating effectively in politically complex and physically dangerous environments.

Simultaneously, American and European sanctions on Iran created additional space for Chinese engagement. As Western companies withdrew from Iran, Chinese firms moved in (Nephew, 2019). Chinese oil companies contracted for Iranian oil; Chinese construction firms undertook infrastructure projects; and Chinese trading companies facilitated Iran's integration into global commerce despite sanctions (USIP, 2023). These developments were tactically uncoordinated, individual companies responding to commercial opportunities yet strategically cumulative, progressively deepening Beijing's regional entrenchment.

Throughout this period, Chinese officials emphasized principles of non-interference and respect for national sovereignty, rhetoric that resonated powerfully with governments weary of Western political conditionality. The Bush administration's explicit rhetoric about democracy promotion created friction with traditional Arab allies uncomfortable with external pressure on their governance practices (Pressman, 2009).

Chinese officials offered an explicit alternative: engagement based on mutual respect and non-interference in internal affairs.

The early 2000s also witnessed the emergence of China's "going out" strategy, a conscious policy initiative encouraging Chinese firms to invest in and operate across the developing world. The Middle East became a crucial arena for this strategy. State-owned enterprises received guidance that they should expand regional presence, secure long-term supply contracts, and build relationships with regional governments (Niblock, 2020). The distinction between state actors and ostensibly private firms blurred in practice, with government providing strategic direction to companies pursuing profit, while companies provided government with intelligence and influence mechanisms.

Energy companies constituted the vanguard of this expansion. China National Petroleum Corporation (CNPC), China National Offshore Oil Corporation (CNOOC), and China Sinopec pursued contracts across the region with determination and resources. Through these companies, China secured access to oil and natural gas reserves and constructed relationships with Gulf governments that extended beyond individual contracts to broader strategic partnerships.

The Belt and Road Initiative: Consolidation and Visibility (2013–Present)

The BRI, announced by Xi Jinping in Kazakhstan in 2013, provided coherence and visibility to China's accumulated investments and relationships across Eurasia and the Middle East. Rather than representing a sudden departure, the BRI consolidated decades of engagement—ideological credibility built through solidarity with liberation movements, energy partnerships forged during the reform era, and commercial experience gained by state enterprises since the 1990s. What the initiative achieved was transforming dispersed projects into a programmatic framework, allowing regional partners to see them as components of a larger vision of connectivity and shared development rather than merely individual commercial transactions. This framing mattered enormously for how regional actors evaluated Chinese engagement and for their willingness to commit to large-scale partnerships.

The scope of the BRI has been vast. It encompasses infrastructure investment in transportation, energy, ports, and telecommunications, with Chinese financing amounting to hundreds of billions of dollars globally.

In the Middle East, emphasis has been on strengthening overland corridors and energy networks. The China–Central Asia–West Asia Economic Corridor, for example, envisions transport and trade facilitation across Central Asia and Iran into the Middle East, while pipelines and energy projects ensure secure flows of oil and gas from Gulf producers to Chinese markets (Beeson & Crawford, 2023).

Equally important, the BRI has succeeded because Middle Eastern states have been active participants in shaping it, not passive recipients. Countries such as Saudi Arabia and the United Arab Emirates have deliberately cultivated ties with Beijing as part of broader diversification strategies aimed at reducing dependence on any single external power. The BRI offered them capital, expertise, and market access without the political conditions that Western development banks imposed. Saudi Vision 2030, for instance, created opportunities for Chinese firms in industrial complexes, renewable energy, and megacity construction (Moshashai et al., 2020). The UAE similarly leveraged Chinese investment to reinforce its role as a regional hub for finance and logistics. In both cases, Chinese engagement aligned with domestic priorities rather than contradicting them.

This historical trajectory reveals three patterns essential for understanding China's contemporary role. First, engagement evolved from symbolic (Maoist solidarity) to material (energy contracts) to systemic (BRI infrastructure). Each phase built upon the previous, creating accumulated credibility and institutional capacity. Second, Chinese statecraft adapted to changing regional conditions, filling gaps left by Western withdrawal (Iraq, Iran), aligning with partner modernization agendas (Saudi Arabia, UAE), and maintaining presence across rivalries (Saudi–Iran, Israel–Arab states). Third, by the BRI era, this engagement exhibited sufficient coordination across Chinese state actors, foreign ministry, development agencies, policy banks, and SOEs, to constitute designed statecraft rather than accumulated accident.

The result is a differentiated regional presence operating through the DSI mechanisms introduced in Sect. 2. Infrastructure embeds Chinese technical standards and operational protocols. Energy partnerships create mutual vulnerabilities binding both parties together. Strategic patience and equidistance allow Beijing to cultivate relationships across rivalries without becoming entangled in zero-sum competitions. These mechanisms function differently depending on partner capacity and political context, as the following section demonstrates through comparison of Saudi Arabia and Iran.

3 Twin Pillars: Previewing Saudi Arabia and Iran

The historical trajectory outlined above produced two distinct partnership models that anchor China's Middle Eastern engagement: Saudi Arabia and Iran. These cases illustrate how DSI adapts to radically different political contexts—one characterized by voluntary alignment between capable states, the other by asymmetric dependence born from isolation and constraint. Together, they demonstrate the flexibility and intentionality underlying China's regional strategy. What follows is a preview of relationships examined in depth in Chaps. 4 and 5.

Saudi Arabia: Partnership by Choice

Saudi Arabia occupies a distinctive position within China's evolving approach to the Middle East. More than a source of energy or a market for exports, the Kingdom represents a deliberate partner in Beijing's effort to design a new model of influence grounded in connectivity, complementarity, and long-term strategic embedding. As the most consequential Arab state, the custodian of Islam's holiest sites, and the region's central node of economic modernization, Saudi Arabia has become the linchpin through which China demonstrates that its diplomacy by design can operate not only in developing or fragile states but also in capable, ambitious powers pursuing their own transformation agendas.

For Beijing, the importance of Saudi Arabia lies in its symbolic and structural value. It is both a reliable partner in an unpredictable region and a testing ground for the BRI's ability to align with local modernization frameworks. The Kingdom's Vision 2030 reform program, an ambitious plan to diversify the economy, build new industries, and transform urban infrastructure, has provided an ideal entry point for China's model of development partnership (Saudi Vision 2030, 2024). Chinese participation does not appear as external intervention but as alignment: the integration of China's global initiative into the domestic priorities of a sovereign state seeking to redefine its future.

For Saudi policymakers, the attraction of China is equally clear. The Kingdom's leadership views Beijing as a necessary and stabilizing counterpart in a world of shifting power centers. While the United States remains an essential security guarantor, it no longer monopolizes Saudi strategic thinking (Scobell & Nader, 2016). China offers a different form of partnership, transactional yet predictable, pragmatic yet transformative. It provides access to advanced technology, infrastructure expertise, and financing mechanisms without the political scrutiny or conditionalities that often accompany Western engagement. This balance allows Riyadh to diversify its external relationships, enhance its bargaining power, and preserve strategic autonomy in a volatile international environment.

The rapid deepening of Sino-Saudi relations over the past three decades exemplifies the success of Beijing's design-oriented diplomacy. When formal diplomatic relations were established in 1990, few could have predicted the extent of alignment that would follow. What began as cautious engagement grounded in commercial pragmatism has matured into a multidimensional partnership linking two ambitious modernization projects—China's BRI and Saudi Arabia's Vision 2030 (Ullah & Xinlei, 2025a). Both frameworks emphasize infrastructure, technology, and state-led development; both seek to translate national revival into global relevance; and both prioritize stability as the foundation of transformation.

DSI in Practice: Infrastructure and Normative Alignment

In practice, this alignment operates through a carefully curated set of projects and initiatives that materialize political intent. The Riyadh Metro has become more than a transportation network; it is an institutional bridge. Chinese engineers and urban planners have introduced technologies and management systems that integrate efficiency, surveillance, and data-driven decision-making—hallmarks of China's urban governance model. Saudi officials and technical staff working alongside Chinese firms acquire not only skills but also exposure to the Chinese approach to development planning. The result is a subtle transfer of norms and expertise that endures long after projects are completed.

China's participation in NEOM, the flagship megacity of Vision 2030, further demonstrates this pattern. NEOM is not merely a construction project but an attempt to materialize a national vision of post-oil modernity (Chen et al., 2018). For China, participation in NEOM secures presence in one of the world's most high-profile transformation efforts, showcasing the sophistication and global competitiveness of its companies. For Saudi Arabia, Chinese involvement provides technical capacity, financing options, and global legitimacy (Martin & Ianchovichina, 2001).

It also embeds Chinese design principles into the Kingdom's emerging technological and urban infrastructure, strengthening the connective tissue of long-term cooperation.

What distinguishes this partnership is its designed interdependence. China's involvement in Saudi projects creates a network of material and institutional linkages that cannot be easily substituted. Urban systems, digital platforms, and energy facilities developed through Chinese participation operate on Chinese standards, technologies, and software ecosystems. Each connection reinforces a web of reliance that simultaneously enhances Saudi development capacity and extends Chinese influence. This is not dependency in the exploitative sense; rather, it is a structured relationship in which both sides derive tangible benefits while China subtly shapes the parameters of cooperation.

Strategic Hedging and Dual-Track Logic

Diplomatically, both countries have managed their relationship with remarkable balance. Riyadh continues to rely on Washington for security and defense, yet it openly welcomes Beijing as a partner in economic transformation. This dual-track strategy is not accidental but deliberate—a product of sophisticated hedging. By cultivating ties with both the United States and China, Saudi Arabia reduces vulnerability to unilateral pressure and signals its capacity to navigate great power competition on its own terms (Eslami & Papageorgiou, 2023). Beijing, for its part, respects these constraints and avoids challenging America's security primacy in the Gulf. Instead, it focuses on domains where its strengths are undeniable: infrastructure, technology, and industrial capacity.

For China, Saudi Arabia's strategic centrality within the Gulf offers not only economic dividends but also political leverage. Engagement with the Kingdom enhances Beijing's credibility across the Arab and Islamic worlds, providing access to regional institutions and forums where Chinese influence has historically been limited. For Saudi Arabia, the partnership embodies an opportunity to shape globalization from within rather than as a passive participant. By engaging China, the Kingdom situates itself at the crossroads of East–West connectivity, transforming from a resource exporter into a regional hub of trade, logistics, and innovation.

Ultimately, the Saudi–Chinese partnership reveals the operational logic of diplomacy by design. It functions through alignment rather than alliance, integration rather than domination, and interdependence rather than coercion. Each initiative—whether a metro line, an industrial park, or a renewable energy venture—serves as both an instrument and a symbol of a deeper strategic architecture. Chapter 4 examines this relationship in depth, analyzing how DSI's four dimensions (spatial, diplomatic, normative, temporal) operate in a context of voluntary partnership between capable states.

Iran: Partnership by Necessity

If Saudi Arabia represents partnership by choice, Iran embodies partnership by necessity. The relationship between Beijing and Tehran reflects an asymmetric interdependence born from structural constraints and strategic calculation rather than voluntary alignment. Where China's engagement with Gulf monarchies is framed as collaboration with capable, resource-rich states pursuing modernization, its relationship with Iran emerges from isolation, sanctions, and endurance. Yet this asymmetry has not diminished its strategic value. For Beijing, Iran offers an anchor point in the northern tier of the Middle East, a state whose defiance of the U.S.-led order reinforces China's narrative of alternative globalization. For Tehran, China functions as an indispensable economic lifeline and political counterweight, a partner whose engagement sustains the viability of resistance.

The 25-year Comprehensive Strategic Partnership (CSP) agreement, signed in March 2021, crystallized this dynamic. While its specific provisions remain opaque, the symbolism was unmistakable. China was willing to formalize long-term cooperation with a state still subject to some of the world's most stringent sanctions (Ullah & Xinlei, 2025a). The agreement signaled not only continuity of engagement but also China's readiness to institutionalize a model of diplomacy that operates in defiance of American constraint. It represented, in effect, the codification of diplomacy by design under conditions of coercive isolation. Fig. 1 maps their relationship.

Asymmetric Dependence and Economic Lifelines

For Tehran, the partnership is not optional. Western sanctions have progressively eroded the country's access to global finance, advanced technology, and investment capital. China occupies the space left vacant by departing Western firms, supplying goods, services, and technologies that sustain the basic functioning of the Iranian economy. Chinese

KEY ASPECT OF CHINA IRAN RELATIONS FRAMINGS:

- Shared civilizational heritage
- Common historical grievances
- Perceived ongoing Western opposition
- Vision of non-Western global cooperation
- Aspiration for regional leadership

Fig. 1 Conceptual framework of the Sino-Iranian relations

state-owned enterprises have invested in energy infrastructure, telecommunications, and transport networks; smaller private actors facilitate trade in essential goods through complex intermediaries and barter systems (Calabrese, 2006). Chinese purchases of Iranian crude, often heavily discounted and routed through indirect channels, provide Tehran with vital foreign exchange revenue. These flows have become structural features of Iran's economy, anchoring its external trade and cushioning it against complete economic isolation.

For Beijing, the logic is more complex but equally deliberate. Iran occupies a unique geographic and strategic position linking the Persian Gulf to Central Asia, the Caucasus, and the Levant. Its ports, railways, and pipelines form critical nodes in the overland corridors envisioned by the BRI. Cooperation with Iran thus supports China's ambition to build a trans-Eurasian network of connectivity that bypasses maritime chokepoints vulnerable to Western naval power. The partnership also yields political dividends: it demonstrates China's capacity to sustain meaningful relations with states marginalized by the Western order, thereby signaling autonomy from American strategic preferences. Engagement with Iran, in this sense, is as much a declaration of principle as a pursuit of material interest.

However, this partnership remains profoundly asymmetrical. While Iran depends heavily on China, the reverse is not true. China's diversification of energy imports across multiple suppliers, Saudi Arabia, Iraq, the UAE, and even Russia, dilutes Tehran's leverage. For Iran, China is a primary market and critical source of technology; for China, Iran is one of several options. This imbalance shapes every negotiation. Iranian officials routinely express frustration over Chinese demands for favorable contract terms, extensive technology transfer, and sovereign guarantees (Garcia & Oskrouchi, 2025). Beijing's negotiating posture reflects confidence derived from its alternatives, while Tehran's bargaining power is constrained by the absence of viable substitutes.

DSI Under Constraint: Infrastructure as Survival

This asymmetry does not imply exploitation but rather explains the logic of DSI under unequal conditions. China's engagement creates systems of connectivity, refineries, railways, and telecommunications grids, that bind Iran into a framework of economic activity centered on Chinese standards and institutions. These connections stabilize Iran's economy in the short term but embed long-term dependencies that limit Tehran's future strategic flexibility. The infrastructure of survival becomes, in time, the architecture of constraint.

The Tehran–Isfahan high-speed rail project provides a compelling case. Although presented as a domestic transportation initiative, the project links Iran's political center to its industrial heartland through Chinese technology, financing, and construction expertise. More significantly, the railway incorporates Chinese signaling systems, rolling stock, and maintenance protocols, thereby establishing long-term technological dependencies that will endure for generations. Each requirement for spare parts, technical assistance, or system upgrades reinforces Iran's reliance on Chinese suppliers whose proprietary knowledge is indispensable to network operation.

Iranian politics intensifies these tensions. Within Tehran's policy circles, the relationship with China is both defended and contested. Hardline factions frame China as a natural ally in the struggle against Western hegemony, emphasizing shared opposition to unilateral sanctions and external interference. Reformist and nationalist voices, however, express unease, accusing the government of mortgaging sovereignty by selling oil at steep discounts and granting opaque concessions to Chinese firms. The debate captures a central paradox of Iranian foreign policy: the desire for autonomy sustained by relationships that constrain it.

From Beijing's perspective, managing these internal dynamics requires caution and discretion. China avoids overt political statements about Iran's domestic or regional behavior, adhering to principles of non-interference that distinguish its diplomacy from Western engagement. It positions itself as a pragmatic partner rather than an ideological ally, maintaining quiet but steady cooperation while minimizing exposure to reputational risk. This deliberate ambiguity allows Beijing to sustain economic ties with Tehran without alienating Gulf monarchies or jeopardizing broader regional relations (Alyahya, 2023).

Strategic Signaling and Geopolitical Balancing

The relationship also possesses a strategic signaling function extending far beyond bilateral ties. By maintaining cooperation with Iran, Beijing communicates to regional and global audiences that it can engage across divides others deem irreconcilable. It sustains partnerships simultaneously with Saudi Arabia and Iran, two regional rivals whose enmity has defined Middle Eastern politics for decades. This balancing act underscores the sophistication of China's diplomacy: it seeks inclusion, not alignment; coexistence, not confrontation (Houghton, 2022). The ability to sustain such parallel relationships reinforces China's image as a power capable of mediating rather than polarizing.

Yet the durability of the Sino-Iranian partnership remains uncertain. Should sanctions be eased or lifted, Tehran would likely recalibrate its external orientation, seeking Western investment and technology that China cannot match. Beijing, too, might adjust its exposure if engagement became politically costly or commercially less advantageous. The relationship, in this sense, is contingent—a structure built for a particular geopolitical moment.

Despite these limits, the partnership's significance should not be underestimated. It exemplifies how China adapts its diplomatic design to varied environments: where state capacity is high, as in Saudi Arabia, it aligns; where isolation prevails, as in Iran, it sustains. Both strategies produce interdependence, but of different kinds. Chapter 5 examines this relationship in depth, analyzing how DSI operates under conditions of asymmetry, isolation, and structural constraint, and what this reveals about the limits and adaptability of China's regional strategy.

Comparative Logic and the Flexibility of DSI

Taken together, the Saudi and Iranian cases highlight the dual architecture of China's diplomacy by design in the Middle East—a strategy that operates through differentiated engagement calibrated to contrasting local conditions. In Saudi Arabia, partnership is an act of choice, structured around mutual ambition, modernization, and prestige. In Iran, it is an act of necessity, structured around endurance, survival, and asymmetric interdependence. Both relationships demonstrate the same underlying logic of DSI, yet each reveals a distinct pathway through which China embeds influence and constructs a durable presence without assuming the burdens of formal alliance or ideological alignment.

Figure 2 illustrates the mechanism of China's DSI in its engagement with Saudi Arabia and Iran. It shows how partner structural conditions shape the deployment of DSI mechanisms, including spatial, temporal, diplomatic, and normative instruments. The diagram also traces how these mechanisms interact with partner capacity to produce observable outcomes and cross-case insights on asymmetry and leverage.

The comparative dynamics can be understood across several dimensions. In terms of engagement logic, Saudi Arabia represents voluntary alignment between capable states pursuing complementary modernization agendas, while Iran reflects constrained partnership where China provides critical lifelines unavailable elsewhere. Regarding energy interdependence, Saudi Arabia exports high-value, stable oil supplies integrated

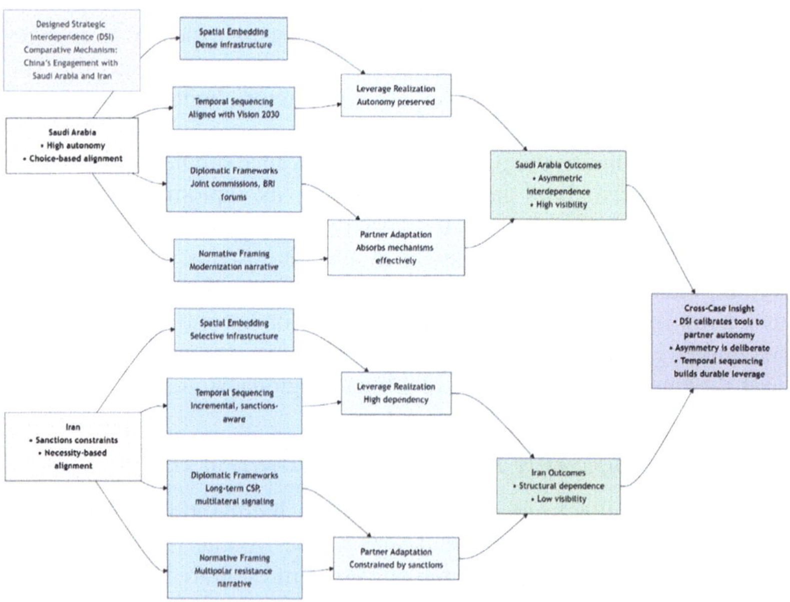

Fig. 2 Comparative logic and the flexibility of DSI

with Chinese downstream markets, whereas Iran sells discounted crude under sanctions, creating asymmetric leverage favoring Beijing. In infrastructure embedding, Saudi projects (Riyadh Metro, NEOM) are highly visible, prestige-driven initiatives with extensive training and technical transfer, while Iranian projects (railways, ports) are more targeted but create equally significant operational dependencies.

Diplomatically, Saudi Arabia retains high autonomy, maintaining U.S. security ties and independent foreign policy, while Iran's autonomy is limited by sanctions and isolation, making it more dependent on Chinese support. Yet both cases demonstrate normative alignment with Chinese principles: Saudi Arabia appreciates economic complementarity and low political conditionality, while Iran frames cooperation as multipolar resistance to Western pressure. Temporally, Saudi engagement is sequenced to align with Vision 2030 milestones, whereas Iranian projects are incremental, synchronized with sanctions constraints and strategic timing.

The Saudi case underscores China's ability to integrate with established, high-capacity states that retain strong ties with Washington but seek strategic diversification. Through Vision 2030, Beijing found not only a framework for economic cooperation but a domestic political project into which its infrastructural and technological diplomacy could be inserted seamlessly. The Iran case, by contrast, reveals how the same design logic functions under constraint. There, Chinese diplomacy operates in the shadows of sanctions, constructing networks of resilience through trade, energy, and technology.

Figure 2 visually maps these comparative dynamics, illustrating how the four dimensions of DSI—spatial, diplomatic, normative, and temporal—operate differently according to local conditions and partner capacity. In Saudi Arabia, DSI manifests through highly visible, prestige-driven projects embedded in Vision 2030, reflecting engagement by choice and enabling deep integration without challenging existing security alignments. In Iran, by contrast, DSI functions under constraint, with China leveraging infrastructure, energy, and technology to sustain strategic presence in an environment marked by sanctions and geopolitical isolation. The visual representation underscores the adaptability and intentional asymmetry of China's regional strategy Fig. 3.

What unites these cases is intentional asymmetry: China adapts the form of interdependence to the structural conditions of each partner. Where resources and legitimacy abound, it embeds through cooperation

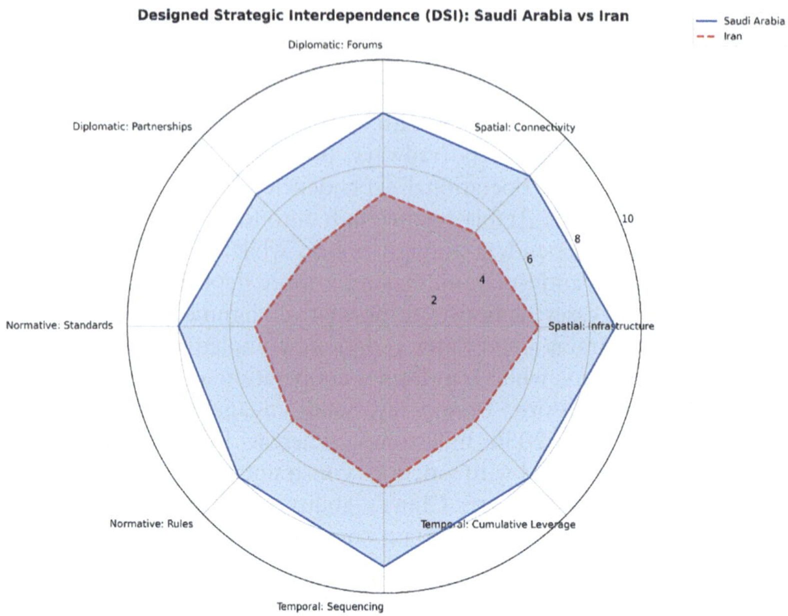

Fig. 3 Comparative visualization of China's designed strategic interdependence in Saudi Arabia and Iran

and prestige projects; where isolation prevails, it embeds through necessity and endurance. This flexibility transforms the BRI from a uniform initiative into an adaptive framework: a platform capable of producing influence under vastly different political and economic conditions. The Saudi–Iran contrast, therefore, reveals the versatility and discipline of Beijing's regional strategy: its capacity to sustain equilibrium across opposing poles of Middle Eastern politics while designing relationships that serve its long-term strategic purposes.

4 Constraints and Limits: The Boundaries of Chinese Influence

To evaluate China's evolving role in the Middle East requires an honest reckoning with the boundaries of its power. The architecture of China's regional engagement, anchored in infrastructure, energy, and strategic patience, has generated significant leverage and embedded influence, yet it also reveals structural limitations that constrain Beijing's ability to shape outcomes in decisive ways. Recognizing these constraints is not to diminish China's achievements but to situate them within the broader asymmetries that still define the global order. The same mechanisms that sustain DSI also expose its limits, particularly in security, political influence, and institutional depth.

Military Incapacity and the Security Gap

The most visible constraint lies in China's limited military capacity to project power into the Middle East. Despite its economic centrality, Beijing remains a secondary actor in the region's security landscape. The United States continues to maintain a military infrastructure developed over seven decades, encompassing forward-deployed aircraft carriers, extensive air and naval bases, advanced defense systems, and alliance networks stretching from the Gulf to the Mediterranean. These arrangements provide the United States with capabilities for rapid intervention, intelligence collection, and coordinated operations with local partners. In comparison, China's presence remains minimal. Its single overseas logistics facility in Djibouti, while often cited as evidence of expanding reach, functions primarily as a support node for maritime operations and humanitarian missions rather than a true power-projection base (Sun & Zoubir, 2021).

This imbalance becomes most evident in times of crisis. When attacks threaten Saudi oil infrastructure, when tensions escalate between Iran and Israel, or when instability spreads across the Red Sea and Gulf waters, regional actors instinctively turn to the United States for protection and reassurance. American military assets provide deterrence and response capabilities that no other external power can match. Chinese calls for restraint and diplomacy carry political significance, but they lack the coercive credibility that comes from demonstrated military capability. In international politics, credible security guarantees remain the ultimate currency of influence, and China's inability to provide them confines its role to one of mediation and persuasion rather than enforcement or deterrence.

Beijing's leaders have long understood this asymmetry and have consciously avoided replicating American-style military entanglement. China's foreign policy principles emphasize non-interference, respect for sovereignty, and preference for political over military solutions. These tenets align with its material interests, which are best served by regional stability rather than interventionist commitments. However, this restraint also creates a paradox. China's economic and infrastructural entanglement increases expectations for it to act as a stabilizing power, yet its chosen instruments of influence diplomacy, trade, and development cannot easily substitute for the deterrent functions of security alliances. In effect, China's regional strategy operates in the shadow of American military dominance, depending on the stability that U.S. security guarantees provide even as it seeks to reduce Washington's economic and normative influence.

Economic Leverage and Political Autonomy

Energy interdependence and infrastructure penetration, although powerful tools of DSI, are similarly bounded in their capacity to shape political behavior when core national interests diverge. Economic leverage does not translate automatically into political compliance. Regional states, while deeply integrated into Chinese supply chains and investment networks, retain significant autonomy in matters of high politics.

Iran, despite its reliance on Chinese markets, continues to pursue regional proxy engagements that often complicate Beijing's preference for stability. Tehran's support for Hezbollah, the Houthis, and various Iraqi militias persists regardless of Chinese concerns about regional volatility. Saudi Arabia, while deepening its economic ties with China, maintains its strategic security relationship with the United States and continues to procure advanced Western defense systems. When Riyadh normalized relations with Israel through the Abraham Accords framework or when it adjusts oil production levels in coordination with OPEC, these decisions reflect calculations about regional security and domestic legitimacy that Chinese economic partnerships cannot override. Egypt and Israel pursue policies in the Eastern Mediterranean that occasionally conflict with Chinese economic or diplomatic interests.

Specific cases illustrate these limits. Chinese investment in Oman's Duqm Port, while substantial, has not prevented Muscat from maintaining its traditional balancing act between regional powers or from hosting joint military exercises with Western forces. Qatar's significant energy exports to China did not constrain Doha's independent foreign policy during the 2017–2021 Gulf rift, when it maintained defiant positions despite economic pressure from Saudi Arabia and the UAE—states that are themselves major Chinese partners. In Egypt, Chinese infrastructure investments have not translated into consistent diplomatic support; Cairo has occasionally sided with Western positions on issues Beijing considers sensitive. These cases demonstrate that infrastructure and trade create influence over economic decisions but rarely dictate outcomes on security or high-politics issues.

This divergence reveals an important distinction between structural power and strategic influence. Structural power allows China to shape the context in which states make choices, but it does not guarantee control over the choices themselves. Infrastructure, trade, and technology embed China deeply within regional economies, yet they cannot compel alignment when partners face existential threats or domestic imperatives. In this sense, China's DSI produces pathways of influence that are broad but shallow, capable of constraining options yet insufficient to dictate outcomes. The durability of American strategic dominance rests precisely on this difference: it combines material entanglement with coercive capacity, while China's model remains anchored in persuasion, participation, and process.

Institutional Depth and Organizational Fragmentation

Another limitation concerns institutional depth and the unevenness of China's regional networks. Although Beijing has signed dozens of cooperation agreements and elevated several relationships to the level of comprehensive strategic partnerships, these frameworks remain largely bilateral and transactional. They lack the kind of multilateral institutionalization that underpins American and European engagement. China has not yet constructed enduring regional security or political institutions comparable to NATO, the EU, or even U.S.-sponsored coalitions (Sarsenbayev & Véron, 2020).

Its regional diplomacy relies instead on flexible arrangements, ad hoc working groups, and summit diplomacy. While this flexibility provides adaptability and avoids the rigidity of formal alliances, it also prevents the formation of binding commitments or collective defense mechanisms. As a result, China's regional presence remains significant but dispersed—its influence diffuses rather than consolidates. When regional crises erupt, there is no "China bloc" that acts in concert or defers to Beijing's coordination. Each bilateral relationship operates on its own logic, limiting China's ability to orchestrate collective action or establish regional norms through institutional channels.

Domestic factors further complicate the expansion of Chinese influence. Beijing's external engagements are often constrained by the need to manage economic slowdown, financial exposure, and reputational risk associated with Belt and Road projects. Concerns about debt sustainability, project delays, and local backlash have led to a more cautious approach to overseas lending (Hurley et al., 2019). In the Middle East, where political volatility and governance deficits pose constant risks, Chinese policymakers must balance ambition with prudence. This cautious stance reinforces the image of China as a pragmatic, economically driven power but limits its ability to act decisively during political or security crises. DSI functions best under conditions of stability and predictability; in volatile environments, its incremental logic faces structural limits.

Differentiated Multipolarity and the Persistence of American Primacy

These constraints also reflect the broader evolution of global order. Multipolarity in the twenty-first century is not characterized by the simple replacement of one hegemon by another, but by the coexistence of multiple powers exercising influence through different instruments. The Middle East exemplifies this differentiated multipolarity. The United States continues to dominate militarily and politically, while China commands increasing economic and technological centrality. Russia intervenes episodically through coercive means, and regional actors assert growing agency within this complex matrix. In such a landscape, no single power can achieve comprehensive dominance. China's rise thus contributes to pluralization rather than the displacement of influence.

This functional differentiation has important implications. China's economic centrality coexists with—rather than replaces—American military preponderance. Regional states navigate this reality by cultivating relationships with multiple powers simultaneously, extracting benefits from each while avoiding exclusive alignment with any. Saudi Arabia exemplifies this logic: it depends on American security guarantees while pursuing economic transformation through Chinese partnership. The UAE positions itself as a financial hub serving both Western and Chinese capital. Egypt receives military aid from Washington while welcoming Chinese infrastructure investment. This hedging behavior limits how far any external power can push regional partners toward exclusive alignment.

The persistence of these limits does not negate the significance of China's achievements. Rather, it situates them within the emerging logic of diplomacy by design. Beijing's strategy in the Middle East is not to replicate Western military architectures but to construct alternative foundations of influence grounded in connectivity, mutual dependence, and systemic embedding. Its strength lies in design, not domination; in interdependence, not intervention. Yet this very design makes its influence contingent on cooperation rather than coercion, and therefore vulnerable to shifts in local agency and external competition.

In this respect, the limits of Chinese influence are integral to understanding its character. Power exercised through design requires acceptance from partners and stability within systems. It advances through projects and partnerships rather than bases or battalions. Its endurance depends on maintaining equilibrium among multiple actors rather than asserting hegemony. China's Middle East engagement, therefore, reveals a new kind of power—ambitious yet constrained, embedded yet cautious, pervasive yet indirect. Recognizing both its strengths and its limitations is essential for grasping how DSI operates in practice and how it contributes to the broader reordering of regional and global systems.

5 Conclusion: From Periphery to Pivot Reconsidered

Understanding China's rise in the Middle East requires recognizing both its structural ingenuity and its enduring constraints. The transformation of China from a peripheral actor to a pivotal force in regional geopolitics marks one of the most consequential reconfigurations of the post–Cold War order. Yet this transformation is not a story of displacement but of differentiation. The region is no longer organized around a single hegemon. Instead, it exhibits a pluralized order where multiple powers including China, the United States, Russia, and Europe exercise influence through distinct mechanisms rooted in their comparative advantages.

Synthesis: The Logic of Diplomacy by Design

China's rise rests on three interlocking foundations that together form the essence of its regional strategy: infrastructure-first diplomacy, energy interdependence, and strategic patience. These principles are underpinned by what this book conceptualizes as DSI, a framework through which Beijing structures durable relationships by shaping material, institutional, and normative linkages over time. Through spatial, diplomatic, normative, and temporal design, China embeds itself into regional systems in ways that gradually accumulate influence without overt domination. This is diplomacy by design—a method of creating influence through architecture rather than coercion.

The question that opened this chapter, whether this represents conscious strategic planning or adaptive learning, finds its answer in recognizing that the distinction ultimately matters less than the outcome. By the BRI era, Chinese engagement exhibited sufficient systematization, cross-institutional coordination, and strategic coherence to constitute designed statecraft. Whether this design emerged from foresight in the 1990s or from accumulated institutional learning across decades, the patterns by 2013 were unmistakable: ministries, state-owned enterprises, and policy banks operated with evident coordination; similar instruments were deployed systematically across diverse political contexts; and Beijing demonstrated sophisticated understanding of how infrastructure, energy, and patience could be combined to produce durable influence. This book demonstrates that China's Middle Eastern engagement, whatever its origins, evolved into something deliberate—a model of statecraft suited to an era where economic centrality can rival military preponderance as a source of global power.

The logic of DSI is vividly demonstrated in China's relationships with Saudi Arabia and Iran. Each represents a distinct pathway through which Beijing constructs and manages interdependence. Saudi Arabia reflects engagement by choice—a partnership between two capable states aligning their development trajectories through Vision 2030 and the BRI. Iran reflects engagement by necessity—a partnership born from constraint in which China provides critical lifelines to a sanctioned and isolated state. Both relationships demonstrate that China's influence does not stem from ideology or alliance, but from deliberate creation of infrastructural, economic, and institutional linkages that embed Beijing's presence deeply yet non-intrusively.

However, the durability of these linkages is neither absolute nor unbounded. The pillars supporting China's rise, infrastructure, energy, and strategic patience, also delineate the boundaries of its reach. Military incapacity remains the most visible constraint. Despite its global ambitions, China lacks the logistical networks, forward-deployed assets, and alliance structures necessary to project sustained force into the Middle East. When regional crises erupt, Middle Eastern governments still turn instinctively toward Washington for reassurance and resolution.

Political and reputational limitations also circumscribe China's influence. Although its emphasis on sovereignty and non-interference appeals to many regional states, this same posture limits its ability to intervene decisively or mediate effectively when tensions escalate. Economic leverage, while substantial, does not always translate into political compliance. Middle Eastern states have demonstrated the capacity to pursue autonomous strategies even when dependent on Chinese markets or technology. Iran continues regional interventions despite Beijing's preference for restraint. Saudi Arabia maintains deep security ties with the United States. Egypt, the UAE, and other regional powers routinely engage multiple partners simultaneously.

In this context, American preponderance persists, albeit within differentiated domains. The United States retains unmatched hard-power capabilities and security relationships that define the region's coercive architecture. China's strength, by contrast, lies in economic connectivity, infrastructure, and long-term planning. Rather than a zero-sum contest, the two powers now operate across complementary and sometimes overlapping spaces. The Middle East thus embodies what may become the defining feature of twenty-first-century multipolarity, functional differentiation of power, where economic centrality and military preponderance coexist within the same strategic environment.

Broader Implications and Contributions

The broader implications of China's transformation are profound. By privileging infrastructure over intervention, development over deterrence, and partnership over patronage, Beijing offers a distinct modality of great power engagement. Whether this model proves more sustainable than the United States' security-led paradigm remains an open question, but its appeal to many developing states is undeniable. It promises autonomy, material benefit, and visible progress without the political costs associated with alignment.

Yet the sustainability of this model depends on maintaining delicate balances: between economic expansion and political restraint, diversification and dependence, global ambition and regional sensitivity. China's Middle Eastern strategy is adaptive rather than revolutionary. It neither seeks to replace existing orders nor to construct new ones from scratch. Instead, it aims to embed itself within existing structures, incrementally reshaping them through practice and presence.

This book contributes to international relations scholarship in three ways. First, it advances a new theoretical framework, Designed Strategic Interdependence, that explains how rising powers can accumulate influence through deliberate construction of economic, technological, and institutional dependencies rather than through military dominance or ideological appeal. DSI bridges structural theories of power with agency-centered analyses of strategic choice, showing how material capabilities are translated into political influence through systematic design. Second, it revises BRI scholarship by moving beyond descriptive accounts of infrastructure projects to analyze the strategic logic underlying Chinese engagement. Rather than treating the BRI as a collection of disconnected initiatives, this book demonstrates how infrastructure, energy, and diplomacy combine to produce systematic patterns of influence calibrated to local political contexts. Third, it illuminates the emerging character of twenty-first-century multipolarity, showing how great power competition increasingly operates through functional differentiation rather than comprehensive rivalry. The Middle East becomes a laboratory for understanding how military preponderance and economic centrality can coexist, creating complex interdependencies that constrain all actors while preventing hegemonic consolidation.

In this light, the story of China's rise in the Middle East is one of transformation without domination. The pivot from periphery to centrality is not linear, and it is certainly not complete. It is an evolving process shaped by opportunity and constraint, by the agency of both external and regional actors. For scholars of international relations, this trajectory reveals the emergence of a new kind of global influence, grounded in connectivity rather than coercion, and in design rather than command.

China's Middle Eastern engagement thus serves as a microcosm for understanding the broader reconfiguration of global order. The future will not be defined by a single hegemon or by simple power transitions, but by complex systems of designed interdependence where influence is shared, negotiated, and continually reconstructed. Recognizing this transformation is essential for comprehending both the limits of American dominance and the nature of China's ascent.

The age of unilateral power in the Middle East has passed. What replaces it is still in formation, but China's rise ensures that the region will no longer be defined solely by Western initiative. It has become a space of convergence, of designed connections, overlapping dependencies, and pluralized authority. Understanding this transformation is not only crucial for Middle Eastern studies but for grasping the architecture of global order now taking shape.

This book is structured to guide readers from context and empirical observation to theoretical innovation and broader implications, offering a coherent narrative that illuminates China's rising influence in the Middle East through the lens of DSI. Each chapter addresses specific facets of China's engagement while collectively demonstrating the strategic logic underpinning Beijing's regional policy.

Chapter 2 introduces the core conceptual framework of Designed Strategic Interdependence, explaining how China deliberately structures influence across four dimensions: spatial, diplomatic, normative, and temporal. This chapter provides the analytical tools for interpreting subsequent chapters, framing China's engagement as systematically designed strategy that generates long-term interdependencies with multiple regional actors simultaneously.

Chapter 3 situates the reader within the historical and contemporary dynamics of Middle Eastern rivalries, focusing on Saudi Arabia and Iran as primary actors. It examines how these states' competing ambitions create both opportunities and constraints for external powers, providing essential context for understanding why China's engagement must be adaptive and calibrated to existing fault lines.

Chapter 4 focuses on China's engagement with Saudi Arabia, analyzing DSI in the context of partnership by choice. It examines how infrastructure projects, energy collaboration, and technical integration create mutually reinforcing dependencies aligned with Vision 2030, demonstrating how Beijing calibrates its approach to respect Saudi sovereignty while establishing durable channels of influence.

Chapter 5 presents the contrasting case of partnership by necessity with Iran, where DSI functions under conditions of sanctions, geopolitical isolation, and constrained capacity. This chapter highlights the asymmetric nature of the relationship and demonstrates DSI's flexibility in navigating contexts of vulnerability, showing how designed interdependence stabilizes relationships even under adverse conditions.

Chapter 6 examines China's role as mediator, particularly in facilitating the 2023 Saudi–Iran rapprochement. It illustrates how DSI extends beyond material projects into the diplomatic sphere, embedding credibility and trust that allow Beijing to support conflict management without relying on coercive capabilities—demonstrating the operational payoff of carefully sequenced strategy.

Chapter 7 synthesizes the patterns of engagement explored in preceding chapters, offering a spatial and strategic mapping of China's Middle Eastern presence. It examines how infrastructure, energy networks, institutional linkages, and operational norms interact to form a contiguous architecture of influence, highlighting the multidimensionality of DSI and how its components converge to produce durable leverage.

Chapter 8 situates China's engagement within broader regional transformations, exploring how DSI has contributed to the emergence of a more pluralized Middle Eastern order in which multiple external powers exert influence through differentiated mechanisms. The chapter analyzes implications for regional sovereignty, multipolarity, and the exercise of power, emphasizing that China's influence operates through integration rather than coercion.

The concluding chapter draws together empirical, theoretical, and analytical insights from the book, reassessing China's position from periphery to pivot while emphasizing both operational successes and inherent constraints. It articulates how infrastructure, energy interdependence, and patient diplomacy constitute a distinctive model of influence, while acknowledging limits imposed by military incapacity, reputational risk, and the persistence of American preponderance. It offers reflections on the broader significance of DSI for global order and the implications of China's model for other regions and future research agendas.

Together, these chapters demonstrate how infrastructure, energy, and patience combine to produce a new model of great power influence—one that reshapes regional order not through military dominance or ideological appeal, but through the deliberate architecture of interdependence. Understanding this transformation is essential for grasping the Middle East's future and the emerging character of global multipolarity.

References

Alterman, J. B., & Garver, J. W. (2008). *The vital triangle: China, the United States, and the Middle East* (Vol. 30). CSIS.

Alyahya, M. (2023, 2023/3/14). China Surges Ahead in Middle East Diplomacy. Barron's. https://www.barrons.com/articles/chinas-economic-recovery-disappoints-bulls-heres-where-they-are-investing-instead-ed070cd0

Beaujard, P. (2019). Tang China and the rise of the silk roads. In P. Beaujard (Ed.), The Worlds of the Indian Ocean: A Global History: Volume 2: From the Seventh Century to the Fifteenth Century CE (Vol. 2, pp. 18–41). Cambridge University Press. https://doi.org/10.1017/9781108341219.002.

Beeson, M., & Crawford, C. (2023). Putting the BRI in perspective: History, hegemony and geoeconomics. *Chinese Political Science Review, 8*(1), 45–62.

Burton, G. (2022). *China and Middle East Conflicts: Responding to War and Rivalry from the Cold War to the Present*. Routledge. https://books.google.de/books?id=8Af3zgEACAAJ

Calabrese, J. (2006). China and Iran: Partners Perfectly Mismatched. *Manuscript, Washington DC: Middle East Institute.*

Chen, J., Shu, M., & Wen, S. (2018). Aligning China's belt and road initiative with Saudi Arabia's 2030 vision: Opportunities and challenges. *China Quarterly of International Strategic Studies, 4*(03), 363–379.

Cordesman, A. H. (2020). China in the Gulf: A New Partnership with Iran?. *Washington, DC: Center for Strategic & International Studies.*

Eslami, M., & Papageorgiou, M. (2023). China's increasing role in the Middle East: Implications for regional and international dynamics. *Georgetown Journal of International Affairs, 2*(6).

Garcia, Z., & Oskrouchi, A. (2025). Beyond geopolitics: The domestic drivers of China-Iran cooperation on the belt and road initiative. The Diplomat. https://thediplomat.com/2025/05/beyond-geopolitics-the-domestic-drivers-of-china-iran-cooperation-on-the-belt-and-road-initiative/

Haghirian, M., & Zaccara, L. (2023). China's economic and political presence in the Middle East and South Asia. *Routledge, Taylor & Francis Group.*

Houghton, B. (2022). China's balancing strategy between Saudi Arabia and Iran: The view from Riyadh. *Asian Affairs, 53*(1), 124–144.

Hurley, J., Morris, S., & Portelance, G. (2019). Examining the debt implications of the belt and road initiative from a policy perspective. *Journal of Infrastructure, Policy and Development, 3*(1), 139–175.

Karsh, E. (2014). The Iran–Iraq War 1980–1988. Bloomsbury Publishing.

Lee, C. J. (2010). *Making a world after empire: The Bandung moment and its political afterlives* (Vol. 11). Ohio University Press.

Martin, W., & Ianchovichina, E. (2001). Implications of China's accession to the World Trade Organisation for China and the WTO. *The World Economy, 24*(9), 1205–1219.

Massad, J. (2018). Against self-determination. *Humanity: An International Journal of Human Rights, Humanitarianism, and Development, 9*(2), 161–191.

Moshashai, D., Leber, A. M., & Savage, J. D. (2020). Saudi Arabia plans for its economic future: Vision 2030, the National Transformation Plan and Saudi fiscal reform. *British Journal of Middle Eastern Studies, 47*(3), 381–401. https://doi.org/10.1080/13530194.2018.1500269

Nephew, R. (2019). China and economic sanctions: Where does Washington have leverage? *Global China*, 3–4.

Niblock, T. (2020). China and the Middle East: A global strategy where the Middle East has a significant but limited place. *Asian Journal of Middle Eastern and Islamic Studies, 14*(4), 481–504.

Pressman, J. (2009). Power without influence: The bush administration's foreign policy failure in the Middle East. *International Security, 33*(4), 149–179.

Sarsenbayev, M., & Véron, N. (2020). European versus American perspectives on the belt and road initiative. *China & World Economy, 28*(2), 84–112.

Saudi Vision 2030 (2024). Vision 2030 Overview Retrieved 8/1/2024 from https://www.vision2030.gov.sa/en/

Scobell, A., & Nader, A. (2016). *China in the Middle East: The wary dragon.* RAND corporation.

Sun, D., & Zoubir, Y. H. (2021). Securing China's 'latent power': The dragon's anchorage in Djibouti. *Journal of Contemporary China, 30*(130), 677–692.

Tang, F. C. (1995). China's petroleum market in the 1990s: Review and challenges to its refining industry. *Energy Exploration & Exploitation, 13*(6), 617–629.

Ullah, A., & Xinlei, L. (2024). Navigating the Persian Gulf security complex: Saudi-Iran rapprochement in an era of great power competition. *East Asia, 40*(3). https://doi.org/10.1007/s12140-024-09430-2

Ullah, A., & Xinlei, L. (2025a). Navigating complex interdependence: An in-depth analysis of Iran and Saudi Arabia's strategic engagement with the BRI in the Middle East. *Chinese Political Science Review, 10*(1), 72–100.

USIP. (2023). Iran and China: A trade lifeline. United States Institute of Peace. Retrieved 8/16/2024 from https://iranprimer.usip.org/blog/2023/jun/28/iran-china-trade-lifeline

Vogel, E. F. (2011). *Deng Xiaoping and the transformation of China.* Harvard University Press.

Westad, O. A. (2005). *The global cold war: Third world interventions and the making of our times*. Cambridge University Press.

Wu, K. (2014). China′ s energy security: Oil and gas. *Energy Policy, 73*, 4–11.

Yoncacı, A. (2023). China's Energy Security in the Gulf Middle East Technical University].

CHAPTER 2

Embedded Influence: The Logic and Consequences of China's Designed Interdependence

1 The Puzzle: Influence Without Dominance

In March 2023, Saudi Arabia and Iran restored diplomatic relations after 7 years of estrangement, and they did so in Beijing. The agreement, brokered by Chinese diplomats through months of patient facilitation, signaled a fundamental shift in Middle Eastern geopolitics. For the first time in modern history, a non-Western power had mediated a breakthrough between the region's two most consequential rivals, states whose enmity has defined Gulf politics for decades through proxy conflicts in Yemen Lebanon, Iraq, and Syria. The breakthrough was unexpected not because reconciliation was impossible, regional dynamics had been shifting for years, but because China accomplished it.

This outcome presents a puzzle for international relations theory. China brokered the Saudi–Iran rapprochement without possessing the instruments traditionally associated with great power mediation. It maintains no formal alliance with either state. It provides no security guarantees comparable to American commitments. It operates a single modest logistics facility in Djibouti rather than the network of bases, aircraft carriers, and forward-deployed forces through which the United States projects power across the Middle East. Beijing cannot credibly threaten military intervention to enforce agreements, nor can it offer defense pacts to incentivize cooperation. Yet its mediation succeeded where others failed, and its regional influence continues expanding.

A. Ullah, *Diplomacy by Design*,
https://doi.org/10.1007/978-981-95-7876-4_2

The puzzle extends beyond this single diplomatic achievement. Across the Middle East, China has become simultaneously indispensable to rival states pursuing incompatible regional visions. It is Iran's largest oil customer and primary source of sanctions-resistant technology, providing economic lifelines that sustain Tehran's capacity to resist American pressure. Simultaneously, it is Saudi Arabia's largest trading partner and a central participant in Vision 2030's modernization projects, embedding Chinese firms, standards, and expertise within the Kingdom's flagship development initiatives. The United Arab Emirates hosts extensive Chinese investment in ports, free zones, and technology sectors. Egypt depends on Chinese financing for infrastructure megaprojects. Turkey maintains robust trade despite periodic diplomatic tensions. Israel pursues technology partnerships even as it manages American security concerns.

This pattern of simultaneous, overlapping partnerships with rivals represents something qualitatively different from traditional great power engagement. Regional states do not perceive Chinese involvement as requiring exclusive alignment or zero-sum choices. They deepen economic ties with Beijing while maintaining—and sometimes strengthening—security relationships with Washington. They welcome Chinese mediation without abandoning other diplomatic channels. They integrate Chinese infrastructure into national development plans without triggering the nationalist backlash or sovereignty concerns that typically accompany extensive foreign involvement. China's presence has become structurally embedded across the region's economic systems, yet it operates without the formal mechanisms, military preponderance, or ideological appeal through which great powers have historically exercised influence.

This empirical reality challenges foundational assumptions in international relations scholarship. How does a rising power construct meaningful influence in a contested region without the traditional instruments of statecraft? What mechanisms enable embedded presence to translate into diplomatic leverage? Why do regional actors accommodate Chinese preferences despite lacking formal obligations to do so? And why has Chinese engagement not triggered the balancing behavior, competitive polarization, or resistance that realist theory predicts accompanies rising power emergence?

Why Existing Theories Fall Short

Realist frameworks emphasizing material capabilities and security competition offer limited explanatory power. Structural realism, in its various forms, predicts that states respond to power shifts through balancing or bandwagoning: they form countervailing coalitions against rising threats or align with stronger powers for protection (Morgenthau, 1948; Waltz, 1979). Yet China's Middle Eastern engagement has generated neither response. Regional states have not formed anti-Chinese coalitions despite Beijing's expanding presence, nor have they bandwagoned by severing American ties and exclusively aligning with China. Instead, they pursue simultaneous partnerships with both powers, extracting benefits from each while avoiding exclusive commitment to either (Mearsheimer, 2001; Ullah & Xinlei, 2025a; Walt, 1990).

Realist theory struggles to explain this pattern because it underestimates how influence can operate through non-military mechanisms. The framework treats military capabilities as the ultimate arbiter of international politics, yet China exercises substantial leverage without credible capacity to project decisive force into the Middle East. Its single Djibouti facility supports logistics and humanitarian operations, not power projection. It provides no security guarantees comparable to American treaty commitments. When regional crises erupt—attacks on Saudi oil facilities, escalation in the Red Sea, confrontation between Iran and Israel—affected parties turn instinctively to Washington for military reassurance, not to Beijing. Yet this military asymmetry has not prevented China from becoming regionally indispensable through economic integration, infrastructural embedding, and diplomatic facilitation.

Liberal institutionalism captures important dynamics but suffers from a different limitation. The tradition emphasizes how institutions, interdependence, and repeated interaction enable cooperation despite anarchy's constraining effects (Keohane, 2005; Nye & Keohane, 1977, pp. 22–24). Complex interdependence theory correctly identifies that economic integration can constrain aggressive behavior and create channels for dialogue (Nye, 1977, pp. 22–24). However, the framework treats interdependence primarily as an emergent property of globalization and market forces rather than recognizing how interdependence can be deliberately designed to serve strategic objectives.

Keohane and Nye developed their framework to explain how interdependence arising from technological change and economic liberalization constrained superpower behavior during détente. They emphasized unintended consequences and system-level effects emerging from decentralized decisions by multiple actors (Keohane, 2005). Chinese engagement in the Middle East, by contrast, reflects deliberate strategic architecture. Infrastructure placements follow calculated decisions about where to establish presence for maximum effect. The sequencing of engagement, basic connectivity, then technology sectors, then digital infrastructure, reflects conscious temporal design building cumulative leverage. The distribution of investments across rival states demonstrates diplomatic design enabling parallel dependencies. This intentional architecture cannot be adequately captured by theories treating interdependence as spontaneous rather than engineered.

Dependency theory, emphasizing asymmetric economic relationships between core and peripheral economies, predicts that massive infrastructure investments and resource extraction agreements create structural dependencies enabling political domination (Cardoso, 1982; Frank, 1967). Applied to Chinese engagement, dependency theory would anticipate that lending, technology provision, and market access generate overwhelming leverage compelling political compliance.

This perspective finds some empirical support in specific cases where Chinese engagement has generated debt sustainability concerns or where economic dependence appears to constrain partner autonomy. However, it fundamentally mischaracterizes broader patterns.It cannot explain why economically powerful states with substantial autonomy, such as Saudi Arabia and the UAE, actively invite and expand Chinese engagement rather than resisting potential dependency. Saudi Arabia possesses massive financial reserves, sophisticated bureaucratic capacity, and diversified international partnerships, yet has systematically deepened ties with China across energy, infrastructure, and technology sectors. This behavior contradicts dependency theory's predictions that powerful states resist relationships potentially compromising sovereignty.

Moreover, dependency theory overstates Chinese control and understates partner agency. Empirical examination reveals that Middle Eastern states negotiate agreements protecting sovereignty, demand technology transfer rather than simple equipment provision, and maintain diversified partnerships preventing excessive reliance on Chinese cooperation. Iran has resisted Chinese demands for exclusive resource access despite severe sanctions; Gulf states have insisted on local content requirements limiting Chinese autonomy; and Egypt has renegotiated disadvantageous terms. This pattern of negotiated engagement contradicts dependency theory's emphasis on structural lock-in and limited peripheral agency. The relationships involve mutual vulnerability and reciprocal dependence, China depends on Middle Eastern energy, Gulf financial flows, and regional stability, creating bidirectional leverage rather than unidirectional subordination.

Soft power theory, emphasizing attraction to values, culture, and political models, similarly falls short (Nye & Power, 2004). China's mediating capacity in the Saudi–Iran rapprochement derived not from Saudi or Iranian admiration for Chinese civilization or desire to adopt Chinese political systems—both states maintain distinctive governance models—but from structural positioning. China had become important enough economically and strategically that its preferences regarding regional relationships mattered, its facilitation proved credible, and its successful brokerage generated benefits including enhanced legitimacy and reduced tensions threatening Chinese economic interests. Influence emerged from embedded relevance rather than ideational attraction.

The Research Question

These theoretical shortcomings point toward a fundamental gap in our understanding of contemporary international politics. How do rising powers construct durable influence in contested regions without traditional instruments of statecraft? Specifically:

> First, through what mechanisms does economic engagement translate into political leverage when military superiority is absent? Infrastructure creates operational dependencies, but how do material linkages generate diplomatic capital? Trade produces mutual interests, but under what conditions does commerce constrain political behavior?
>
> Second, why does deliberately designed interdependence prove more consequential than spontaneously emergent interdependence? What distinguishes strategic architecture from organic market integration, and how does intentional sequencing amplify influence that random transactions cannot achieve?
>
> Third, how do rising powers embed themselves across adversarial networks without triggering polarization? Why do rival states

tolerate simultaneous external partnerships that conventional alliance theory suggests should provoke exclusionary competition?
Fourth, what are the scope conditions and limitations of influence exercised through embedding rather than coercion? When does designed interdependence produce durable leverage, and when do dependencies prove reversible or politically insufficient?

This chapter introduces DSI as an analytical framework addressing these questions. DSI explains how rising powers deliberately construct influence through four interlocking dimensions, spatial, diplomatic, normative, and temporal design, that collectively embed external presence within partner states' economic systems, developmental trajectories, and strategic calculations. The framework specifies mechanisms through which infrastructure becomes political leverage, identifies scope conditions determining when these mechanisms operate effectively, and provides observable indicators enabling systematic empirical analysis.

DSI is not a theory of harmony eliminating conflict or resolving deep antagonisms through cooperation. Rather, it explains how managed tension can be strategically sustained and moderated through deliberate structural design. By embedding themselves within multiple rivals' economies simultaneously, external powers create switching costs discouraging disruption, establish institutional channels facilitating communication, and generate constituencies favoring stability. Influence operates through altered incentive structures rather than hierarchical authority, through embedded relevance rather than coercive dominance, and through designed interdependence rather than imposed subordination.

This chapter proceeds in four steps. Section 2 elaborates DSI theory, specifying its four dimensions, explaining how they interact, establishing scope conditions, and providing observable indicators. Section 3 illustrates each mechanism through brief empirical snapshots demonstrating how spatial, diplomatic, normative, and temporal design operate in practice. Section 4 compares DSI systematically with alternative theoretical frameworks, clarifying what DSI explains that existing theories cannot. Section 5 examines scope conditions and limitations, specifying when DSI works versus fails, addressing measurement challenges, and considering normative implications. Together, these sections establish DSI as a framework for understanding how influence increasingly operates in multipolar regional contexts where traditional instruments of statecraft prove insufficient, counterproductive, or unavailable.

2 Designed Strategic Interdependence: Theory and Mechanisms

Designed Strategic Interdependence offers a framework for understanding how rising powers construct durable influence in contested regional environments through the deliberate engineering of economic, technological, and institutional dependencies. At its core, DSI begins from a straightforward but powerful premise: interdependence is not merely an emergent property of globalization resulting from market forces and technological change, but can be intentionally architected to serve strategic purposes through conscious decisions about what to build, where to invest, whom to engage, and how to sequence initiatives over time.

States possessing appropriate capabilities and pursuing particular objectives can design architectures of connectivity that create durable channels of influence operating through altered incentive structures rather than threatened coercion. In doing so, they construct environments in which others' choices are shaped not by explicit demands backed by punishment threats, but by structural entanglement making certain behaviors costly and others attractive. This represents a shift from hierarchical control to embedded relevance, from episodic intervention to sustained presence, and from imposed order to designed interdependence.

DSI differs fundamentally from spontaneous interdependence in three respects. First, it involves deliberate spatial positioning: infrastructure is placed strategically to maximize both economic efficiency and political leverage, creating physical dependencies that prove difficult to reverse. Second, it operates through calibrated intensity: dependencies are deep enough to generate meaningful reliance yet diversified enough across multiple partners to avoid catastrophic overexposure. Third, it functions through temporal sequencing: engagement builds incrementally, with each phase establishing trust and operational familiarity that enable deeper integration in subsequent stages.

Where classical realism conceptualizes influence primarily as a function of superior capabilities enabling control through coercion, DSI treats influence as a function of relevance—the degree to which a state becomes integral to others' economic functioning and developmental trajectories. Where liberal institutionalism assumes interdependence emerges spontaneously from market integration, DSI treats interdependence as a product of purposeful design reflecting conscious strategic choices. And where soft power emphasizes attraction to values and voluntary emulation, DSI grounds power in material embeddedness—the capacity to shape incentives through infrastructural presence and operational dependencies that make disruption costly regardless of normative affinity.

Spatial Design: Infrastructure as an Anchoring Mechanism

Spatial design captures the strategic logic through which infrastructure transcends its conventional economic role and becomes a durable mechanism of geopolitical anchoring. Rather than serving merely as an input for market integration, cost reduction, or growth facilitation, infrastructure under a spatial design lens functions as a structural device that embeds foreign actors within the territorial and institutional fabric of host states. This embedding produces forms of material entrenchment that complicate disengagement and transform external commercial presence into a long-term geopolitical fixture (Aschauer, 1989). Scholarship in international political economy increasingly recognizes the spatiality of power projection, noting that physical installations, standards, and networks create institutional and political environments that both constrain and enable state preferences (Cowen, 2014; Farrell & Newman, 2019). Infrastructure is, therefore, not simply a capital-intensive asset but an instrument of strategic positioning that stabilizes external presence even in the face of diplomatic volatility.

The anchoring effect of spatial design operates through a precise and identifiable causal mechanism rooted in the creation of technical lock-in. Infrastructure projects generate enduring dependencies through engineering specifications, operational protocols, proprietary technologies, and maintenance requirements that bind host states to the systems of external suppliers for decades. Ports calibrated to specific container dimensions, railways reliant on unique signaling architectures, telecommunications platforms built on proprietary software ecosystems, and energy grids dependent on specialized components all establish technical baselines that cannot be easily substituted. These dependencies operate through three mutually reinforcing pathways.

First, switching costs become pronounced as replacing technically specialized infrastructure requires substantial capital, planning, and expertise. Second, operational continuity must be maintained throughout any attempted transition, meaning that parallel systems must run temporarily or that disruptions become politically intolerable. Third, network effects magnify the embeddedness of these systems as the value of each individual project increases when integrated into a broader technical architecture, rendering isolated replacement inefficient or dysfunctional (Arthur, 1994; Pierson, 2000).

Technical dependencies alone, however, do not fully explain spatial design's durability. Infrastructure projects produce domestic political constituencies that benefit materially from continued foreign involvement. Workers, subcontractors, firms, municipal authorities, and sectoral bureaucracies develop vested interests that align with the infrastructure's uninterrupted operation. These constituencies generate a politics of continuity that insulates external actors from volatility in high-level diplomacy. This dynamic contrasts sharply with political sensitivities surrounding foreign military installations, which often trigger nationalist anxieties and sovereignty concerns (Cooley & Nexon, 2020). Civilian infrastructure instead delivers widely distributed, tangible economic value, generating stakeholders who defend established arrangements even when the geopolitical relationship between states becomes strained.

Spatial design becomes empirically observable through identifiable patterns in the geography, standards, and governance of infrastructure projects. Concentration at strategic chokepoints, logistical corridors, or connectivity hubs reveals deliberate efforts to shape flows of goods, energy, and information. The adoption of technical standards that diverge from or are incompatible with those of rival suppliers signals an intention to create long-term dependencies. Multi-decade operation and maintenance contracts requiring external engineers, technicians, and proprietary systems reveal the presence of ongoing reliance rather than one-off transfers of technology. Sequential project expansions demonstrate cumulative path dependence, where initial successes legitimize further involvement in more complex or sensitive sectors such as digital infrastructure, energy systems, and smart city architectures. Finally, multi-sectoral anchoring, where logistics, communications, energy, and finance become interdependent, creates dense cross-linkages that render disengagement politically and economically prohibitive. These indicators align with broader scholarly understandings of infrastructural power, standard-setting, and geoeconomic statecraft (Hopewell, 2020; Mann, 2008).

Spatial design does not operate automatically; its effectiveness depends on specific domestic and systemic conditions. Host states with limited capacity to construct or maintain infrastructure of comparable scale or complexity are more likely to accept long-term foreign involvement. When projects align with national development priorities such as industrial diversification, urban expansion, or digital transformation, political resistance diminishes and foreign participation becomes institutionally normalized. The absence of competitive suppliers, especially when Western or regional alternatives are politically constrained or commercially uncompetitive, enhances the attractiveness of external infrastructure providers. Authoritarian or technocratic governance systems also facilitate spatial design by enabling rapid decision-making, suppressing domestic contestation, and accelerating project approval processes. Crucially, spatial design requires time; technical and institutional dependencies mature over long horizons, typically a decade or more. Scholarship on path dependence and infrastructural governance highlights that such temporal depth is essential for systems to become effectively irreversible (Mahoney, 2000; Slater & Smith, 2016).

Despite its anchoring potential, spatial design faces inherent limitations. First, large-scale infrastructure demands substantial upfront capital and long amortization periods, reducing scalability and making states vulnerable to financial risks. Second, infrastructural engagement can trigger nationalist backlash if local actors interpret it as neo-colonial or sovereignty-eroding, particularly when transparency is lacking or foreign involvement becomes highly visible. Third, dependencies, though durable, are not absolute. With sufficient political determination, fiscal resources, and international support, states can replace or diversify away from foreign systems, as demonstrated in cases where governments have nationalized infrastructure assets or pursued aggressive supplier diversification. Finally, although spatial design generates economic leverage, this leverage rarely translates directly into security influence. Infrastructure embeds presence, but it does not necessarily provide coercive tools comparable to military alliances or basing agreements. For this reason, scholars warn against assuming linear conversion of economic entrenchment into strategic alignment (Deng, 2022; Guldi, 2022).

The Mecca–Medina high-speed railway exemplifies the operational logic and strategic implications of spatial design. Completed in 2018 by Chinese firms, the project connects Islam's holiest cities and carries substantial symbolic weight for Saudi Arabia's political identity and religious legitimacy. Chinese involvement in this culturally sensitive endeavor reflects an unusually high level of trust, while the railway itself embeds Chinese engineering standards, signaling systems, and maintenance regimes into the core of the kingdom's transport network. The continued functioning of the system depends on Chinese technical expertise, specialized spare parts, and software updates (Arabia, 2024). These requirements institutionalize long-term relationships between Chinese firms, Saudi agencies, and local constituencies that depend on the railway's operation. The credibility established through the project subsequently enhanced Chinese participation in broader development initiatives, including the Riyadh Metro and NEOM. This progression illustrates how initial infrastructural anchoring can open pathways for sequential expansion into even more strategic domains, consistent with theoretical expectations regarding path dependence and infrastructural entrenchment.

Diplomatic Design: Structured Ambiguity and Parallel Dependencies

Diplomatic design captures the strategic logic through which rising powers construct political relationships and institutional frameworks that enhance influence while allowing partners to retain substantial autonomy. Rather than relying on traditional alliance structures dependent on binding commitments, exclusive alignments, or explicit security guarantees, diplomatic design emphasizes calibrated engagement that stretches across rival actors simultaneously. This approach avoids the polarizing dynamics inherent in binary alliance choices and positions the external power as a versatile and acceptable interlocutor for states that are themselves locked in regional rivalries. In contrast to classical alliance theory, which highlights commitment, credibility, and entrapment risks (Morrow, 1994; Snyder, 1997), diplomatic design relies on ambiguity, flexibility, and distributed forms of interdependence to cultivate staying power without provoking balancing behavior. This modality resonates with contemporary scholarship on hedging, nonalignment, and geoeconomic statecraft, all of which emphasize the advantages of preserving maneuverability amid systemic uncertainty (Cheng-Chwee, 2008; Katada, 2020).

The mechanism underpinning diplomatic design operates through two mutually reinforcing principles. The first is structured ambiguity, which grants strategic flexibility by avoiding rigid, codified commitments that would otherwise constrain options or trigger zero-sum alignments. By maintaining relationships with rival states without imposing alliance obligations, external powers escape the reputational costs and strategic entrapment risks associated with formal security guarantees. Structured ambiguity enables an actor to present itself not as a partisan threat but as a benign facilitator whose neutrality is rooted not in normative claims but in institutional design and policy choices. In this sense, ambiguity becomes a resource that broadens diplomatic access and reduces the likelihood that deepening ties with one actor will provoke antagonism from others. Scholars of nonalignment and hedging have long observed that such calibrated flexibility allows states to navigate contested regions without signaling hostile intent (Goh, 2005).

The second principle is parallel dependencies: a condition in which rival states rely simultaneously on the same external actor for economic, technological, financial, or infrastructural cooperation. These overlapping partnerships create indirect moderating pressures. When states entangled in regional rivalry recognize that escalatory behavior could endanger valuable cooperation with a shared partner, they gain incentives for restraint even without explicit coercion. Parallel dependencies thus operate as a stabilizing structure, not through overt enforcement but through the anticipation of economic and diplomatic opportunity costs. Unlike alliance-based deterrence, which depends on credible threats of punishment, parallel dependencies rely on the logic of mutual forbearance embedded in shared interests. This mechanism converts regional fragmentation into strategic leverage. Instead of choosing sides and reinforcing cleavages, the external power cultivates broad but non-exclusive relationships, weaving a web of overlapping ties that produce influence precisely because they do not demand alignment. This dynamic aligns with emerging work on multiplex diplomacy and geoeconomic governance, which underscores the stabilizing effects of cross-cutting interdependencies in competitive environments (Kahler, 2011; Paul, 2018).

Diplomatic design becomes empirically visible through a set of interrelated diplomatic and institutional patterns. The most prominent indicator is the maintenance of simultaneous, comprehensive partnerships with rival states: relationships that extend across trade, investment, technology, high-level political exchanges, and development planning, even when the partners themselves are locked in intense geopolitical competition. High-level diplomatic engagement persists despite mutual hostility among partners, demonstrating the external actor's capacity to sustain dialogue across fractured regional environments. Institutional frameworks such as joint commissions, strategic dialogues, and multi-year cooperation mechanisms further regularize these relationships, embedding them in bureaucratic routines rather than episodic diplomatic initiatives.

The ability to mediate disputes or facilitate dialogue among rival states arises from credibility built through consistent engagement with each side, rather than from coercive leverage or security guarantees. Diplomatic design also entails an avoidance of formal military alliances or explicit commitments that could compromise neutrality. In public rhetoric, external actors emphasize neutrality, facilitation, non-interference, and pragmatic problem-solving, framing their role as supportive rather than directive. This narrative coherence reinforces the underlying institutional logic of ambiguity and parallel engagement.

Diplomatic design requires particular structural and regional conditions to operate effectively. It is most successful in regions characterized by overlapping rivalries and plural security orders, where no single power can impose hegemonic dominance and where states seek external partners for hedging, diversification, or strategic reassurance. When a rising power possesses substantial economic capabilities but lacks overwhelming military preponderance, its engagement is less likely to be perceived as threatening or escalatory, making it an attractive partner for multiple sides simultaneously. The approach also depends on rivals maintaining minimal communication channels and sharing a basic interest in avoiding uncontrolled escalation, even if their long-term goals remain incompatible.

Diplomatic design thrives in political environments where states value economic modernization, market access, or technological cooperation, but are reluctant to enter formal alliances that would restrict autonomy or provoke domestic and regional backlash. These conditions mirror broader findings in the literature on hedging and limited alignment, which emphasize that states gravitate toward flexible partnerships when systemic uncertainty is high and alliance commitments are costly.

Despite its advantages, diplomatic design faces important limitations. Strategic ambiguity, while enabling flexibility, can undermine credibility with partners seeking clear commitments during crises. Parallel engagement across rivals also limits the depth of cooperation achievable with any single actor, as deep alignment with one party risks alienating another. Mediation capacity, though often celebrated, is structurally generated rather than leader-dependent; it ebbs quickly if the underlying configuration of parallel dependencies shifts. Moreover, diplomatic design cannot compel settlement or enforce compliance. It can create conducive conditions for dialogue, but it cannot substitute for the political will of the disputing parties themselves. Its influence is facilitative rather than determinative. This distinction matters: while diplomatic design can reduce incentives for escalation, it lacks the coercive instruments associated with traditional security architecture and therefore cannot resolve conflicts when parties remain entrenched or ideologically opposed.

China's simultaneous partnerships with Saudi Arabia and Iran exemplify the logic and practice of diplomatic design (Kaye, 2022). For decades, Riyadh and Tehran have competed across Yemen, Lebanon, Iraq, Syria, and the broader Gulf, viewing one another as existential rivals with incompatible regional visions. Despite this antagonism, both states maintain deep engagement with Beijing. Saudi Arabia is China's leading Gulf trading partner and a central node in China's economic participation in Saudi Vision 2030. Iran, constrained by sanctions and diplomatic isolation, relies on China for energy purchases, investment, and sanctions-resistant technology. These relationships are intentionally non-exclusive: neither partnership necessitates the exclusion of the other, and both derive value from Chinese economic, technological, and infrastructural cooperation. This dual embedding generated the structural position that enabled China's facilitation of the 2023 Saudi–Iran rapprochement. Beijing did not impose a settlement nor exert coercive leverage; rather, both sides viewed it as a credible facilitator because each had cultivated significant yet non-aligned dependencies. This episode illustrates how diplomatic design converts overlapping partnerships into opportunities for mediation and regional stabilization, consistent with theoretical expectations of structured ambiguity and parallel dependencies.

Normative Design: Sovereignty, Non-Interference, and Operational Trust

Normative design constitutes the ideational and discursive foundation through which external powers structure expectations, cultivate legitimacy, and enable long-term cooperation in politically sensitive or contested environments. Whereas spatial and diplomatic designs operate through material anchoring and strategic flexibility, normative design provides the principled framework that renders these other mechanisms politically acceptable and operationally stable. It does so by embedding engagement within a set of shared principles most prominently sovereignty, non-interference, equality, and mutual benefit that resonate deeply with many postcolonial states.

These principles offer a discursive repertoire that allows external actors to cultivate influence without resorting to coercion, explicit conditionality, or binding alliances, while enabling partners to frame cooperation as an exercise of autonomous agency rather than the product of external pressure. Contemporary scholarship in global governance, development politics, and international relations highlights the growing importance of normative congruence, framing effects, and legitimacy in enabling cooperation among actors with divergent political systems and interests (Acharya, 2014; Finnemore, 1996; Lake et al., 2021). Normative design, therefore, functions as the connective tissue that binds material engagement to political acceptability.

The operation of normative design rests on two interrelated processes: legitimation and the reduction of transaction costs. Legitimation occurs when engagement is framed through principles that reflect partner-state preferences, political identities, and historical experiences. By emphasizing sovereignty, non-interference, and mutual benefit, external actors reduce domestic and elite resistance within partner states, allowing governments to defend cooperation as a voluntary choice aligned with national interests. This resonates particularly in regions where historical memory of colonial subordination or externally imposed political conditionality has produced skepticism toward Western-led governance agendas. Normative congruence thus creates political cover for elites to deepen cooperation without appearing to concede authority or legitimacy to external actors.

The second process transaction cost reduction stems from the predictability that consistent normative principles provide. When external engagement is anchored in clear commitments to non-interference and respect for domestic political autonomy, partners gain greater confidence that cooperation will remain stable despite leadership turnover, regime transformation, or regional crises. This predictability reduces the perceived risk of future political demands, moral pressure, or governance conditionality, thereby facilitating long-term infrastructural, diplomatic, and technological commitments. The effect mirrors findings in institutionalist scholarship that emphasize how shared norms reduce uncertainty, enhance trust, and sustain durable cooperation in anarchic or volatile settings (Johnston, 2001; Keohane, 1984). When infrastructure agreements, investment deals, and strategic partnerships are explicitly framed as non-political and non-conditional, states with fragile or contested domestic politics perceive engagement as less threatening and more sustainable across political cycles.

The normative architecture that underpins this mode of engagement emerged in response to decades of Global South frustration with Western conditionality. Structural adjustment programs imposed by the IMF and World Bank during the 1980s and 1990s linked financial support to liberalization, privatization, and fiscal austerity, often producing significant social dislocation and political instability (Stiglitz, 2017). Similarly, foreign aid and trade preferences from Western donors frequently carried governance, transparency, and human rights conditions that constrained recipient autonomy and empowered external oversight mechanisms. These experiences contributed to what scholars have described as a "postcolonial politics of sovereignty," in which Global South states seek external partnerships that respect domestic political autonomy and reject intrusive monitoring (Hobson & Sharman, 2005).

In this context, alternative engagement models that foreground sovereignty, equality, and non-interference acquire normative resonance and political durability. Normative design thus responds to historically rooted demands for recognition, agency, and policy space, transforming these normative expectations into a strategic asset.

Normative design is empirically identifiable through a pattern of discursive commitments, contractual provisions, and diplomatic practices. External actors consistently emphasize sovereignty, equality, and non-interference in official statements, bilateral agreements, and multilateral forums. Cooperation is structured without political conditionality, avoiding explicit linkage to governance reforms, human rights benchmarks, or democratization metrics. Infrastructure, energy, and trade agreements frequently maintain formal host-state ownership and limit external oversight, reinforcing the perception that engagement respects political autonomy. External partners often sustain cooperation despite domestic political upheavals, coups, or regime transitions, signaling that engagement is anchored in principles rather than particular regimes or ideological affinities. Diplomatic language remains markedly non-judgmental, eschewing moralizing rhetoric or prescriptive demands regarding domestic governance. These observable patterns align with research on alternative development partnerships and non-Western foreign policy norms emphasizing low conditionality and respect for sovereignty (Brautigam, 2009).

Normative design functions most effectively in political environments where sovereignty and autonomy possess heightened symbolic and strategic significance. Partners who have experienced Western conditionality as coercive or destabilizing tend to favor normative frameworks that shield domestic politics from external scrutiny. Authoritarian and semi-authoritarian regimes find such arrangements particularly attractive, as they grant access to economic and infrastructural support without exposing domestic governance practices to international criticism or conditional reforms.

Regions where national identity and postcolonial narratives foreground autonomy—such as the Middle East, Africa, and parts of Southeast Asia—provide fertile ground for normative design. Its success also requires that the rising power promoting these norms refrains from pursuing ideological projects that demand political transformation or regime change abroad. When external engagement does not hinge on ideological alignment, partners perceive the normative commitments as credible and durable.

Normative design nonetheless faces significant limitations. A strict non-interference posture can inadvertently enable repression, elite corruption, or destabilizing policies by shielding domestic actors from external accountability. This can undermine long-term stability, thereby reducing the reliability of infrastructural or diplomatic cooperation. Moreover, the absence of conditionality limits the external actor's leverage when partners engage in activities that threaten regional stability or contravene the external actor's broader strategic interests. Normative consistency also becomes difficult to uphold when core economic or geopolitical interests are at stake, creating tensions between principled commitments and pragmatic imperatives. Critics therefore argue that non-interference may function as rhetorical cover for geoeconomic expansion rather than as a genuinely principled stance, a tension widely noted in debates on norm diffusion and competing conceptions of global order (Foot & Walter, 2010).

China's long-standing engagement with Iran illustrates normative design operating under constraint. Despite extensive Western sanctions targeting Iran's nuclear program, ballistic missile development, and regional activities, Chinese trade and investment persisted, consistently framed through principles of sovereignty and non-interference. This normative positioning resonated strongly with Iranian political elites, who interpreted Western pressure as illegitimate intrusion into domestic and regional affairs. By providing energy markets, infrastructure partnerships, technological cooperation, and diplomatic recognition without demanding concessions on governance or regional policy, China embedded itself as a dependable partner in the Iranian political economy.

The 2021 CSP formalized this relationship, signaling a long-term commitment built on mutual benefit rather than conditional assistance. China did not shield Iran from the consequences of sanctions entirely, nor did it endorse Iran's regional behavior; instead, it maintained a principled stance that sustained cooperation through periods of intense geopolitical pressure. This case demonstrates how normative design creates operational trust and conditions under which infrastructure, diplomacy, and parallel dependencies can function even amid severe international contestation.

Temporal Design: Sequencing, Patience, and Cumulative Leverage

Temporal design captures the strategic management of time as a resource for long-term influence-building. Unlike approaches that emphasize immediate returns, rapid conditionality, or short-term diplomatic gains, temporal design relies on pacing, sequencing, and layering engagements across extended horizons. It treats influence not as the product of singular interventions but as the cumulative outcome of repeated interactions, progressive deepening, and institutional consolidation. This temporal sensitivity distinguishes rising power engagement from Western modalities driven by electoral cycles, bureaucratic turnover, and short-term political incentives.

In international political economy and strategic studies, scholars increasingly note that time constitutes a form of structural power: the ability to wait, invest patiently, and bind others to extended sequences of cooperation generates advantages unavailable to actors operating under shorter decision horizons (Pierson, 2004). Temporal design thus transforms time from a constraint into a strategic asset, allowing influence to accrue organically through demonstrated reliability and institutional embedding rather than through coercive or disruptive means.

Temporal design operates through two mutually reinforcing processes. The first is path dependency: early decisions regarding infrastructure, standards, and institutional frameworks set trajectories that shape future choices by creating sunk costs, operational familiarity, and network effects. Initial infrastructural or economic engagements provide the material foundations upon which later, more sophisticated forms of cooperation can be built. As each layer of engagement—whether ports, industrial zones, telecommunications architecture, or financial interoperability—accumulates, the economic and political costs of reversal rise, making disengagement progressively less attractive. This logic echoes established findings in historical institutionalism, which highlight how early design choices generate increasing returns, lock-in effects, and long-term structural consequences (Arthur, 1994).

The second mechanism is cumulative trust-building. Gradual engagement across decades allows external actors to demonstrate operational competence, reliability, and predictability. Early low-risk or low-visibility projects provide proof-of-performance while minimizing political exposure for both sides. Successful implementation in these early phases generates elite confidence and domestic constituencies that support continued cooperation, enabling expansion into progressively more sensitive or strategically salient sectors such as digital infrastructure, finance, advanced manufacturing, or security-adjacent technologies. Through repeated, consistent delivery, temporal design reduces perceived risk and fosters a durable sense of partnership. This dynamic aligns with scholarship on strategic reassurance, economic statecraft, and trust formation, which emphasizes that credibility accumulates incrementally rather than through singular commitments (Kydd, 2005).

Temporal design rests on a distinct conception of strategic time. Instead of seeking rapid influence gains, it acknowledges that durable political and economic embedding requires patience, adaptability, and endurance across generational horizons. Rising powers pursuing temporal strategies invest in long-term political relationships, capacity-building initiatives, and multi-decade infrastructure plans that outlast leadership transitions both at home and abroad. By operating outside the constraints of electoral cycles, they sustain continuity across projects and maintain stable expectations among partners. This approach resonates with analyses of long-horizon planning in developmental states and geoeconomic strategy, where extended time horizons become essential to achieving structural transformation (Fukuyama, 2011).

Temporal design is observable through several consistent patterns in sequencing, duration, and strategic rhetoric. Engagement often begins with foundational projects such as energy trade, transport corridors, or industrial zones, before advancing into technologically complex or institutionally sensitive areas like 5G networks, artificial intelligence, smart city systems, or currency arrangements. Long-term contracts for infrastructure operation and maintenance, frequently spanning 20–30 years, institutionalize endurance and ensure continuous technical involvement over time.

External actors maintain engagement through partner-state political transitions, economic crises, or regional upheavals, signaling consistency rooted in long-term strategy rather than short-term opportunism. Pilot projects are deliberately coordinated with larger-scale initiatives, demonstrating iterative learning and cumulative scaling. Diplomatic discourse regularly invokes themes such as "strategic patience," "long-term partnership," or "shared future," reinforcing the temporal structure underpinning engagement.

Temporal design is most effective under particular domestic and systemic conditions. First, the rising power must possess political stability, bureaucratic continuity, and fiscal capacity sufficient to sustain multi-decade commitments. Second, partner states must prioritize long-term development over short-term crisis response, allowing patience to generate political and economic returns. Third, the relationship should be insulated from disruptive electoral cycles or abrupt ideological shifts, enabling continuity across administrations. Fourth, early projects must deliver tangible benefits that build constituencies favoring continued engagement; without demonstrable early gains, path dependency and trust-building cannot take root. Finally, regional environments with slow-moving strategic dynamics provide fertile ground for temporal design, as they allow influence to accumulate without requiring disruptive interventions.

Despite its advantages, temporal design faces important limitations. Influence accumulated gradually can be disrupted rapidly by geopolitical shocks, domestic upheaval, or sudden shifts in regional alignments. Long time horizons limit the ability to respond to urgent crises or security contingencies, making temporal design vulnerable to actors with more flexible or coercive tools. Maintaining consistency across decades demands substantial domestic political and economic commitment, which may be challenged by leadership changes, economic downturns, or public opposition to long-term foreign investments. Temporal design also depends on partners' continued willingness to engage; rapid political realignments or nationalist backlashes can destabilize long-standing sequences of cooperation. Finally, delayed payoffs can create pressures within the rising power's domestic political system, especially if investments generate uncertain or uneven returns.

Saudi Arabia's evolving engagement with China exemplifies the cumulative logic of temporal design. The relationship began with basic energy trade in the 1990s and early 2000s, establishing commercial credibility and minimal political risk. During the 2000s and 2010s, cooperation expanded into foundational infrastructure ports, industrial zones, and transportation systems, demonstrating technological capability and operational reliability. These earlier phases created a platform for subsequent expansion into advanced technology sectors, including 5G telecommunications, smart city infrastructure, and digital services integral to Saudi Arabia's national modernization agenda. More recently, financial integration has deepened through discussions on yuan-denominated oil contracts and participation in alternative payment systems, embedding China into sectors central to Saudi Arabia's long-term transformation. Each stage reinforced the next, creating a cumulative sequence of trust, capacity, and path-dependent reliance. Vision 2030's explicit incorporation of Chinese participation reflects decades of patient engagement that gradually constructed the structural conditions for comprehensive partnership.

Mechanism Interactions: How Dimensions Combine

The four dimensions of DSI do not function as isolated mechanisms but interact in patterned, mutually reinforcing ways that generate forms of influence unattainable through any single dimension alone. DSI therefore operates as an integrated system in which spatial, diplomatic, normative, and temporal components strengthen one another across sequential and cross-cutting pathways. These interactions produce synergies that magnify the cumulative effect of each mechanism, organizing influence not through dominance or hierarchy but through layered embeddedness. Understanding these pathways is essential for explaining how interdependence is intentionally constructed and sustained.

A primary interaction flows from spatial design into diplomatic design. Physical infrastructure generates tangible benefits that cultivate goodwill, while embedding technical and operational presence creates recurrent points of official contact. These everyday bureaucratic and managerial interactions widen political access and enable sustained relationship management. Competent project delivery then strengthens reputational trust, inviting expanded cooperation. Gwadar Port in Pakistan is a paradigmatic illustration: beyond its logistical and economic significance, continuous Chinese operation facilitated deeper diplomatic coordination on regional connectivity, demonstrating how spatial design opens durable political channels.

A second pathway runs from diplomatic design into normative design. Parallel engagement with rival states requires legitimating principles that explain why relationships need not be exclusive. Structured ambiguity—maintaining ties with antagonistic partners without binding commitments—depends on normative framing that emphasizes sovereignty, flexibility, and non-interference. Mediation capacity derives from this credibility: rivals cooperate with the same external partner because they believe political relationships are not instruments of coercion. The Saudi–Iran rapprochement mediated by Beijing reflects this mechanism: China's diplomatic access to both parties rested on stable normative commitments that reassured each side of its neutrality.

A third pathway moves from normative design into spatial design. Normative principles, especially sovereignty, mutual benefit, and non-interference, provide the discursive legitimacy that enables large-scale infrastructure embedding without triggering domestic backlash. When cooperation is framed as an autonomous national decision rather than external imposition, political resistance diminishes. This legitimacy also insulates infrastructure projects during crises. In Iran, for instance, Chinese infrastructural partnerships persisted through sanctions and international pressure precisely because leaders framed them as expressions of sovereign economic strategy, thereby shielding them from nationalist contestation.

The fourth and most encompassing pathway is the temporal mechanism, which amplifies all other dimensions. Time allows spatial dependencies to mature, diplomatic relationships to institutionalize, and normative commitments to accrue credibility. Sequential engagement produces a layered architecture of interdependence: early low-risk projects demonstrate reliability; subsequent initiatives expand into more sensitive sectors; long-term contracts ensure continuity; and decades of cumulative interaction produce path dependency that makes reversal costly. Temporal design thus acts as the adhesive that binds all other mechanisms together.

These interactions produce threshold effects. DSI does not succeed through dominance in a single dimension but requires minimum levels of intensity across multiple mechanisms. Spatial presence without diplomatic follow-through yields limited political leverage; diplomatic flexibility without normative anchoring appears opportunistic; normative rhetoric without infrastructural delivery lacks credibility; and temporal patience without strategic positioning generates shallow influence. Effective DSI therefore requires moderate-to-high strength across at least three dimensions simultaneously, allowing each mechanism to reinforce the others.

To visualize these dynamics, Table 1 summarizes the core interaction pathways.

Scope Conditions: When DSI Works and When It Fails

Although DSI provides a powerful account of influence-building, its effectiveness is contingent on specific structural and political conditions. These scope conditions clarify when designed interdependence generates meaningful leverage and when it fails to take hold.

Partner characteristics constitute the most fundamental determinants. DSI is most successful when partner states lack domestic capacity in capital-intensive sectors such as infrastructure, digital networks, or advanced manufacturing. Limited indigenous capabilities increase the attractiveness of external provision and decrease the feasibility of disentanglement once dependencies mature. Authoritarian or technocratic regimes offer further advantages, as insulated decision-making allows leaders to commit to long-term relationships without facing electoral volatility. States seeking strategic autonomy—especially those dissatisfied with Western conditionality—tend to embrace DSI's sovereignty-based normative framing. Partners must also possess resources or markets that justify sustained engagement: energy exporters, states with geostrategic chokepoints, or large consumer economies.

Conversely, DSI faces constraints where partners possess strong domestic industrial capacity, operate through transparent democratic processes, maintain exclusive security alignments with rival powers, or lack sufficient strategic or economic value to warrant multi-decade investment. In such contexts, one or more DSI dimensions will be structurally inhibited.

External competition further shapes DSI's feasibility. The approach thrives in environments where Western powers have withdrawn, deprioritized economic engagement, or focused primarily on security provision. Fragmented regional landscapes facilitate parallel partnerships and reduce the likelihood of forced alignment. In contrast, active competition by the

Table 1 Interaction pathways within designed strategic interdependence

Interaction	*Causal pathway*	*Empirical manifestation*	*Failure mode*
Spatial → Diplomatic	Infrastructure generates political access by creating material benefits and regular bureaucratic contact points	Port or transport projects produce recurrent bilateral dialogue and deeper diplomatic channels	Infrastructure without diplomatic follow-through yields minimal political leverage
Diplomatic → Normative	Parallel engagement requires legitimating principles to justify non-exclusivity; ambiguity must be normatively grounded	Engagement with rivals is framed through non-interference and neutrality; mediation becomes credible	Ambiguity without normative framing appears opportunistic and undermines trust
Normative → Spatial	Legitimacy reduces opposition to foreign infrastructure and protects projects during crises	Sovereignty-based discourse lowers nationalist resistance and sustains cooperation	Normative rhetoric without consistent practice erodes credibility and invites backlash
Temporal → Cumulative (all dimensions)	Patience amplifies spatial, diplomatic, and normative mechanisms through sequential layering	Sectoral deepening over decades generates path dependency and structural integration	Impatience leads partners to doubt long-term commitment, weakening embeddedness

United States, the European Union, Japan, India, or Gulf powers—particularly when backed by coordinated financing and political pressure—can constrain DSI's reach. DSI is therefore most effective in vacuums where traditional powers have reduced their footprint.

Issue-area variation introduces a third set of constraints. DSI generates strong influence in economic, infrastructural, and regulatory sectors where embeddedness produces tangible switching costs. Diplomatic facilitation also benefits from DSI's multi-vector engagement and neutrality. However, leverage is far weaker in security, ideological, and core sovereignty issues, where existential concerns override material interdependence. This asymmetry explains why states deeply embedded in DSI often maintain autonomous foreign policy positions in security matters.

Temporal dynamics produce the final set of scope conditions. DSI requires long horizons: in the first 5 years, leverage remains limited; between 5 and 15 years, operational integration expands; and after 15 years, path dependencies typically solidify. However, the slow accumulation of influence makes DSI vulnerable to rapid geopolitical disruptions. In crises requiring immediate security commitments, DSI's gradual mechanisms cannot substitute for coercive tools or formal alliances. The very temporality that empowers DSI also limits its crisis utility.

Observable Indicators: Measuring DSI Presence and Intensity

For DSI to operate as a falsifiable and comparable theoretical framework, it must be measurable. This section identifies observable indicators that allow analysts to detect the presence and intensity of DSI across cases.

Presence indicators establish whether each dimension is active.

Spatial Design

- Infrastructure contracts exceeding USD $1 billion.
- Long-term operation or maintenance agreements (10+ years).
- Adoption of technical standards incompatible with alternative suppliers.
- Multi-sector involvement in at least three domains.

Diplomatic Design

- Existence of a comprehensive strategic partnership.
- Annual (or near-annual) high-level visits.
- Parallel diplomatic engagement with rivals.
- Evidence of credible mediation or facilitation.

Normative Design

- Consistent sovereignty or non-interference rhetoric.
- Absence of political conditionality.
- Sustained engagement across leadership transitions.
- Diplomatic defense against external criticism.

Temporal Design

- Relationship duration exceeding a decade.
- Sequential progression from basic to advanced sectors.
- Multi-decade project contracts.
- Continuous engagement during crises.

Intensity indicators evaluate how strongly each dimension is expressed. A four-tier scoring system (0–3) yields a composite DSI intensity score:

0 = absent.
1 = minimal (1–2 indicators).
2 = moderate (3–4 indicators).
3 = high (5 + indicators).

DSI Intensity Score =
(Spatial + Diplomatic + Notmative + Temporal)÷4

Applied empirically, China–Saudi Arabia scores extremely high (11/12), while China–Egypt scores moderate (8/12), illustrating how the framework distinguishes cases systematically.

To complement this scoring tool, the matrix given in Table 2 captures the structure of the measurement logic.

DSI provides a coherent framework for understanding how rising powers engineer interdependence in fragmented, multipolar regions. It advances four core theoretical claims. First, interdependence can be intentionally designed; it is neither accidental nor spontaneous. Second, influence emerges through embedded indispensability rather than coercive dominance. Third, DSI's dimensions operate synergistically, producing

Table 2 DSI intensity measurement matrix

Dimension	*Low (1)*	*Moderate (2)*	*High (3)*
Spatial	One sector; limited contracts	Multi-sector; some long-term agreements	Multi-sector; large-scale projects; standards adoption
Diplomatic	Irregular engagement	Strategic partnership; periodic visits	Parallel rival engagement; mediation role
Normative	Occasional sovereignty rhetoric	Consistent non-interference framing	Strong normative alignment; diplomatic shielding
Temporal	<10 years; limited sequencing	10–20 years; visible sectoral progression	20+ years; multi-decade contracts; crisis endurance

cumulative effects far greater than their individual contributions. Fourth, effectiveness depends on structural and political scope conditions that determine when DSI can take root.

The framework contributes conceptual clarity by disaggregating interdependence into four mechanisms, offers causal precision by specifying their interaction pathways, and establishes empirical testability through clear indicators and measurement matrices. The subsequent sections provide the empirical applications (Sect. 3), theoretical comparisons (Sect. 4), and analysis of limitations and failures (Sect. 5) necessary for establishing DSI as a robust tool for analyzing contemporary statecraft.

3 Mechanism Illustrations: DSI in Practice

The preceding section elaborated DSI's four dimensions as analytical concepts, specifying their causal mechanisms, interaction pathways, and scope conditions. However, theoretical abstraction requires empirical grounding to demonstrate how these mechanisms operate in practice. This section provides brief illustrations of spatial, diplomatic, normative, and temporal design through concrete cases, showing how infrastructure becomes political leverage, how parallel dependencies enable mediation, how normative principles reduce transaction costs, and how sequential engagement accumulates influence over time. These illustrations are not comprehensive case studies—such analysis appears in subsequent chapters—but rather targeted snapshots demonstrating each dimension's operational logic through observable evidence.

Spatial Design in Action: Gwadar Port and Strategic Positioning

Gwadar Port in Pakistan exemplifies how deliberate infrastructure placement generates enduring strategic relevance that transcends commercial functionality. Located on the Arabian Sea coast of Balochistan Province, Gwadar occupies a position of exceptional geographic significance. It sits near the Strait of Hormuz through which substantial portions of global energy supplies transit, provides access to Central Asian markets through overland corridors, and offers China alternative maritime routes reducing dependence on the Malacca Strait chokepoint vulnerable to interdiction during potential conflicts.

China's engagement with Gwadar began in the early 2000s when Chinese firms constructed the port's initial phase, completing the facility in 2007 (Anwar & Hussain, 2023). However, the port's strategic significance materialized fully only after its integration into the China–Pakistan Economic Corridor announced in 2013 as the BRI's flagship project. CPEC transformed Gwadar from an isolated commercial facility into a node within a comprehensive connectivity network linking Pakistan's coast to China's western provinces through highways, railways, and energy pipelines. This integration created network effects amplifying individual infrastructure significance: Gwadar's utility depends partly on road and rail connections to Kashgar in Xinjiang, which themselves depend on Pakistani government cooperation maintaining security and operational continuity (Lin & Iftikhar, 2024). The infrastructure thus generates overlapping dependencies binding China, Pakistan's federal government, Balochistan provincial authorities, and local communities into relationships where disruption imposes costs on all parties.

The port's technical specifications and operational arrangements further exemplify spatial design's strategic logic. China Overseas Port Holding Company operates Gwadar under a 40-year lease agreement providing substantial operational control while Pakistan retains formal sovereignty. The operational protocols, management systems, and technical standards deployed at Gwadar reflect Chinese practices and specifications, creating dependencies on Chinese expertise for maintenance, upgrades, and troubleshooting. Port equipment, container handling systems, and digital management platforms require proprietary software and specialized technical knowledge that Pakistani authorities cannot easily replicate or replace with alternative suppliers (Talpur et al., 2023). These technical dependencies operate quietly, generating leverage without requiring explicit political demands or threatened coercion.

Moreover, Gwadar's development has created domestic constituencies within Pakistan possessing material stakes in continued Chinese engagement. The port generates employment for local workers, provides commercial opportunities for regional businesses, and contributes to provincial development budgets through taxes and fees. Balochistan's provincial government views Gwadar as central to economic transformation aspirations, creating political actors who defend the project against critics alleging sovereignty compromise or environmental damage (Wang et al., 2024). This constituency-building dimension of spatial design proves particularly valuable during periods of diplomatic tension or political transition, when bureaucratic and economic stakeholders advocate for relationship continuity regardless of broader political calculations.

The Gwadar case also illustrates spatial design's limitations and vulnerabilities. Security challenges, including separatist violence targeting Chinese workers and infrastructure, have repeatedly disrupted operations and generated tensions between Pakistani and Chinese officials over responsibility for protection. Local communities have protested environmental degradation, displacement, and limited employment opportunities, complicating political narratives about mutual benefit (Anwar & Hussain, 2023). Operational profitability has proven elusive, with the port handling far less cargo than projected, raising questions about commercial viability independent of strategic significance. These challenges demonstrate that spatial design, while powerful, cannot overcome fundamental security deficits, governance failures, or economic miscalculations that undermine projects despite their strategic positioning.

Diplomatic Design in Action: The Saudi–Iran Rapprochement

The March 2023 restoration of Saudi-Iranian diplomatic relations, facilitated by Chinese mediation in Beijing, provides compelling evidence of how diplomatic design operates through parallel dependencies and structured ambiguity. The rapprochement ended 7 years of formal estrangement during which the two regional powers engaged in proxy conflicts across Yemen, Lebanon, Iraq, and Syria, with sectarian rhetoric intensifying and direct military confrontation appearing increasingly plausible. Yet within weeks of Chinese-hosted negotiations, the rivals announced agreement to reestablish embassies, respect sovereignty, and refrain from interference in each other's internal affairs (Ullah & Xinlei, 2024).

China's mediating capacity emerged not from superior military capabilities enabling imposed settlements, nor from normative authority legitimizing particular outcomes, but from structural positioning accumulated through decades of parallel engagement. By 2023, China had become Saudi Arabia's largest trading partner, a central participant in Vision 2030 infrastructure projects, and a crucial technology provider for telecommunications and renewable energy systems. Simultaneously, China functioned as Iran's primary export market for oil despite sanctions, a major source of infrastructure financing and technology transfer, and a diplomatic partner providing political cover in international forums. These dual embedding created conditions enabling mediation that actors aligned exclusively with one side could not achieve (ibid.).

The rapprochement's facilitation illustrates diplomatic design's operational mechanisms. Chinese officials provided neutral venues in Beijing physically removed from regional tensions, managed logistics enabling discrete negotiations away from media scrutiny, and offered face-saving formulas allowing both parties to claim diplomatic victory domestically. Crucially, China did not impose settlement terms or threaten consequences for non-compliance. Rather, it facilitated dialogue that both parties had independently concluded served their interests, with Beijing's role limited to creating conditions enabling breakthrough when political calculations aligned (Ullah & Xinlei, 2025b).

The mediation's success derived partly from structured ambiguity characterizing China's regional engagement. By avoiding exclusive alignment with either party and maintaining consistent principles of non-interference across all relationships, Beijing positioned itself as acceptable facilitator rather than threatening partisan. Saudi officials trusted that Chinese involvement would not advantage Iranian interests at Saudi expense; Iranian leaders similarly believed Chinese mediation would not subordinate their security concerns to Saudi preferences. This mutual confidence, while perhaps fragile, proved sufficient to enable initial dialogue that might otherwise have been politically impossible due to fears that engaging with rivals could signal weakness or compromise core interests.

The rapprochement also reveals diplomatic design's limitations. China's facilitation did not resolve underlying sources of Saudi-Iranian rivalry, including sectarian differences, competing regional ambitions, divergent relationships with Western powers, or conflicting visions of regional order. The agreement addressed symptoms through diplomatic normalization but left structural causes unaddressed. Subsequent months demonstrated that restored diplomatic relations did not end proxy conflicts, eliminate mutual suspicions, or produce substantive cooperation on contested regional issues. Rather, it created channels for communication and established norms discouraging direct escalation while permitting continued competition through indirect means.

Moreover, the mediation's success depended on broader geopolitical shifts creating incentives for accommodation independent of Chinese efforts. Saudi Arabia faced international criticism over Yemen intervention and sought regional stability enabling economic transformation. Iran confronted intensifying sanctions pressure and domestic unrest, making regional tensions increasingly costly. Both states calculated that diplomatic normalization offered advantages—reduced conflict expenditures, enhanced international legitimacy, opportunities for economic cooperation—worth the risks of engaging adversaries. China's mediation proved consequential not because it compelled accommodation against parties' preferences but because it provided mechanisms facilitating outcomes both sides independently sought. This reveals both diplomatic design's power in creating enabling conditions and its limitations when fundamental interests diverge or when structural conflicts persist.

Normative Design in Action: China–Iran Engagement Under Sanctions

China's sustained engagement with Iran throughout decades of escalating Western sanctions exemplifies how normative design operates through consistent application of sovereignty and non-interference principles. Since the 1979 Islamic Revolution, Iran has faced varying degrees of international isolation, with sanctions intensifying dramatically after 2006 when the UN Security Council imposed measures targeting Iran's nuclear program. Subsequent unilateral American sanctions, particularly after 2018 when the Trump administration withdrew from the JCPOA, sought to economically strangle Tehran through secondary sanctions threatening any entity conducting business with Iranian counterparts (Ullah & Xinlei, 2025c).

Throughout these periods, China maintained infrastructure investment, technology transfer, and energy trade with Iran, explicitly framing engagement through sovereignty principles and rejecting extraterritorial application of unilateral sanctions. Chinese officials consistently articulated that cooperation with Iran represented legitimate exercise of sovereign rights, that unilateral sanctions lacked international legal foundation, and that China would not permit external actors to dictate its foreign economic relationships. This normative positioning resonated powerfully with Iranian political elites across factional divides, who viewed Western sanctions as illegitimate interference aimed at regime change and welcomed Chinese partnership as validation of Iran's autonomous development path.

The 2021 signing of a 25-year CSP between China and Iran formalized this relationship, signaling long-term commitment operating through mutual benefit rather than conditional assistance. While the agreement's specific provisions remain partially opaque, its symbolic significance proved substantial. At a moment when Iran faced maximal international isolation with pandemic-induced economic crisis compounding sanctions pressure, China's willingness to institutionalize cooperation provided political legitimacy and economic lifeline simultaneously. The agreement's emphasis on infrastructure development, technology cooperation, and energy partnerships embedded through sovereignty-respecting frameworks directly reflected normative design principles.

Operationally, normative design's effectiveness in the Iran case derived from consistency between rhetoric and practice. Chinese firms continued operating in Iran despite American threats of secondary sanctions, demonstrating that non-interference commitments were not merely diplomatic courtesy but operational reality. State-owned enterprises maintained presence in Iranian energy sectors, financed infrastructure projects, and supplied technology for telecommunications and transportation systems. While the scale of engagement fluctuated based on sanctions intensity and commercial viability, the fundamental commitment to partnership persisted regardless of Western pressure or international condemnation of Iranian policies.

This normative consistency generated operational trust enabling cooperation in sensitive sectors where Western withdrawal created vacuums. Iranian authorities welcomed Chinese involvement in projects that directly advanced national development priorities—railways connecting industrial centers, ports facilitating trade, renewable energy installations supporting economic diversification—precisely because engagement occurred without political conditionality demanding governance reforms, nuclear concessions, or regional restraint. Infrastructure became instruments of autonomous development rather than channels for external leverage, legitimizing projects politically and insulating them from nationalist criticism that might otherwise accompany extensive foreign involvement.

However, the Iran case also exposes normative design's limitations and generates legitimate concerns about its consequences. By providing economic partnerships without political scrutiny, China's engagement arguably enables authoritarian resilience and reduces pressure for domestic reforms that might enhance accountability or respect for human rights (Zheng, 2016). Technology transfers in telecommunications and surveillance systems raise questions about complicity in repressive practices when equipment and expertise are deployed for social control. Energy partnerships sustaining regime finances potentially prolong conflicts and proxy interventions that destabilize the broader region, contradicting stated Chinese preferences for stability.

Moreover, normative design creates strategic constraints when partners pursue policies threatening Chinese interests or generating instability affecting Chinese investments. Iran's regional interventions, support for proxy forces, and confrontational rhetoric toward adversaries periodically complicate Chinese diplomatic positioning and risk entangling Beijing in conflicts it seeks to avoid. China's normative commitment to non-interference limits capacity to pressure Tehran toward moderation when Iranian actions undermine regional stability upon which Chinese infrastructure and energy security depend. The tension between normative consistency and strategic pragmatism proves difficult to resolve: abandoning non-interference would undermine credibility with all partners observing Chinese behavior for signals about reliability, yet tolerating destabilizing partner actions potentially compromises the very stability that DSI requires to function effectively.

Temporal Design in Action: China–Saudi Strategic Evolution

The evolution of Sino-Saudi relations from initial diplomatic recognition in 1990 through contemporary comprehensive partnership exemplifies temporal design's cumulative logic. The relationship progressed through distinct phases, with each stage building upon previous engagement and creating conditions enabling subsequent deepening. This sequential evolution demonstrates how patient, systematically structured engagement over decades generates influence that rapid approaches cannot replicate.

The initial phase during the 1990s focused primarily on energy trade. Saudi Arabia emerged as a reliable crude oil supplier for China's rapidly industrializing economy, while China provided a growing market as Western consumption stagnated. This commercial foundation established basic trust and operational familiarity without requiring political alignment or strategic commitments. Chinese and Saudi officials developed routine channels for communication, technical personnel gained experience working across cultural differences, and both governments recognized mutual commercial benefits from sustained partnership.

The second phase during the 2000s expanded beyond energy into basic infrastructure cooperation. Chinese construction firms won contracts for industrial facilities, housing projects, and transportation infrastructure within Saudi Arabia. These projects demonstrated Chinese technical competence, cost-effectiveness, and reliability in delivering complex undertakings on schedule and within budget. Success in basic infrastructure generated invitations for expanded cooperation, with Saudi authorities increasingly viewing Chinese firms as capable partners for ambitious development initiatives rather than merely as commercial contractors.

The third phase following 2016 coincided with Saudi Arabia's launch of Vision 2030, the comprehensive economic transformation strategy aimed at diversifying beyond petroleum dependence and building knowledge-based industries. China positioned itself as central partner in Vision 2030's implementation, offering infrastructure financing, technology transfer, and expertise in sectors from renewable energy to smart city development. Chinese involvement in flagship projects including NEOM, the futuristic megacity envisioned as centerpiece of post-oil Saudi economy, embedded Beijing within initiatives upon which Saudi leadership has staked regime legitimacy and national prestige (Yang et al., 2020).

The most recent phase involves integration into strategically sensitive sectors including digital infrastructure, financial systems, and advanced technology. Huawei's deployment of 5G telecommunications networks across Saudi urban centers, despite sustained American pressure to exclude Chinese technology, reflects deepened trust and operational integration transcending commercial transactions. Discussions of yuan-denominated oil contracts, joint development of petrochemical facilities in China, and cooperation in artificial intelligence and biotechnology signal expansion into domains with profound strategic implications.

This temporal progression illustrates several key principles of temporal design. First, each phase built credibility enabling subsequent expansion into more sensitive sectors. Initial success in basic commercial exchange generated trust facilitating infrastructure cooperation; demonstrated competence in infrastructure created opportunities for technology partnership; and proven reliability in technology sectors opened pathways into strategic domains. Second, the sequencing created cumulative dependencies difficult to reverse. Energy trade established material interdependence; infrastructure embedded operational protocols and technical standards; and technology integration created systemic dependencies on Chinese platforms and expertise. Third, the relationship survived political transitions and regional crises precisely because decades of engagement created constituencies with material stakes in continuity. Saudi business communities, government technocrats, and provincial administrators all benefited from Chinese partnership, generating political support transcending individual leadership preferences.

However, temporal design's effectiveness in the Saudi case also depended on favorable conditions that are not universally present. Saudi Arabia's authoritarian governance enabled long-term commitments without electoral constraints or public accountability mechanisms demanding immediate returns. Vision 2030 provided a multi-decade development framework into which Chinese sequential engagement naturally integrated. The Kingdom's resource wealth ensured it could attract Chinese attention and sustain expensive infrastructure projects despite uncertain short-term profitability. Alignment between Chinese economic capabilities and Saudi development priorities created genuine mutual benefits rather than exploitative dependencies. These conditions enabled temporal design to function effectively, but their absence in other contexts limits the strategy's applicability and success rates.

Integrated Mechanisms: The Mecca–Medina High-Speed Railway

Some projects illustrate multiple DSI dimensions operating simultaneously, demonstrating how spatial, diplomatic, normative, and temporal mechanisms interact synergistically. The Mecca–Medina high-speed railway exemplifies this integrated approach. Completed in 2018 by Chinese firms at a cost exceeding ten billion dollars, the railway connects Islam's two holiest cities, serving millions of pilgrims annually during Hajj and throughout the year for Umrah.

Spatially, the railway embeds Chinese engineering standards, operational protocols, and maintenance requirements into Saudi Arabia's core transportation infrastructure. The system employs Chinese signaling technology, rolling stock manufactured by Chinese state-owned enterprises, and management software requiring ongoing technical support from Chinese specialists. Continued operation depends on spare parts, system upgrades, and troubleshooting expertise that Saudi authorities cannot easily source from alternative suppliers without massive costs and extended service disruptions (CCGTN, 2021). This technical lock-in generates enduring dependencies operating through material necessity rather than political coercion.

Diplomatically, Chinese involvement in such a culturally and religiously sensitive project signaled extraordinary trust between governments. Connecting Islam's holiest sites carries profound symbolic significance, and Saudi willingness to entrust this responsibility to Chinese firms rather than exclusively to Muslim-majority countries or Western corporations with longer regional histories reflected confidence in Chinese competence and reliability. The project's success enhanced China's reputation across the Islamic world, demonstrating capacity to deliver complex infrastructure respectfully navigating cultural sensitivities.

Normatively, the railway project embodied principles of sovereignty and mutual benefit consistently emphasized in Chinese engagement. Saudi authorities retained ownership and regulatory control, Chinese firms operated through contracts negotiated between sovereign equals, and the project advanced Saudi development priorities articulated in national plans rather than external agendas (Lesutis, 2020). This framing insulated the project from nationalist criticism that might otherwise accompany extensive foreign involvement in such symbolically important infrastructure.

Temporally, the railway represented a critical juncture in sequenced engagement. Its successful completion built upon decades of prior cooperation establishing China's credibility as reliable partner. Chinese firms had proven competence through earlier projects before receiving opportunity to undertake this prestigious and technically demanding initiative.

Success, in turn, generated invitations for expanded participation in even more strategic sectors including NEOM development, Riyadh Metro construction, and renewable energy initiatives central to Vision 2030. Each phase reinforced the next, creating cumulative trust and operational integration difficult for competitors to replicate through sudden entry.

The Mecca–Medina railway thus demonstrates how DSI operates as an integrated system rather than as discrete, independent mechanisms. Infrastructure placement creates material dependencies; diplomatic frameworks enable politically sensitive cooperation; normative principles legitimate foreign involvement; and temporal sequencing allows trust to accumulate and capabilities to demonstrate. When these dimensions align, the resulting influence proves remarkably durable, embedding external presence within partner development trajectories in ways resistant to disruption from political volatility or competitive challenges. The following section examines how this integrated approach compares with alternative frameworks for understanding contemporary statecraft, clarifying DSI's distinctive analytical contributions and empirical insights.

4 Comparative Logic: What DSI Explains That Alternative Theories Cannot

Having elaborated DSI's conceptual architecture and illustrated its operational mechanisms through empirical examples, this section positions the framework within existing theoretical debates. The goal is not to dismiss alternative approaches as obsolete but rather to clarify DSI's distinctive analytical contributions by specifying what it explains that existing frameworks cannot adequately capture. This comparative exercise proceeds through systematic examination of four dominant theoretical traditions—realism, liberal institutionalism, dependency theory, and soft power—identifying their explanatory limits and demonstrating how DSI addresses gaps these frameworks leave unresolved.

DSI Versus Realism: Influence Without Military Dominance

Realist theories, in their various forms, predict that rising powers expand influence primarily through military buildup, alliance formation, and coercive capabilities enabling them to compel compliance or deter opposition (Waltz, 1979, p. 88). Structural realists emphasize material capabilities and balance-of-power dynamics, arguing that states respond to power shifts through balancing coalitions or bandwagoning with stronger actors (Waltz, 1979, pp. 126–128). Offensive realists contend that great powers inevitably pursue regional hegemony to maximize security (Mearsheimer, 2001, pp. 30–31), while defensive realists argue that security-seeking behavior can trigger arms races and competitive spirals even when states prefer cooperation (Waltz, 1979, pp. 91–93).

Applied to China's Middle Eastern engagement, realist frameworks would predict several observable patterns. First, as Chinese power grows, regional states should form countervailing coalitions to balance against potential Chinese dominance, particularly given China's growing economic presence and strategic investments. Second, China should pursue military preponderance in the region through base acquisitions, naval deployments, and alliance formation to secure its expanding economic interests. Third, traditional American partners should face pressure to choose between Washington and Beijing as rivalry intensifies, generating polarization and bloc formation. Fourth, Chinese influence should correlate directly with military capabilities and willingness to threaten or use force.

The empirical record contradicts each prediction. Regional states have not formed anti-Chinese coalitions despite Beijing's expanding presence. Instead, they pursue simultaneous partnerships with multiple powers, deepening ties with China while maintaining security relationships with the United States. Saudi Arabia, the UAE, Egypt, and other traditional American partners have expanded Chinese economic engagement without abandoning American security cooperation, demonstrating hedging strategies rather than exclusive alignment. Even states with reasons to fear Chinese influence—such as smaller Gulf monarchies concerned about potential hegemonic ambitions—have welcomed Chinese investment and infrastructure rather than mobilizing resistance.

China has not pursued military dominance commensurate with its economic presence. Its single modest logistics facility in Djibouti serves humanitarian and anti-piracy operations rather than power projection. It maintains no formal security alliances, provides no defense guarantees comparable to American treaty commitments, and cannot credibly threaten military intervention to protect investments or compel compliance. When regional crises erupt, attacks on Saudi oil facilities, Red Sea shipping disruptions, and Iran–Israel escalation, affected parties seek

American military reassurance, not Chinese intervention. Yet this military asymmetry has not prevented China from becoming regionally indispensable through economic integration and diplomatic facilitation.

Moreover, Chinese influence appears uncorrelated with coercive capabilities. Beijing's mediation facilitating the Saudi–Iran rapprochement succeeded not because China could threaten punishment for non-compliance but because it offered neutral facilitation valued by both parties. Its capacity to convene negotiations derived from structural positioning accumulated through parallel economic relationships rather than from superior military power enabling imposed settlements. Regional actors accommodate Chinese preferences not because they fear military consequences but because disrupting economic partnerships would impose material costs they prefer to avoid.

DSI explains these patterns by demonstrating how influence can be constructed through embedded interdependence rather than coercive dominance. Infrastructure creates dependencies that generate leverage without requiring military superiority. Parallel diplomatic engagement enables mediation without demanding exclusive alignment. Normative principles reduce resistance by respecting sovereignty rather than threatening it. Temporal patience allows influence to accumulate gradually rather than requiring immediate assertion through force. These mechanisms operate through altered incentive structures and structural positioning rather than through threatened violence or hierarchical authority.

What realism misses, and what DSI captures, is that influence in contemporary multipolar contexts increasingly derives from relevance rather than dominance. States possessing capacity to embed themselves within others' economic systems, developmental trajectories, and institutional frameworks can shape behavior without commanding superior military capabilities. This does not render military power irrelevant, security guarantees and coercive capabilities remain consequential in specific domains, but it demonstrates that economic and infrastructural mechanisms can generate meaningful influence operating through distinct causal pathways that realist frameworks systematically underestimate.

DSI Versus Liberal Institutionalism: Designed Versus Emergent Interdependence

Liberal-institutionalist theories emphasize how international institutions, economic interdependence, and repeated interaction enable cooperation despite international anarchy (Keohane, 1984, p. 49). Complex interdependence theory, developed by Keohane and Nye, argues that multiple channels of interaction, reduced salience of military force in certain issue areas, and absence of a clear hierarchy among issues generate cooperation and constrain conflict (Keohane & Nye, 1977, 29–30). Institutional liberalism highlights how organizations and regimes reduce transaction costs, provide information, and create frameworks for iterated cooperation (Keohane & Martin, 1995, pp. 42–45).

These frameworks capture important dynamics observable in Chinese engagement. Infrastructure projects create operational dependencies; trade relationships generate shared economic interests; and institutional forums establish communication channels. Complex interdependence correctly identifies that economic integration can constrain aggressive behavior and facilitate dialogue. Liberal theories also anticipate that sustained interaction builds trust, reduces uncertainty, and creates norms encouraging cooperation over time.

However, liberal frameworks suffer from a crucial analytical limitation: they treat interdependence primarily as an emergent property of globalization and market forces rather than recognizing how interdependence can be deliberately designed to serve strategic objectives. Keohane and Nye developed their framework to explain how interdependence arising from technological change, economic liberalization, and transnational connections constrained great power behavior during détente. They emphasized unintended consequences and system-level effects emerging from decentralized decisions by multiple actors pursuing their own interests without coordinating strategies.

Chinese engagement in the Middle East, by contrast, reflects conscious strategic architecture rather than spontaneous market integration. Infrastructure placements follow calculated decisions about where to establish presence for maximum strategic effect rather than responding randomly to commercial opportunities. The sequencing of engagement, beginning with basic connectivity, expanding into technology sectors, and deepening into digital infrastructure, reflects deliberate temporal design building cumulative leverage rather than accidental progression. The distribution of investments across rival states demonstrates diplomatic design enabling parallel dependencies rather than market forces randomly distributing capital. The emphasis on sovereignty and non-interference constitutes normative design generating political capital rather than emerging organically from commercial transactions.

The counterfactual clarifies the distinction. If Chinese engagement reflected only market forces and organic interdependence, we would observe investment concentrating in most profitable sectors regardless of strategic significance, infrastructure development responding to immediate commercial returns without regard to long-term positioning, engagement patterns varying randomly across political contexts without systematic adaptation to local conditions, and temporal progression following profit maximization rather than trust-building and sequential deepening. Instead, we observe systematic patterns suggesting conscious design: infrastructure positioned at strategic chokepoints despite uncertain profitability, sustained engagement in politically complex environments where purely commercial actors withdraw, calibrated adaptation to partner characteristics enabling relationships across diverse political systems, and patient accumulation of influence through sequential engagement building trust before expanding into sensitive sectors.

DSI thus extends liberal institutionalism by demonstrating that interdependence is not merely a constraint on state behavior emerging spontaneously from globalization but can function as an instrument of statecraft deliberately architected to maximize influence. States can design the infrastructure, institutions, and sequencing of engagement to create dependencies that serve strategic purposes while generating legitimate mutual benefits. This designed character transforms interdependence from passive condition into active strategy, from unintended consequence into deliberate construction.

What liberal institutionalism misses, and what DSI captures, is the intentional architecture underlying certain forms of interdependence and the strategic calculation informing decisions about what to build, where to invest, and how to sequence initiatives. Recognizing this design dimension does not invalidate liberal insights about cooperation under interdependence but enriches understanding by incorporating the conscious engineering of interdependence itself as a mechanism through which rising powers construct influence in multipolar contexts.

DSI Versus Dependency Theory: Mutual Vulnerability versus Asymmetric Exploitation

Dependency theory, emerging from Latin American structuralist scholarship, emphasizes asymmetric economic relationships between core and peripheral economies generating systematic exploitation and political subordination. The framework foregrounds mechanisms through which powerful states extract resources from weaker partners, lock peripheral economies into disadvantageous production patterns, and employ economic leverage to compel political compliance. Applied to Chinese engagement, dependency theory would predict that massive infrastructure investments, long-term resource extraction agreements, and technology provision create structural dependencies enabling Chinese political domination over partner states.

This perspective finds some empirical support in cases where Chinese lending has generated debt sustainability concerns, where infrastructure projects appear to serve Chinese strategic interests more transparently than host country development needs, or where economic dependence constrains partner autonomy on issues Beijing considers vital. Critics citing debt-trap diplomacy arguments invoke dependency logic, contending that China deliberately extends unsustainable loans to acquire strategic assets when partners default or to leverage debt obligations for political compliance.

However, dependency theory fundamentally mischaracterizes broader patterns of Chinese engagement in several crucial respects. First, it cannot adequately explain why economically powerful states with substantial autonomy actively invite and expand Chinese engagement rather than resisting potential dependency. Saudi Arabia possesses massive financial reserves, sophisticated bureaucratic capacity, and diversified international partnerships, yet has systematically deepened economic ties with China across energy, infrastructure, and technology sectors. This behavior contradicts dependency theory's predictions that powerful states would resist relationships potentially compromising sovereignty or creating asymmetric vulnerabilities. The Kingdom's Vision 2030 strategy explicitly incorporates Chinese participation as desirable partnership contributing to developmental objectives rather than as threatening subordination requiring resistance.

Second, dependency theory overstates Chinese control and understates partner agency in shaping relationship terms. Empirical examination reveals that Middle Eastern states negotiate agreements protecting sovereignty, demand technology transfer rather than simple equipment provision, and maintain diversified partnerships preventing excessive reliance on Chinese cooperation. Iran has resisted Chinese demands for exclusive resource access despite severe sanctions constraining alternatives. Gulf states have insisted on local content requirements and operational control provisions limiting Chinese autonomy. Egypt has renegotiated terms when initial agreements proved disadvantageous. This pattern of negotiated engagement contradicts dependency theory's emphasis on structural lock-in and limited peripheral agency.

Third, dependency theory cannot explain mutual vulnerability and reciprocal dependencies characterizing many Chinese partnerships. China depends on Middle Eastern energy supplies for economic functioning, on Gulf financial flows for development financing, and on regional stability for BRI success. This mutual exposure creates bidirectional leverage rather than unidirectional subordination, enabling partner states to extract concessions and shape Chinese behavior in ways dependency theory's asymmetric framework cannot accommodate. When Saudi Arabia adjusts oil production affecting global prices and Chinese import costs, when Iran threatens regional stability disrupting Chinese infrastructure, or when UAE financial flows shift toward competing powers, these actions constrain Chinese options and demonstrate that relationships involve negotiated interdependence rather than simple extraction.

DSI addresses these limitations by conceptualizing interdependence as potentially mutual rather than inherently asymmetric. While power imbalances exist and influence relationships, DSI recognizes that rising powers often create dependencies that bind themselves as well as partners. China's energy security depends on Gulf supplies; its BRI success requires regional stability; and its technological standards gain value from widespread adoption requiring partner cooperation. These mutual vulnerabilities generate incentives for sustained partnership and restraint from exploitative behavior that would provoke resistance or relationship termination.

Moreover, DSI explains why powerful states voluntarily deepen engagement despite potential vulnerabilities. Dependency theory treats such behavior as irrational or evidence of elite corruption, but DSI demonstrates that states rationally pursue partnerships creating mutual dependencies when they gain tangible benefits, infrastructure accelerating development, technology enhancing capabilities, and markets enabling diversification, that outweigh costs of increased exposure. The framework thus moves beyond zero-sum assumptions implicit in dependency theory, recognizing that interdependence can generate genuine mutual benefits even while creating leverage opportunities for all parties.

What dependency theory misses, and what DSI captures, is that contemporary interdependence relationships often involve negotiated arrangements where both parties possess exit options, bargaining power, and capacity to shape terms rather than simple subordination of weak by strong. Recognizing this negotiated character and mutual vulnerability does not deny power asymmetries or exploitation risks but provides more nuanced understanding of how influence operates through designed interdependence rather than coercive extraction.

DSI Versus Soft Power: Material Embedding Versus Ideational Attraction

Joseph Nye's influential concept of soft power emphasizes how states exercise influence through attraction to their values, culture, and political models rather than through coercion or payment. Soft power operates when others want what a state wants, adopting its preferences voluntarily because they find its culture appealing, its values admirable, or its political system worthy of emulation (Joseph S. Nye Jr, 2004; Nye & Power, 2004). This contrasts with hard power relying on military force or economic inducements to compel or purchase compliance.

Applied to Chinese engagement, soft power theory would predict that influence derives from growing global attraction to Chinese civilization, admiration for its developmental model, or desire to emulate its political system. Chinese cultural diplomacy, Confucius Institutes, media expansion, and promotion of harmonious world order rhetoric would function as primary influence mechanisms, generating voluntary alignment through ideational appeal rather than material coercion.

However, China's Middle Eastern influence appears substantially disconnected from soft power mechanisms. Regional actors do not appear motivated by attraction to Chinese culture, values, or political models. Saudi Arabia maintains its Islamic identity and monarchical governance without desiring Chinese political emulation. Iran preserves its revolutionary Islamic system fundamentally incompatible with Chinese secular authoritarianism. Neither state seeks to adopt Chinese language, embrace Chinese cultural practices, or model domestic institutions on Chinese templates. Public opinion surveys reveal limited Middle Eastern admiration for Chinese civilization relative to Western or Islamic reference points.

China's mediating capacity in the Saudi–Iran rapprochement derived not from ideational attraction but from structural positioning. Both parties valued Chinese facilitation not because they admired Chinese values or aspired to Chinese political models but because Beijing had become economically indispensable, because its non-interference principles reduced political costs of engagement, and because its parallel relationships with both sides made it acceptable intermediary. The mediation succeeded through material embeddedness rather than normative appeal.

Similarly, Chinese infrastructure's influence operates through operational dependencies rather than voluntary emulation. When Middle Eastern states adopt Chinese technical standards in telecommunications, transportation, or energy systems, this reflects not admiration for Chinese engineering philosophy but rather practical calculations about cost-effectiveness, financing availability, and compatibility with existing Chinese-built systems. The dependencies are material—technical lock-in, switching costs, operational continuity requirements—rather than ideational.

DSI explains influence through mechanisms distinct from soft power. Spatial design generates leverage through infrastructure embedding creating material dependencies. Diplomatic design enables mediation through structural positioning rather than normative authority. Normative design operates through sovereignty rhetoric reducing resistance rather than through cultural attraction generating voluntary alignment. Temporal design accumulates influence through patient sequential engagement rather than through ideational persuasion inspiring emulation.

This does not mean soft power is irrelevant. China invests substantially in cultural diplomacy, media presence, and public diplomacy initiatives suggesting Beijing values ideational influence. However, the primary mechanisms generating Chinese influence in the Middle East operate through material embeddedness rather than cultural attraction, through designed interdependence rather than voluntary emulation, and through structural positioning rather than normative appeal.

What soft power theory misses, and what DSI captures, is that influence can be constructed through material mechanisms creating dependencies that constrain choices regardless of normative affinity or cultural attraction. States cooperate with China not primarily because they admire Chinese civilization but because infrastructure dependencies, energy relationships, and economic integration make cooperation rational and disruption costly. This material embeddedness operates through distinct causal pathways that soft power frameworks systematically overlook by focusing exclusively on ideational mechanisms.

The comparative analysis reveals DSI's unique explanatory power. DSI is not a universal theory replacing all alternatives. Realist insights remain valuable for understanding security competitions and military conflicts. Liberal institutionalism illuminates cooperation dynamics within established multilateral frameworks. Dependency theory highlights exploitation risks in asymmetric relationships. Soft power theory explains influence derived from cultural attraction where such mechanisms operate. However, DSI addresses a distinct analytical space these frameworks leave undertheorized: how rising powers systematically engineer interdependence to construct influence in multipolar regional contexts where traditional instruments prove insufficient, counterproductive, or unavailable.

The framework's analytical contribution lies in specifying mechanisms through which infrastructure, diplomacy, norms, and temporal sequencing combine to generate influence operating through designed interdependence. By identifying scope conditions, interaction effects, and observable indicators, DSI enables systematic empirical analysis of patterns that existing frameworks explain inadequately. The following section examines where DSI's explanatory power encounters limits, specifying conditions under which the framework's mechanisms fail to generate influence and addressing normative implications of influence exercised through designed interdependence.

5 Scope and Limits: When DSI Fails and What It Reveals

Having elaborated DSI's conceptual architecture, illustrated its operational mechanisms, and positioned it within existing theoretical debates, this final section confronts the framework's boundaries. No theory explains all outcomes across all contexts, and DSI is no exception. Specifying when and why the framework's mechanisms fail to generate influence proves as analytically important as demonstrating where they succeed. This section examines three dimensions of limitation: empirical failures where DSI mechanisms did not produce expected outcomes, measurement challenges complicating systematic operationalization, and normative implications raising questions about whether influence exercised through designed interdependence proves desirable even when effective. Together, these limitations establish DSI's scope conditions, clarify its analytical boundaries, and acknowledge tensions between explanatory power and normative evaluation.

When DSI Fails: Lessons from Malaysia, Myanmar, and Sri Lanka

DSI's mechanisms do not guarantee influence. Several cases illustrate conditions under which infrastructure investments, diplomatic engagement, normative appeals, and patient sequencing fail to generate anticipated leverage or produce outcomes contradicting DSI's logic.

Malaysia provides instructive evidence of DSI's limits when domestic political transitions empower actors skeptical of Chinese engagement. Following the 2018 electoral defeat of Prime Minister Najib Razak's government, the incoming Mahathir administration immediately scrutinized BRI projects negotiated under the previous regime. The East Coast Rail Link, a signature infrastructure project linking Malaysia's west coast to eastern states, faced cancellation amid allegations of inflated costs, excessive debt burdens, and insufficient benefits for Malaysian development. Chinese firms had invested substantial resources in planning and initial construction, employing spatial design logic by positioning the railway to connect Malaysian production centers with regional trade networks. Yet political transition exposed the project's vulnerability to domestic contestation.

After protracted renegotiations, Malaysia secured significant cost reductions and revised terms, demonstrating that Chinese infrastructure investments do not automatically generate irreversible dependencies or constrain partner sovereignty when domestic political will mobilizes against perceived unfavorable arrangements. The case reveals several conditions limiting DSI effectiveness. First, electoral democracies with competitive politics can generate leadership changes that repudiate predecessors' commitments, particularly when opposition parties campaign on nationalist platforms questioning foreign partnerships. Second, when projects lack transparent benefits visible to domestic constituencies, they become politically vulnerable regardless of technical lock-in or switching costs. Third, partner states with sophisticated negotiating capacity can extract concessions during implementation when initial terms prove disadvantageous, demonstrating that dependencies remain partially reversible through determined renegotiation backed by credible threats of project cancellation.

Myanmar similarly illustrates DSI's fragility during acute political crises requiring rapid responses incompatible with patient temporal design. China invested decades building relationships with Myanmar's military and civilian governments, financing infrastructure including the Kyaukpyu deep-water port and multiple hydroelectric projects, and positioning itself as Myanmar's primary external partner through consistent engagement transcending domestic political volatility. Yet the February 2021 military coup that overthrew the elected government and subsequent brutal crackdown on protesters exposed Chinese diplomatic design's limitations when partners pursue policies generating international condemnation and domestic resistance.

China's initial response, avoiding explicit condemnation of the coup and maintaining engagement with the military junta, protected immediate economic interests and preserved access to strategic infrastructure. However, this stance generated significant reputational costs, with civil society actors across Myanmar and the broader region viewing Chinese non-interference as complicity in military repression. Moreover, ongoing instability, armed resistance, and economic disruption threatened Chinese infrastructure investments whose viability depended on stability that the coup shattered. The case demonstrates that DSI mechanisms optimized for stable or gradually changing political environments prove brittle during acute crises demanding immediate moral positioning or when partner actions trigger sustained domestic resistance undermining the operational continuity upon which infrastructure dependencies rely.

Sri Lanka's experience with the Hambantota Port project became emblematic of debt-trap diplomacy allegations, though the actual dynamics prove more complex than critics suggest. Chinese financing enabled port construction in a region lacking adequate maritime infrastructure, employing spatial design logic by positioning facilities to serve Indian Ocean shipping lanes. However, the port generated insufficient commercial revenue to service debt obligations, and Sri Lanka's broader fiscal crisis compounded by multiple factors, including tax cuts, economic mismanagement, and global commodity price fluctuations, created unsustainable debt burdens. In 2017, Sri Lanka agreed to a 99-year lease transferring operational control to a Chinese state-owned enterprise in exchange for debt relief, generating accusations that China deliberately extended predatory loans to acquire strategic assets.

The reality reveals both DSI's effectiveness and its limitations. Chinese financing did create dependencies that Sri Lankan governments could not easily escape, validating DSI's premise that infrastructure generates enduring leverage. However, the case also exposed how poorly designed projects lacking commercial viability or adequate demand forecasting can generate political backlash undermining broader relationship legitimacy. Domestic opposition portrayed the port lease as sovereignty surrender, nationalist rhetoric mobilized against Chinese presence, and subsequent Sri Lankan governments faced pressure to scrutinize or renegotiate Chinese projects. The case demonstrates that spatial design's effectiveness depends on projects delivering tangible benefits justifying their costs; when infrastructure becomes visible symbol of debt burden rather than development catalyst, political protection evaporates regardless of technical dependencies.

These failure cases reveal common patterns limiting DSI effectiveness. First, domestic political accountability mechanisms including competitive elections, free media, and civil society mobilization can generate opposition that reverses or renegotiates arrangements when perceived as disadvantageous, particularly when projects lack transparent benefits or when economic difficulties make debt burdens politically salient. Second, acute political crises requiring rapid responses expose temporal design's brittleness; patient accumulation of influence over decades cannot substitute for immediate crisis management capacity or moral authority enabling decisive intervention. Third, projects lacking commercial viability or adequate demand forecasting generate political vulnerabilities regardless of technical lock-in, as partners question value and seek renegotiation when costs exceed benefits. Fourth, normative design's emphasis on non-interference proves constraining when partners pursue destabilizing policies generating international condemnation or domestic resistance, limiting capacity to pressure moderation when strategic interests demand it.

Measurement Challenges: Operationalizing DSI Empirically

Beyond empirical failures, DSI faces significant measurement challenges complicating systematic operationalization and comparative analysis across cases. Three methodological difficulties warrant acknowledgment.

First, distinguishing designed interdependence from spontaneous market integration proves difficult without access to internal decision-making processes. When Chinese firms invest in Middle Eastern infrastructure, how do researchers determine whether placements reflect conscious strategic calculation versus commercial opportunism responding to market signals? Official rhetoric emphasizing strategic partnership may mask purely profit-driven decisions, while genuinely strategic investments may be publicly framed as commercial transactions to reduce political sensitivity. Without access to classified planning documents or elite interviews revealing actual decision-making logic, attributing intentionality remains partially speculative.

This challenge becomes acute when analyzing temporal sequencing. DSI posits that sequential engagement builds cumulative influence through deliberate staging, yet observed patterns could reflect path-dependent market dynamics where initial successes generate subsequent opportunities without conscious long-term design. Demonstrating that 1990s energy trade was causally linked to 2020s technology partnerships requires evidence that early planners anticipated later outcomes and structured initial engagements accordingly, evidence rarely available in public sources.

Second, measuring influence itself proves methodologically fraught. DSI claims that designed interdependence generates leverage shaping partner behavior, but how do researchers distinguish influence from coincidental preference alignment? When Saudi Arabia accommodates Chinese preferences on particular issues, does this reflect genuine leverage from economic dependencies, or would Saudi policies have been identical absent Chinese engagement due to independent strategic calculations? Establishing counterfactuals enabling causal inference about influence proves difficult without experimental variation impossible in international relations.

Moreover, influence operates across multiple dimensions, economic policy, diplomatic positioning, and technology standards, requiring composite measurement aggregating diverse outcomes. A state may accommodate Chinese preferences on trade while resisting on security, complicating assessment of whether DSI has succeeded or failed. Developing valid indicators measuring influence across domains while accounting for issue-area variation remains an ongoing methodological challenge requiring careful case-by-case analysis rather than simple quantitative metrics.

Third, scope conditions require precise specification to enable falsification, yet existing formulations remain partially ambiguous. DSI posits effectiveness varies with partner characteristics, external competition, issue areas, and temporal dynamics, but exact thresholds determining when conditions favor or undermine DSI mechanisms remain underspecified. At what point does democratic accountability become sufficiently strong to constrain infrastructure dependencies? How intense must external competition n become before DSI advantages disappear? Which specific security issues prove resistant to economic leverage? Without precise specification, the framework risks unfalsifiability where any outcome can be post-hoc rationalized as consistent with scope conditions.

These measurement challenges do not invalidate DSI but require humility about empirical claims and careful methodological attention in subsequent research. Researchers employing the framework should triangulate multiple data sources, use process tracing to establish causal mechanisms linking DSI dimensions to influence outcomes, conduct comparative analysis examining variation across cases with different scope conditions, and remain attentive to alternative explanations attributing observed patterns to factors beyond designed interdependence. Observable indicators in Sect. 2.4 provide starting points, but systematic operationalization requires continued methodological refinement as the framework undergoes empirical testing.

Normative Implications: Power, Accountability, and Development

Beyond empirical and methodological limitations, DSI raises normative questions about whether influence exercised through designed interdependence proves desirable even when effective. Three concerns warrant serious consideration.

First, DSI's emphasis on non-interference and sovereignty respect, while appealing to states valuing autonomy, can enable authoritarian resilience by providing economic partnerships shielding regimes from accountability pressures. When China finances infrastructure, provides technology, and offers diplomatic support without conditioning assistance on governance reforms, human rights compliance, or democratic transitions, it reduces incentives for authoritarian regimes to liberalize or become more accountable to populations. Critics contend this makes China complicit in sustaining repressive systems, with infrastructure and technology potentially deployed for surveillance, social control, and repression rather than solely for developmental purposes.

This critique carries force particularly regarding technology transfers. When Chinese firms provide telecommunications equipment, surveillance systems, or social media monitoring capabilities to authoritarian partners, these technologies can enhance state capacity for population control as readily as for development administration. The normative principle of non-interference becomes problematic when it facilitates technology provision enabling human rights violations. DSI's analytical framework treats effectiveness and ethics as separate questions, focusing on explaining influence mechanisms rather than evaluating their moral implications, but scholars and policymakers must grapple with normative tensions even while recognizing analytical distinctions.

Second, infrastructure financing through long-term loans creates debt sustainability concerns that disproportionately burden vulnerable populations when projects fail to generate anticipated revenues. While Sri Lanka's experience with Hambantota Port involved complex factors beyond Chinese predation, the outcome demonstrates real risks: when infrastructure proves commercially unviable, governments face debt distress requiring austerity measures, reduced social spending, or asset transfers affecting citizens who derived no direct benefits from projects. The distributional consequences of infrastructure dependencies warrant normative scrutiny even when aggregate economic effects prove positive.

Moreover, decision-making processes surrounding major infrastructure projects in authoritarian or weakly institutionalized contexts often lack transparency, enabling corruption and elite enrichment at public expense. When projects involve non-competitive bidding, opaque contract terms, or limited public consultation, they risk serving elite interests rather than broader developmental needs. DSI's analytical framework focuses on how infrastructure generates influence rather than evaluating whether it advances equitable development, but normative assessment requires examining distributional impacts and governance quality alongside influence mechanisms.

Third, designed interdependence creates asymmetric vulnerabilities that constrain partner sovereignty despite formal equality rhetoric. When states become dependent on Chinese infrastructure, technology, and markets, their decision-making autonomy narrows even without explicit Chinese demands. Partners must consider Chinese preferences when formulating policies affecting bilateral relationships, anticipating potential disruption costs, and moderating positions that might jeopardize valuable partnerships. This self-censorship operates through structural constraints rather than overt coercion, making dependencies potentially more insidious than explicit conditional assistance that at least makes power asymmetries visible.

The tension between formal sovereignty and operational autonomy proves particularly acute for smaller or economically vulnerable states with limited alternatives. While Saudi Arabia or UAE can leverage multiple partnerships maintaining genuine autonomy despite Chinese dependencies, states like Laos, Cambodia, or certain African countries possess fewer options and face steeper costs from relationship disruption (Ross, 1992; Womack, 2003). DSI's scope conditions acknowledge this variation, but normative evaluation must consider whether influence mechanisms that respect sovereignty formally while constraining autonomy practically prove ethically defensible.

These normative concerns do not invalidate DSI as analytical framework, which aims to explain rather than justify influence mechanisms. However, they demand that scholars and policymakers employing the framework remain attentive to ethical dimensions alongside explanatory power. Understanding how designed interdependence operates proves essential for both supporters seeking to replicate successful strategies and critics seeking to mitigate problematic consequences. Subsequent empirical chapters examine these dynamics through detailed case analysis, testing DSI's explanatory claims while remaining cognizant of normative complexities surrounding influence exercised through infrastructure, technology, and patient engagement.

References

Acharya, A. (2014). *The end of American world order* (Vol. 6). Polity Press.

Anwar, U., & Hussain, Z. (2023). Game changer for Pakistan: Significance of Gwadar for Pakistan economy & factors of underutilization of Gwadar port. *Journal of Nautical Eye and Strategic Studies, 3*(1), 110–126.

Arabia, G. O. S. (2024). *Vision 2030*. https://www.vision2030.gov.sa/en/

Arthur, W. B. (1994). *Increasing returns and path dependence in the economy*. University of Michigan Press.

Aschauer, D. A. (1989). Is public expenditure productive? *Journal of Monetary Economics, 23*(2), 177–200.

Brautigam, D. (2009). *The dragon's gift: The real story of China in Africa*. Oxford University Press.

Cardoso, F. H. (1982). Dependency and development in Latin America. In *Introduction to the sociology of "developing societies"* (pp. 112–127). Springer.

CCGTN. (2021). *Chinese-built Mecca-Medina high-speed railway changes the appearance of Saudi Arabia's cities*. CCGTN. https://news.cgtn.com/news/2022-12-11/Mecca-Medina-High-speed-Railway-changes-the-appearance-of-Saudi-Arabia-1fGg6FEumbe/share_amp.html

Cheng-Chwee, K. (2008). The essence of hedging: Malaysia and Singapore's response to a rising China. *Contemporary Southeast Asia: A Journal of International and Strategic Affairs, 30*(2), 159–185.

Cooley, A., & Nexon, D. (2020). *Exit from hegemony: The unraveling of the American global order*. Oxford University Press.

Cowen, D. (2014). *The deadly life of logistics: Mapping violence in global trade*. University of Minnesota Press.

Deng, Y. (2022). *China's strategic opportunity*. Cambridge University Press.

Farrell, H., & Newman, A. L. (2019). Weaponized interdependence: How global economic networks shape state coercion. *International Security, 44*(1), 42–79.

Finnemore, M. (1996). *National interests in international society*. Cornell University Press.

Foot, R., & Walter, A. (2010). *China, the United States, and global order*. Cambridge University Press.

Frank, A. G. (1967). *Capitalism and underdevelopment in Latin America* (Vol. 93). New York University Press.

Fukuyama, F. (2011). *The origins of political order: From prehuman times to the French Revolution*. Profile Books.

Goh, E. (2005). *Meeting the China challenge: The US in Southeast Asian regional security strategies*. East-West Center Washington.

Guldi, J. (2022). *The long land war: The global struggle for occupancy rights*. Yale University Press.

Hobson, J. M., & Sharman, J. C. (2005). The enduring place of hierarchy in world politics: Tracing the social logics of hierarchy and political change. *European Journal of International Relations, 11*(1), 63–98.

Hopewell, K. (2020). *Clash of powers: US-China rivalry in global trade governance*. Cambridge University Press.

Johnston, A. I. (2001). Treating international institutions as social environments. *International Studies Quarterly, 45*(4), 487–515.

Joseph S., & Nye Jr. (2004). *Soft Power: The Means to Success in World Politics*. New York: Public Affairs.

Kahler, M. (2011). *Networked politics: Agency, power, and governance*. Cornell University Press.

Katada, S. N. (2020). *Japan's new regional reality: Geoeconomic strategy in the Asia-Pacific*. Columbia University Press.

Kaye, D. D. (2022). America's role in a post-American Middle East. *The Washington Quarterly, 45*(1), 7–24.

Keohane, R. O. (1984). *After hegemony: Cooperation and discord in the world political economy*. Princeton University Press.

Keohane, R. O. (2005). *After hegemony: Cooperation and discord in the world political economy*. Princeton University Press.

Keohane, R. O., & Martin, L. L. (1995). The promise of institutionalist theory. *International Security, 20*(1), 39–51.

Kydd, A. H. (2005). *Trust and mistrust in international relations*. Princeton University Press.

Lake, D. A., Martin, L. L., & Risse, T. (2021). Challenges to the liberal order: Reflections on international organization. *International Organization, 75*(2), 225–257.

Lesutis, G. (2020). How to understand a development corridor? The case of Lamu Port-South Sudan–Ethiopia-Transport corridor in Kenya. *Area, 52*(3), 600–608.

Lin, W., & Iftikhar, R. (2024). CEPC and Gwadar port: Viabilities and challenges. *Annals of Human and Social Sciences, 5*(2), 575–581.

Mahoney, J. (2000). Path dependence in historical sociology. *Theory and Society, 29*(4), 507–548.

Mann, M. (2008). Infrastructural power revisited. *Studies in Comparative International Development, 43*(3), 355–365.

Mearsheimer, J. (2001). *The tragedy of great power politics/John J. Mearsheimer*. W. W. Norton.

Morgenthau, H. (1948). *Politics among nations: The struggle for power and peace*. Alfred A. Knopf.

Morrow, J. D. (1994). *Game theory for political scientists*. Princeton University Press.

Nye, J., & Power, S. (2004). *The means to success in world politics*. Public Affairs.

Paul, T. V. (2018). *Restraining great powers: Soft balancing from empires to the global era*. Yale University Press.

Pierson, P. (2000). Increasing returns, path dependence, and the study of politics. *American Political Science Review, 94*(2), 251–267.

Pierson, P. (2004). *Politics in time: History, institutions, and social analysis*. Princeton University Press.

Robert O., Keohane & Joseph S. Nye Jr. (1977). *Power and Interdependence: World Politics in Transition*. Boston: Little, Brown and Company.

Ross, R. S. (1992). China and post-Cambodia Southeast Asia: Coping with success. *The Annals of the American Academy of Political and Social Science, 519*(1), 52–66.

Slater, D., & Smith, N. R. (2016). The power of counterrevolution: Elitist origins of political order in postcolonial Asia and Africa. *American Journal of Sociology, 121*(5), 1472–1516.

Snyder, G. (1997). *Alliance politics*. Cornell University Press.

Stiglitz, J. E. (2017). *Globalization and its discontents revisited: Anti-globalization in the era of Trump*. W. W. Norton.

Talpur, A. R., Ahmed, J., & Katohar, H. A. (2023). Development of Gwadar port: A plight for Fisherfolk community. *Journal of Development and Social Sciences, 4*(3), 202–211.

Ullah, A., & Xinlei, L. (2024). Navigating the Persian Gulf security complex: Saudi-Iran rapprochement in an era of great power competition. *East Asia, 41*(3), 273–300. https://doi.org/10.1007/s12140-024-09430-2

Ullah, A., & Xinlei, L. (2025a). Great power divergence: Military primacy versus economic engagement in the Israeli-Palestinian conflict: A theoretical reexamination of realist paradigms. *Chinese Political Science Review*, 1–28. https://doi.org/10.1007/s41111-025-00287-1

Ullah, A., & Xinlei, L. (2025b). Navigating complex interdependence: An in-depth analysis of Iran and Saudi Arabia's strategic engagement with the BRI in the Middle East. *Chinese Political Science Review, 10*(1), 72–100.

Ullah, A., & Xinlei, L. (2025c). Systemic constraints and state behavior: A neorealist perspective on China's BRI and Iran's strategic calculations. *Iranian Studies, 58*(3), 526–547.

Walt, S. M. (1990). *The origins of alliance*. Cornell University Press.

Waltz, K. (1979). *Theory of international politics*. McGraw.

Wang, B., Dong, K., Zhong, W., & Zhao, C. (2024). Can high-quality energy development and energy security achieve a win-win situation? The case of China. *Economic Analysis and Policy, 83*, 17–28.

Womack, B. (2003). Asymmetry and systemic misperception: China, Vietnam and Cambodia during the 1970s. *Journal of Strategic Studies, 26*(2), 92–119.

Yang, Z., Du, L., & Ding, L. (2020). The China-Saudi Arabia (Jizan) industrial park under the Belt and Road Initiative. *Asian Journal of Middle Eastern and Islamic Studies, 14*(4), 528–537.

Zheng, C. (2016). China debates the non-interference principle. *The Chinese Journal of International Politics, 9*(3), 349–374.

CHAPTER 3

Proxy Wars and Rivalry: The Saudi–Iranian Contest for the Middle East

1 The Historical Roots of the Rivalry

The modern Saudi–Iranian rivalry cannot be understood through the narrow lens of the 1979 Revolution alone. Its foundations were laid decades earlier, during the formative periods when both states emerged as centralized monarchies controlling vast oil wealth and claiming leadership over competing visions of Islamic legitimacy. While their parallel trajectories toward petro-state power created structural similarities, the paths they followed also planted the seeds of future confrontation. Understanding how Saudi Arabia and Iran became regional powers reveals why their rivalry proved so persistent and why it resisted resolution for over four decades.

Parallel State Formation and the Seeds of Competition

The foundation of the modern Saudi state under Abdul Aziz Ibn Saud's leadership between 1914 and 1932 involved a sophisticated combination of military conquest, tribal alliance-building, and strategic partnership with Great Britain. As Al-Enazy (2010) documents, Ibn Saud transformed a collection of feuding tribes into a unified kingdom through careful navigation between competing imperial powers while building domestic coalitions that could sustain centralized rule. The Anglo-Saudi Treaty of

A. Ullah, *Diplomacy by Design*,
https://doi.org/10.1007/978-981-95-7876-4_3

Darin in 1915 provided crucial external support for Ibn Saud's territorial ambitions against Ottoman-backed rivals, establishing patterns of great power involvement in Arabian affairs that would shape Saudi foreign policy for generations (Al-Enazy, 2010).

The Saudi state's consolidation depended critically on Ibn Saud's alliance with the Wahhabi religious movement, which provided ideological legitimacy for conquest and unification. This partnership created a distinctive governance model where monarchical authority derived legitimacy from custodianship of Islam's holiest sites and strict adherence to Wahhabi interpretations of Islamic law (Al-Rasheed, 2010). The formal establishment of the Kingdom of Saudi Arabia in 1932 marked the culmination of this process, creating a state whose very identity rested on claims to represent authentic Sunni Islam and to protect the sacred geography of Mecca and Medina (Wynbrandt, 2010).

Iran's path to modern statehood followed different trajectories but produced remarkably similar outcomes. The Pahlavi dynasty, established by Reza Khan in 1925, pursued authoritarian modernization that paralleled developments in Saudi Arabia while reflecting distinctly Persian cultural traditions. Like Ibn Saud, Reza Shah consolidated power through military campaigns that pacified tribal regions and created effective centralized control over previously fragmented territories. The construction of the Trans-Iranian Railway in 1938 symbolized Iran's commitment to modernization and national integration, demonstrating state capacity for mobilizing resources toward major developmental projects (Chehabi, 1998).

Yet Iran's historical experience differed from Saudi Arabia's in ways that would later fuel rivalry. Iran possessed a longer history as a unified state, a larger and more diverse population, and a tradition of Persian imperial grandeur that shaped elite self-conceptions and regional ambitions. These asymmetries created different sources of national pride and regional influence. While Saudi Arabia derived legitimacy from religious custodianship and tribal confederation, Iran's nationalism drew on imperial legacy and cultural sophistication stretching back millennia.

The discovery and development of oil resources transformed both states but in ways that accentuated their differences as much as their similarities. Saudi Arabia's oil discovery at Dammam in 1938 came relatively late in its state formation process, allowing the monarchy to incorporate petroleum revenues into existing governance structures (Clifford, 1976). The establishment of Aramco in 1944 created institutional frameworks for managing oil wealth that strengthened rather than disrupted the Al Saud family's political dominance. Oil revenues funded rapid modernization, comprehensive welfare programs, and military capabilities while reinforcing monarchical legitimacy through state provision of public goods (Jones, 2010).

Iran's petroleum experience followed a more turbulent path that generated lasting grievances against foreign control. The Anglo-Persian Oil Company's dominance over Iranian oil development created resentments that erupted during the 1951–1953 nationalization crisis. Prime Minister Mohammad Mossadegh's attempt to assert Iranian control over petroleum resources and his subsequent overthrow through CIA-orchestrated intervention established patterns of anti-Western nationalism and suspicion of foreign interference that would profoundly influence Iranian political culture (Abrahamian, 2018; Byrne & Gasiorowski, 2015). The restoration of the Shah consolidated American influence while also deepening domestic opposition to foreign domination.

Under Mohammed Reza Shah Pahlavi, Iran experienced rapid economic development and emerged as a regional power with global ambitions. The White Revolution's reforms in land distribution, women's rights, and industrialization modernized Iranian society while generating social tensions that contributed to revolutionary pressures. The Shah's Iran developed one of the world's most advanced military forces and pursued independent foreign policy initiatives that sometimes conflicted with American preferences, including support for oil price increases during the 1970s that enriched the Kingdom but complicated Western economic interests (Hambly, 1963).

By the late 1970s, both Saudi Arabia and Iran had become oil-rich monarchies maintaining close relationships with the United States while asserting increasing independence in foreign policy. Both benefited enormously from rising oil prices, using petroleum revenues to fund ambitious development programs and build military capabilities that enhanced regional influence. Both maintained conservative social orders despite rapid economic modernization. These structural similarities created conditions for either cooperation or competition.

Yet differences in their development trajectories created potential sources of conflict that would become acute after 1979. Iran's larger population, more diversified economy, and longer historical experience as a unified state provided certain advantages in regional competition. Its revolutionary and nationalist political culture, shaped by the

Mossadegh experience and suspicion of foreign control, differed fundamentally from Saudi Arabia's conservative monarchical traditions and close Western alignment. Saudi Arabia's control over Islam's holiest sites provided unique religious authority that Iran could not match, while Iran's Persian imperial heritage and Shi'a theological traditions offered alternative sources of regional influence (Nasr, 2007).

The governance structures established during this formative period also planted seeds of future rivalry. The Saudi monarchy's legitimacy derived from Wahhabi religious authority and custodianship of holy sites, creating a state whose identity was inseparable from claims to represent authentic Sunni Islam. Iran's Pahlavi monarchy, by contrast, derived authority from nationalist modernization and Persian imperial legacy rather than religious credentials. These different legitimation strategies meant that when Iran's political order transformed in 1979, it would produce a revolutionary ideology directly challenging Saudi claims to Islamic leadership.

The rentier economic model both states adopted during this period created parallel but distinct vulnerabilities. As Hertog (2007, 2017) and Luciani (2017) demonstrate, rentier states face inherent challenges in developing non-oil economic sectors and creating sustainable employment for growing populations. Both Saudi Arabia and Iran used oil revenues to provide extensive welfare benefits and subsidies that fostered political stability through fiscal distribution rather than democratic participation. Yet this model also created long-term dependencies on volatile global oil markets and made both states vulnerable to price fluctuations that could trigger fiscal crises and political instability.

The stage was thus set by the late 1970s for either unprecedented cooperation or destructive rivalry between the Middle East's two most powerful oil-producing states. Both had modernized rapidly, both had accumulated substantial military capabilities, both maintained important relationships with global powers, and both harbored ambitions for regional leadership. Whether their parallel trajectories would generate partnership or conflict depended ultimately on political developments within each country and the broader regional context within which they operated.

The 1979 Iranian Revolution would decisively resolve this question, transforming what might have been a natural partnership between wealthy oil monarchies into one of the most destructive and persistent conflicts in modern Middle Eastern history. The revolution replaced Iran's pro-Western monarchy with a theocratic regime explicitly committed to exporting revolutionary ideology and challenging existing regional orders. For Saudi Arabia, this represented an existential threat to everything the Kingdom represented. The rivalry that emerged was therefore not merely a competition between neighboring states but a fundamental clash over political legitimacy, religious authority, and the future direction of the Islamic world. Understanding this transformation requires examining not only the revolutionary changes within Iran but also how those changes intersected with Saudi strategic calculations and broader regional dynamics to produce a rivalry that would define Middle Eastern geopolitics for four decades.

2 The Impact of the 1979 Revolution: The Genesis of Modern Saudi–Iranian Antagonism

The 1979 Iranian Revolution represents the most consequential moment in modern Middle Eastern geopolitics, fundamentally altering not merely Iran–Saudi relations but precipitating a seismic shift that would define regional power dynamics for four decades (Therme, 2016). This extraordinary upheaval, which displaced the pro-Western Pahlavi monarchy and established an Islamic theocracy under Ayatollah Ruhollah Khomeini, generated multifaceted implications for bilateral relations between these emerging regional powers.

The revolution marked a paradigmatic break from established political orders, challenging prevailing models of state legitimacy and inspiring transnational networks of mobilization. For Saudi Arabia, the Iranian Revolution was not a neighboring country's internal affair but an existential challenge to everything the Kingdom represented. Khomeini's revolutionary ideology, grounded in the establishment of Islamic governance through jurisprudential sovereignty (*Velayat-e Faqih*), transcended conventional Westphalian notions of state sovereignty and posed a direct ideological challenge to the Saudi monarchical system (Dabashi, 2017).

What made Khomeini's vision so threatening was its universalist ambition. Unlike traditional nationalist revolutions that sought to transform only their own societies, the Islamic Revolution explicitly proclaimed its intention to export its model across the Muslim world. Khomeini famously declared that Islam knows no borders, and this was not rhetoric but a declaration of ideological war against existing Muslim governments, particularly those like Saudi Arabia that derived legitimacy from different interpretations of Islamic governance.

Khomeini's revolutionary ideology was fundamentally grounded in what Adib-Moghaddam (2017) terms transcendent political theology, a framework postulating the universality of Islamic governance beyond nation-state constraints. As Dabashi (2017) explains, this ideological construct represented an unprecedented synthesis of classical Twelver Shi'a jurisprudence and modern political theory, resulting in a hybrid governance model that challenged both Western democratic frameworks and traditional Sunni conceptions of political authority.

The doctrine of Velayat-e Faqih, positioning the Supreme Jurisprudent as the embodiment of both spiritual and temporal authority, represented what Brumberg (2001) identifies as a theological-political rupture in Islamic governance theory. This doctrinal innovation directly contested alternative models of Islamic sovereignty, particularly the Saudi monarchy's Wahhabi-legitimized rulership, which rested on fundamentally different interpretations of the relationship between religious authority and political power (Brumberg, 2001).

Saudi Arabia's Threefold Crisis

The propagation of Iran's revolutionary ideology precipitated an unprecedented ontological security crisis within the Saudi strategic establishment, manifesting across three critical dimensions that threatened the foundations of Saudi state identity.

The revolutionary doctrine challenged not merely the political legitimacy of the Saudi monarchy but its ontological security as custodian of Islamic orthodoxy and guardian of Islam's holiest sites. For a kingdom whose entire identity centered on leading the Muslim world, Iran's claim to represent true Islam was catastrophic. The Saudi establishment suddenly confronted a revolutionary state claiming superior Islamic credentials despite being led by Shi'a clerics whom Saudi Wahhabi doctrine had traditionally marginalized. Khomeini's Iran presented an alternative model of Islamic governance that was simultaneously more populist, more revolutionary, and more appealing to oppressed Muslim populations worldwide than the Saudi monarchy's conservative approach.

The Saudi response to perceived Iranian ideological expansionism culminated in the urgent formation of the Gulf Cooperation Council (GCC) in 1981 (Ali, 1988). This represented far more than a typical regional security arrangement. It was essentially a counter-revolutionary alliance designed to contain and neutralize Iranian influence. The GCC's formation marked the beginning of what would become a permanent security dilemma in the Persian Gulf. Every Iranian action would be interpreted through the lens of revolutionary expansionism, while every Saudi response would be seen by Iran as evidence of counter-revolutionary conspiracy. This dynamic created a self-reinforcing cycle of mistrust and competition that defined the region for decades.

Perhaps most threatening to Saudi internal security was the revolution's potential to inspire the Kingdom's own Shi'a minority, concentrated primarily in the oil-rich Eastern Province. The revolution's reverberations extended beyond Iran's borders, resonating powerfully with Shi'a populations across the region, including within Saudi Arabia. As Matthiesen (2014) demonstrates, the mobilization of these communities, directly inspired by Iran's revolutionary rhetoric and organizational success, exacerbated existing sectarian tensions within Saudi Arabia and other Gulf states (Matthiesen, 2014). The Saudi regime suddenly faced the prospect of a fifth column within its borders, potentially supported and directed by a hostile revolutionary government in Tehran.

The Saudi response involved dramatically intensified efforts to suppress domestic Shi'a activism while simultaneously augmenting religious soft power through massive increases in funding for global Islamic institutions and Wahhabi missionary movements. This dual strategy of domestic repression and international religious competition became a defining feature of Saudi policy throughout the 1980s and beyond.

Institutionalizing Confrontation

The post-revolutionary period was characterized by persistent cycles of acute diplomatic tension punctuated by short-lived attempts at rapprochement. These cycles followed a predictable pattern: crisis escalation, mediation attempts, superficial engagement, renewed tensions, and eventual breakdown. The 1987 Mecca incident, in which over 400 Iranian pilgrims were killed during clashes with Saudi security forces, illustrates the fusion of religious symbolism and geopolitical rivalry. As Keynoush (2016) documents, Iranian pilgrims staged politically charged demonstrations during Hajj, prompting a severe Saudi response. For Riyadh, the incident represented unacceptable politicization of Islam's holiest rituals. For Tehran, it symbolized Saudi suppression of authentic Islamic expression (Keynoush, 2016). This event exemplifies how religious sites and rituals became contested spaces embedded within broader strategic rivalries, serving as arenas for symbolic as well as material confrontation.

The revolution also transformed regional alliance structures in ways that extended far beyond bilateral relations. Saudi Arabia moved decisively to consolidate Arab support against Iran, leveraging financial resources, religious authority, and diplomatic networks to build a coalition containing revolutionary influence. The Kingdom provided massive financial assistance to Iraq during the Iran–Iraq War, viewing Baghdad as an essential buffer against revolutionary expansion. This support, exceeding 25 billion dollars, demonstrated Saudi Arabia's willingness to commit enormous resources to counter the Iranian threat (Rakipoğlu, 2017).

Iran, for its part, developed asymmetric strategies for projecting influence despite conventional military limitations. The establishment of relationships with non-state actors, most notably Hezbollah in Lebanon, provided Tehran with capabilities for regional intervention that did not require conventional force projection. These proxy relationships became essential components of Iranian strategy, allowing influence that transcended material constraints and geographical distance. The cultivation of these networks during the 1980s established patterns that would define regional competition for decades.

The ideological dimension of the rivalry also had profound effects on Islamic discourse globally. Both Saudi Arabia and Iran invested heavily in promoting their respective interpretations of Islamic governance, funding religious institutions, training clergy, and disseminating literature across the Muslim world. This competition for Islamic legitimacy transformed religious debates into geopolitical contests, with theological disputes often serving as proxies for strategic competition. The result was a polarization of Islamic discourse along sectarian lines that had lasting consequences for Muslim communities worldwide.

By the end of the 1980s, the Saudi–Iranian rivalry had crystallized into a durable pattern that would persist with remarkable consistency through subsequent decades. The revolution had transformed what might have been cooperative relations between oil-rich monarchies into a zero-sum competition for regional dominance. The contest encompassed military, economic, ideological, and diplomatic dimensions, creating a comprehensive rivalry that shaped virtually every aspect of Middle Eastern geopolitics.

The structural persistence of this antagonism requires explanation beyond proximate causes. The revolution created what international relations scholars term a security dilemma, where actions taken by one state to enhance its security inevitably threaten the other, generating a spiral dynamics that proved difficult to escape. Saudi efforts to contain revolutionary influence appeared to Iran as an aggressive encirclement. Iranian attempts to build regional influence appeared to Saudi Arabia as existential threats requiring vigorous response. This dynamic generated escalation even when neither party desired confrontation, as defensive measures triggered counter-responses that deepened mistrust and hostility.

Moreover, the rivalry became institutionalized within the domestic political structures of both states. In Saudi Arabia, the Iranian threat narrative provided justification for military expenditures, regional interventions, and domestic security measures. In Iran, confrontation with Saudi Arabia and its Western allies became integral to revolutionary identity and regime legitimacy. Political leaders on both sides derived domestic benefits from maintaining rivalry, creating incentives that reinforced antagonism even when strategic logic might have counseled restraint.

The 1979 Revolution thus established patterns that would govern Saudi–Iranian relations for over four decades. It transformed potential partners into bitter rivals, created security dilemmas that generated perpetual escalation, and embedded sectarian narratives into political competition. Yet the revolution alone cannot fully explain the rivalry's persistence and intensity. The following sections examine how this antagonism manifested through proxy warfare, economic competition, and sectarian mobilization, creating a comprehensive system of rivalry that proved remarkably resistant to resolution. Understanding these mechanisms is essential for grasping why the 2023 rapprochement represented such a significant departure from established patterns, and how China's DSI framework offered tools for managing rivalry that traditional diplomacy could not provide.

3 The Emergence of Proxy Warfare

In the wake of escalating ideological, political, and sectarian rivalries, Iran and Saudi Arabia increasingly turned to indirect methods of influence, giving rise to a new paradigm of regional competition: proxy warfare. Confronted with the prohibitive costs and catastrophic risks of direct military confrontation, both states invested in complex networks of client actors, non-state militias, and allied governments to project power and advance strategic objectives across the Middle East.

This proxy dimension transformed local conflicts into arenas of broader geopolitical struggle. Each confrontation became both a tactical contest and a symbolic theater in which Tehran and Riyadh sought to undermine one another's influence while consolidating their own regional standing. By leveraging sectarian loyalties, ideological affinities, and political patronage, Iran and Saudi Arabia institutionalized a form of competition that was at once diffuse, resilient, and deeply destabilizing. Proxy warfare thus emerged not merely as a military strategy but as a defining feature of Iranian-Saudi rivalry, a mode of engagement that systematically reshaped the architecture of regional conflict and redefined the parameters of Middle Eastern power politics.

The Saudi–Iranian rivalry has unfolded less through direct confrontation than through a series of interlinked proxy wars that institutionalized competitive interference across the Middle East. Beginning with the Iran–Iraq War, which established the logic of indirect engagement and external patronage, this rivalry evolved through successive conflicts that embedded sectarian, ideological, and geopolitical dimensions into local struggles. Understanding how proxy warfare operates requires examining both its historical evolution and its contemporary manifestations across different theaters, revealing patterns that distinguish this form of competition from traditional interstate conflict.

4 Foundations of Proxy Competition: The Iran–Iraq War (1980–1988)

The Iran–Iraq War represents the first major proxy confrontation in the Saudi–Iranian rivalry, establishing patterns that would define regional competition for decades. The conflict, while formally fought between two sovereign states, rapidly assumed the characteristics of a broader contest between Saudi Arabia and revolutionary Iran (Karsh, 2014). Saudi Arabia became Iraq's principal financial and logistical patron, extending billions of dollars in credit, arms support, and diplomatic backing to Saddam Hussein's regime.

As Ullah et al. (2024) emphasize, Riyadh's stance reflected layered strategic calculations rather than simple sectarian alignment. At the ideological level, revolutionary fervor emanating from Tehran posed an existential threat to hereditary monarchies and conservative governance structures across the Gulf. The prospect of revolutionary ideology spreading beyond Iran's borders particularly alarmed Saudi Arabia, which feared internal mobilization and regional instability. At the geopolitical and economic levels, the war coincided with acute volatility in global hydrocarbon markets, compelling Riyadh to leverage vast oil wealth as a tool of strategic influence, supporting Iraq while attempting to stabilize regional energy supply and maintain control over pricing dynamics. This era institutionalized a petro-political dimension to the Saudi–Iranian rivalry, where energy resources were deployed explicitly as instruments of regional power projection and strategic patronage.

The human and material costs were staggering, with casualties estimated between several hundred thousand and over a million, and economic losses accumulating into hundreds of billions of dollars. Despite this devastation, Riyadh considered the expenditure strategically acceptable. By underwriting Baghdad's war effort, Saudi Arabia pursued a calculated strategy of attrition against Tehran, aiming to exhaust Iran militarily, economically, and politically while curtailing its ability to export revolutionary ideology. Financial assistance to Iraq exceeded 25 billion dollars, a figure unprecedented in scale and indicative of Riyadh's determination to instrumentalize Iraq as a geopolitical buffer and safeguard the broader Arab heartland from perceived revolutionary encroachment. The following Figure illustrates the composition of Saudi financial support to Iraq, highlighting the distribution across direct cash aid, oil subsidies, and arms financing (Rakipoğlu, 2017).[1]

The war established a proxy warfare template that would influence subsequent regional conflicts. Saudi support for Iraq demonstrated how external powers could engage indirectly to achieve strategic objectives, mitigating direct confrontation while projecting influence. This approach relied on financial, logistical, and intelligence support alongside selective diplomatic advocacy, enabling Saudi Arabia to shape conflict dynamics without committing ground forces directly.

Moreover, the Iran–Iraq War and subsequent tensions set a precedent for the durability and adaptability of proxy competition in the region. Riyadh and Tehran learned to maintain influence and pursue strategic

[1] Data compiled by the author from multiple sources, including policy analyses, archival estimates, and scholarly literature.

objectives through intermediaries, client networks, and indirect interventions, a pattern that would later shape conflicts in Lebanon, Syria, Yemen, and beyond. The war highlighted how long-term strategic planning, financial leverage, and ideological positioning could sustain rivalries, even in the absence of direct military confrontation, laying the foundation for competitive interference, a permanent state of low-level but persistent conflict across multiple regional theaters Fig 1.

In sum, the Iran–Iraq War represents more than a bilateral conflict; it was the formative stage of enduring Saudi–Iranian proxy competition, establishing patterns of indirect engagement, sectoral influence, and regional maneuvering that continue to inform contemporary Middle Eastern geopolitics. It provides a critical lens through which to understand subsequent proxy wars, the rise of dual-track engagement strategies, and the operational logic of DSI discussed in later chapters. By blending ideological concerns, geopolitical calculations, and economic leverage, Riyadh's approach during this war exemplifies the sophistication and longevity of proxy strategy that would define the region for decades.

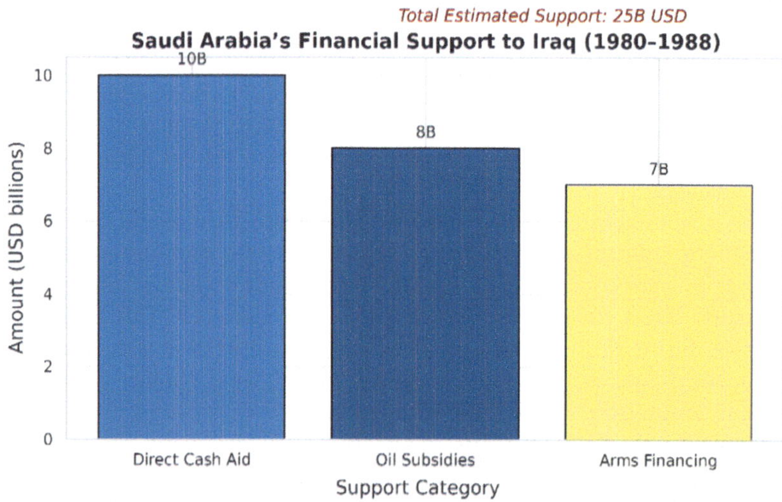

Fig. 1 Estimated Saudi financial support to Iraq during the Iran–Iraq war (1980–1988)

Civil War Interventions: Syria and Yemen as Crucibles of Competition

Syria: Forward Defense and Asymmetric Advantage

The Syrian Civil War, initially emerging from domestic political grievances against authoritarian rule, rapidly evolved into perhaps the most complex proxy conflict in modern Middle Eastern history. Research by Phillips (2020) demonstrates how the Assad regime's alignment with Iran's axis of resistance precipitated Saudi intervention, transforming localized unrest into a comprehensive theater for regional power competition. Berti and Paris (2014) argue that this transformation reflected both powers' perception of Syria as critical to their regional aspirations (Berti & Paris, 2014).

Iran's approach to the Syrian conflict represents what strategists term forward defense, the projection of defensive capabilities far from Iranian territory to prevent threats from reaching Iran's borders. This strategy has proven remarkably effective and cost-efficient, allowing Iran to challenge Saudi and American influence throughout the region while avoiding confrontation that might trigger overwhelming retaliation. Iran's implementation has been comprehensive and sophisticated, encompassing deployment of IRGC military advisors providing tactical and strategic guidance to Syrian forces, systematic mobilization of transnational Shi'a militias from Iraq, Afghanistan, and Pakistan, and provision of substantial financial assistance estimated at over 15 billion dollars annually to sustain the Syrian government through the conflict's most challenging phases (Cordesman & Kleiber, 2007).

The Iranian intervention in Syria also served as a laboratory for developing and testing new forms of proxy warfare that combine conventional military support with irregular warfare tactics, information operations, and economic reconstruction programs designed to create permanent Iranian influence. The establishment of Iranian military bases, weapons production facilities, and logistical networks in Syria represents a fundamental shift in Iranian strategic capabilities, providing Tehran with forward-deployed assets that can threaten Israeli territory and project power throughout the Eastern Mediterranean.

Saudi Arabia implemented an equally sophisticated but ultimately less successful strategy encompassing extensive material support to opposition groups, ambitious diplomatic initiatives designed to isolate the Assad regime internationally, and comprehensive economic measures designed to alter Damascus's strategic calculus and force regime change through economic pressure. The Saudi approach initially focused on supporting what they termed moderate opposition forces through massive arms transfers, training programs, and financial assistance estimated at several billion dollars annually (Wehrey, 2014).

Therefore, the Saudi–Iranian rivalry has contributed to what Lynch (2016) describes as a new Arab Cold War, characterized by proxy conflicts and the weakening of state institutions. This competition has profound implications for regional stability and the potential for conflict resolution. The internationalization of regional conflicts, particularly in Syria, has introduced additional complexities to the Saudi–Iranian rivalry. The involvement of global powers has both constrained and enabled regional actors' pursuit of their strategic objectives. The engagement of Saudi Arabia and Iran in contested zones illustrates the instrumental role of confessional identities in regional geopolitical dynamics. The Sunni–Shia dialectic transcends the internal political configurations of nations such as Syria, Yemen, and Lebanon, exerting influence on the broader Middle Eastern geopolitical landscape, where demographic compositions serve as critical variables.

A nuanced comprehension of these dynamics is imperative for analyzing contemporary conflicts and their implications for regional stability.[2] To elucidate these confessional dimensions, a comparative demographic analysis of Sunni and Shia populations across various Middle Eastern states proves instructive. The following demographic distribution data provides a quantitative framework for understanding the context within which Saudi and Iranian strategic influences operate throughout the region Fig. 2.

However, the Kingdom's strategy was hampered by fundamental challenges: the fragmented nature of the Syrian opposition, difficulty controlling proxy forces once armed and trained, and superior organizational capabilities of Iranian-backed forces. Saudi diplomatic efforts to isolate Syria included extensive lobbying in international forums, suspension of diplomatic relations, and attempts to build international coalitions for intervention. These efforts achieved some symbolic success but failed to generate the level of international support necessary to force regime change or significantly constrain Iranian involvement.

Yemen: The Limits of Conventional Intervention

[2] Map: Sunni and Shina- The World of Islam, PBS (2024).

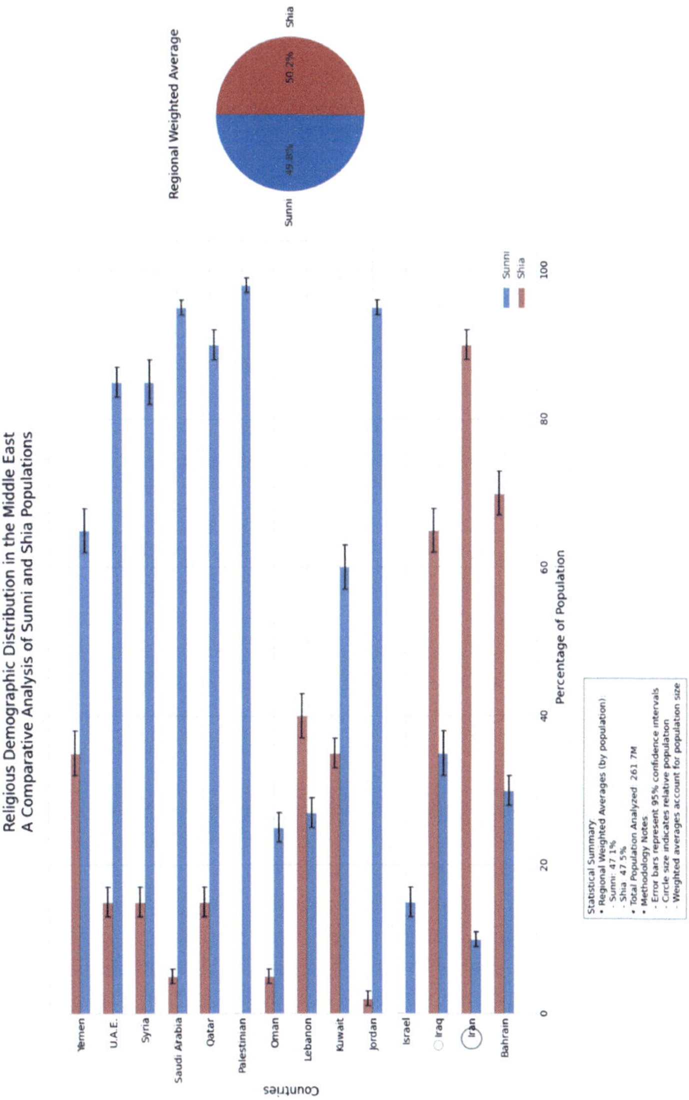

Fig. 2 Sunni and shia population in the middle east

The Yemen Civil War represents the most visible manifestation of Saudi–Iranian proxy confrontation, transforming local grievances into regional battlegrounds with global implications. The conflict demonstrates how sectarian narratives can be imposed upon complex tribal and political dynamics, how economic warfare becomes intertwined with military conflict, and how the instrumentalization of human suffering serves broader strategic objectives.

The seeds of Yemen's current crisis were sown in 2011, as popular uprisings swept across the Arab world. The departure of Ali Abdullah Saleh created a power vacuum that his successor, Abdrabbuh Mansur Hadi, proved unable to fill. Into this void stepped the Houthis, a Zaidi Shi'a movement from Yemen's northern highlands that had evolved from a cultural preservation organization into an armed political movement. Their seizure of Sanaa in September 2014 set in motion events that would draw the region's major powers into Yemen's internal struggles, systematically transforming what had been a complex but essentially domestic civil conflict into an arena for broader strategic competition with devastating humanitarian consequences (Orkaby, 2017).

For Saudi Arabia, the Houthis' advance represented what Crown Prince Mohammed bin Salman described as an intolerable threat to the Kingdom's fundamental security interests. The prospect of a Shi'a-dominated regime on its southern border, potentially aligned with Iran and capable of threatening Saudi territory, struck at the heart of Saudi Arabia's most basic strategic concerns. Operation Decisive Storm, launched in March 2015, saw Saudi warplanes filling Yemeni skies while a comprehensive naval blockade tightened around Yemen's ports (Buys & Garwood-Gowers, 2019).

The operation was conceived as a demonstration of Saudi Arabia's emergence as a regional power capable of independent military action. Crown Prince Mohammed bin Salman envisioned a quick, decisive campaign that would restore the internationally recognized government, eliminate the Iranian-backed Houthi threat, and establish Saudi Arabia's credentials as the region's dominant military power. Yet the Saudis found themselves drawn into a conflict far more complex and intractable than initially envisioned, revealing fundamental gaps between Saudi strategic ambitions and military capabilities.

The Houthis proved remarkably resilient opponents, their fighters hardened by years of guerrilla warfare against government forces and sustained by a combination of local support, tribal alliances, and increasingly sophisticated external assistance. Tehran, sensing an opportunity to challenge Saudi influence at relatively low cost while opening a new front in the broader regional competition, gradually increased support to the Houthis movement (Zimmerman, 2022). IRGC advisers provided crucial tactical guidance while sophisticated weaponry, from ballistic missiles to armed drones to naval mines, began appearing in Houthi arsenals through smuggling networks that proved remarkably resistant to interdiction efforts.

The Iranian support strategy was carefully calibrated to maximize strategic impact while minimizing direct exposure. Unlike in Syria, where Iran deployed significant ground forces, the Yemen intervention relied primarily on weapons transfers, technical assistance, and training programs that allowed Tehran to maintain plausible deniability while achieving substantial strategic objectives. The war quickly assumed dimensions that transcended Yemen's borders. Houthi missiles began arcing toward Riyadh and other Saudi cities while their drones struck at the Kingdom's vital oil infrastructure, including the devastating September 2019 attacks on Aramco facilities that temporarily halved Saudi oil production.

As the war dragged on with no clear military resolution in sight, Yemen's civilian population paid an unconscionable price. The Saudi-led coalition's naval and air blockade, ostensibly intended to prevent Iranian arms shipments, also effectively choked off essential civilian supplies to a country that imported over 90 percent of its food and most of its fuel and medical supplies. Famine stalked the land as agricultural production collapsed and food prices soared beyond ordinary families' reach. The systematic bombing of civilian infrastructure, including markets, hospitals, schools, and water treatment facilities, destroyed the basic foundations of modern life. Over 377,000 people have died in the conflict, with more than 70 percent of deaths resulting from indirect causes such as lack of food, health services, and infrastructure (Sowers & Weinthal, 2021).

The Yemen conflict fundamentally reshaped regional understanding of military power and strategic effectiveness. Saudi Arabia's intervention, originally intended as a decisive demonstration of strength, has instead exposed severe limitations of conventional military power against determined guerrilla opponents and the vulnerability of modern infrastructure to asymmetric attacks. The war has drained Saudi coffers with estimates of military expenditure exceeding 200 billion dollars, while damaging the Kingdom's international reputation and failing to achieve primary strategic objectives.

For Iran, Yemen has provided what strategists term a strategic dividend, a relatively low-cost opportunity to challenge Saudi influence, demonstrate capability to project power far from its borders, and impose significant costs on its regional rival. Iranian expenditure in Yemen has been estimated at less than 20 million dollars annually, representing perhaps the most cost-effective proxy warfare campaign in modern history. Yet neither side can claim true victory in any meaningful sense.

Domestic Uprisings and Regional Intervention—The Bahrain Case

The Bahraini uprising of 2011 demonstrates the extent to which regional geopolitical rivalries penetrate domestic political arenas and influence internal outcomes through coercive, financial, and diplomatic mechanisms. When thousands of Bahrainis gathered at Pearl Roundabout on 14 February 2011, they articulated long-standing structural grievances that had shaped Bahrain's political environment for decades (Mueller, 2023). The protesters demanded constitutional reform, the reduction of monarchical authority, greater political inclusion for the Shi'a majority population, and an end to discriminatory governance practices that had entrenched sectarian stratification within state institutions (Gray, 2011). These demands challenged the core foundations of the Al Khalifa ruling dynasty and threatened to unsettle a security order that was already deeply embedded in regional power structures.

For Saudi Arabia and its Gulf partners, the uprising was never perceived as a purely domestic phenomenon. Bahrain is geographically linked to Saudi territory through the King Fahd Causeway and occupies a position of strategic significance due to its role as host to the United States Fifth Fleet. Consequently, the stability of the island is central to Saudi security thinking. Riyadh has long regarded Bahrain as a buffer zone, a strategic extension of its own political sphere, and a space where Shi'a political mobilization could directly influence the dynamics of Saudi Arabia's Eastern Province (Matthiesen, 2020). In this context, the Bahraini protests were viewed not only as a challenge to monarchical authority but also as a potential opportunity for Iran to derive influence from Shi'a political empowerment. This perception, rather than evidence of Iranian direction, shaped Saudi strategic calculations (Wehrey, 2013).

This interpretation provided the political justification for a direct regional intervention. On 14 March 2011, Saudi Arabia and the United Arab Emirates deployed troops under the Gulf Cooperation Council's Peninsula Shield Force following a request from the Bahraini monarchy (Bronner & Slackman, 2011). Gulf officials framed the deployment as a collective security operation designed to protect critical infrastructure and preserve regional stability. Iran, by contrast, condemned the intervention as an externally imposed suppression of legitimate political demands. These competing narratives highlighted the transformation of the Bahrain crisis into a site of geopolitical contestation between Saudi Arabia and Iran, each advancing mutually exclusive claims regarding sovereignty, legitimacy, and security (Mabon 2020).

The intervention facilitated an extensive campaign of repression. Bahraini security forces, supported by Gulf military units, dismantled protest encampments, including the symbolic center at Pearl Roundabout. Hundreds of activists, medical workers, journalists, and human rights defenders were arrested, while independent media outlets were shut down. A state of emergency expanded the coercive capacity of the security services, and the removal of the Pearl Monument signified the regime's determination to erase the physical and symbolic markers of collective dissent. According to the Bahrain Independent Commission of Inquiry, the crackdown resulted in 46 deaths, widespread torture, thousands of dismissals from employment, and the institutionalization of practices that violated domestic and international legal standards (Bahrain Independent Commission of Inquiry, 2011).

The Bahrain case illustrates the structural nature of regional dependence in the Gulf. The deployment of the Peninsula Shield Force reflected the material infrastructures of dependence that tie smaller Gulf states to Saudi Arabia through joint security mechanisms, intelligence networks, and financial support arrangements. Simultaneously, the judicialization of dissent through mass trials, citizenship revocations, and restrictions on media freedom created institutional entanglements that increasingly aligned Bahrain's internal governance with the security imperatives of Riyadh and Abu Dhabi (Ulrichsen, 2016). Fiscal support packages and energy cooperation further deepened Bahrain's reliance on external financial resources, allowing Gulf states to reinterpret domestic political mobilization as a threat to regional stability rather than a legitimate expression of popular political aspiration.

Despite the scale of repression, the intervention did not achieve rapid or sustainable stabilization. Although public demonstrations were suppressed, the underlying political crisis persisted. Opposition movements became fragmented, underground networks expanded, and sectarian divisions hardened as both the government and various political actors relied on competing narratives of insecurity and existential threat. The result was not the restoration of political order but the consolidation of a long-term model of security governance that elevated repression above reform and entrenched a regional approach to internal dissent that continues to shape the political trajectory of Bahrain and the wider Gulf.

Comparative Patterns: The Logic of Proxy Warfare

Examining these conflicts comparatively reveals systematic patterns distinguishing proxy warfare from traditional interstate competition. Three dynamics emerge as particularly significant for understanding how the Saudi–Iranian rivalry operates and why it proved so resistant to resolution.

First, proxy warfare enables strategic competition while limiting escalation risks. By engaging through intermediaries rather than directly, both Saudi Arabia and Iran avoided catastrophic confrontation that might trigger devastating retaliation or international intervention. This allowed sustained competition across multiple theaters without the existential risks accompanying direct military conflict. Iran's support for Houthis, Hezbollah, and Syrian forces projected power far beyond what its conventional military capabilities could achieve through direct intervention. Saudi Arabia's financial backing for Iraqi forces, Syrian opposition groups, and Bahraini security demonstrated how economic resources could be converted into strategic influence without committing Saudi troops to combat.

Second, proxy relationships prove remarkably resilient but difficult to control. Once established, proxy networks develop their own internal logic, economic interests, and political dynamics that can persist even when original strategic rationales shift. Hezbollah evolved from Iranian proxy into an independent political-military force capable of pursuing objectives sometimes divergent from Tehran's preferences. Syrian opposition groups supported by Saudi Arabia fragmented into competing factions whose actions often undermined Saudi strategic goals. This demonstrates a fundamental paradox of proxy warfare: it provides influence without requiring direct commitment, but this same indirectness limits control over proxy behavior.

Third, proxy warfare systematically embeds sectarian identities into political competition. While the rivalry originated in strategic and ideological disputes rather than primordial sectarian hatred, both states instrumentalized confessional identities to mobilize support and legitimize intervention. Over time, this strategy reshaped the social and economic fabric across the region. Previously integrated communities fragmented, parallel economies emerged along sectarian lines, and identity increasingly determined access to resources, mobility, and political participation. The structural entrenchment of sectarianism created enduring obstacles to regional cohesion, ensuring that reconciliation requires dismantling entire ecosystems of identity-based politics and patronage.

These patterns reveal why proxy warfare proved so durable and why traditional diplomatic approaches struggled to resolve underlying conflicts. Proxy relationships created vested interests in continued competition among non-state actors, local factions, and even bureaucratic constituencies within Saudi and Iranian state structures, who benefited from sustained rivalry. The economic dimensions of proxy warfare, including smuggling networks, parallel markets, and war profiteering, generated constituencies opposed to peace. The sectarian mobilization that proxy warfare required and reinforced created social cleavages that persisted long after particular conflicts ended.

Understanding these dynamics is essential for grasping how China's DSI framework offers alternative approaches to managing regional competition. Unlike traditional great power interventions that often reinforced zero-sum dynamics by aligning with one side against another, DSI operates through creating overlapping dependencies that constrain all parties simultaneously. Infrastructure connectivity, energy interdependence, and economic integration generate incentives for restraint that operate regardless of sectarian identity or ideological orientation. The question subsequent chapters explore is whether these economic mechanisms can gradually transform incentive structures that proxy warfare created, substituting material interdependence for military competition as the organizing logic of regional order.

5 Energy Rivalry and the Geoeconomics of Sanctions

The Saudi–Iranian rivalry cannot be fully understood through the prism of sectarianism alone. While ideological contestation provided cultural scaffolding of hostility, the deeper foundations of antagonism were rooted in the material economy of energy and the geopolitical management of sanctions. For over three decades, hydrocarbons and the financial regimes surrounding them were weaponized as tools of competition, shaping not only bilateral relations between Riyadh and Tehran but also the structure of regional and global energy markets. To ignore this dimension would reduce a systemic conflict into purely cultural confrontation. Energy and economics were the very arteries through which this rivalry pulsed, and sanctions became the constrictive ligatures tightening Iran's ability to project power.

Understanding this economic dimension proves essential for grasping how China's DSI framework operates, particularly its energy interdependence mechanism. Where Saudi–Iranian competition weaponized energy markets to impose costs on rivals, DSI seeks to create mutual vulnerabilities through energy trade that constrain aggressive behavior and generate incentives for cooperation. The contrast between these approaches reveals fundamentally different logics of how energy relationships shape regional order.

Oil as Strategic Leverage—Asymmetric Market Power

Saudi Arabia entered the rivalry with a singular structural advantage: its unmatched capacity within OPEC and global oil markets to influence prices through production adjustments. With proven reserves exceeding 260 billion barrels and technical ability to adjust production levels on relatively short notice, Riyadh could unilaterally shape price trajectories in ways Tehran could not (Cildir, 2019). Iran, constrained by sanctions, outdated infrastructure, and need for foreign investment, lacked this flexibility. This asymmetry transformed oil from a shared resource into an instrument of economic warfare.

The 1980s oil price collapse provides the clearest example of this dynamic. As Iran struggled to recover from the Iran–Iraq War, Saudi overproduction contributed to a steep decline in oil revenues that devastated Tehran's already fragile economy. Far from being an accidental byproduct of market fluctuations, this reflected a calculated strategy by Riyadh to ensure Iran remained encircled by economic scarcity (Gately et al., 1986). The pattern repeated in subsequent decades. During the 2010s, when international sanctions tightened against Iran over its nuclear program, Saudi Arabia again expanded production to guarantee global supply remained uninterrupted, thereby neutralizing Iran's leverage and preventing oil price escalation that might have mitigated sanctions impact on Tehran (Borszik, 2016).

This capacity to shape global oil economy gave Saudi Arabia enduring edge in the rivalry. Whereas Iran's oil and gas resources were potential sources of strategic power, Saudi Arabia's were operational instruments deployed in real time (Ullah & Xinlei, 2025a). The asymmetry meant that while Tehran sought to use hydrocarbons to attract investment and generate revenue, Riyadh used them as geopolitical weapon. The rivalry thus became not only a contest over who possessed resources but over who could manipulate global market architecture surrounding those resources.

From the perspective of economic statecraft theory, Saudi strategy exemplifies what Baldwin terms positive and negative sanctions operating simultaneously (Baldwin, 2020). Positive sanctions involved Saudi Arabia guaranteeing stable energy supplies to Western allies, thereby strengthening strategic partnerships and securing political support. Negative sanctions involved using production capacity to suppress prices when doing so would inflict maximum damage on Iranian fiscal position. This dual approach maximized Saudi leverage while minimizing costs to the Kingdom itself, as expanded production during periods of falling prices still generated substantial revenues given Saudi Arabia's low extraction costs.

The effectiveness of this strategy is derived from structural features of global oil markets that created asymmetric vulnerabilities. Iran's economy depends far more heavily on oil exports as percentage of GDP and government revenues than Saudi Arabia's more diversified economy. Tehran also lacks Saudi Arabia's financial reserves to weather extended periods of low prices. These asymmetries meant identical price movements imposed dramatically different costs on the two rivals, allowing Saudi Arabia to weaponize market conditions in ways that systematically favored the Kingdom while constraining Iranian capabilities.

Sanctions as Structural Containment

Sanctions augmented the energy asymmetry dramatically. From aftermath of the 1979 revolution onward, Iran was progressively subjected to waves of U.S. and multilateral sanctions that restricted its ability to export oil, access capital markets, and import critical technologies for energy development. These sanctions were not static but evolved into comprehensive regime that penetrated virtually every sector of Iranian economy (Ullah & Xinlei, 2025b). By the 2010s, Iran's oil exports had been reduced by more than half, foreign direct investment had collapsed, and even basic financial transactions were channeled through costly and inefficient mechanisms.

Saudi Arabia's role in sustaining this pressure was neither passive nor secondary. Riyadh positioned itself as indispensable guarantor of energy security for Western powers seeking to isolate Iran. Each time sanctions reduced Iranian exports, Saudi Arabia compensated by increasing its own production, ensuring global supply chains remained uninterrupted. This alignment reassured Washington and European capitals that sanctioning Iran would not trigger energy crises. In effect, Saudi Arabia acted as structural enabler of the sanction regime, transforming Iran's energy endowment from asset into stranded liability.

Moreover, Riyadh actively lobbied in Western capitals for maintenance of strict sanctions on Tehran, framing Iran not merely as destabilizing regional actor but as systemic threat to international order. By presenting itself as both energy stabilizer and political ally, Saudi Arabia created durable coalition of interests ensuring Iran's economic isolation endured for decades. The costs imposed on Tehran were staggering. By some estimates, Iran lost more than 100 billion dollars in potential oil revenues between 2010 and 2020 due to sanctions and price suppression (Jeffrey, 2016; Rühl, 2022). These figures capture not merely lost profits but foregone developmental opportunities, schools unbuilt, industries undeveloped, and technologies never acquired.

The interplay between Saudi oil policy and international sanctions created vicious cycle for Iran. Every attempt by Tehran to break out of isolation, whether through energy partnerships with Asia, barter agreements, or clandestine export channels, was met with countermeasures limiting their impact (Ullah & Xinlei, 2025a). Meanwhile, Riyadh leveraged oil wealth to fund regional interventions, modernize military, and underwrite alliances with Western powers. The net result was that the same energy system that should have facilitated shared prosperity instead entrenched mutual hostility.

This geoeconomic contest did not merely affect the two rivals. It reshaped the broader Middle East. Energy market volatility, sanctions-induced trade distortions, and the diversion of financial resources into proxy wars undermined the region's developmental prospects (Jeroudi, 2024). The Middle East thus became not a hub of energy-fueled modernization but a theater where hydrocarbons financed endless conflict. Crucially, this rivalry prevented the emergence of coordinated regional energy frameworks that might have turned the Gulf into a collective powerhouse for economic integration. Instead, hydrocarbons were weaponized, transforming a potential engine of cooperation into the fuel of competition.

Strategic Consequences and Structural Lock-in

From Riyadh's perspective, this strategy was brutally effective. By aligning oil policy with sanctions regime, Saudi Arabia ensured Iran remained financially constrained and strategically contained. The Kingdom also solidified its position as indispensable partner for Western powers, enhancing global leverage and securing military and political support. At domestic level, the Iranian threat narrative justified vast defense expenditures and allowed monarchy to portray itself as guardian not only of Sunni Islam but also of global energy stability.

Yet this came at cost. The emphasis on oil as political weapon deepened Saudi dependence on hydrocarbons at the very moment when global transitions toward renewable energy were accelerating. Billions of dollars that could have been invested in diversification were instead funneled into sustaining rivalry whose material returns were diminishing. The paradox was that Saudi Arabia both strengthened its immediate strategic position and undermined long-term economic security.

For Iran, costs were heavier. The sanctions regime and Saudi oil strategies collectively imposed constraints that reshaped Iran's domestic political economy. Tehran was forced to develop sanctions-resistant structures, including barter trade networks, indigenous technological initiatives, and reliance on non-Western partners such as China and Russia. While these measures provided degree of resilience, they also entrenched inefficiencies, corruption, and economic distortions. More importantly, they diverted Iranian resources into survival strategies rather than developmental transformation.

At strategic level, Iran compensated for economic weakness by doubling down on asymmetric military tools, proxies, militias, and regional alliances that required relatively modest financial outlays but produced significant geopolitical returns. In this sense, geoeconomic pressure contributed directly to militarization of Iran's regional strategy. What Iran lost in economic strength, it sought to regain in security depth. The long-term effect was consolidation of political economy built not for growth but for resistance.

The combined effect of energy rivalry and sanctions left structural legacy that continues to shape the Middle East. Two of the world's most resource-rich states became locked in competition that systematically diverted wealth away from development and into confrontation (Riedel, 2016). Hydrocarbons were transformed from instruments of shared prosperity into mechanisms of coercion. Sanctions, rather than moderating behavior, entrenched hostility by forcing Iran into more radical strategies of survival and by cementing Saudi Arabia's reliance on external patrons.

Alternative Logics: From Weaponization to Interdependence

The Saudi–Iranian experience with energy competition reveals both the power and the limits of economic statecraft when deployed as weapon rather than as connector. Energy relationships generated substantial leverage for Saudi Arabia, enabling containment of Iranian influence and reinforcement of Western alliances. Yet this same weaponization prevented the emergence of regional energy interdependence that might have created mutual vulnerabilities constraining conflict.

China's approach to energy relationships in the Middle East operates through fundamentally different logic, one that seeks to create designed interdependence rather than strategic dominance. By becoming simultaneously indispensable to both Saudi Arabia and Iran as energy customer, technology provider, and infrastructure partner, Beijing constructs overlapping dependencies that generate incentives for restraint. Where Saudi–Iranian energy competition was zero-sum, with one party's gain necessarily representing the other's loss, Chinese energy relationships with both states create positive-sum dynamics where all parties benefit from stability and suffer from disruption.

This alternative logic manifests through several mechanisms. First, China's massive and growing energy demand provides reliable market for both Saudi and Iranian exports, reducing competition over market share that fueled previous rivalry. Second, Chinese investments in energy infrastructure, refining capacity, and petrochemical industries create long-term operational dependencies that transcend spot market transactions. Third, China's willingness to engage both parties simultaneously, without demanding exclusive alignment, allows both Saudi Arabia and Iran to pursue Chinese partnerships without triggering zero-sum competition.

The energy interdependence mechanism within DSI thus operates not through weaponizing energy relationships but through creating mutual exposure that raises costs of disruption for all parties. When Saudi Arabia and Iran both depend on Chinese energy markets, both possess incentives to avoid conflicts that might jeopardize those relationships. When Chinese infrastructure and technology become embedded in both countries' energy sectors, both acquire stakes in regional stability that enables continued operation of that infrastructure. This does not eliminate rivalry or resolve underlying sources of tension, but it creates countervailing pressures that moderate behavior and generate openings for diplomatic initiatives that pure confrontation forecloses.

The contrast between these approaches, *energy as weapon* versus *energy as connector*, illuminates broader questions about how economic relationships shape regional order. The Saudi–Iranian experience demonstrates that resource wealth alone does not generate prosperity or stability when embedded within frameworks of strategic competition. Resources become assets or liabilities depending on how relationships surrounding them are structured. When energy relationships operate through zero-sum competition, they fuel conflict. When structured through mutual interdependence, they can constrain escalation and create foundations for cooperation.

Analysts have argued that Gulf states' tendency to politicize energy policy, using oil production and pricing as strategic tools, has hindered regional economic integration and long-term growth (Al-Sarihi, 2025; Sweidan, 2021). Had these countries pursued coordinated, market-driven energy strategies focused on diversification and stability, regional GDP per capita could have been significantly higher. While precise estimates vary, some studies suggest improved cooperation and reform could have boosted economic performance by double-digit margins. The opportunity costs of weaponizing energy thus extended far beyond bilateral

Saudi–Iranian relations to encompass regional development prospects for the entire Gulf.

Understanding this energy dimension proves essential for grasping both the depth of Saudi–Iranian antagonism and the potential for transformation through alternative approaches. The rivalry was sustained not merely by ideological differences or proxy conflicts but by systematic economic warfare that prevented cooperation and entrenched hostility. Yet the same energy relationships that fueled decades of conflict also provide pathways for creating interdependence that could gradually transform incentive structures. Whether DSI's energy mechanism can succeed where traditional approaches failed depends on its ability to create mutual vulnerabilities sufficiently substantial to constrain aggressive behavior while generating tangible benefits that make cooperation rational for all parties.

6 The Structural Persistence of Rivalry—and the Conditions for Transformation

The endurance of the Saudi–Iranian rivalry for over four decades constitutes one of the most defining structural realities of modern Middle Eastern geopolitics. Far from a transient episode, this antagonism became deeply institutionalized, shaping domestic political structures, security doctrines, and regional alignments in both states. Understanding why this rivalry proved so persistent, and why the 2023 rapprochement represented a genuine departure rather than another temporary pause, requires synthesizing the multiple dimensions of competition examined in preceding sections and identifying the structural changes that created openings for transformation.

Mechanisms of Rivalry Persistence

The Saudi–Iranian rivalry persisted not because of irrational hatred or intractable cultural differences but because it served functional purposes for multiple actors and became embedded in regional structures through self-reinforcing mechanisms. Four dynamics proved particularly important in sustaining antagonism across decades.

First, the rivalry generated domestic political legitimacy for both regimes. For Iran, confrontation with Saudi Arabia and its Western allies became integral to revolutionary identity and regime legitimacy. The narrative of resistance against arrogant powers, externally directed and internally maintained, provided justification for economic hardship imposed by sanctions, political repression of domestic opposition, and concentration of power in clerical institutions. Political leaders derived tangible benefits from maintaining rivalry, as external threats unified domestic constituencies and deflected attention from governance failures or economic mismanagement.

For Saudi Arabia, the Iranian threat narrative provided comparable domestic benefits. It justified vast military expenditures, enabled regional interventions presented as defensive necessities, and reinforced the monarchy's legitimacy as guardian not only of Sunni Islam but also of Gulf security and stability. The rivalry allowed the Kingdom to position itself as indispensable regional anchor and essential Western ally, enhancing its international standing while generating domestic support through appeals to security imperatives and religious duty.

Second, the rivalry created vested interests in continued competition among non-state actors and bureaucratic constituencies. Proxy warfare generated economic opportunities for smuggling networks, arms dealers, and local factions whose livelihoods depended on sustained conflict. Iranian Revolutionary Guard Corps elements benefited from regional interventions that enhanced their domestic political power and economic interests. Saudi defense establishments and regional allies developed institutional stakes in maintaining threat perceptions justifying continued resource flows and political influence. These constituencies actively resisted reconciliation efforts that might eliminate their raison d'etre or reduce their access to resources and power.

Third, the rivalry became embedded in regional alliance structures and institutional frameworks that proved difficult to reconfigure. The GCC was founded explicitly to counter Iranian influence, creating institutional architecture predicated on shared threat perception. Iran's axis of resistance, linking Tehran with Damascus, Hezbollah, and various Iraqi militias, similarly depended on sustained confrontation with Saudi Arabia and its allies for coherence and purpose. These alliance structures created path dependencies where changing course required not merely bilateral agreement between Riyadh and Tehran but coordinated shifts across multiple actors with divergent interests and limited central control.

Fourth, the rivalry generated security dilemmas that produced spiral dynamics resistant to rational management. Actions taken by one party to enhance security inevitably appeared threatening to the other, triggering counter-responses that deepened mistrust and generated escalation even when neither party desired confrontation. Saudi efforts to contain revolutionary influence through military buildups, alliance formation, and proxy support appeared to Iran as aggressive encirclement requiring vigorous response. Iranian attempts to build regional influence through proxy networks and asymmetric capabilities appeared to Saudi Arabia as existential threats justifying preventive action. These dynamic generated self-reinforcing cycles where defensive measures triggered offensive interpretations producing escalatory counter-moves.

These mechanisms collectively created what might be termed destructive equilibrium, a stable pattern of rivalry that imposed enormous costs on all parties yet proved remarkably resistant to transformation. The rivalry was not irrational but reflected rational responses by multiple actors to structural conditions and incentive frameworks that made cooperation difficult and competition rewarding. Breaking this equilibrium required not merely diplomatic skill or temporary alignment of interests but fundamental changes in structural conditions altering cost-benefit calculations for all relevant actors.

Structural Changes Enabling the 2023 Rapprochement

The March 2023 restoration of diplomatic relations between Saudi Arabia and Iran, mediated by China in Beijing, represented more than symbolic gesture or tactical pause in ongoing competition. It reflected structural changes in regional and global contexts that altered incentive structures sustaining four decades of rivalry. Four developments proved particularly significant in creating conditions enabling rapprochement.

First, American strategic retrenchment reduced external reinforcement of the rivalry. For decades, U.S. security guarantees to Gulf monarchies and maximum pressure campaigns against Iran reinforced zero-sum dynamics by providing Saudi Arabia with external backing, enabling aggressive regional postures while simultaneously driving Iran toward asymmetric strategies and proxy warfare. The gradual American pivot away from Middle Eastern engagement, accelerated under successive administrations from Obama through Biden, reduced Washington's willingness to underwrite Saudi regional interventions or maintain comprehensive pressure on Iran. This created strategic uncertainty for both Riyadh and Tehran, generating incentives to explore regional arrangements less dependent on unreliable external patrons.

Second, the Yemen stalemate demonstrated limits of military solutions and imposed unsustainable costs. Saudi Arabia's intervention, originally conceived as quick demonstration of regional dominance, instead revealed fundamental limitations of conventional military power against determined irregular opponents. After eight years of fighting, over 200 billion dollars expended, and immense reputational damage, the Kingdom controlled no more territory than when intervention began while facing regular Houthi attacks on Saudi infrastructure and cities. For Iran, while Yemen provided a cost-effective opportunity to challenge Saudi influence, the conflict also demonstrated diminishing returns as international attention to humanitarian catastrophe and growing war weariness among regional populations created pressures for de-escalation. Both parties independently concluded that continued confrontation in Yemen generated costs exceeding benefits.

Third, economic pressures created demand for regional stability enabling developmental priorities. Saudi Arabia's Vision 2030 modernization program, upon which Crown Prince Mohammed bin Salman staked his legitimacy and the Kingdom's future, required sustained economic growth, foreign investment, and regional stability. Continued rivalry diverted resources from development priorities, deterred international investors concerned about security risks, and constrained economic partnerships that regional tensions complicated. For Iran, decades of sanctions and economic isolation had generated severe developmental deficits, youth unemployment, and social pressures threatening regime stability. Both states faced domestic imperatives favoring regional stability over continued confrontation.

Fourth, China's enhanced regional presence provided credible facilitation mechanisms. Unlike previous mediation attempts by Western powers or international organizations perceived as biased toward one party, China had systematically built relationships with both Saudi Arabia and Iran through decades of patient engagement. By 2023, China had become Saudi Arabia's largest trading partner, a central participant in Vision 2030 infrastructure projects, and a crucial technology provider. Simultaneously, China functioned as Iran's primary oil customer despite sanctions, a major source of infrastructure financing, and a diplomatic partner providing political cover in international forums. This dual embedding created structural conditions enabling mediation that actors aligned exclusively with one side could not achieve. China possessed neither desire nor capability to impose settlement terms, but its material presence and demonstrated commitment to engagement with both parties generated credibility enabling facilitation when political conditions aligned.

These structural changes did not eliminate underlying sources of rivalry or resolve fundamental disagreements over regional order, sectarian mobilization, or ideological legitimacy. They did, however, alter cost-benefit calculations sufficiently to make diplomatic normalization rational for both parties at a particular historical moment. The rapprochement succeeded not because rivalry had become obsolete but because continuing confrontation had become counterproductive for both states given their respective strategic circumstances and developmental priorities.

From Rivalry Management to Designed Interdependence

Understanding these structural changes illuminates how China's DSI framework offers tools for managing rivalry that traditional diplomacy struggled to provide. Where conventional mediation approaches focused on resolving disputes through negotiated agreements backed by external guarantees, DSI operates through creating material dependencies that alter incentive structures making sustained confrontation increasingly costly.

The connection between rivalry dimensions analyzed in this chapter and DSI mechanisms elaborated in Chapter 2 becomes explicit when examining how each dimension might be addressed through designed interdependence.

Military proxy competition, which generated enormous costs and humanitarian catastrophes while failing to produce decisive outcomes for either party, can be moderated through spatial design. Infrastructure connectivity creates shared interests in regional stability, as disruption threatens investments, trade flows, and development projects that both parties value. Chinese-built ports, railways, industrial zones, and energy facilities create constituencies within both Saudi Arabia and Iran, government officials, business communities, and regional populations, with material stakes in preventing conflicts that might damage or destroy this infrastructure. While spatial design cannot eliminate proxy warfare, it raises costs of escalation and creates counterweights to military constituencies favoring confrontation.

Sectarian mobilization, which weaponized religious identities to justify intervention and delegitimize rivals, can be mitigated through normative design. China's consistent emphasis on sovereignty, non-interference, and mutual benefit provides alternative framework for legitimizing engagement that does not require sectarian justification. When partnerships are defended through appeals to national development rather than religious duty, when cooperation is framed as sovereign choice rather than sectarian obligation, political space opens for relationships transcending confessional divides. Normative design does not eliminate sectarian identities but reduces their salience in determining state behavior and strategic calculations.

Energy competition, which weaponized hydrocarbon markets to impose costs on rivals and prevented emergence of coordinated regional frameworks, can be transformed through energy interdependence. By becoming simultaneously essential to both Saudi and Iranian energy sectors as customer, investor, and technology provider, China creates mutual vulnerabilities that constrain aggressive behavior. When both parties depend on Chinese markets for exports, Chinese financing for development, and Chinese technology for modernization, both acquire incentives to avoid disruptions that might jeopardize those relationships. Energy interdependence thus transforms hydrocarbons from weapons of competition into foundations for cooperation.

Institutional rivalry, which prevented emergence of regional frameworks for dialogue and coordination, can be addressed through diplomatic design. China's willingness to maintain parallel partnerships with competing actors, avoiding exclusive alignments that force zero-sum choices, demonstrates alternative model for great power engagement in contested regions. By cultivating relationships across rivalries without demanding subordination or exclusive loyalty, external powers can create channels for communication and coordination that bloc-based alliance systems foreclose. The 2023 rapprochement itself exemplifies this logic, as China's structural positioning enabled facilitation precisely because Beijing maintained credibility with both parties simultaneously.

These connections between rivalry dimensions and DSI mechanisms reveal how material interdependence can gradually transform regional order without requiring resolution of underlying ideological or strategic disagreements. DSI does not aim to eliminate rivalry, which may persist in attenuated forms for generations, but rather to manage it through creating countervailing pressures that moderate behavior and expand space for cooperation. The transformation is not from confrontation to friendship but from destructive competition to managed coexistence.

References

Abrahamian, E. (2018). A history of modern Iran. *(No Title)*.

Al-Enazy, A. H. (2010). The creation of Saudi Arabia: Ibn Saud and British Imperial policy, 1914–1927. *(No Title)*.

Ali, A.-J. K. (1988). *The Gulf cooperation council (GCC) and regional integration: An analysis of cultural origins, political evolution, and collective security*. The Catholic University of America.

Al-Rasheed, M. (2010). A history of Saudi Arabia. Cambridge university press.

Al-Sarihi, A. (2025). Energy transition in the Gulf: Best practices and limitations.

Bahrain Independent Commission of Inquiry. 2011. Report of the Bahrain Independent Commission of Inquiry.

Baldwin, D. A. (2020). *Economic statecraft* (New edition ed.).

Berti, B., & Paris, J. (2014). Beyond sectarianism: Geopolitics, fragmentation, and the Syrian civil war. *Strategic Assessment, 16*(4), 21–34.

Borszik, O. (2016). International sanctions against Iran and Tehran's responses: Political effects on the targeted regime. *Contemporary Politics, 22*(1), 20–39.

Bronner, E., & Slackman, M. (2011). Saudi troops enter Bahrain to help put down unrest. *The New York Times, 14*, A1.

Brumberg, D. (2001). *Reinventing Khomeini: The struggle for reform in Iran*. University of Chicago Press.

Buys, E., & Garwood-Gowers, A. (2019). The (Ir) relevance of human suffering: Humanitarian intervention and Saudi Arabia's operation decisive storm in Yemen. *Journal of Conflict and Security Law, 24*(1), 1–33.

Byrne, M., & Gasiorowski, M. J. (2015). *Mohammad Mosaddeq and the 1953 coup in Iran*. Syracuse University Press.

Chehabi, H. E. (1998). The pahlavi period. Iranian Studies, 31(3–4), 495–502.

Cildir, S. (2019). How Saudi-Iranian Oil Rivalry has been Shaped by American Power. *Academic rigour (Journalistic flair)*.

Clifford, R. L. (1976). The Arabian American oil company. *Asian Affairs, 7*(2), 178–182.

Dabashi, H. (2017). *Theology of discontent: The ideological foundation of the Islamic revolution in Iran*. Routledge.

Gately, D., Adelman, M., & Griffin, J. M. (1986). Lessons from the 1986 oil price collapse. *Brookings Papers on Economic Activity, 1986*(2), 237–284.

Gray, M. (2011). *A theory of'late rentierism'in the Arab states of the Gulf*. CIRS Occasional Papers.

Hambly, G. R. (1963). Aqa Mohammad khan and the establishment of the Qajar dynasty. *Journal of the Royal Central Asian Society, 50*(2), 161–174.

Hertog, S. (2007). Shaping the Saudi state: Human agency's shifting role in rentier-state formation. *International journal of Middle East studies, 39*(4), 539–563.

Hertog, S. (2017). The political economy of distribution in the Middle East: Is there scope for a new social contract? *Development Policy, 88*(7), 88–113.

Jeffrey, J. (2016). The JCOPA'S regional impacts: Sinking confidence in the US balancing role,. The Washington Institute for Near East Policy.. https://www.washingtoninstitute.org/policy-analysis/jcpoas regional-impact-sinking-confidence-us-balancing-role.

Jeroudi, L. (2024). *Energy geopolitics in a fragmented world: A comparative analysis of Europe and the Middle East*. TRENDS Research & Advisory.

Jones, T. C. (2010). *Desert kingdom: How oil and water forged modern Saudi Arabia*. Harvard University Press.

Karsh, E. (2014). *The Iran–Iraq War 1980–1988*. Bloomsbury Publishing.

Keynoush, B. (2016). *Saudi Arabia and Iran: Friends or foes?* Springer.

Luciani, G. (2017). Oil rent and regional economic development in MENA. *Combining economic and political development: the experience of MENA*, 211–230.

Matthiesen, T. (2014). *The other Saudis: Shiism, dissent and sectarianism* (Vol. 46). Cambridge University Press.

Matthiesen, T. (2020). *Sectarian gulf: Bahrain, Saudi Arabia, and the Arab spring that wasn't*. Stanford University Press.

Mueller, C. (2023). Memory politics in Bahrain: The invocation of the early modern past in the aftermath of the February 14, 2011 uprising. *History & Memory, 35*(1), 141–170.

Nasr, S. V. R. (2007). *The Shia revival: How conflicts within Islam will shape the future*. WW norton & Company.

Orkaby, A. (2017). Yemen's humanitarian nightmare: The real roots of the conflict. *Foreign Affairs, 96*(6), 93–101.

Phillips, C. (2020). *The battle for Syria: International rivalry in the new Middle East*. Yale University Press.

Rakipoğlu, M. (2017). Revisiting the saudi position during the Iran-Iraq war through the lens of balance of threat theory. *Ortadoğu Etütleri, 9*(1), 118–134.

Rühl, C. (2022). Energy sanctions and the global economy: Mandated vs unilateral sanctions. *International Economics and Economic Policy, 19*(2), 383–399.

Sweidan, O. D. (2021). The environmental and energy policies to enable sustainable consumption and production in the Gulf cooperation council countries. *Clean Technologies and Environmental Policy, 23*(9), 2639–2654.

Therme, C. (2016). SAUDI ARABIA AND IRAN. POWER AND RIVALRY IN THE MIDDLE EAST, Simon Mabon, Londres, IB Tauris, 2016, 298 pages. *Politique étrangère*(3), XXXV-XXXV.

Ullah, A., & Xinlei, L. (2025a). Navigating complex interdependence: An in-depth analysis of Iran and Saudi Arabia's strategic engagement with the BRI in the Middle East. *Chinese Political Science Review, 10*(1), 72–100.

Ullah, A., & Xinlei, L. (2025b). Systemic constraints and state behavior: A neorealist perspective on China's BRI and Iran's strategic calculations. *Iranian Studies*, 1–22.

Ulrichsen, K. (2016). *The United Arab Emirates: Power, politics and policy-making*. Routledge.

Wehrey, F. (2013). Bahrain's decade of discontent. *Journal of Democracy, 24*(3), 116–126.

Wehrey, F. (2014). Gulf calculations in the Syrian conflict. *Carnegie Articles, 9.*

Wynbrandt, J. (2010). *A brief history of Saudi Arabia*. Infobase Publishing.

Zimmerman, K. (2022). *Yemen's Houthis and the expansion of Iran's Axis of resistance*. American Enterprise Institute.

CHAPTER 4

Beyond Oil: China's Infrastructural Entanglement with Saudi Arabia

Saudi Arabia's Vision 2030 has fundamentally altered the Kingdom's approach to international partnerships. No longer content to exchange oil for revenue under Western security guarantees, Crown Prince Mohammed bin Salman seeks to transform Saudi Arabia into a diversified, technology-driven economy capable of thriving in a post-carbon world. This ambition created both opportunity and necessity: opportunity to leverage competition among global powers for favorable partnerships, and necessity to rapidly acquire infrastructure, technology, and industrial capacity that decades of rentier governance failed to develop domestically.

China's BRI arrived at precisely this moment of Saudi reinvention. For Beijing, the Kingdom represents a test case for whether DSI can operate with autonomous, wealthy partners who possess alternatives, a sharp contrast to dependent states like Iran, where necessity drives engagement. For Riyadh, China offers what Western partners increasingly cannot or will not provide: patient capital, rapid implementation, advanced technology, and crucially, cooperation unconstrained by human rights conditionalities or governance prescriptions. The resulting partnership reflects mutual recognition of complementary interests, but it is Saudi Arabia's strategic requirements under Vision 2030 that structure the terms of engagement, not simply China's BRI blueprint.

A. Ullah, *Diplomacy by Design*,
https://doi.org/10.1007/978-981-95-7876-4_4

1 Energy as Strategic Foundation: The Evolution of Sino–Saudi Relations

The relationship between China and Saudi Arabia has long been defined by a foundational economic logic: energy interdependence. Since the formal establishment of diplomatic relations in 1990, Beijing and Riyadh have cultivated a pragmatic partnership grounded in complementary material needs. China, the world's largest crude oil importer, relies on Saudi Arabia's vast hydrocarbon reserves to sustain its industrial growth and energy security. Saudi Arabia, in turn, has found in China a stable and expanding market, its single largest oil customer offering consistent demand insulated from the political volatility and normative conditionalities that have periodically strained Riyadh's ties with Western partners. This energy partnership contained strategic dimensions from its inception, with both sides seeking to reduce vulnerabilities in their respective geopolitical positions.

Energy trade has functioned as a sequencing mechanism for the evolution of Sino–Saudi cooperation. Early reliance on crude exports created commercial interdependence and political trust, which later enabled China to participate in industrial and infrastructure projects within the Kingdom. Table 1 illustrates the trajectory of energy trade alongside key joint projects and strategic milestones.[1]

In recent years, the character of this relationship has undergone a qualitative transformation (Fulton, 2022). What began as an energy-centered trade partnership has evolved into a multidimensional strategic engagement encompassing defense coordination, technology transfer, financial integration, and above all, infrastructure diplomacy. This broadening reflects mutual recognition of shifting structural realities. For Saudi Arabia, dependence on a single commodity has become not only economically untenable but politically constraining. The volatility of global oil

[1] Crude import volumes are expressed in million barrels. Values for 2005–2015 are estimated based on historical trade patterns, China's overall crude import growth, and Saudi Arabia's market share among top suppliers. Figures for 2016–2025 are derived from reported import volumes in tones converted to barrels (1 tons $\approx$ 7.33 barrels) and projections based on trade trends and partial-year customs data. Key projects and initiatives reflect publicly reported joint ventures, refinery and petrochemical projects (e.g., YASREF, Fujian complex), and bilateral energy agreements, showing both upstream supply and downstream industrial integration. All volumes are rounded to nearest five million barrels for clarity.

Table 1 Energy trade and strategic projects in Sino–Saudi relations

Period	*Saudi Crude Imports to China (million barrels)*	*Key Joint Projects/ Initiatives*	*Strategic Significance*
2005–2010	150–200	Early supply agreements and expansion of long-term contracts with Sinopec and CNPC	Foundation of long-term crude supply relationships and strengthening of energy trade contracts amid China's rising demand
2011–2015	250–290	Development and planning of Yanbu Aramco Sinopec Refining Company (YASREF)	Deepening downstream integration and industrial cooperation in refining and petrochemicals
2016–2020	300–450	YASREF operational; pilot projects for Fujian refinery & petrochemical ventures	Maturation of bilateral energy ties, with increased downstream integration and strategic energy cooperation
2021–2023	580–629	Expansion of Fujian refinery & petrochemical projects; long-term supply agreements	Peak downstream cooperation, major Saudi–Chinese refinery and petrochemical JVs, diversification of energy cooperation beyond crude trade
2024–2025	566–582	New Aramco–Sinopec JV in Fujian and YASREF expansion	Strategic pivot to diversified crude sourcing, continued industrial integration, and strengthening of overall energy partnership

markets and accelerating energy transition threaten the fiscal sustainability of rentier governance, compelling the Kingdom to reimagine its development model (Al-Tamimi, 2013).

China, for its part, has sought to diversify its energy suppliers, reduce exposure to geopolitical risk, and extend its BRI into the Gulf, both to secure supply chains and to project influence through non-military means. Yet Beijing's engagement operates responsively, capitalizing on opportunities that Saudi transformation creates rather than imposing a preconceived template. Chinese firms and financial institutions have proven remarkably adept at aligning their offerings with Saudi Arabia's evolving needs: patient capital when Western banks hesitated, rapid construction when timelines compressed, and advanced technology when conditionalities constrained Western alternatives.

This divergence in structural imperatives gives the relationship an asymmetrical but complementary logic. For Riyadh, the Chinese capital and technology are instruments for transforming oil wealth into diversified growth. For Beijing, Saudi Arabia is a partner through which to test the viability of DSI in an advanced, strategically autonomous, and globally connected state. The energy nexus remains the foundation, but it has been gradually overlaid with infrastructural, digital, and financial layers that transform a commercial bond into a multidimensional strategic web. These cases demonstrate that energy is not merely a commercial commodity but the strategic foundation that enables institutional embedding, technological transfer, and long-term operational influence.

The strategic role of energy differs across contexts. In Iran, Chinese engagement has been largely reactive, driven by U.S. sanctions that constrained Tehran's access to global markets. Energy trade there functions primarily as a lifeline rather than a strategic foundation. By contrast, in Saudi Arabia, energy interdependence is proactive and deliberately sequenced. Riyadh leverages its energy exports to attract infrastructure and technology investments, while Beijing uses energy as a platform to cultivate long-term influence, operational integration, and institutional interdependence (Soltani, 2023). This contrast underscores the capacity of energy to function either as a reactive instrument or as a deliberate strategic foundation, depending on the agency of the actors involved.

DSI interprets interdependence as intentional statecraft: a calibrated configuration of linkages designed to align partner incentives with strategic objectives. Beijing's engagement with Riyadh illustrates this process vividly. The relationship followed a carefully sequenced trajectory: beginning with energy trade to establish trust and commercial credibility; expanding into industrial and infrastructural cooperation to anchor a durable physical presence; and advancing into digital systems and governance technologies that extend influence into the informational and administrative realms. Each phase deepens mutual reliance and reduces the feasibility of abrupt disengagement, transforming what was once a market-based interdependence into a designed architecture of structural power.

In this sense, DSI operationalizes what Susan Strange identified as structural power: the capacity to shape the frameworks within which others operate, rather than merely influencing outcomes within them (Strange, 1988). Infrastructure diplomacy becomes the material mechanism through which structural power is exercised. As Barnett and Duvall later argued, such power operates not through coercion or explicit hierarchy but through the infrastructural embedding of norms, standards, and dependencies that silently shape behavior (Barnett & Duvall, 2005). By embedding Chinese firms, technologies, and operational standards into Saudi Arabia's modernization agenda, Beijing is not merely trading goods; it is subtly shaping the Kingdom's pathways of globalization and development.

Infrastructure, in this sense, has emerged as the material expression of the Sino–Saudi relationship (Foley, 2023). Chinese state-owned and private firms are now integral to Saudi Arabia's modernization, participating in projects that range from telecommunications and renewable energy to industrial zones and logistics corridors. These projects are not isolated investments but cumulative commitments that embed Chinese standards, technologies, and expertise within Saudi development frameworks. Once embedded, such systems are difficult to replace, creating enduring operational interdependencies and aligning long-term incentives.

This embeddedness also carries normative implications. Whereas Western partnerships have often been conditioned on governance reforms, transparency standards, or political liberalization, Chinese cooperation proceeds under the banner of non-interference and mutual respect for sovereignty. This normative posture resonates deeply with Saudi leadership, offering a model of modernization unconstrained by external prescriptions. In doing so, it not only reinforces the legitimacy of Saudi governance but also advances Beijing's broader normative agenda—promoting an alternative model of development that privileges sovereignty, stability, and pragmatism over liberal conditionality.

2 Sequencing Influence: Energy to Infrastructure

By the late 2000s, both Saudi Arabia and China recognized that energy trade alone, while stabilizing, was structurally limited. Oil, by its very nature, is fungible and globally priced; it generates exchange but not exclusivity. Trade in hydrocarbons could provide wealth and familiarity, but not necessarily strategic depth. A relationship confined to energy trade risked stagnation. For Riyadh, the volatility of oil prices and the accelerating global transition toward renewables underscored the perils of excessive dependence on a single export. For Beijing, vulnerabilities associated with maritime chokepoints, especially the Strait of Hormuz, exposed the fragility of its supply routes. In both capitals, policymakers began to look beyond oil for mechanisms that could embed the relationship in more durable and multidimensional structures (Daojiong, 2005).

Infrastructure emerged as the mechanism to transform commercial exchange into strategic depth. Through financing, constructing, and operating critical systems such as ports, power grids, and telecommunications networks, China could embed itself as a co-architect of Saudi modernization rather than remaining merely a consumer of Saudi oil. The BRI (2013) and Vision 2030 (2016) provided aligned frameworks for this shift, with both initiatives emphasizing connectivity, industrial diversification, and technology transfer as pathways to economic transformation.

This infrastructural turn operationalizes what this book terms DSI. Unlike liberal institutionalist accounts (Keohane & Nye, 1977) that treat interdependence as an unintended by-product of market integration, DSI interprets it as intentional statecraft: the calibrated embedding of economic, technological, and infrastructural systems within a partner's developmental trajectory to create material, institutional, and symbolic dependencies that align incentives and constrain exit options. Infrastructure becomes the vehicle through which influence is constructed, not through coercion, but through the gradual reconfiguration of what is possible, practical, and preferable.

China's Saudi engagement exemplifies this sequencing: energy trade established trust (Phase 1), physical infrastructure anchored Chinese presence (Phase 2), and digital systems extended influence into governance realms (Phase 3). Each phase deepens reliance and constrains exit options, transforming market-based exchange into designed structural power.

This incremental approach has been instrumental in shifting the relationship from transactional exchange to structural entanglement. It has allowed Beijing to project influence through what may be termed *infrastructural quiet power*, a form of authority exercised not through coercion or conditionality, but through the normalization of dependency. Once Chinese standards, logistics systems, and data architectures become integral to a partner's economy, they generate a form of path dependence that is both material and cognitive: policies and institutions evolve around embedded systems that are difficult, and often costly, to replace.

The contrast with Iran is instructive in this respect. In Tehran, Chinese infrastructure investments are typically framed as lifelines, mechanisms for survival amid sanctions and international isolation. Dependencies there emerge from necessity: China functions as the indispensable external actor that enables Iran to sustain its economy under duress. In Riyadh, however, the logic is inverted. Infrastructure is not a survival mechanism but an aspirational instrument, a means of achieving technological sophistication, economic diversification, and global prestige. Dependencies here are voluntary, rooted in ambition rather than constraint. This divergence underscores the flexibility and context-sensitive adaptability of DSI as a strategic framework: the same instruments of engagement, credit lines, infrastructure projects, and technology transfers can produce very different forms of entanglement depending on whether they are calibrated to contexts of vulnerability or aspiration.

This process also mirrors the dynamics identified by Barnett and Duvall (2005) in their typology of productive and structural power, where authority is exercised through the constitution of social and material relations that shape actors' capacities and identities. In the Saudi case, Chinese infrastructural presence is not limited to physical assets but extends to discursive legitimacy.

In sum, the transition from energy interdependence to designed strategic interdependence marks a transformative juncture in Sino–Saudi relations. What began as a pragmatic exchange—oil for revenue—has evolved into a deliberate, sequenced architecture of interdependence. The partnership now operates on multiple registers: material (through infrastructure and trade), institutional (through joint ventures and regulatory harmonization), and symbolic (through the co-narration of modernization and sovereignty).

This evolution illustrates the book's central argument: interdependence, when deliberately designed and strategically sequenced, operates as a mechanism of structural power that shapes not only economic outcomes but the very architecture of choice itself. In Saudi Arabia, China has moved beyond its role as an energy consumer to become embedded in the systems that will define the Kingdom's future. Chinese firms do not simply build infrastructure; they establish the technical standards for 5G networks, the operational protocols for automated ports, the data architectures for smart cities, and the supply chains for renewable energy systems. Each choice made today in NEOM's design, in telecommunications procurement, or in hydrogen production technology narrows the range of alternatives available tomorrow. By shaping the material and institutional foundations of Saudi modernization, China acquires influence that persists independently of diplomatic agreements or political alignments. The infrastructure itself becomes the instrument of power, encoding dependencies into the everyday functioning of the Saudi economy and state.

3 The Physical Architecture of Interdependence

Energy trade created the foundation for Sino–Saudi relations; strategic sequencing transformed commodity exchange into infrastructural integration. The concrete manifestations of that transformation now anchor China's presence within Saudi Arabia's modernization through physical systems that outlast political cycles, shape economic geography, and constrain future strategic alternatives. Ports, power grids, industrial complexes, and digital networks function as durable structures through which dependencies crystallize and influence becomes embedded in the material fabric of the state.

China's infrastructural engagement operates across three interconnected domains: NEOM's comprehensive development as a laboratory for integrated Chinese participation, energy infrastructure linking hydrocarbon systems to renewable technologies, and logistics networks that reposition Saudi Arabia within China's global connectivity corridors. Each domain demonstrates how infrastructure translates strategic intent into material reality, creating operational dependencies and path dependencies that function independently of diplomatic agreements or leadership preferences.

NEOM as Laboratory for Comprehensive Integration

NEOM, announced in 2017 as the flagship of Vision 2030, exemplifies the convergence of domestic transformation and infrastructure diplomacy. It seeks not merely to expand urban space but to create a new economic geography: a $500-billion complex of futuristic cities, renewable energy systems, advanced manufacturing centers, and logistics corridors designed to diversify Saudi Arabia's economy and position it as a global leader in post-carbon innovation. The project signals the Kingdom's ambition to modernize and execute megaprojects that meet global benchmarks, with its success crucial to the credibility of Vision 2030.

For China, NEOM offers an unparalleled opportunity to showcase the global reach of the BRI. Beyond providing construction and financing, the initiative embeds Chinese technologies, standards, and strategic influence into Saudi Arabia's developmental trajectory. NEOM serves as a laboratory where capabilities in renewable energy, digital governance, and industrial design can be integrated into the physical and institutional blueprint of Saudi modernity (Boretti & Castelletto, 2022). Participation thus represents more than contractual engagement; it is co-authorship in shaping the Kingdom's future.

Spanning approximately 26,500 square kilometers along the northwestern coast, NEOM envisions high-tech cities, AI hubs, renewable energy complexes, and advanced industrial clusters. While its projected cost of over half a trillion dollars makes it one of the largest planned developments in history, its true significance lies in its message: NEOM embodies Saudi Arabia's post-oil vision, signaling its intent to lead in technology, logistics, and sustainable development (Veghese, 2025).

Realizing these ambitions within the compressed timeframe of Vision 2030 requires capabilities few global actors can supply. Western firms possess advanced technologies but face reputational constraints following the Khashoggi crisis, regulatory burdens stemming from compliance and environmental assessments, financing obstacles linked to governance conditionalities, and capacity limitations that slow simultaneous deployment across multiple sites. Chinese state-owned enterprises offer a contrasting set of advantages: integrated delivery combining design, financing, construction, and operations; speed developed through experience with massive national projects; cost competitiveness enabled by subsidies and policy bank financing; political flexibility without governance conditionalities; and unparalleled capacity to mobilize labor and capital at scale.

Chinese involvement in NEOM spans several core domains. In renewable energy infrastructure, Chinese firms dominate solar and wind markets, supplying multi-gigawatt installations such as the Al Shuaibah photovoltaic plant and contributing to the renewable power systems necessary for NEOM's planned green hydrogen production (Enerdata, 2024). In digital infrastructure, Chinese companies, most prominently Huawei and Alibaba Cloud, provide the communications backbone, cloud computing architecture, smart city management systems, and surveillance technologies that underpin NEOM's cognitive city model. These systems create high switching costs data flows, operational logic, and technological ecosystems become intertwined with Chinese platforms, making future disengagement costly and technically disruptive.

The depth of Chinese participation is substantial, yet Saudi Arabia exerts considerable agency. Through technology diversification, joint venture requirements, regulatory oversight, financial independence, and contractor competition, Saudi authorities prevent any singular actor from dominating critical systems. This ensures that Chinese presence, while extensive, remains embedded within a framework ultimately controlled by Saudi institutions.

Chinese renewable energy companies such as Power-China and the China Energy Engineering Corporation contribute to NEOM's solar and wind complexes, embedding Chinese technological standards in the Kingdom's emerging green energy grid (China, 2024). Port operators like COSCO and China Harbor Engineering Company have participated in the design of logistics and maritime hubs that will connect NEOM to global trade networks. At the same time, digital infrastructure firms such as Huawei are developing data centers and smart city systems that are central to NEOM's governance model (ACIEP, 2024).

Each sector reinforces the others. Energy infrastructure powers digital systems; digital systems manage industrial efficiency; ports and logistics link both to global markets. The result is integration rather than simple cooperation. Chinese involvement becomes embedded in the functional logic of the project itself. Saudi success becomes partly dependent on Chinese participation, and Chinese influence derives not from overt leverage but from indispensability. This is the essence of designed interdependence: influence achieved through embedded relevance rather than through coercive control.

China's engagement with NEOM also highlights a distinctive quality of its foreign policy, namely, political flexibility. While Western governments and corporations have approached NEOM with caution because of concerns over feasibility, regulatory uncertainty, and reputational risk, Beijing has pursued a pragmatic approach. Chinese policymakers and companies frame NEOM not as a political risk but as a commercial and technological opportunity. This flexibility gives China a comparative advantage in contexts where other actors hesitate (Yusuf & Abdulmohsen, 2022).

Beijing's willingness to engage without imposing political or normative conditions has allowed Chinese companies to assume privileged positions in NEOM's implementation. Chinese participation now extends from renewable energy installations to port and logistics development and from digital systems to the physical infrastructure of the planned *Line City* (Wang, 2021).

Through these activities, Chinese firms have embedded elements of China's technological and regulatory ecosystem within Saudi Arabia's development framework. This advantage, however, has its limits. Western caution has not resulted in Western absence. American, European, and Japanese firms remain active in NEOM's energy and design sectors, contributing architectural, financial, and engineering expertise. Moreover, the Saudi state has deliberately structured NEOM's governance to prevent overdependence on any single foreign partner (Burton, 2021). This hedging strategy ensures that while China is indispensable in certain sectors, it cannot dominate the project's overall trajectory.

From the perspective of DSI, this outcome demonstrates the reciprocal agency of host states. Designed interdependence functions most effectively when partners have limited alternatives. Saudi Arabia's financial autonomy and geopolitical weight allow it to retain strategic flexibility. The Kingdom welcomes Chinese engagement to accelerate its modern ization process, but resists any degree of reliance that could constrain its sovereignty. The result is a dynamic equilibrium: China gains embedded presence without exclusive control, while Saudi Arabia benefits from Chinese capabilities without political subordination.

Chinese participation validates Saudi Arabia's modernization agenda at both domestic and international levels. It signals that Vision 2030 is supported by credible international partners and that its aspirations are technologically feasible. For Beijing, this reciprocal validation is equally valuable. Each collaboration reinforces China's image as a provider of developmental modernity, capable of exporting both infrastructure and governance solutions that align with the needs of non-Western partners (Samoudi, 2025). The symbolism operates across multiple levels. Economically, NEOM represents diversification; politically, it conveys agency; and diplomatically, it demonstrates autonomy from Western tutelage. Chinese involvement increases all three of these narratives, allowing Riyadh to project itself as an independent, confident actor within a multipolar world.

NEOM also exemplifies a broader transformation in international relations: the rise of infrastructural power as a key form of global influence. Whereas twentieth-century diplomacy centered on treaties, alliances, and military bases, twenty-first-century influence increasingly operates through the material systems that sustain everyday life. Energy grids, data centers, ports, and digital networks are now the arenas in which strategic influence is constructed. Through NEOM, China demonstrates how infrastructural entanglement can serve as a durable foundation for influence. By shaping the technologies that power Saudi cities, the grids that transmit energy, and the logistics corridors that connect markets, Beijing becomes integrated into the operational heart of Saudi development. This form of influence is subtle and cumulative. It depends not on overt coercion but on path dependency, as Chinese systems become normalized as essential components of national development.

Whether this partnership evolves into genuine structural interdependence remains uncertain. Saudi Arabia's hedging strategy and financial autonomy limit Beijing's leverage. Yet China's embedded presence within NEOM's technological and infrastructural systems guarantees a form of enduring relevance. NEOM is therefore not only a bilateral project but also a microcosm of broader transformations in world politics, where ambition, design, and diplomacy intersect within the built environment.

Chinese Roles in NEOM's Core Components

China has emerged as a pivotal partner in shaping NEOM's ambitious infrastructure and energy agenda. The energy dimension forms the structural foundation of NEOM's development. Planners have consistently emphasized that the project will be powered entirely by renewable sources, with particular focus on solar and wind, supplemented by large-scale hydrogen production (Farag, 2018). For Saudi Arabia, this orientation responds to both external and internal imperatives. Externally, the global transition toward low-carbon energy threatens the long-term viability of oil-based revenues, making diversification an economic and political necessity. Internally, sustained domestic energy consumption, encouraged by long-standing subsidies, has eroded the Kingdom's export capacity and exposed the inefficiency of hydrocarbon dependence. By grounding NEOM in renewable energy, Riyadh signals its intent to move from being a supplier of fossil fuels to becoming a leader in sustainable energy innovation.

China's participation in this transformation is both practical and strategic. Chinese companies dominate the global solar photovoltaic supply chain, from polysilicon processing to module manufacturing (Dong et al., 2016). They also lead in deploying large-scale wind farms and in advancing technologies of energy storage (Zhang et al., 2023). Within NEOM, enterprises such as the State Grid Corporation of China and the China Energy Engineering Corporation have positioned themselves as potential partners in constructing the renewable backbone of the city. Their appeal to Riyadh lies in two main factors. First, these firms have repeatedly demonstrated their ability to deliver at scale and within compressed timelines, a critical attribute for a project of NEOM's magnitude. Second, Chinese technology is markedly cost-competitive, often undercutting European and North American alternatives. This blend of efficiency, affordability, and execution capacity makes Chinese participation not only expedient but structurally advantageous to Saudi Arabia's ambitions.

Within this energy framework, hydrogen has emerged as the most innovative and strategically significant component. NEOM is intended to host one of the largest green hydrogen facilities in the world, producing hydrogen through electrolysis powered entirely by renewable energy. The project envisions positioning Saudi Arabia as a global supplier of hydrogen-based fuel, aligning the Kingdom's future with the decarbonized energy economy (Yong et al., 2025).

Chinese firms have shown growing interest in this dimension, leveraging their experience in electrolyzer technology, hydrogen storage systems, and fuel cell manufacturing. While European and Japanese companies maintain a strong presence in hydrogen innovation, China's integrated approach—linking hydrogen to broader industrial ecosystems and logistics—offers a competitive advantage. Should Saudi Arabia succeed in exporting hydrogen at a commercial scale, the supporting infrastructure of pipelines, storage facilities, and transport networks will likely bear significant Chinese technological and operational imprints. Through this channel, Beijing embeds itself not only in Saudi Arabia's energy transition but in the global architecture of the emerging hydrogen economy.

The second pillar of NEOM's architecture is the smart city complex. Conceived as a network of interconnected urban zones, NEOM seeks to integrate artificial intelligence, autonomous transportation, the internet of things, and digital governance into daily life (Abdelhady, 2024). The aim is to create what planners describe as cognitive cities, where data-driven management optimizes energy efficiency, mobility, and service delivery. For Saudi Arabia, this model has both economic and political functions. Economically, it serves to attract global talent and investment, positioning NEOM as a laboratory of technological innovation. Politically, it reinforces state control by enabling advanced surveillance and monitoring capabilities unavailable in traditional urban infrastructure.

Chinese technology companies are particularly well-suited to this agenda. Huawei and ZTE, already entrenched in Gulf telecommunications through the rollout of 5G networks, have expanded their expertise in fiber optics, cloud computing, and data management to the Saudi market (Dahdal & Ghafar, 2025). Huawei has signed multiple agreements to develop smart city solutions that integrate energy efficiency with security and governance systems. For Riyadh, these partnerships offer not only technical capacity but also political convenience. Western firms often face regulatory and reputational challenges when providing surveillance technologies to authoritarian regimes; Chinese companies operate without such constraints and market their systems as turnkey solutions that combine administrative control with technological efficiency. In this context, Chinese participation becomes essential to Saudi Arabia's vision of smart urban governance.

The implications of Chinese engagement in NEOM's digital infrastructure reach far beyond the project itself. Once embedded, technological standards, whether in telecommunications, cloud architecture, or surveillance systems, tend to be path-dependent and costly to replace. By establishing these standards at the inception of NEOM's development, China ensures a long-term presence in the Kingdom's digital ecosystem.

This dynamic represents the essence of infrastructure diplomacy: influence generated not through overt political alignment but through the quiet consolidation of technological dependencies that shape the everyday functioning of governance.

The third pillar of NEOM's development concerns industrial transformation. Beyond futuristic architecture and digital grids, NEOM aspires to serve as a hub for advanced manufacturing, logistics, and research-intensive industries (Fadel & Mohamed, 2025). Planned facilities include sectors such as aerospace, robotics, pharmaceuticals, and clean technology, integrated with transport and logistics systems that connect to global markets. Here again, the logic of partnership intersects with China's comparative advantages. Chinese state-owned enterprises possess extensive experience in constructing industrial parks and special economic zones, both domestically and through the BRI. For these firms, NEOM offers a platform not only to build but to integrate their global supply chains into Saudi Arabia's emerging industrial landscape. Construction firms such as China State Construction Engineering Corporation and technology firms involved in robotics and artificial intelligence have already expressed interest in anchoring production facilities and research partnerships within NEOM's designated industrial zones.

This industrial expansion signifies a broader reconfiguration of Sino–Saudi economic relations. Historically, the partnership revolved around the simple exchange of oil for capital. With NEOM, the structure of the relationship evolves toward multidimensional engagement, in which Saudi Arabia provides market access, political stability, and strategic location, while China supplies infrastructure, technology, and institutional expertise. The exchange thus shifts from extraction to co-production. The Kingdom's aspiration to diversify and China's pursuit of embedded influence meet within a framework of mutually reinforcing interdependence.

When examined collectively, China's roles in NEOM's three foundational components, renewable energy, smart cities, and industrial zones, reveal the operational logic of DSI. These are not isolated commercial contracts but interconnected layers of engagement that tie Chinese capabilities to Saudi Arabia's national transformation. For Riyadh, Chinese involvement is a pragmatic choice that ensures speed, scale, and affordability. For Beijing, the benefits extend far beyond profit margins. Through these projects, China shapes the standards, systems, and physical infrastructures that define Saudi Arabia's participation in the twenty-first-century economy. The relationship becomes self-reinforcing, producing a partnership that is resilient to short-term political fluctuations.

Yet Saudi Arabia's leadership has been cautious in managing this interdependence. The Kingdom has consistently avoided excessive reliance on any single external actor. While Western participation in NEOM has been constrained by reputational and regulatory concerns, it has not disappeared. American firms remain active in energy, European companies contribute to architectural and engineering design, and Japanese corporations occupy specialized technological niches. Riyadh has structured NEOM's governance to ensure maximum flexibility, thereby maintaining leverage over all foreign partners (Burton, 2021).

From the perspective of DSI, this represents an important structural limitation. Designed interdependence yields its strongest influence when alternatives are either unavailable or prohibitively costly. Saudi Arabia's financial strength and geopolitical standing allow it to maintain multiple options, thereby constraining Beijing's ability to convert infrastructural presence into political leverage.

The Reordering of Regional Connectivity

China's influence also expands through logistics networks that reshape the Kingdom's spatial integration with global trade. Ports, railways, and multimodal corridors determine how goods move, which markets connect efficiently, and which states become indispensable nodes in global commerce. Through its role in developing Saudi Arabia's logistics infrastructure, China indirectly shapes regional economic geography.

China's role in Saudi port development illustrates these dynamics with remarkable clarity. The engineering, procurement, and construction contract for NEOM's Container Terminal 1, awarded to China Harbour Engineering Arabia, reflects more than a commercial opportunity. It signifies China's embedding within one of the most strategically significant maritime gateways of the Red Sea. Similarly, Shanghai Zhenhua Heavy Industries (ZPMC) has supplied Saudi Arabia's first fully automated cranes for the Oxagon industrial complex, introducing advanced Chinese technologies into the Kingdom's logistics systems (SGP, 2024). Each of these projects extends Chinese presence from design and construction to long-term maintenance, software integration, and operational management. The cumulative effect is a layered form of dependency that is not easily unwound, as Chinese firms become integral to the Kingdom's logistical infrastructure.

The technical architecture of these engagements reveals why such dependencies are resilient. Automated port operations depend not only on physical hardware but also on proprietary software, algorithmic systems, and data networks that manage container flows, berthing schedules, and real-time supply chain integration (Notteboom & Yang, 2017). ZPMC's cranes, for example, operate within a digital ecosystem that requires continuous updates, maintenance, and interoperability services provided by Chinese suppliers. Once these systems are installed, operational continuity depends on access to Chinese technology and technical expertise. This produces what might be described as operational lock-in, a form of dependency that persists long after construction is complete. Even if Saudi Arabia were to seek diversification in suppliers, the technical and financial costs of shifting to alternative systems would be significant, ensuring Beijing's continued relevance within the Kingdom's logistics architecture.

Beyond hardware, Chinese participation also influences the standards that govern global trade. International logistics depends as much on invisible digital protocols, customs procedures, container tracking, and freight management platforms as on visible infrastructure. These standards have long reflected Western dominance, shaped by firms in Europe, Japan, and the United States. By promoting alternative platforms through companies such as COSCO and China Merchants Group, Beijing introduces its own operational norms into Saudi logistics systems (SPA, 2025). Once adopted, such standards tend to be path-dependent and costly to replace, creating a subtler but equally durable form of dependence. The adoption of Chinese systems thus represents a transfer of influence exercised not through overt political leverage but through the technical codes and procedures that structure international commerce. Infrastructure becomes a vector through which regulatory environments and logistical norms are gradually aligned with China's global networks.

These developments unfold within a competitive geopolitical environment. The Arabian Peninsula sits at the intersection of some of the world's most contested maritime corridors. India has supported the development of Iran's Chabahar port as a counterweight to Chinese investment in Gwadar, while the United States has advanced the India–Middle East–Europe Corridor (IMEC) as an alternative framework for connectivity that includes Saudi Arabia (Das, 2024). European operators maintain a strong presence in the Gulf through established hubs such as Dubai's Jebel Ali Port. In this crowded landscape, China's participation in Saudi infrastructure reflects not only bilateral cooperation but also a broader struggle over who defines the future geography of global trade. Each contract, each logistics partnership, becomes an instrument through which competing powers seek to inscribe their presence into the material foundations of regional order.

Competition also manifests at the corporate level. Chinese companies are known for their speed, scalability, and willingness to undertake complex projects under compressed timelines (Rodrigue, 2020). Yet they do not operate uncontested. European port operators bring long-standing expertise in logistics management and regulatory compliance, American firms offer advanced automation and cybersecurity capabilities, and Japanese companies contribute precision engineering and quality assurance developed over decades of industrial experience.

This diversity of competitors provides Riyadh with the ability to hedge its partnerships. By balancing multiple providers and playing them against one another, Saudi authorities can extract more favorable terms and prevent overdependence on any single partner (Ulrichsen, 2018). This dynamic exposes one of the limitations of DSI: interdependence generates leverage most effectively in monopolistic conditions, but where competition thrives, the capacity to translate infrastructural presence into political influence becomes diluted.

If Chinese firms succeed in embedding themselves deeply in the Kingdom's port infrastructure, their influence will extend well beyond the Saudi market into the wider architecture of Mediterranean–Indian Ocean trade. The significance of this position has been reinforced by recent disruptions in global shipping, such as the 2021 blockage of the Suez Canal by the Ever Given, which halted traffic for nearly a week and exposed the vulnerability of chokepoint-dependent supply chains (Colon & Hochrainer-Stigler, 2023; Verschuur & Hall, 2024).

Saudi Arabia's logistics vision also extends beyond the coast into the interior. Vision 2030 emphasizes the development of cross-country transport corridors linking the Gulf with the Red Sea, transforming the Kingdom into a land bridge between the Indian Ocean and the Mediterranean. The construction of railways and highways across the desert is central to this ambition. Here again, Chinese firms hold a comparative advantage due to their experience with large-scale desert rail projects, such as those in Central Asia and North Africa. Companies like China

Railway Construction Corporation and China Railway Group offer integrated packages combining technical expertise, project financing, and rapid implementation. Should they become the primary contractors for these corridors, they would effectively control the connective tissue of the Kingdom's internal and transnational transport systems. In such a scenario, Saudi domestic integration would simultaneously advance China's broader connectivity strategy.

The scope of Sino–Saudi cooperation across these sectors can be summarized as follows (Table 2).[2]

The durability of these investments underscores the profound diplomatic weight of infrastructure. Political alignments and security partnerships can shift with leadership changes or policy realignments, but infrastructure endures for decades, shaping the material realities of power. Ports, railways, and logistics systems become physical conduits through which influence circulates. For Saudi Arabia, this permanence offers both opportunity and constraint. Collaboration with China accelerates development and grants access to technology and financing, yet it also embeds dependencies that are not easily reversed. For Beijing, these same structures generate quiet but lasting influence, rooted not in rhetoric or coercion but in the enduring presence of steel, concrete, and digital systems.

Seen in this light, Saudi Arabia's logistics ambitions represent more than a program of modernization. They are central to the reordering of regional connectivity. The BRI adapts flexibly to Riyadh's domestic aspirations, while simultaneously serving Beijing's global strategy of building redundancy, setting standards, and projecting influence. Yet the Kingdom's ability to hedge between partners ensures that China's leverage remains qualified rather than absolute. What emerges is a contested landscape of infrastructure diplomacy, where influence is embedded in the physical and digital flows that sustain the global economy. Beijing's

[2] The data compiled in the table is drawn from a range of authoritative sources, including peer-reviewed journal articles, official government releases, institutional reports, and verified news platforms. These include publications from Sustainability, Energy Reports, Renewable and Sustainable Energy Reviews, and policy briefings from the Observer Research Foundation (ORF), Carnegie Endowment, CNAS, and Daleel News. Each entry reflects publicly documented cooperation between China and Saudi Arabia under the Belt and Road Initiative and Vision 2030, with emphasis on infrastructure, energy, digital systems, and strategic diplomacy. All references have been cross-verified for factual accuracy and relevance to the 2022–2025 period.

Table 2 Major China–Saudi Arabia joint projects under the Belt and Road Initiative and Vision 2030 (2022–2025)

Sector	*Project/Initiative*	*Description*
Port Infrastructure	Port of NEOM- Container Terminal 1	China Harbour Engineering Arabia awarded EPC contract for marine services and terminal infrastructure
Green Hydrogen	NEOM Green Hydrogen Project—Oxagon	Chinese firms (e.g., Sungrow, Envision Energy) supplying solar inverters and wind turbines for $8.7B hydrogen hub
Solar Energy	Al Shuaibah PV Power Plant (2.6 GW)	Developed by China Energy Engineering Group; world's largest single-site PV plant under construction
Petrochemicals	Gulei Refining & Petrochemical Complex (Phase II)	Sinopec–Aramco joint venture; $9.74B investment in Fujian with export links to Saudi Arabia
Digital Infrastructure	Huawei Smart City & AI Deployment in NEOM	Huawei involved in NEOM's digital backbone, including cloud, surveillance, and smart governance systems
Industrial Automation	Oxagon Port Automation—ZPMC Cranes	Shanghai Zhenhua Heavy Industries (ZPMC) delivered Saudi Arabia's first fully automated port cranes
Transport Logistics	Multimodal Export Corridor: Nanchang–Xiamen–Saudi Arabia	Facilitates petrochemical exports from China to Saudi Arabia via Maritime Silk Road
Strategic Diplomacy	China-Brokered Iran–Saudi Rapprochement (2023)	Diplomatic breakthrough hosted in Beijing, reshaping regional alignments
Financial Cooperation	$50B PIF–Chinese Financial Institutions Agreements	Signed during Xi Jinping's 2022 visit to Riyadh; supports industrial and infrastructure investment
Education & Talent	Xiamen University–Saudi Chemical Industry Exchange	Saudi graduates trained in China's chemical sector, enhancing bilateral human capital ties

success in embedding itself within Saudi Arabia's transformation represents one of the most sophisticated forms of contemporary influence. Whether Riyadh can maintain equilibrium within this entanglement will be a defining factor in the future balance of connectivity and power across the Red Sea, the Indian Ocean, and the Mediterranean.

4 The Convergence of Digital and Green Infrastructure in Sino–Saudi Strategy

If China's ports, railways, and energy networks form the visible structure of its external infrastructure strategy, its digital systems represent the invisible network that binds everything together. Digital infrastructure functions like the nervous system of modern governance. It is hidden, deeply interconnected, and central to state capacity and economic development. This dynamic appears most clearly in Saudi Arabia, where Vision 2030 places digital transformation at the heart of national modernization. For China, the digital realm is both a commercial arena and a strategic opening. The Digital Silk Road (DSR), which promotes Chinese digital technologies, standards, and governance approaches, aligns directly with Saudi ambitions to build smart cities, expand digital government, and establish the Kingdom as a regional leader in artificial intelligence and cloud computing.

The DSR represents the most advanced form of digital statecraft. Unlike physical infrastructure that creates visible geographic dependence, digital systems create structural dependence inside the operational logic of state administration and economic management (Shen, 2018). Once a country adopts a certain digital standard or platform, switching becomes extremely difficult. Moving data across systems is technically demanding. Retraining personnel disrupts established routines. Integrating new systems with older ones introduces friction and risk (Mayer-Schönberger & Cukier, 2013). Digital networks also operate faster and on a far larger scale than physical infrastructure. They enable continuous data collection, algorithmic decision-making, and wide-ranging surveillance capabilities that transform how governments interact with societies (Zuboff, 2019). Through the DSR, China exports not only technology but also data architectures, institutional habits, and governance principles.

Why Saudi Arabia Embraces Chinese Digital Infrastructure

Saudi Arabia offers an unusually favorable environment for Chinese digital engagement. Vision 2030 presents digital transformation as the main tool for economic diversification and public sector reform. Institutions such as the National Transformation Plan, the Saudi Data and Artificial Intelligence Authority, and the National Cybersecurity Authority are designed to develop a state that manages both efficiency and social control through data-driven methods (He, 2022). This combination reflects the Chinese experience, where digital technologies have strengthened state effectiveness and reinforced controlling governance. The shared orientation toward governance has created political confidence between Beijing and Riyadh, which helps sustain cooperation in the digital sphere.

Saudi enthusiasm for Chinese technology reflects both strategic calculation and ideological affinity. The Kingdom's digital transformation serves two related goals. The first is economic, since Saudi leaders hope to build a knowledge-based economy as oil revenues decline. The second is political, since digital tools enhance the government's ability to manage society and maintain stability. The ambitions of Vision 2030 require technologies that are sophisticated yet flexible enough to support strong state authority. Western firms often cannot provide this combination because many of their technologies are shaped by democratic norms that emphasize privacy, transparency, and user rights (Triolo et al., 2020).

This asymmetry in engagement is partly structural. Since the Snowden revelations, European publics have become acutely sensitive to the political implications of digital infrastructure (Greenwald, 2014). The 2018 murder of Jamal Khashoggi intensified these sensitivities, making Western technology companies wary of being complicit in potential human rights violations. American firms, constrained by congressional oversight and reputational risk, have largely avoided projects involving surveillance or data governance. Chinese firms, in contrast, face no such domestic constraints. Their international expansion is framed as a matter of state policy and economic necessity, supported by both financing and diplomatic cover from Beijing (He, 2022). This asymmetry has given China's digital enterprises a decisive competitive advantage in markets where governance models prioritize control and efficiency over transparency and liberal norms.

The implications extend far beyond commerce. Digital infrastructure is not politically neutral; it encodes standards, dependencies, and operational logics that shape how information is stored, transmitted, and secured. Huawei's 5G networks, already deployed in major Saudi cities, form the backbone of future technologies such as autonomous vehicles, telemedicine, and smart grids (Zhentian, 2024). Once these platforms are embedded, replacing them becomes technically prohibitive and economically costly. Switching away from Huawei would require dismantling the very networks upon which national data and communications depend.

This produces a form of structural dependency more binding than traditional alliances, since it operates at the infrastructural level of state functionality rather than at the level of policy preference.

Beyond telecommunications, Chinese firms are actively constructing Saudi Arabia's digital backbone in cloud computing, artificial intelligence, and surveillance. Alibaba Cloud has partnered with local entities to build hyperscale data centers that support both government and commercial operations (Alghannam, 2025). These facilities are not neutral storage sites but critical nodes in a global data ecosystem through which questions of sovereignty, cybersecurity, and data governance are negotiated. Huawei and Dahua have also supplied surveillance systems for urban management, integrating facial recognition, predictive policing, and traffic monitoring into the fabric of Saudi urban life. For Riyadh, these technologies promise efficiency and control; for Beijing, they expand the reach of the DSR into sensitive domains where Western actors remain reluctant to engage.

From a DSI perspective, this represents the most advanced form of interdependence: designed digital entanglement. Once Chinese systems become embedded in Saudi governance processes, they create dependencies that cannot easily be disentangled without jeopardizing critical functions. This form of dependency is self-reinforcing. Every update, every cloud migration, and every software patch deepens the technical and institutional reliance on Chinese ecosystems. In this sense, the DSR operates as both infrastructure and diplomacy, fusing technical integration with strategic alignment.

The geopolitical context makes this even more significant. The United States has exerted pressure on allies to exclude Chinese firms from critical networks, warning that such participation poses security risks (Bu, 2024). The European Union has issued guidelines against high-risk vendors, and India has imposed outright bans on Chinese digital technologies. Against this backdrop, Saudi Arabia's embrace of Chinese digital providers signals strategic defiance and growing confidence in pursuing an independent technological path. Riyadh's hedging strategy, maintaining ties with Western providers while deepening cooperation with Chinese firms, illustrates how middle powers navigate great-power competition to maximize autonomy. Yet in the digital domain, such hedging is inherently constrained.

Digital ecosystems, unlike physical infrastructure, demand interoperability and standardization. A national telecommunications system cannot simultaneously operate Huawei and Ericsson architectures without major technical friction. Cloud systems cannot easily migrate between Alibaba and Amazon Web Services, and surveillance networks cannot seamlessly integrate Chinese and Western protocols. As a result, once Saudi Arabia commits to a given digital supplier, it effectively locks itself into that ecosystem for years, if not decades (de Seta, 2023). In DSI terms, this creates a high-density interdependence: a condition where alternatives are technically possible but economically and politically prohibitive.

In practical terms, Chinese technology also offers compelling economic and technical benefits. Huawei's 5G systems are usually significantly cheaper than their European competitors. Chinese firms supply complete digital ecosystems that include hardware, software, cloud services, and applications. They can deliver large-scale projects at high speed. Despite ongoing concerns about security risks, Chinese telecommunications, cloud computing platforms, and artificial intelligence tools operate at a level of quality that satisfies Saudi technical requirements. For a country pursuing a rapid national transformation, this combination of price, speed, and capability is highly attractive.

Green Infrastructure: China's Role in Saudi Arabia's Post-Oil Transition

As Saudi Arabia seeks to position itself as a leader in post-oil sustainable energy, China has emerged as a critical partner, providing expertise, technology, and investment in renewable energy and green hydrogen production. Chinese firms are instrumental in delivering the solar, wind, and hydrogen infrastructure that underpins Riyadh's vision of a diversified, low-carbon economy.

Within this context, China's participation in renewable energy and green infrastructure becomes strategically significant. The Kingdom's aspiration to lead in hydrogen, solar, and smart grids provides Beijing with a laboratory to showcase its technological leadership, while Riyadh benefits from access to Chinese capital, expertise, and industrial capacity. The partnership represents a form of diplomacy by design, in which long-term interdependence is created through infrastructural choices that lock-in relationships for decades. Green infrastructure becomes a mechanism for producing mutual dependency, where the architecture of the energy transition itself becomes a vehicle of influence.

Marketed as a model for sustainable living, Saudi Arabia's flagship green initiatives pledge to operate on 100% renewable energy, reflecting some of the most ambitious efforts in the global energy transition (Chaziza, 2025). Its design seeks to project Saudi Arabia as a leader in the global green economy capable of transcending its hydrocarbon legacy (Wang et al., 2022). By inviting Chinese companies into the energy ecosystem, Riyadh demonstrates pragmatic recognition of these capabilities. Yet this cooperation also binds the Kingdom to Chinese technologies, standards, and supply chains, creating dependencies Vision 2030 seeks to transcend.

The centerpiece of Saudi Arabia's green aspirations is its plan to become a global leader in hydrogen production. Chinese participation in hydrogen research, electrolyzer manufacturing, and infrastructure development positions Beijing as an indispensable partner (NEOM, 2023). China has already rolled out hydrogen pilot projects domestically, integrating fuel cells into transport networks and industrial (Zhang et al., 2023).

Partnership with Chinese firms offers Riyadh both technical capability and access to markets. China's demand for clean fuels is projected to surge as it seeks to decarbonize its heavy industries and transport sectors. The prospect of exporting hydrogen to China creates a new pattern of energy interdependence. Whereas in the oil era Saudi Arabia exported hydrocarbons to power industrial growth, in the hydrogen era it could export green energy eastward to sustain China's own transition. In both cases, infrastructure serves as the material expression of geopolitical alignment.

Hydrogen cooperation therefore alters the geopolitics of energy in ways that echo, yet depart from, the oil age. In the twentieth century, Saudi Arabia's strategic importance rested on the flexibility of its oil supply to the United States, Europe, and Asia. In the twenty-first century, hydrogen could play a similar role, binding producers and consumers through fixed infrastructural links and long-term contracts. If China becomes the dominant technology supplier and Saudi Arabia the leading producer, the bilateral relationship will evolve into a new form of structural interdependence—an energy-for-technology compact that mirrors the oil-for-security dynamic of the past but in a post-carbon context.

Solar power constitutes another major field of cooperation. Saudi Arabia's deserts receive some of the world's highest levels of solar irradiance, making large-scale photovoltaic generation economically viable. Yet previous efforts faltered due to high costs and limited institutional capacity. The entry of Chinese firms such as JinkoSolar and LONGi has altered the landscape (Bellini, 2023). These companies deliver solar capacity at a competitive cost and speed unmatched by Western competitors. They also bring access to integrated supply chains supported by China's manufacturing base and financing institutions. Through the BRI, Chinese development banks offer concessional loans and turnkey packages that accelerate project implementation.

Wind power also features prominently in Saudi diversification plans. NEOM's coastal geography offers strong wind resources, and Chinese turbine manufacturers have already supplied equipment for projects in other Gulf states (SGP, 2023). Wind complements solar by providing generation at different times of the day, contributing to a more balanced renewable mix. By engaging Chinese firms, Saudi planners tap into an ecosystem of suppliers and engineers who have already deployed wind at scale across Asia and Africa. Chinese turbines spinning in the Saudi desert would mark not only technological progress but also the visible manifestation of Beijing's role in powering the Kingdom's future.

Grid modernization is the often-overlooked yet indispensable component of this transition. Renewable energy requires grids that can handle variability, distribute power efficiently, and integrate storage systems. China's State Grid Corporation has pioneered ultra-high voltage transmission lines and smart grid technologies. Its involvement in Saudi Arabia represents the transfer of an entire philosophy of energy management. State Grid has long promoted the idea of a global energy internet, in which renewable energy is transmitted seamlessly across borders (SCAMP, 2020). By partnering with State Grid, Saudi Arabia aligns itself with this vision, positioning its energy infrastructure within a transnational network largely shaped by Chinese engineering and standards.

The geopolitical implications of this green partnership are far-reaching. Saudi Arabia has long been courted by Western states seeking to promote renewable energy cooperation, yet political frictions and technology transfer concerns have slowed progress (Barnes & Jaffe, 2006). China offers a different model: partnership framed as mutual modernization rather than conditional assistance. This appeal is not only economic but ideological. By working with China, Riyadh asserts its autonomy in choosing partners, rejecting the notion that energy transition must follow Western templates. For Beijing, embedding itself in Saudi Arabia's most high-profile renewable projects positions it as a co-architect of the Kingdom's post-oil identity. Influence is thus exercised not through rhetoric but through kilowatts, turbines, and transmission lines.

At a broader level, Chinese engagement in Saudi green infrastructure challenges prevailing assumptions about the geopolitics of energy transition. Western discourse often assumes that decarbonization will diminish the strategic importance of the Middle East by reducing global dependence on hydrocarbons (Proedrou, 2025). The reality may be more complex. If Saudi Arabia becomes a leading exporter of hydrogen and renewable energy, its geopolitical relevance will persist, albeit in transformed ways. And if Chinese firms and technologies form the backbone of this new energy economy, Beijing will have secured a long-term stake in the region's strategic future. Rather than fading into irrelevance, the Middle East may reemerge as the nexus of a new green energy order, with China and Saudi Arabia at its center.

Diplomacy by design operates here in subtle ways. The materiality of green infrastructure creates enduring linkages that outlast political cycles. Just as pipelines locked European states into Soviet gas during the Cold War, Saudi Arabia's hydrogen pipelines or smart grid standards could tie its energy future to Chinese technology for decades. The design of these systems is not neutral; it encodes dependencies into the everyday functioning of the economy. By participating in these projects, China embeds itself into the architecture of Saudi Arabia's future, shaping the very pathways of its post-oil development.

Regional comparisons reinforce this logic. In the UAE, renewable projects are often partnered with Western firms such as Siemens or EDF, embedding European technologies and standards. In Oman and Egypt, Chinese firms have already secured contracts for green hydrogen facilities, creating a patchwork of influence across the Middle East. Saudi Arabia's choice to work extensively with Chinese partners places it within this broader regional landscape of green infrastructure diplomacy. The Kingdom seeks to hedge by maintaining ties with Western energy companies, yet the scale and cost advantages of Chinese firms tilt the balance toward Beijing. The competition for standard-setting in the region is therefore not merely commercial but strategic, determining whose technologies and protocols will dominate the future energy economy.

The partnership is not without vulnerabilities. Dependence on Chinese supply chains for critical minerals such as lithium, cobalt, and rare earths exposes Saudi Arabia to potential disruptions. Cybersecurity risks emerge from the integration of Chinese smart grid technologies, raising concerns about data sovereignty and operational control. Yet these vulnerabilities are integral to the very logic of designed interdependence: they generate both leverage and constraint. For Saudi Arabia, the challenge lies in balancing the efficiency and scale of Chinese partnerships with the strategic resilience that diversification provides. For Beijing, the challenge lies in managing its growing entanglement without provoking counterbalancing from rival powers.

In the end, the renewable energy partnership between China and Saudi Arabia exemplifies the evolution of infrastructure diplomacy in the age of decarbonization. The energy transition does not erase geopolitics; it reconfigures it. By embedding its technology, standards, and supply chains within Saudi Arabia's green transformation, Beijing achieves structural presence without military bases or formal alliances. Riyadh leverages Chinese capabilities to accelerate its modernization while attempting to preserve autonomy. Whether this balance can endure will depend on the very infrastructures that both states have designed together.

5 Strategic Convergence and Bounded Interdependence

Sino–Saudi infrastructure cooperation unfolds across physical, digital, energy, and logistics networks, yet its strategic weight stems less from any single sector than from the cumulative effect of their interaction. Vision 2030 created an institutional and political environment that invited deeper external partnerships, and Beijing proved especially adept at aligning its own connectivity agenda with Riyadh's reform priorities. At the same time, this interdependence remains intentionally circumscribed. Saudi policymakers have welcomed Chinese capital, technology, and project delivery while preserving room to maneuver vis-à-vis other great powers and safeguarding critical domains. Understanding this balance—between convergence and constraint—also reveals how the Saudi approach diverges from that of other Gulf states, some of which have embraced tighter, more exclusive linkages, while others maintain more rigid boundaries.

Vision 2030 as Enabling Structure for Chinese Engagement

Vision 2030 did not originate from Chinese strategic thinking, yet it produced structural incentives that rendered Chinese participation increasingly consequential. Announced in 2016, the initiative seeks to reconfigure the Kingdom's political economy by diminishing dependence on hydrocarbon revenues, expanding private sector employment, broadening non-oil fiscal sources, and repositioning Saudi Arabia as a central node in global investment flows. Realizing these objectives requires the concurrent development of airports, industrial complexes, logistics corridors, renewable energy systems, digital infrastructure, and large-scale urban projects. The cumulative scope of these undertakings necessitates extraordinary concentrations of capital, expertise, and organizational capacity.

The Saudi reform program created five functional requirements. It demanded scale sufficient for the execution of multiple multi-billion-dollar initiatives at the same time; velocity adequate to meet politically compressed timelines; integrative capacities that could supply comprehensive, turnkey project solutions; political discretion that avoids intrusive conditionalities; and temporal patience that can accommodate extended or uncertain returns. These requirements reflect the political logic underpinning Vision 2030. The authority of Mohammed bin Salman is contingent upon demonstrable progress within a relatively narrow window of time, which renders delays politically costly and constrains the viability of gradualist, institution-first development pathways.

Western firms possessed advanced engineering capabilities but confronted mounting constraints. After the Khashoggi killing, American and European corporations faced reputational liabilities, regulatory scrutiny, and politically sensitive oversight that disincentivized visible engagement with Saudi flagship projects. Compliance regimes concerning corruption and environmental standards slowed implementation. Fluctuating United States policy signals and congressional opposition elevated political risk for long-horizon investments. Japanese and South Korean firms offered high-quality outputs but lacked the financial depth to underwrite expansive, cross-sectoral undertakings without reliance on Western financial institutions, which would have reintroduced conditionalities. India lacked the capital, institutional coordination, and bureaucratic coherence required for projects of comparable magnitude. Neighboring Gulf states functioned as competitors rather than complementary partners.

Chinese state capitalism corresponded more closely to the structural demands of Vision 2030. Chinese state-owned enterprises demonstrated the capacity to mobilize labor, capital, and equipment with exceptional immediacy, an ability facilitated by substantial domestic surplus capacity and insulated from short-term commercial pressures. Chinese policy banks supplied concessional finance with minimal political stipulations. Chinese firms had established a record of completing very large infrastructure projects within highly compressed timeframes that Western firms rarely attempted. Beijing's non-interference doctrine removed governance and human rights conditionalities, while the Belt and Road Initiative provided a macro-strategic framework supportive of projects with speculative or long-term revenue horizons, including components of NEOM, The Line, and emerging hydrogen industries.

Leadership continuity accentuated these complementarities. Mohammed bin Salman and Xi Jinping operate within governance structures that permit extended planning horizons. This configuration reduces policy volatility and enables sequential commitments that are difficult to maintain within political systems governed by electoral turnover.

However, the same attributes that render Chinese engagement attractive also generate structural vulnerabilities. As Vision 2030 becomes increasingly intertwined with Chinese finance, technology, and execution capacity, Saudi planners face exposure to potential Chinese leverage. Any deceleration of project implementation, restrictions on technology transfer, or shifts in Chinese industrial policy would have significant implications for Saudi development trajectories and could impose domestic political costs. Consequently, Saudi authorities attempt to preserve strategic optionality through continued engagement with Western, Japanese, and South Korean firms, even when such partners are constrained by regulatory or political considerations.

The resulting configuration is interdependent yet asymmetric. Vision 2030 generates demand that aligns uniquely with Chinese capabilities, and Chinese participation facilitates progress at a pace that Saudi leadership deems politically essential. Nevertheless, China's regional connectivity strategy would proceed through other Gulf partners if Saudi cooperation diminished. Saudi Arabia, by contrast, would encounter substantial difficulty replicating the combination of financial breadth, operational speed, and integrated project delivery that Chinese institutions currently provide.

Defense Cooperation and the Persistence of Security Asymmetry

Economic cooperation between Saudi Arabia and China has expanded at a significant pace, yet it has not transformed the Kingdom's foundational security alignment. Defense ties between the two states have grown in scope, although they remain constrained by structural factors that reflect American dominance in advanced military technologies and in regional security provision.

Saudi Arabia has procured Chinese unmanned aerial vehicles, particularly the Wing Loong series, primarily because Washington maintains stringent restrictions on the export of such systems. These platforms have been deployed along the Saudi–Yemen frontier and are supported by technology transfer arrangements that permit local assembly. Chinese involvement in missile production facilities has likely contributed to the Kingdom's indigenous ballistic missile capabilities, although in ways calibrated to remain within technical and legal parameters that avoid explicit treaty violations. Joint ventures in defense manufacturing, training programs for Saudi engineers, and limited joint exercises have enhanced operational familiarity without indicating a shift in strategic orientation.

Nuclear cooperation exhibits similarly dual-use characteristics. Chinese firms have conducted geological surveys and advanced proposals for reactor construction under terms that are considerably more flexible than those offered by the United States. Beijing's willingness to provide assistance without the stringent nonproliferation conditions that Washington typically requires aligns with Saudi preferences to preserve strategic freedom of action in future nuclear decision-making.

Such cooperation introduces forms of dependency. Military platforms require continuous access to compatible munitions, spare parts, maintenance services, and software updates. These requirements generate long-term technical and logistical relationships that are difficult to unwind. The training of Saudi personnel on Chinese systems further embeds operational practices that increase the cost of switching suppliers.

These dependencies, however, remain secondary. For its core security needs, Saudi Arabia continues to rely on capabilities that China cannot feasibly provide. American aircraft, missile defense systems, satellite intelligence, and naval power remain substantially superior to Chinese equivalents. The United States possesses an established record of defending Gulf monarchies, most visibly during the 1991 Gulf War and through its ongoing military presence. China, by contrast, refrains from formal security commitments and demonstrates no inclination to extend military guarantees. The principal threats facing Saudi Arabia, particularly from Iran and associated non-state actors, require high-end capabilities and integrated intelligence support that only the United States can credibly supply.

Interoperability requirements within the Gulf Cooperation Council further anchor Saudi military forces within a security architecture oriented around American standards and systems. A significant shift toward Chinese equipment in sensitive domains would impede coordination with regional partners. Moreover, American political pressure imposes an additional constraint. Washington has repeatedly signaled that excessive defense cooperation with China could jeopardize access to advanced U.S. platforms and broader security cooperation.

Saudi Arabia has therefore adopted a segmentation strategy. It acquires lower-end and politically sensitive systems from China, relies on the United States for high-end capabilities central to deterrence and warfighting, and supplements its overall defense portfolio with European systems that diversify procurement without challenging the centrality of the American partnership.

From the perspective of theories of developmental–security interdependence, this configuration illustrates that economic ties do not automatically generate corresponding shifts in security alignments when existential or high-stakes considerations are involved. Infrastructure and economic cooperation can create forms of leverage, but they cannot substitute for credible security guarantees. China's policy of avoiding military commitments allows its partners to retain their reliance on American security provision, which Saudi Arabia perceives as essential. This arrangement remains viable only insofar as strategic competition between the United States and China does not force exclusive alignment choices. If Washington were to impose such a binary, Saudi hedging strategies would encounter severe and potentially unsustainable constraints.

Financial Integration's Conspicuous Absence

Chinese infrastructure engagement in Saudi Arabia is extensive, yet financial integration between the two states remains limited. Despite a decade of Chinese initiatives aimed at promoting the use of the renminbi in oil trade through the petroyuan mechanism, Saudi Arabia continues to price and settle nearly all of its hydrocarbon exports in United States dollars.

A currency swap line was established between Riyadh and Beijing in 2016, and high-level diplomatic engagement has underscored the potential advantages of renminbi-denominated transactions. Substantive adoption, however, has not materialized. The Saudi riyal remains pegged to the dollar, the Kingdom's foreign exchange reserves remain overwhelmingly dollar-denominated, and global commercial transactions continue to rely on established dollar-based networks.

This divergence illustrates the distinction between greenfield and brownfield domains. Chinese infrastructure initiatives succeed where new systems can be constructed de novo, allowing integration without displacing entrenched incumbents. By contrast, international finance is deeply institutionalized around the dollar. Oil pricing benchmarks, derivatives and futures markets, correspondent banking systems, hedging mechanisms, and reserve management all presuppose dollar-denominated flows. Path dependency and network effects render systemic change both costly and complex.

Adopting the renminbi for oil exports to China would necessitate the development of new financial instruments, entail additional currency risk, and generate conversion costs. Dollar-denominated obligations across imports, debt service, and investment portfolios would produce structural mismatches. Furthermore, potential reactions from the United States impose additional constraints. Washington has signaled that any substantial departure from dollar settlement in oil trade would be interpreted as a strategic challenge, with repercussions spanning financial and security domains.

This case exemplifies the limits of intentionally constructed strategic interdependence. Even extensive infrastructure engagement cannot displace systemic financial structures that are defended by a dominant power. Chinese leverage is effective in domains where incumbent systems are weak or absent. In contrast, the global financial architecture remains firmly anchored to the dollar, and neither Saudi Arabia nor its Gulf neighbors have ventured beyond this structural boundary.

Comparing Gulf Responses to Chinese Infrastructure Diplomacy

Saudi Arabia's engagement with China occurs within a regional context in which Gulf states confront comparable development pressures but pursue divergent strategies.

The United Arab Emirates has also deepened its economic ties with China across ports, digital infrastructure, manufacturing, and renewable energy. Initiatives at Khalifa Port, the extensive deployment of Huawei equipment in commercial networks, and joint industrial investment funds exemplify significant cooperation. Nonetheless, Emirati engagement exhibits a more calibrated balance. Formalized security ties with the United States and expanded intelligence and defense cooperation following Israeli normalization provide structural anchors. The UAE has adopted stricter regulatory standards for sensitive digital infrastructure and maintains diversified partnerships that mitigate dependence on any single external actor. Its federal political structure generates institutional checks that constrain executive discretion, fostering a more cautious approach to foreign alignment than that observable in Saudi Arabia.

Kuwait illustrates the constraining effect of domestic politics on Chinese engagement. Parliamentary oversight imposes transparency requirements and legislative veto points absent in the Saudi system. Chinese bids for major infrastructure projects have encountered scrutiny concerning debt implications, geopolitical risks, and procurement standards. These institutional constraints, combined with Kuwait's sustained dependence on U.S. security guarantees following the 1991 invasion, limit the scope and scale of Chinese involvement.

Oman demonstrates an alternative pattern. Muscat has welcomed Chinese investment in Duqm Port and associated industrial zones. At the same time, the Sultanate maintains diversified security relationships with the United States and the United Kingdom and pursues an independent foreign policy shaped by its strategic location on the Arabian Sea. While economic pressures increase Omani receptivity to Chinese financing, engagement is treated as one component of a broader, balanced external strategy.

Comparative analysis highlights several structural factors that explain variation in Gulf engagement with China. Political systems shape decision-making. Centralized governance in Saudi Arabia permits rapid, large-scale Chinese integration, whereas parliamentary or federal institutions in Kuwait and the UAE impose procedural constraints. Security dependencies influence strategic latitude. States with acute reliance on U.S. protection adopt more cautious approaches to Chinese involvement. Economic capacity affects bargaining leverage. Wealthier states can extract favorable terms and avoid excessive indebtedness, whereas fiscally constrained actors display greater openness to Chinese financing. Development ambitions and implementation timelines further condition the scope of engagement. The compressed timelines of Vision 2030 generated exceptional demand for capabilities that Chinese actors are uniquely positioned to deliver.

Saudi Arabia represents an exceptional case in the region because these structural and political factors converge to facilitate unusually deep engagement. Autocratic consolidation, fiscal capacity, ambitious reform objectives, and geopolitical confidence collectively enable engagement at a scale unmatched elsewhere in the Gulf. Nevertheless, regional comparison also underscores shared constraints. No Gulf state has materially reduced its security reliance on the United States, nor has any significantly altered oil pricing or settlement away from the dollar. All pursue hedging strategies within structural boundaries imposed by American power and the entrenched architecture of global finance.

6 The Limits and Leverage of Designed Interdependence

Chinese infrastructure engagement in Saudi Arabia encompasses material, digital, logistics, and energy domains. Yet documenting physical or institutional presence is not synonymous with demonstrating influence. The central analytical question for the theory of designed strategic interdependence is whether such embedded positions meaningfully shape Saudi behavior or impose constraints on its autonomy.

The petroyuan case illustrates the limits of infrastructure interdependence in generating compliance. Despite the deepest Chinese presence in the history of Sino–Saudi relations, Riyadh has resisted Beijing's efforts to denominate oil sales in renminbi. China pursued this objective through a combination of currency swap arrangements, policy bank financing linked to broader cooperative initiatives, and high-level diplomatic engagement. The implicit expectation was that Saudi Arabia would reciprocate infrastructure support with financial alignment, advancing Chinese ambitions for currency internationalization.

Saudi authorities, however, determined that renminbi pricing imposed unacceptable costs. Such a shift risked destabilizing the riyal's dollar peg, complicating financial operations, and undermining relations with the United States. The Kingdom's substantial wealth, access to alternative sources of finance, and capacity to self-fund projects meant that Chinese displeasure did not threaten core national interests. Even in the event of a partial withdrawal by Chinese firms or financiers, Saudi Arabia retained viable alternatives among Western and Asian partners, albeit at higher financial or operational cost. Infrastructure dependence alone was therefore insufficient to compel financial or strategic concessions.

This case demonstrates that designed strategic interdependence produces leverage primarily under conditions of scarcity, high switching costs, and when the political costs of resistance exceed those of compliance. Where core sovereign interests are at stake and credible alternatives exist, infrastructure interdependence does not override state agency.

A second domain, 5G deployment, demonstrates a more nuanced outcome. Saudi Arabia faced concurrent pressure from the United States to exclude Huawei and from China to adopt Huawei exclusively. The Kingdom responded with a segmentation strategy, deploying Huawei technology in commercial and consumer networks where its comparative advantages were strongest, while retaining Western suppliers for sensitive government and critical infrastructure systems. This dual architecture increased operational complexity and technical inefficiencies, yet it allowed Saudi Arabia to preserve strategic relationships with both major powers. In this instance, China achieved partial influence, as its prior 4G investments increased the cost of exclusion, yet Saudi strategic priorities and resources prevented exclusive dependence. The case exemplifies bounded leverage: Chinese infrastructure shaped the structure of choice without fully determining outcomes.

These examples reveal five mechanisms through which infrastructure diplomacy generates leverage, each mediated by partner characteristics. First, switching cost escalation occurs as systems become embedded. Second, operational interdependence generates disruption risks if systems are withdrawn. Third, normative alignment, particularly through non-interference principles, cultivates political and institutional compatibility. Fourth, temporal lock-in arises from long equipment lifecycles and multi-decade project horizons. Fifth, network effects emerge as systems integrate into broader Chinese technological and logistical architectures. For Saudi Arabia, the cost-bearing capacity provided by wealth, combined with diversification strategies across multiple suppliers and parallel systems, reduces vulnerability along all five dimensions.

Across these mechanisms, leverage is mediated by partner wealth, availability of alternatives, and the degree of strategic autonomy. States lacking financial resources or political options face more acute constraints, while wealthy and strategically positioned states can resist pressures that would bind less capable partners.

Overall, the Saudi case indicates that designed strategic interdependence should be conceptualized as a variable condition rather than a uniform outcome. Infrastructure diplomacy can produce influence, yet its effectiveness depends upon sectoral context, partner characteristics, and the interaction of embedded mechanisms. Saudi Arabia occupies an intermediate category: China has secured structural presence and partial influence across several domains, but limits remain significant because the Kingdom possesses alternatives, substantial financial capacity, and strong security ties with the United States. For less autonomous and financially constrained states, Chinese leverage is likely to be far more pronounced. For highly autonomous advanced economies, the potential for infrastructure-induced influence is comparatively limited.

In conclusion, Saudi Arabia exemplifies both the opportunities and the limits of contemporary Chinese infrastructure diplomacy. The Kingdom's experience underscores that while infrastructure engagement can shape strategic environments, it does not automatically translate into compliance, particularly for states with substantial resources, diversified partnerships, and credible security guarantees. Chinese leverage is contingent, bounded, and sectorally mediated; it is strongest where incumbency is weak and alternatives are scarce, and weakest where wealth, autonomy, and allied support provide resilient buffers. The Saudi case thus illustrates the conditional and context-dependent nature of influence in designed strategic interdependence, offering critical insight for understanding the broader regional implications of China's global infrastructure strategy.

In sum, Sino–Saudi engagement illustrates a complex interplay between infrastructure presence, economic interdependence, and strategic autonomy. Across material, digital, energy, and logistics domains, China has established a substantial structural footprint, enabling accelerated progress on Vision 2030 while aligning with Saudi development imperatives. Defense and nuclear cooperation demonstrate the selective boundaries of influence: economic leverage does not automatically translate into security dependence, particularly when core sovereign interests intersect with credible U.S. guarantees. Financial integration, exemplified by the petroyuan case, underscores the limits of infrastructure diplomacy in entrenched global systems where alternative options, path dependencies, and geopolitical pressures constrain compliance. Comparative analysis within the Gulf further clarifies that domestic political institutions, security dependencies, and fiscal capacity mediate the scope and pace of Chinese engagement, highlighting why Saudi Arabia occupies an exceptional position in the region.

Collectively, these cases demonstrate that designed strategic interdependence operates as a conditional mechanism. Leverage emerges where alternatives are scarce, switching costs are high, and the political costs of resistance exceed those of compliance. It remains bounded where partner wealth, diversified capabilities, and allied relationships preserve autonomy. Saudi Arabia exemplifies the middle ground: China achieves structural presence and partial influence, yet significant limits persist due to the Kingdom's financial resources, strategic diversification, and enduring U.S. security ties. This analysis underscores that infrastructure diplomacy, while powerful, is neither uniform nor deterministic. Its effects are contingent upon partner characteristics, sectoral contexts, and the broader strategic environment, offering critical insights into the opportunities and constraints of China's global engagement in highly autonomous and strategically significant states.

References

Abdelhady, M. A. (2024). Policies and legislation enabling sustainable technologies in the public transport infrastructure in NEOM. *Sustainable Development, 32*(5), 5602–5610.

ACIEP. (2024). *Chinese companies spearhead development of Saudi NEOM Future city*. Arab-China Institute for Economics and Policy. https://www.aciep.net/en/2024/02/05/chinese-companies-spearhead-development-of-saudi-neom-future-city/

Al-Tamimi, N. M. (2013). *China-Saudi Arabia relations, 1990–2012: Marriage of convenience or strategic alliance?* Routledge.

Alghannam, H. (2025). *How China aligned itself with Saudi Arabia's vision 2030*. Carnegie Endowment for International Peace.

Barnes, J., & Jaffe, A. M. (2006). The Persian Gulf and the geopolitics of oil. *Survival, 48*(1), 143–162.

Barnett, M., & Duvall, R. (2005). Power in international politics. *International Organization, 59*(1), 39–75. https://doi.org/10.1017/S0020818305050010

Bellini, E. (2023). *Saudi Arabia to power green hydrogen project with 2.2 GW of solar*. PV Magazine. https://www.pv-magazine.com/2023/08/10/saudi-arabia-to-power-green-hydrogen-project-with-2-2-gw-of-solar/

Boretti, A., & Castelletto, S. (2022). Opportunities of renewable energy supply to NEOM city. *Renewable Energy Focus, 40*, 67–81.

Bu, Q. (2024). Behind the Huawei sanction: National security, ideological prejudices or something else? *International Cybersecurity Law Review, 5*(2), 263–300. https://doi.org/10.1365/s43439-024-00112-6

Burton, G. (2021). China's three level game in the Middle East. *Asian Journal of Middle Eastern and Islamic Studies, 15*(2), 189–204.

Chaziza, M. (2025). From oil to renewables: China's role in Gulf cooperation council energy transition. *Asian Affairs, 56*(3), 566–593.

China, P. (2024). *Saudi Arabia NEOM project achieves major milestones*. Power China. Retrieved 10 May 2025 from https://en.powerchina.cn/2024-02/20/c_828656.htm

Colon, C., & Hochrainer-Stigler, S. (2023). Systemic risks in supply chains: A need for system-level governance. *Supply Chain Management: An International Journal, 28*(4), 682–694.

Dahdal, A. M., & Ghafar, A. A. (2025). The digital silk road: "Tech-diplomacy" as a paradigm for understanding technological adoption and emerging digital regulations in MENA. *Asian Journal of Law and Society, 12*(2), 163–188.

Daojiong, Z. (2005). China's energy security and its international relations. *The China and Eurasia Forum Quarterly, 3*, 39–54.

Das, D. (2024). Revisiting the contours of the evolving Middle Eastern order through the India-Middle East-EU Corridor: Mapping India's scopes and limitations. *Asian Journal of Political Science, 32*(1), 35–56.

de Seta, G. (2023). China's digital infrastructure: Networks, systems, standards. *Global Media and China, 8*(3), 245–253.

Dong, L., Liang, H., Gao, Z., Luo, X., & Ren, J. (2016). Spatial distribution of China's renewable energy industry: Regional features and implications for a harmonious development future. *Renewable and Sustainable Energy Reviews, 58*, 1521–1531.

Enerdata. (2024). *inkoSolar will supply 1 GW of solar for the NEOM hydrogen project in Saudi Arabia*. Enerdata. https://www.enerdata.net/publications/daily-energy-news/jinkosolar-will-supply-1-gw-solar-neom-hydrogen-project-saudi-arabia.html

Fadel, E. H., & Mohamed, A. B. (2025). *Neom City: A paradigm shift in urban development and economic transformation*.

Farag, A. A. (2018). The story of NEOM city: Opportunities and challenges. In S. Attia, Z. Shafik, & A. Ibrahim (Eds.), *New cities and community extensions in Egypt and the Middle East: Visions and challenges* (pp. 35–49). Springer.

Foley, S. (2023). Saudi Arabia's relations with China. In *Routledge companion to China and the Middle East and North Africa* (pp. 333–359). Routledge.

Fulton, J. (2022). *Routledge Handbook on China-Middle East Relations*. Routledge Abingdon.

Greenwald, G. (2014). *No place to hide: Edward Snowden, the NSA, and the US surveillance state*. Macmillan.

He, A. (2022). *The digital Silk Road and China's influence on standard setting* (No. 264). CIGI Papers.

Mayer-Schönberger, V., & Cukier, K. (2013). *Big data: A revolution that will transform how we live, work, and think*. Houghton Mifflin Harcourt.

NEOM. (2023). *NEOM Green Hydrogen company completes financial close at a total investment value of USD 8.4 billion in the world's largest carbon-free green hydrogen plant*. NEOM News Room. https://www.neom.com/en-us/newsroom/neom-green-hydrogen-investment

Notteboom, T., & Yang, Z. (2017). Port governance in China since 2004: Institutional layering and the growing impact of broader policies. *Research in Transportation Business & Management, 22*, 184–200.

Proedrou, F. (2025). The geopolitics of the global energy transition. In *EU energy geopolitics: Strategic premiums, challenges, and dilemmas in the global energy transition era* (pp. 23–48). Springer.

Robert O. Keohane., & Joseph S. Nye Jr. (1977). *Power and Interdependence: World Politics in Transition*. Boston: Little, Brown and Company.

Rodrigue, J.-P. (2020). *The geography of transport systems*. Routledge.

Samoudi, A. (2025). China and the Persian Gulf: A new era of strategic cooperation. In *Implications, prospects, and challenges in China's global south strategy* (pp. 305–334). IGI Global Scientific Publishing.

SCAMP. (2020). *Saudi Arabia signs smart grid deal with China's state grid, land-grab continues*. World Energy. https://www.world-energy.org/article/6138.html

SGP. (2023). *Envision energy awarded 1.67 GW wind turbine contract for NEOM green hydrogen project*. Saudi Gulf Projects. https://www.saudigulfprojects.com/2023/06/envision-energy-awarded-1-67-gw-wind-turbine-contract-for-neom-green-hydrogen-project/

SGP. (2024). *Hassan Allam, El Seif and China Harbour awarded a major contract by Port of NEOM*. Saudi Gulf Projects (SGP). https://www.saudigulfprojects.com/2024/07/hassan-allam-el-seif-and-china-harbour-awarded-a-major-contract-by-port-of-neom/

Shen, H. (2018). Building a digital silk road? Situating the internet in China's belt and road initiative. *International Journal of Communication, 12*, 19.

Soltani, E. (2023). *How China became Saudi Arabia's largest trading partner*. Visual Capitalist. Retrieved July 31, 2024 from https://www.visualcapitalist.com/cp/how-china-became-saudi-arabias-largest-trading-partner/

SPA. (2025). *Saudi Arabia strengthens industrial ties with China in industry and mining*. Saudi Press Agency. https://www.spa.gov.sa/en/N2407267

Strange, S. (1988). *Strange states and markets*. Frances Pinter.

Triolo, P., Allison, K., Brown, C., & Broderick, K. (2020). The digital silk road: Expanding China's digital footprint. *Eurasia Group, 8*, 1–13.

Ulrichsen, K. C. (2018). *The changing security dynamics of the Persian Gulf*. Oxford University Press.

Veghese, J. (2025). Saudi Arabia hits reset on NEOM: Did costs for 'the line' spiral out of control? *Gulf News*. https://gulfnews.com/business/property/saudi-arabias-neom-hits-reset-are-costs-for-the-line-spiraling-out-of-control-1.500205617

Verschuur, J., & Hall, J. (2024). Systemic impacts of disruptions at maritime chokepoints. *Nature Communications, 16*(1), 10421.

Wang, Y. (2021). *The Line from NEOM*. The Urban Tech Hub. https://atlasofurbantech.org/cases/sau-neom-theline/

Wang, Y., Chao, Q., Zhao, L., & Chang, R. (2022). Assessment of wind and photovoltaic power potential in China. *Carbon Neutrality, 1*(1), 15.

Yong, R., Hussain, S., & Gibbs, H. (2025). Hydrogen energy trading networks in China: Economic viability, technological advancements, and environmental sustainability. *International Journal of Hydrogen Energy, 109*, 789–801.

Yusuf, N., & Abdulmohsen, D. (2022). Saudi Arabia's NEOM project as a testing ground for economically feasible planned cities: Case study. *Sustainability, 15*(1), 608.

Zhang, H., Gao, S., & Zhou, P. (2023). Role of digitalization in energy storage technological innovation: Evidence from China. *Renewable and Sustainable Energy Reviews, 171*, Article 113014.

Zhentian, T. (2024). *Middle East: Leading the 5.5G era and striding towards an intelligent world*. Huawei. https://www.huawei.com/en/huaweitech/publication/202401/middle-east-leading-5ga-era

Zuboff, S. (2019). *The age of surveillance capitalism: The fight for a human future at the new frontier of power*. PublicAffairs.

CHAPTER 5

China's Infrastructure Diplomacy in Iran: Strategic Lifeline Under Constraint

1 Infrastructure as Political Agency

Infrastructure remains undertheorized in international relations scholarship despite its profound political consequences. Economists treat it as neutral scaffolding, the technical foundation upon which markets function. Political scientists often overlook it entirely, focusing instead on military capability, diplomatic rhetoric, or financial flows. Yet infrastructure, including ports, railways, pipelines, and grids, ranks among the most durable and politically consequential instruments of statecraft precisely because it resists reversal. A port carved into a coastline cannot be uprooted. A railway corridor reconfigures spatial economies for generations. A power plant embeds energy dependence into the rhythms of daily governance. Once such systems are built, political choices narrow. Disengagement becomes costly, and alignment becomes structural.

This durability makes infrastructure a form of embedded leverage, a type of influence that derives not from immediate pressure but from the gradual accumulation of irreversible commitments. Unlike sanctions that can be lifted, loans forgiven, or treaties abandoned, infrastructure creates permanent entanglement. It operates through the logic of sunk costs: once states have reoriented trade routes or energy supply chains around foreign-built systems, the political and economic costs of disengagement rise dramatically. The result is a quiet but profound recalibration of diplomatic incentives, where maintaining favorable ties with the infrastructure

A. Ullah, *Diplomacy by Design*,
https://doi.org/10.1007/978-981-95-7876-4_5

provider becomes less a choice than a structural necessity (Baldwin, 2020; Hirschman, 1980).

Yet this leverage is contingent rather than absolute. States routinely push back even when deeply tied into major infrastructure deals. Recent cases from Malaysia, Myanmar, and Sri Lanka demonstrate that strategic investments cannot fully neutralize domestic constraints or political resistance (Brautigam, 2020; Ramachandran, 2019). Infrastructure statecraft, then, is powerful but far from deterministic.

What varies fundamentally is the context within which infrastructure operates. The same mechanisms of embedded leverage produce markedly different outcomes depending on whether a state enters infrastructure partnerships from a position of strategic choice or structural desperation. This distinction between designed engagement and constrained dependence structures the analytical framework of this chapter and indeed the entire book.

Consider the contrast between Saudi Arabia and Iran. Saudi Arabia approached Chinese infrastructure investment from a position of relative strength. Possessing vast hydrocarbon wealth, sitting astride global shipping lanes, and maintaining sophisticated diplomatic relationships with multiple powers simultaneously, Riyadh could evaluate infrastructure partnerships against competing offers from the United States, Europe, and other regional actors (Alterman & Garver, 2008). The result has been carefully calibrated engagement: Chinese investment in projects like NEOM and Aramco technology partnerships, coupled with active diplomatic hedging and maintenance of U.S. security ties (Fulton, 2019). For Saudi Arabia, Chinese infrastructure represents one option among several, a means of accelerating strategic ambitions rather than surviving in their absence. The relationship is designed, selective, and ultimately subordinate to broader calculations of national interest.

Iran's position differs fundamentally. Decades of Western sanctions, nuclear restrictions, and financial isolation have progressively narrowed the country's options. Access to Western capital markets is blocked. Technology transfer is restricted. International banking channels are constrained. Within this narrowing corridor of possibility, China has become not one choice among many but the indispensable partner of last resort. When Iran needs financing for energy infrastructure or port expansion, Beijing is often the sole source willing to provide it. When Iranian firms require technology in telecommunications or renewable energy, Chinese companies fill gaps left by Western restrictions. This is not strategic choice but structural necessity, a distinction that proves analytically crucial throughout the analysis.

The theoretical framework underpinning this book, DSI, illuminates precisely this distinction. DSI posits that China deliberately sequences infrastructure projects, financial instruments, and technological integration to move partner states from independence through deepening interdependence toward locked-in structural dependency. Each phase is designed to increase the costs of disengagement while decreasing the partner's capacity to access alternatives. The framework explains why some partnerships remain managed and reversible while others calcify into something closer to subordination.

Yet the Iran case also reveals the limits of DSI as a framework of pure strategy. A state under comprehensive sanctions does not enter infrastructure partnerships on equal terms. The asymmetries are so pronounced that dependency becomes less a product of careful design and more a consequence of coercion from without. China's leverage over Iran is real, but it is shadowed by constraints: Iran's economic weakness limits its utility as a market; its political volatility threatens project viability; and Beijing's need for energy imports means it cannot afford Iran's complete collapse (Erickson & Strange, 2016). Moreover, Iran has not been entirely passive. It has sought to hedge its dependence on China through simultaneous engagement with Russia, India, and regional corridors, attempting to preserve fragments of autonomy even within a fundamentally constrained position.

Before examining these dynamics in depth, we must situate China's approach within the broader tradition of infrastructure diplomacy. The use of infrastructure as a political instrument extends back at least to the mid-twentieth century. The Marshall Plan, launched in 1948, rebuilt Europe's transport networks, factories, and energy systems, embedding Western Europe into an economic order centered on American capital and trade flows (Steil, 2018). The Soviet Union pursued parallel strategies, exporting dams, industrial complexes, and pipelines to satellite states and newly independent postcolonial countries. The Aswan High Dam in Egypt, completed with Soviet assistance after the United States withdrew support, epitomized this logic (Time, 1992). Infrastructure became an ideological artifact, binding Egypt into a broader narrative of socialist modernization and Soviet partnership.

The United States, too, leveraged infrastructure strategically in the Middle East. Pipelines constructed in Saudi Arabia, Kuwait, and Iraq during the mid-twentieth century served not only commercial purposes but strategic ends, cementing U.S. ties to monarchies whose survival was closely linked to oil exports (Painter, 2014). Later, the construction of air bases, telecommunications systems, and desalination plants reinforced Washington's security and economic architecture throughout the Gulf (Roberts, 2025). Each runway or refinery was simultaneously an engineering project and a diplomatic investment, embedding American influence in the region's daily functioning. These precedents underscore two enduring truths. First, infrastructure has long been wielded as a tool of alignment, shaping not only economies but also strategic orientations. Second, each great power adapted its infrastructural diplomacy to its broader ideological project: liberal modernization for the United States, socialist development for the Soviet Union.

Yet these Cold War precedents differed from China's contemporary approach in two fundamental ways. First is scale and scope. Whereas the Marshall Plan concentrated on Western Europe and Soviet projects were dispersed across a smaller circle of allies, the BRI is global in ambition, spanning continents and binding together states as disparate as Iran, Saudi Arabia, Egypt, and the UAE into overlapping circuits of connectivity (Blanchard & Flint, 2017). Second is its pragmatic idiom of power. Unlike Cold War infrastructural diplomacy, which was overtly ideological, Chinese initiatives are framed in pragmatic language: connectivity, development, win–win cooperation. This rhetorical strategy allows Beijing to pursue strategic entrenchment while appearing apolitical, positioning itself as a benign partner unconcerned with regime type or domestic politics (Caskey, 2024). The absence of ideological conditionality renders Chinese engagement strategically flexible, capable of serving states with radically different political systems and regional alignments.

This dual innovation, global scale and pragmatic idiom, allows China to operate across fragmented regional landscapes without triggering the zero-sum anxieties that often accompany great power competition. In the Middle East, where external powers have historically aligned along sectarian or ideological lines, Beijing's infrastructural diplomacy offers an alternative model: one that privileges connectivity over confrontation and integration over division. Yet this very flexibility also generates ambiguity. The BRI's ability to embed China within competing regional blocs raises questions about the long-term implications of such entanglements. Does infrastructural neutrality mask strategic ambition? Can pragmatic engagement remain sustainable in the face of deepening geopolitical rivalries?

What happens when Chinese interests in one regional actor conflict with those in another?

These questions underscore the need to interpret the BRI not merely as a developmental initiative but as a strategic grammar, a language through which China articulates its global presence, negotiates influence, and redefines the contours of international order. Infrastructure, in this context, is not simply a means to an end but a medium of diplomacy itself, a form of inscription through which power is materialized, legitimized, and sustained (Ho, 2020). The Middle East has historically been a testing ground for infrastructural statecraft. From the Aswan Dam to U.S.-backed Gulf pipelines, the region has experienced firsthand how concrete and steel serve as the grammar of allegiance. Yet the BRI reconfigures this tradition. Rather than using infrastructure to pull states into ideological blocs, China employs it to cultivate what might be termed multipolar entanglement, simultaneously financing both sides of regional rivalries, creating overlapping dependencies that position Beijing not as a partisan ally but as an indispensable stakeholder embedded in the region's architecture itself.

In doing so, China transforms infrastructure into a form of embedded mediation. By simultaneously financing Iranian railways and Saudi megaprojects, Beijing does not resolve the Saudi–Iranian rivalry directly. Rather, it builds material circuits that render long-term disengagement costly for both, thereby nudging them toward accommodation through structural incentive rather than diplomatic pressure. Infrastructure becomes diplomacy not through formal negotiation but through the structural logic of interdependence—what this monograph terms Designed Strategic Interdependence.

The Iran case proves particularly revelatory of this logic operating under extreme constraint. Unlike Saudi Arabia, where Chinese infrastructure supports strategic ambition, Iran represents infrastructure operating as a lifeline. Decades of sanctions, isolation, and restricted access to global finance have made Beijing not merely a preferred partner but the indispensable alternative to economic collapse. The dynamics of power and dependence that emerge in such conditions differ fundamentally from those of the Saudi case.

2 China's Infrastructure Engagement in Iran: Railways and Ports

Iran's relationship with China's BRI reflects a convergence of geographic potential and political necessity. Tehran's engagement stems not from confident calculation but from structural constraint. Western sanctions have systematically excluded Iran from global capital markets, technology networks, and financial systems. Within this context of isolation, China represents not one option among many but often the only available partner willing to provide infrastructure financing, technological transfer, and market access. The question is not whether the terms are ideal, but whether they are necessary. For Tehran, necessity trumps symmetry.

These dynamic challenges conventional frameworks for analyzing asymmetric partnerships. Dependency theorists emphasize how unequal exchange perpetuates underdevelopment and constrains autonomous policy choices (Cardoso, 1982). Realist scholars stress how weaker states can leverage asymmetric relationships to enhance security and extract concessions from more powerful partners (Womack, 2003). The Sino-Iranian case fits neither model cleanly. Iran's engagement with China reflects strategic acceptance of constrained options. Tehran recognizes the asymmetries but judges them preferable to the alternatives: continued isolation, infrastructural decay, and regional marginalization would impose far steeper costs. This represents the DSI framework operating under conditions of necessity, where the weaker party consciously accepts embedding in exchange for capabilities it cannot otherwise acquire.

Iran's Geographic Centrality and Infrastructure Deficit

Iran occupies a singular position within the BRI's strategic geography. Its location at the crossroads of Central Asia, South Asia, and the Middle East offers multidirectional corridors: from the Persian Gulf to the Caspian, from the Indian Ocean to the Mediterranean, and from Xinjiang to Europe. This geospatial centrality renders Iran indispensable to any transcontinental connectivity vision. Moreover, its resource endowments, including oil, gas, minerals, and increasingly rare earth elements, remain vast but underleveraged due to decades of sanctions and diplomatic isolation. The result is a paradox that shapes Iran's entire contemporary strategic position: a country rich in assets but poor in infrastructure, geopolitically central yet economically peripheral.

Classical geopolitical theory identified the Iranian plateau as part of the heartland, whose control would determine Eurasia's political order (Mackinder, 2004). More recent scholarship has emphasized Iran's role as a potential land bridge connecting energy-rich Central Asia with the Persian Gulf and beyond (Amineh & Houweling, 2005). Yet geography alone does not determine strategic significance; it must be activated through infrastructure. Iran's geographic potential has remained latent precisely because sanctions, conflict, and underinvestment have prevented the construction of transport corridors, energy networks, and digital systems that would convert location into connectivity (Zweig & Jianhai, 2005). The BRI offers Iran the means to finally realize this geographic potential, transforming theoretical centrality into operational connectivity.

For Iranian policymakers, Chinese investment promises not only capital infusion but also technological transfer, logistical integration, and access to diversified markets. In a context where Western engagement remains constrained by sanctions and political mistrust, China emerges as a pragmatic alternative. The calculus is not merely economic but existential. Without external partners willing to operate in sanctioned environments, Iran risks infrastructural stagnation, energy bottlenecks, and regional marginalization. Chinese-built railways, ports, energy systems, digital networks, and industrial parks are strategic lifelines, enabling Tehran to modernize without capitulating to Western conditionality.

China has carefully calibrated its Iranian engagement across distinct phases, each building upon and reinforcing the previous one. Beginning with energy imports to establish commercial credibility during the 1990s and 2000s, the relationship expanded into infrastructure projects as sanctions isolated Iran from Western partners in the 2010s, and has now advanced into digital and strategic sectors that promise deeper integration. For Iran, this sequencing has normalized Chinese presence across multiple sectors, making Beijing not an occasional partner but a systemic fixture in the country's economy and governance.

Rather than pursuing simultaneous engagement across all sectors, which might trigger nationalist backlash or create concentrated vulnerabilities, China has proceeded incrementally. Energy partnerships created trust and commercial relationships. As Western sanctions intensified, these relationships matured into infrastructure investments (Cordesman, 2020). Now, with Iran more isolated than at any point since the revolution, digital integration and industrial embedding proceed with minimal political friction. Each phase creates constituencies within Iran with material interests in continued cooperation, making disengagement progressively more costly at both elite and subnational levels.

The Tehran–Mashhad Railway Corridor

The Tehran–Mashhad rail modernization illustrates the dual logic of development and diplomacy with particular clarity. Long considered the backbone of Iran's passenger and freight network, the line connects the political heart of the country to its religious and demographic centers, and extends further toward Afghanistan and Central Asia (Tianyang, 2019). For decades, it has suffered from chronic congestion, slow speeds, and outdated equipment. Chinese firms, led by the China Railway Engineering Corporation and supported by CRRC, entered with a comprehensive modernization plan: electrifying the corridor, upgrading signaling systems, and improving overall capacity and speed. On the surface, the project addresses Iran's domestic developmental needs, promising faster travel between Tehran and Mashhad, more efficient freight movement, and reduced dependence on road transport.

Yet beneath these utilitarian justifications lies a distinct geopolitical calculus. Once electrified and linked to trans-Caspian and Central Asian routes, the line will serve as a major conduit for Chinese goods flowing westward. It embeds Iran into the China-Central Asia-West Asia Economic Corridor, one of the six recognized arteries of the BRI, repositioning Tehran not as an isolated state but as a node in transcontinental connectivity (Jinbo, 2022). For Iran, this promises a way to bypass maritime chokepoints and sanctions-sensitive shipping lanes. For China, it offers redundancy in supply chains and overland resilience against external disruptions that might affect maritime routes.

Moreover, the project serves as a signaling mechanism between the two states, demonstrating China's willingness to invest in high-risk environments and Iran's openness to long-term infrastructural entanglement. This mutual signaling reinforces trust, normalizes Chinese presence, and gradually shifts the perception of China from transactional partner to strategic stakeholder.

Table 1 presents a structured overview of China's involvement in the renewal of the Tehran–Mashhad Railway under the BRI:

Table 1 China's Renewal of the Tehran–Mashhad railway under the belt and road initiative

Project component	*Description*	*Estimated cost (USD)*	*Strategic purpose*
Electrification of Tehran–Mashhad line	Upgrade from diesel to electric trains	$1.72 billion	Improve speed, reduce emissions, and modernize infrastructure
High-speed rail integration	Introduce faster trains and reduce travel time	Included in electrification budget	Enhance passenger experience and regional connectivity
Station modernization	Renovate terminals and service facilities	TBD	Improve comfort and operational efficiency
Cargo corridor enhancement	Link Mashhad to Sarakhs-Razi transit route	TBD	Strengthen Iran's role in East–West trade
BRI financing via China Eximbank	RMB 10.07 billion pledged	$1.72 billion	Deepen Sino-Iranian strategic ties and infrastructure diplomacy

Unlike maritime routes, which remain vulnerable to naval blockades, piracy, and chokepoint closure, overland rail corridors offer what strategists term hedged connectivity (Cooley, 2012). For China, heavily dependent on sea lanes controlled by the U.S. Navy, diversification into land corridors reduces systemic vulnerability (Erickson & Strange, 2015). The Tehran–Mashhad line, when fully integrated with Central Asian networks, provides an alternative route for Chinese exports to reach European and Middle Eastern markets, reducing dependence on the Suez Canal and Malacca Strait (Peyrouse, 2016). For Iran, railway modernization addresses chronic transport bottlenecks that constrain economic growth, but it also serves a defensive function. In the event of renewed sanctions or military conflict that might disrupt Gulf shipping, overland routes offer alternative connectivity to maintain trade flows and supply chains.

Historically, the Tehran–Mashhad project echoes earlier episodes of railway diplomacy in Eurasia. The Trans-Siberian Railway, completed by

Tsarist Russia in the early twentieth century, was not merely a developmental initiative but a strategic instrument to project power into East Asia (Marks, 2020). Similarly, the Berlin-Baghdad Railway, pursued by Imperial Germany before World War I, aimed to link Central Europe with the Persian Gulf, challenging British maritime dominance and reshaping regional alignments (McMeekin, 2010). Both cases demonstrate how railways transcend their economic functions to become geopolitical tools, reconfiguring trade routes, altering power balances, and embedding influence.

The Tehran–Mashhad modernization fits squarely within this lineage of railway statecraft. Ostensibly framed as a domestic transport upgrade, it is fundamentally about repositioning Iran within Eurasian connectivity and embedding Chinese infrastructure standards across a strategically vital corridor. As Chinese firms electrify tracks, install signaling systems, and integrate logistics platforms, they do more than build railways. They shape the operational architecture through which Iran connects to the world. They establish technical standards that future infrastructure must conform to. They create constituencies of Chinese technicians, Iranian engineers trained in Chinese methods, and logistical operators accustomed to Chinese systems. Each of these elements reinforces the others, making disengagement or alternative technological paths progressively more difficult.

Chabahar Port and Regional Competition

The Chabahar Port and its associated railway projects highlight a similar interplay of domestic and diplomatic objectives with additional layers of regional competition. Chabahar is Iran's only deep-water port on the Gulf of Oman, and its location outside the Strait of Hormuz grants it exceptional strategic value. For years, India pursued its development as a counterbalance to Pakistan's Gwadar, which is deeply tied to China through the China-Pakistan Economic Corridor. Yet delays, underinvestment, and the constant shadow of U.S. sanctions eroded Indian momentum (Lasker, 2025). More recently, Chinese logistics actors have shown greater interest: in early 2023, China launched a direct container line to Chabahar, reducing transshipment costs and travel times. While this does not yet mirror the scale of Chinese investment in Gwadar, it signals a subtle but potentially consequential rebalancing in regional port competition (Iran News, 2023).

Iranian authorities have accelerated the linkage of Chabahar to the domestic rail network through the Chabahar-Zahedan line, currently under construction with completion projected for mid-2026. This railway is designed to integrate the port with Iran's wider hinterland and, ultimately, with Central Asian corridors. For Tehran, Chabahar is a gateway to the Indian Ocean that promises autonomy from Gulf politics and greater access to Afghanistan and beyond (Times, 2023). For Beijing, participation in Chabahar offers both a hedge against overreliance on Gwadar and a foothold in a port system that could rival Gulf Arab hubs.

This apparent contradiction makes strategic sense: by maintaining stakes in both ports, China reduces vulnerability to political instability in either Pakistan or Iran, ensures redundancy in Indian Ocean access, and complicates efforts by other powers to contain Chinese maritime expansion. For Iran, Chinese interest in Chabahar provides leverage in negotiations, allowing Tehran to play Chinese and Indian investment against each other to secure better terms. However, this leverage is constrained by sanctions, which limit Iran's ability to attract sufficient capital from either source. The result is a triangular dynamic wherein China, India, and Iran each pursue partly overlapping, partly competing interests, with infrastructure development proceeding incrementally rather than transformatively (Ullah & Xinlei, 2025).

The strategic geography of Chabahar amplifies its significance. Located approximately 72 kilometers from Gwadar, Chabahar provides direct access to Afghanistan's southern provinces and, via the Chabahar-Zahedan railway, to the broader Iranian rail network that connects westward to Turkey and Europe and northward to Central Asia (Brewster, 2014). This positioning makes Chabahar a potential competitor to Gulf Arab ports like Dubai's Jebel Ali for Afghan transit trade and for transshipment between South Asia and Central Asia. Indian involvement in Chabahar has been explicitly motivated by the desire to circumvent Pakistan, which has historically restricted Indian overland access to Afghanistan and Central Asia. China's entry into this space thus intersects with multiple geopolitical fault lines: Sino-Indian competition, Iran–Pakistan relations, Afghanistan's post-2021 political trajectory, and the broader contest for influence in Central Asia.

In this context, infrastructure becomes more than a conduit for commerce; it becomes a cartographic intervention, discussed comprehensively in Chapter 7. Each rail spur and port expansion redraw the map of regional influence, shifting the gravitational pull of trade, diplomacy, and strategic alignment. Chabahar is not simply a port but a platform for geopolitical choreography, where rival powers maneuver through logistics rather than military posturing (Ramani, 2020).

The scope and character of China's infrastructural engagement becomes clearer through examination of specific initiatives. Table 2 presents major Belt and Road projects currently active in Iran, illustrating how engagement spans multiple sectors in ways that create interlocking dependencies:

Chabahar demonstrates how weak states navigate limited agency by leveraging location, courting rival investors, and embedding themselves in overlapping connectivity schemes. For China, the port illustrates the utility of flexible engagement: investing without exclusivity, embedding influence without overt alignment, and shaping regional order through infrastructural presence rather than ideological projection. The Chinese presence in Chabahar does not exclude Indian participation; rather, it adds another layer of complexity, another point of interdependence, another reason for both China and India to maintain stakes in Iranian connectivity.

Chabahar is best understood as a strategic laboratory for infrastructural diplomacy under constraint. It reveals how states like Iran navigate severely limited options by leveraging geographic assets, courting competing investors, and embedding themselves in multiple connectivity schemes that reduce vulnerability to any single patron. For Beijing, Chabahar demonstrates the utility of what might be termed polymorphic engagement: the capacity to maintain simultaneous stakes in competing infrastructure projects without contradiction or commitment to either side. For New Delhi, it presents a persistent challenge: the need to compete with Chinese capital while respecting Indian strategic interests in Iran. The result is infrastructure that serves multiple masters, absorbs multiple investments, and advances multiple interests simultaneously, creating a genuinely multipolar node within the broader architecture of Asian connectivity.

3 Energy Interdependence: The Material Foundation of Strategic Alignment

The Sino-Iranian relationship began not with grand strategic visions or infrastructural diplomacy but with the mundane imperative of energy security. In the early 1990s, as China transitioned from oil exporter to

Table 2 China-Led BRI infrastructure projects in Iran (2022–2025)

Project	*Chinese/Iranian partners*	*Main activities*	*Status/timeline*	*Strategic significance*
Tehran–Mashhad high-speed rail modernization	China Railway Engineering Corp (CRRC)	Upgrade of key passenger/freight corridor; electrification, speed and capacity improvements	Announced; part of broader railway electrification plans; expected incremental completion through mid-2020s	Links to Central Asia; improves domestic mobility; reduces isolation from sanctions
Chabahar port expansion and Chabahar-Zahedan Railway	Chinese logistics firms (increasing interest), Indian participation; Iranian government	Port logistics expansion; container terminals; linking port to domestic rail network (Zahedan)	Direct shipping line started (2023); Chabahar-Zahedan rail planned/under construction to connect port to national network by 2025; port capacity expansion underway to mid-2020s	Offers alternative to Gulf transit, counters Gwadar; strengthens Iran's oceanic access; strategic for trade with Afghanistan, Central Asia

(continued)

Table 2 (continued)

Project	*Chinese/Iranian partners*	*Main activities*	*Status/timeline*	*Strategic significance*
Mining/rare earth and minerals collaboration	Chinese private firms, IMIDRO (Iranian Mines & Mining Industries Dev. and Renovation Org.)	Joint extraction, processing, downstream industries (copper, rare earths, lithium); mining-linked solar/energy plants adjacent to mines	Some MoUs and pilot sites active 2024–2025; completed mining/mineral projects worth $1.3B in recent 10-month period; employment generated	Secures resource supply chains for China; helps Iran diversify export base and bypass some sanctions; builds industrial capacity
Energy sector/grid modernization and smart infrastructure	Sinopec, CNPC, State Grid (China); Iranian ministries	Refinery upgrades; grid improvements; smart-metering; telecom and smart city pilots; digital infrastructure in major cities	MoUs since 2022; varying rates of rollout due to sanctions and financing constraints; deployment in cities like Mashhad, Isfahan, Qom; pilot programs ongoing	Dual use potential; enhances domestic stability; technological alignment; standard setting in ICT/hardware

net importer, Iranian crude offered a reliable source uncomplicated by the political sensitivities that constrained access to Gulf Arab supplies. For Iran, facing increasing Western pressure and seeking to diversify its customer base beyond Europe, China represented a vast and growing market with minimal political conditionality. This initial energy relationship, pragmatic and transactional, laid the commercial foundation upon which subsequent strategic alignment would be constructed.

Three decades later, energy remains the material bedrock of Sino-Iranian relations. It provides the economic rationale that justifies continued engagement despite geopolitical risks, the financial flows that enable infrastructure investments, and the mutual vulnerability that constrains both parties from abandoning the relationship entirely. Understanding China's infrastructure diplomacy in Iran requires recognizing that railways, ports, and digital systems are built atop an energy partnership whose scale and durability shape the terms of all other engagements.

The Evolution of Energy Trade: From Opportunism to Dependency

China's energy imports from Iran have followed a trajectory that mirrors the broader relationship's evolution from opportunistic commerce to structural interdependence. In the 1990s, Chinese purchases of Iranian crude were modest, constituting a small fraction of both China's total imports and Iran's total exports. The relationship was characterized by spot transactions rather than long-term contracts, reflecting mutual uncertainty about its durability (Calabrese, 2006).

The early 2000s witnessed dramatic expansion. China's surging energy demand, driven by rapid industrialization and urbanization, coincided with Iran's need to compensate for declining European purchases as nuclear tensions escalated. By the mid-2000s, China was a significant importer of Iranian crude oil, with imports forming a growing share of its total oil supplies, though exact volumes and ranking among suppliers varied by source. This figure would fluctuate considerably over subsequent years in response to sanctions pressures, but the fundamental pattern was established: China provided Iran with a market when Western buyers withdrew, while Iran provided China with supply diversity that reduced dependence on potentially hostile Gulf Arab states (Garver, 2015).

The 2012 intensification of Western sanctions, particularly the European Union's oil embargo and restrictions on SWIFT banking access, proved a watershed. Iranian oil exports plummeted from 2.5 million barrels per day in 2011 to approximately 1.1 million barrels per day by 2013 (EIA, 2014). Yet China's purchases, while reduced, continued throughout this period, providing Iran with essential hard currency flows when alternatives had evaporated. Chinese state-owned enterprises, particularly CNPC and Sinopec, negotiated discounted prices and payment arrangements that circumvented Western financial restrictions, including barter deals wherein oil deliveries were offset against Chinese goods and services rather than dollar-denominated payments.

The 2015 JCPOA temporarily normalized Iran's energy sector, allowing increased exports and attracting renewed international interest. Chinese imports surged to approximately 655,000 barrels per day by 2016, their highest level in years. More significantly, Chinese companies positioned themselves to capitalize on the opening by negotiating contracts for long-delayed energy development projects, particularly in Iran's underexploited gas fields (Ullah & Xinlei, 2025, p. 534).

The U.S. withdrawal from the JCPOA in 2018 and reimposition of secondary sanctions again reshaped the energy relationship. Western companies and many Asian buyers withdrew from the Iranian market to avoid American penalties. China's official imports dropped precipitously as major state firms sought to maintain access to U.S. markets and financial systems. Yet evidence suggests that substantial unofficial trade continued through independent refiners operating outside the formal banking system, transported via ship-to-ship transfers and falsified documentation (Ullah & Xinlei, 2025, p. 545). Estimates of actual Chinese purchases during this period vary widely, from official figures of near-zero to independent assessments suggesting 200,000 to 400,000 barrels per day continued flowing through informal channels.

This cat-and-mouse dynamic, wherein official statistics understate actual trade volumes, illustrates a crucial dimension of the energy relationship: its resilience despite external pressure. The economic incentives for both parties, Iranian revenue needs and Chinese supply diversity, prove sufficiently powerful to sustain transactions even when formal mechanisms are blocked.

Beyond Oil: Natural Gas and the South Pars Field

Although oil trade frequently dominates public and policy attention, natural gas constitutes an equally significant component of energy interdependence, with potentially more substantial long-term strategic implications. Iran holds the world's second-largest proven natural gas reserves, a substantial portion of which is concentrated in the South Pars field, shared with Qatar in the Persian Gulf. Nonetheless, decades of sanctions and chronic underinvestment have left these resources significantly underexploited relative to their potential.

Chinese energy companies entered Iranian gas development in the early 2000s, initially as junior partners in projects led by European firms. The 2009 withdrawal of Total from the South Pars Phase 11 development, prompted by U.S. sanctions pressure, created an opportunity for CNPC to assume operatorship. The $4.7 billion contract represented China's largest energy investment in Iran at the time and signaled Beijing's willingness to accept risks that Western companies refused (Cordesman et al., 2014; Kashfi, 2014).

The project's subsequent history illustrates both the opportunities and limitations of energy cooperation under sanctions. Development proceeded slowly, hampered by restrictions on accessing specialized equipment, insurance complications, and financing constraints. By 2020, more than a decade after contract signing, the project had achieved production but at levels well below original projections. CNPC scaled back its involvement significantly during the 2018 sanctions reimposition, effectively suspending major development activities to protect its global operations from U.S. penalties.

Yet the strategic logic of Chinese involvement in Iranian gas development extends beyond immediate commercial returns. Natural gas, unlike oil, requires dedicated pipeline infrastructure or liquefaction facilities, creating physical interdependencies that oil tankers avoid. Plans for potential gas pipelines connecting Iranian fields to Chinese western provinces via Pakistan or Central Asian routes, while frequently discussed and never implemented, represent a long-term vision wherein energy flows become embedded in fixed infrastructure rather than flexible maritime trade (Amineh & Houweling, 2005). Such infrastructure, if realized, would create dependencies far more durable than current oil trade arrangements, binding both parties into relationships that resist rapid disengagement.

China's parallel development of liquefied natural gas (LNG) import infrastructure creates additional potential for Iranian gas exports, though U.S. sanctions currently foreclose this option. Should geopolitical circumstances shift, Iran's proximity to Chinese markets and its vast reserves position it as a natural long-term supplier, particularly as China seeks to reduce coal dependence and diversify away from Australian and U.S. LNG sources.

Energy Infrastructure and Technology Transfer

Beyond purchasing hydrocarbons, Chinese engagement in Iran's energy sector encompasses infrastructure development and technology transfer that embed deeper dependencies. Chinese companies have participated in refinery upgrades, petrochemical plant construction, and energy grid modernization across Iran. These projects, while individually smaller in scale than major oil or gas field developments, collectively reshape Iran's energy infrastructure in ways that privilege Chinese standards, technologies, and expertise.

Sinopec's involvement in the Abadan refinery modernization exemplifies this pattern. The refinery, one of Iran's oldest and largest, required substantial upgrading to process heavier crude grades and meet environmental standards. Western sanctions prevented access to European or American refining technology, creating an opening for Chinese firms. Sinopec provided equipment, technical expertise, and training that enabled the refinery's continued operation and expansion. The project embedded Chinese refining standards and created ongoing maintenance dependencies wherein Sinopec remains the obvious partner for future upgrades due to its intimate knowledge of the installed systems (Tunnicliffe, 2018).

Similar patterns emerge across Iran's energy sector. Chinese-manufactured turbines in power plants, Chinese pipeline monitoring systems in oil and gas networks, and Chinese automation technologies in petrochemical facilities create distributed dependencies that parallel those visible in telecommunications and transportation infrastructure. Each installation generates requirements for spare parts, software updates, and technical support that reinforce commercial relationships and create constituencies for continued cooperation.

The technology transfer dimension proves particularly significant. Iranian engineers trained on Chinese refining equipment, energy sector managers familiar with Chinese project management methodologies, and technical institutions that have adopted Chinese industry standards create human capital dependencies that persist beyond individual projects. When Iran undertakes new energy infrastructure, the path of least resistance increasingly leads to Chinese partners whose technologies are familiar, whose standards are already embedded, and whose financing remains available when alternatives are foreclosed by sanctions.

One of the most innovative and strategically significant dimensions of Sino-Iranian energy relations is the development of oil-for-infrastructure barter arrangements that circumvent Western financial restrictions. These mechanisms, while opaque and difficult to quantify precisely, represent adaptations to sanctions pressure that simultaneously solve Iranian financing challenges and Chinese payment obstacles while deepening interdependence.

The basic structure involves Iran delivering crude oil to Chinese companies, which then offset the value against Chinese construction projects, equipment supplies, or manufactured goods provided to Iran. This avoids dollar transactions that might trigger U.S. secondary sanctions and banking restrictions that prevent normal commercial settlements. For Iran, it provides access to infrastructure development despite its exclusion from international capital markets. For China, it secures oil supplies while deploying surplus industrial capacity in construction, manufacturing, and engineering services.

The Tehran–Mashhad railway electrification discussed earlier exemplifies this pattern. Rather than conventional project financing through international banks, the arrangement reportedly involves Chinese firms receiving payment through allocated shares of Iranian oil exports. Similar mechanisms appear to underpin various infrastructure, industrial, and technology projects across Iran, though the opacity of these arrangements prevents precise quantification of their scale.

These barter arrangements carry profound implications for the durability of Sino-Iranian ties. They create financial interdependencies that operate outside the reach of Western sanctions, establishing parallel economic circuits that reduce vulnerability to external pressure. They also generate incentive structures wherein Chinese construction firms, equipment manufacturers, and trading companies develop material stakes in continued Iranian oil flows, creating domestic Chinese constituencies that advocate for maintaining energy relations even when geopolitical circumstances might otherwise recommend caution.

From Iran's perspective, oil-for-infrastructure swaps represent both opportunity and constraint. They provide access to development resources otherwise unavailable, but they also reduce transparency, complicate accounting, and potentially undervalue Iranian assets if negotiated from positions of desperation. The terms of such arrangements remain largely secret, preventing independent assessment of whether they reflect fair market values or represent discounted transactions that favor Chinese counterparties exploiting Iranian isolation.

Energy as Mutual Vulnerability and Strategic Constraint

The energy relationship's most strategically significant characteristic is the mutual vulnerability it creates, constraining both parties' ability to fully exploit their advantages or abandon the partnership despite its asymmetries. For China, Iranian energy supplies provide valuable diversity in a global market where alternative suppliers may be unreliable or politically problematic. Gulf Arab states, while larger exporters, maintain close security ties with the United States that could constrain their willingness to supply China during Sino-American crises. Russian supplies, while growing, concentrate risk in a single northern corridor vulnerable to geopolitical tensions. Iranian crude, despite sanctions complications and quality variations, offers a hedging option that reduces systemic vulnerability.

This dependence gives Iran residual leverage that constrains Chinese behavior even within an otherwise asymmetric relationship. Beijing cannot simply abandon Iran without risking energy security, particularly during periods of global supply tightness or regional instability. Iranian officials understand this dynamic and occasionally signal willingness to redirect exports toward other markets or reduce production if Chinese terms become too unfavorable, though the credibility of such threats remains limited given the absence of alternative buyers willing to defy sanctions comprehensively.

For Iran, energy exports to China represent not merely revenue but economic survival under sanctions. Chinese purchases provide hard currency that enables essential imports, supports currency stability, and sustains regime legitimacy through public spending. The economic costs of losing Chinese energy markets would be catastrophic for a regime already struggling with inflation, unemployment, and public discontent.

This asymmetric dependence constrains Tehran's negotiating leverage and forces acceptance of terms that might otherwise be rejected.

Yet the relationship's mutual vulnerability creates a stability of its own. Neither party can afford complete disengagement, and both benefit from continued cooperation despite ongoing tensions over specific terms. This produces what might be termed stabilized asymmetry: a relationship characterized by clear power imbalances but sustained by mutual needs that constrain the stronger party from fully exploiting its advantages and prevent the weaker party from abandoning cooperation despite its disadvantages.

The energy foundation thus shapes all other dimensions of Sino-Iranian relations. Infrastructure projects become financially viable through energy barter. Technology transfer proceeds because energy revenues create demand for industrial development. Digital systems find customers because energy exports generate the foreign exchange needed to purchase them. The entire edifice of strategic alignment rests upon the material base of energy interdependence, a foundation that proves remarkably durable precisely because it reflects fundamental economic necessities rather than ephemeral political preferences.

This energy bedrock distinguishes the Sino-Iranian relationship from China's engagement with states like Saudi Arabia or the UAE, where infrastructure partnerships supplement rather than substitute for diversified economic relations. In Iran's case, energy interdependence came first, created the commercial trust and financial mechanisms necessary for subsequent infrastructure diplomacy, and continues to anchor a relationship that might otherwise prove too risky for Chinese firms or too asymmetric for Iranian acceptance. Railways carry freight and passengers, but they are built on revenues from oil wells. Smart cities process data, but they are powered by gas turbines. The material grammar of infrastructure diplomacy, in Iran's case, is written in hydrocarbons.

4 The Digital Silk Road: Technology, Standards, and Systemic Lock-In

If China's infrastructural engagement with Iran were measured solely by the tonnage of rail freight or the cubic meters of natural gas transported through pipelines, the relationship would appear substantial but ultimately conventional. What distinguishes Beijing's approach, however, is the parallel construction of a digital infrastructure that operates beneath the surface of conventional economic metrics yet carries implications far exceeding those of physical projects. The Digital Silk Road (DSR) represents China's most sophisticated and potentially transformative vector of influence in Iran, not because it moves goods or energy but because it structures the very systems through which information flows, governance operates, and social control is exercised.

Digital infrastructure differs fundamentally from physical infrastructure in its capacity to embed continuous dependencies. A railway, once built, can theoretically be operated by different companies using compatible rolling stock. A port can accommodate ships from any nation. But digital systems resist such fungibility. They create ecosystems wherein hardware, software, training, maintenance, and future upgrades become inextricably linked to the original provider. This characteristic makes digital infrastructure particularly valuable as an instrument of strategic influence, generating dependencies that compound over time rather than remaining static after initial construction (Bashirov et al., 2025).

Huawei, ZTE, and Digital Infrastructure Deployment

Huawei's role in Iran merits close analytical attention due to its centrality in China's global digital expansion strategy. The company has contributed to telecommunications infrastructure, supported 5G network trials, and participated in smart city initiatives in urban centers such as Mashhad and Isfahan. Huawei has also facilitated technician training through regional partnerships and ICT workshops (Hamza et al., 2024). These activities position Huawei not merely as a commercial vendor but as a key enabler of Iran's digital ecosystem. Operating simultaneously as a technology provider, training institution, and infrastructure partner, Huawei embeds influence across multiple dimensions.

ZTE's involvement in Iran's telecommunications sector has contributed to the expansion of fiber optic infrastructure and broadband connectivity. As a supplier of switching equipment, optical transmission systems, and network management platforms, ZTE has supported Iran's efforts to modernize its digital backbone. The adoption of Chinese technical standards and proprietary systems represents a long-term technological commitment with implications for interoperability, maintenance, and future upgrades (Azad, 2024).

The strategic significance of digital infrastructure lies in its capacity to embed long-term dependencies that surpass the temporal impact of physical construction. When Chinese companies deploy 5G networks across Iranian urban centers, install fiber-optic backbones connecting provincial hubs, and introduce smart city platforms, these actions transcend mere commercial transactions. They constitute the establishment of technical standards, the creation of proprietary ecosystems, and the induction of systemic lock-in effects (Bashirov et al., 2025).

Unlike a railway that can be operated by different entities once constructed, digital systems resist such fungibility. They involve encryption protocols, data architectures, and network effects that bind users to their original platforms (Mueller, 2010). An Iranian government ministry that adopts Chinese enterprise software faces escalating costs with each year of use: migrating data, retraining personnel, and restructuring workflows around new systems. This is digital path dependency in its purest form, wherein early technological choices foreclose future alternatives.

Digital lock-in operates with particular intensity because it combines technical switching costs with organizational inertia and institutional memory. An Iranian agency that has invested five years in Chinese systems has reorganized its internal procedures, trained its personnel, and embedded Chinese protocols into its daily operations. Changing systems at that point would require not just technical conversion but institutional reorganization. This makes digital dependencies more durable than most physical infrastructure, and therefore more strategically valuable from Beijing's perspective.

The mechanism operates at multiple levels simultaneously. At the technical level, Chinese systems establish standards for data formatting, encryption protocols, and network architecture that subsequent technologies must conform to or integrate with. At the organizational level, Iranian ministries develop workflows, reporting structures, and decision-making processes optimized for Chinese platforms. At the human capital level, Iranian IT professionals acquire skills specific to Chinese technologies, creating labor market dynamics that reinforce continued use of those systems. These layered dependencies operate synergistically, making disengagement progressively more costly as integration deepens.

Moreover, digital systems exhibit network effects wherein value increases with adoption. As more Iranian government agencies adopt compatible Chinese systems, inter-agency coordination becomes easier, data sharing more efficient, and integration more valuable. This creates positive feedback loops wherein each additional adoption makes alternative systems less attractive, even if they might offer superior technical capabilities. The result is technological momentum that can persist for decades, independent of the original strategic calculations that prompted initial adoption.

For Iranian authorities navigating international isolation and domestic pressure, Chinese digital technologies offer something approaching a developmental shortcut. Rather than building indigenous capacity from scratch or waiting for Western firms willing to defy sanctions, Tehran can acquire sophisticated capabilities immediately. Smart city platforms promise improved traffic management, energy efficiency, and public service delivery. Advanced telecommunications infrastructure enables economic modernization and connectivity with global markets. These are not trivial benefits for a state struggling against the economic strangulation of sanctions and the political challenge of delivering material improvements to a skeptical population.

Yet these technologies arrive with capabilities that extend well beyond urban management or economic efficiency. Chinese firms like Huawei, Dahua, and Hikvision have pioneered integrated surveillance systems that combine facial recognition with behavioral analysis and predictive policing, systems refined through extensive deployment in domestic Chinese contexts and now packaged as safe city solutions for export markets (Feldstein, 2019). For a regime facing periodic unrest and seeking enhanced tools of social control, such capabilities align with strategic imperatives. The provision of surveillance infrastructure thus creates dependency in the most sensitive domains of state security, establishing ongoing relationships around training, system maintenance, software updates, and operational expansion that bind Chinese firms to Iranian security services far more intimately than commercial contracts suggest.

Surveillance, Cybersecurity, and Strategic Asymmetry

The dual-use character of digital infrastructure merits particular analytical attention. The same 5G network that enables economic connectivity enables surveillance capability. The smart city platform that improves traffic flow also enables population monitoring. The data centers that accelerate commerce also facilitate data collection. These are not separate systems but integrated architectures wherein the infrastructure for development simultaneously functions as infrastructure for control.

Chinese firms involved in Iran's cybersecurity infrastructure gain intimate knowledge of the country's digital vulnerabilities, network architectures, and critical information systems. While cybersecurity relationships are typically framed in benign terms, they create conditions wherein the security provider maintains detailed information about the protected system (Akram, 2024). In the context of a strategic partnership, this knowledge becomes a form of strategic asymmetry: Beijing understands Iran's digital defenses while remaining opaque regarding its own. This asymmetry extends beyond technical capacity to encompass strategic advantage; Beijing gains foreknowledge of Iranian capabilities, vulnerabilities, and likely responses in scenarios of digital conflict.

Chinese firms have deployed facial recognition systems in Iranian cities, integrated these with existing CCTV networks, and begun piloting behavior prediction algorithms for law enforcement use (Cilluffo, 2013). While initiatives like the Mashhad smart city project emphasize efficiency and improved municipal services, these developments in broader Iranian urban surveillance highlight the potential for such technologies to be repurposed for monitoring and control.

This digital embedding carries consequences that transcend material dependency and enter the realm of ideational influence. Technologies are never neutral vessels; they embody the assumptions, priorities, and governance models of their creators. Chinese digital systems reflect a political context that prioritizes comprehensive data collection, algorithmic governance, and state interests over individual privacy (de Seta, 2023). As Iranian authorities integrate these platforms into their own governance structures, they do not merely acquire technical capabilities but import the operational logic embedded within them. Over time, this can produce a form of institutional isomorphism wherein Iranian digital governance comes to resemble its Chinese counterpart not through conscious ideological alignment but through the gradual convergence imposed by shared technological infrastructure.

The mechanism operates subtly but with profound implications. An Iranian administrator working within a Chinese data architecture makes decisions constrained and enabled by the system's design. If the system prioritizes certain data inputs, those become the information the administrator works with. If the system is optimized for state surveillance, the administrator learns to think in terms of population monitoring. This represents what might be termed technocratic isomorphism: the alignment of governance practices not through ideological conversion but through technical absorption.

The digital domain does not operate in isolation from physical and industrial infrastructures. The two dimensions reinforce and enable each other in ways that multiply their individual effects. Industrial parks constructed in Yazd, Kerman, and other provincial centers represent the terrestrial complement to digital engagement. These facilities support light manufacturing, logistics, and agro-processing, contributing to Iran's effort to diversify beyond hydrocarbon dependence while generating employment in historically marginalized regions. Their immediate economic impact matters, but their deeper significance lies in creating distributed constituencies with material stakes in continued Chinese engagement (Mohammadi et al., 2025). Local governments, business communities, and workers in these provinces become advocates for maintaining favorable relations with Beijing, generating subnational political pressure that constrains Tehran's foreign policy options.

This spatial diffusion of Chinese presence reflects a calculated strategy that diverges from the concentrated mega-projects typical of earlier developmental assistance models. Rather than pursuing a handful of highly visible flagship initiatives that risk triggering nationalist backlash, China's distributed industrial development approach generates multiple points of engagement. Each site produces localized benefits and political support while remaining below the threshold of national controversy.

The industrial park model also facilitates subtler forms of influence through technology transfer and standard diffusion. Chinese manufacturing equipment, quality control protocols, and production management systems become embedded in Iranian factories. Workers trained in Chinese industrial practices carry these techniques into the broader Iranian economy, creating spillover effects that extend far beyond the parks themselves (Lin & Wang, 2017). This represents productive embedding: Chinese influence extending into the granular details of industrial organization in ways that prove remarkably durable precisely because they operate at levels too mundane to attract political attention.

Contrast with Saudi Arabia and Implementation Challenges

The contrast with Chinese digital engagement in Saudi Arabia illuminates the distinctive character of the Iranian experience. In Saudi Arabia, Chinese digital involvement in Vision 2030 projects occurs alongside American technology companies, Japanese partners, and European firms. Competition prevents any single technological ecosystem from achieving dominance. Huawei's role in Saudi 5G deployment is significant but not monopolistic (Alfayad, 2019). In Iran, by contrast, sanctions exclude Western technology companies from most domains. Huawei operates without meaningful competition. This absence of competition combined with Iran's acute technological isolation produces genuine monopolistic lock-in rather than shared technological governance.

Yet for all the sophistication of China's digital strategy and the structural logic driving Iranian acceptance, implementation has proceeded unevenly. Many announced smart city projects have encountered delays. 5G rollout has proceeded more slowly than initially projected. Sanctions complications have restricted the availability of specialized components for certain systems. Iranian regulatory environments, often unclear and subject to shifting policy priorities, have created uncertainty regarding ongoing commitments and investments.

These implementation challenges reveal a crucial limitation: infrastructure matters only to the extent that it actually functions and generates expected benefits. A 5G network that provides unreliable service or smart city systems that fail to deliver promised efficiency gains can undermine rather than strengthen bilateral relationships. The strategic value of digital infrastructure depends on technical performance and functional integration, not merely on its existence or Chinese involvement in its construction.

Nonetheless, the trajectory of China's digital engagement in Iran appears set to intensify. Plans for cloud computing infrastructure, artificial intelligence deployment in governance, and expanded smart city initiatives suggest that the scope of digital integration will expand significantly over the remainder of the 2020s and into the 2030s. Each expansion deepens technical dependencies, increases constituencies with stakes in continued cooperation, and locks in standards that shape how Iranian governance operates. Over a thirty-year timeframe, digital infrastructure could come to constitute the fundamental nervous system of Iranian governance, operating according to Chinese protocols and maintained through Chinese expertise.

The DSR in Iran represents a crucial frontier of great power competition. It demonstrates how influence operates through seemingly benign technological cooperation that generates profound strategic asymmetries. It shows how infrastructure statecraft extends beyond physical projects to encompass the invisible but vital systems through which modern states operate. And it reveals how China has adapted traditional statecraft to the digital age, achieving through information networks what earlier empires achieved through railroad networks: the embedding of one state's power within another's fundamental infrastructure.

China's digital engagement in Iran operates within a broader regional pattern that reveals how the same infrastructural logic produces different outcomes depending on partner constraints. The contrast with Saudi Arabia proves particularly instructive. In Saudi Arabia, Chinese digital involvement in Vision 2030 projects occurs alongside American technology companies, Japanese partners, and European firms. Competition prevents any single technological ecosystem from achieving dominance. Huawei's role in Saudi 5G deployment is significant but not monopolistic (Alfayad, 2019). Smart city initiatives feature multiple technological architectures rather than unified Chinese standards. This competitive environment prevents lock-in of the intensity visible in Iran.

In Iran, by contrast, sanctions exclude Western technology companies from most domains. Huawei operates without meaningful competition (Takeyh & Maloney, 2011). ZTE's fiber optic standards become the default infrastructure. Chinese cybersecurity firms gain near-monopolistic roles in strategic sectors. This absence of competition combined with Iran's acute technological isolation produces a different outcome: genuine monopolistic lock-in rather than shared technological governance.

The difference between Saudi Arabia and Iran in infrastructure mirrors their broader engagement with the BRI: in Saudi Arabia, Chinese investment represents one option among many, deployed to accelerate ambitious strategic goals while maintaining relationships with other major powers. In Iran, it represents the only available option, accepted out of necessity rather than strategic confidence. This asymmetry explains why dependencies in Iran reach far greater intensity than in Saudi Arabia despite superficially similar projects.

Similar patterns emerge across the region. The UAE maintains diverse technological partnerships, preventing excessive dependence on any single provider. Egypt, while increasingly reliant on Chinese infrastructure financing, retains relationships with European and Japanese firms in key sectors. Pakistan, despite deep integration through the China-Pakistan Economic Corridor, maintains significant Western military ties that constrain Chinese technological dominance. Iran stands apart in the depth and breadth of its infrastructural dependence, a product not of Chinese coercion but of Western exclusion that has progressively narrowed Tehran's options.

These regional variations underscore that DSI operates differently across varying contexts. Where states possess alternatives, they can manage Chinese engagement to prevent excessive dependency. Where states face comprehensive isolation, as Iran does, Chinese infrastructure becomes not one pathway among several but the primary lifeline available. The resulting relationships differ fundamentally in character, durability, and strategic implications.

5 Designed Strategic Interdependence: Infrastructure as Strategic Alignment

The transformation of Sino-Iranian ties from minimal strategic depth to one of the most consequential alignments of the twenty-first century is not accidental. It is the product of deliberate calibration, structural necessity, and geopolitical opportunity. Tehran needs Beijing more than Beijing needs Tehran, yet this very asymmetry has deepened the relationship. Iran's prolonged international isolation, exacerbated by U.S. sanctions, regional rivalries, and exclusion from Western-led financial systems, has pushed it further into China's orbit. What began as transactional engagement has matured into infrastructural entrenchment, energy interdependence, and strategic synchronization.

The relationship's evolution demonstrates how structural necessity can produce strategic alignment without requiring ideological affinity or explicit political commitment. The first phase, spanning the 1990s to early 2000s, emphasized energy trade. China became Iran's largest oil customer while Iranian crude provided Beijing with diversified supply sources beyond the volatile Persian Gulf Arab states (Calabrese, 2006). This phase established commercial credibility and mutual benefit without demanding deep political alignment.

The second phase, roughly 2010 to 2020, witnessed the expansion of Chinese engagement into infrastructure as Western sanctions intensified. As Western technology companies, engineering firms, and financial institutions withdrew from Iran, Chinese counterparts filled the vacuum. This was not altruism but strategic opportunism: Beijing leveraged Iran's exclusion to establish deep presence in infrastructure sectors that in normal circumstances would remain contested among multiple international competitors.

The third phase, spanning 2020 to the present, involves comprehensive integration across energy, infrastructure, minerals, digital systems, and strategic coordination, institutionalized through the 25-Year Agreement (Ullah & Xinlei, 2025). Chinese presence has become systemic rather than sectoral. Chinese technologies, standards, and financing mechanisms now anchor multiple dimensions of Iran's economy simultaneously. Beijing no longer enters as a contractor providing specific services but as an architect of Iran's broader modernization.

This sequencing illustrates DSI with particular clarity. Each phase reinforced the previous one, producing cumulative dependencies that now constitute a strategic partnership far greater than the sum of individual projects. The logic mirrors other geopolitical realignments driven by external pressure. Just as U.S. containment of Russia inadvertently accelerated Moscow's strategic embrace of Beijing, American sanctions compelled China to seek alternative partners, routes, and resource bases. Iran, with its vast mineral wealth, strategic geography, and defiant posture toward the West, became a natural candidate for deepened engagement. The result is a convergence not born of ideological affinity but of structural necessity and shared opposition to Western hegemony.

Yet this parallel has limits that merit explicit acknowledgment. The Sino-Russian alignment, while driven partly by shared opposition to U.S. hegemony, involves two major powers with comparable military capabilities and overlapping interests in Eurasia. The Sino-Iranian relationship, by contrast, is fundamentally asymmetric: China is a global power with options; Iran is a regional power with constraints. This asymmetry makes the relationship more fragile but also, paradoxically, more binding for Iran. Having few alternatives, Tehran must invest more heavily in managing the relationship and accepting terms that a more powerful partner might resist.

DSI provides analytical leverage for understanding not only the Sino-Iranian case but also broader patterns in contemporary international relations. Traditional theories of alliance formation emphasize shared threats, ideological affinity, or balance-of-power calculations (Waltz,

1979). DSI suggests an alternative pathway: alignment through infrastructure, wherein states become bound together not through formal treaties or military commitments but through the accumulated material interdependencies created by deliberate, sequenced investment. This form of alignment is simultaneously more flexible and more durable than traditional alliances. It is more flexible because it requires no explicit political commitments, allowing both parties to maintain official positions of independence while deepening practical integration. It is more durable because infrastructure creates sunk costs and switching costs that persist regardless of diplomatic rhetoric or leadership changes, binding states together through material facts rather than political promises.

DSI also functions differently across varying power hierarchies. In relationships between relative equals, such as China's engagement with Russia or major European states, designed interdependence must be more balanced to prevent either party from exploiting the other excessively. In relationships marked by stark asymmetry, such as China-Iran or China-Pakistan, DSI can proceed more rapidly and comprehensively because the weaker party has limited capacity to resist unfavorable terms and the stronger party can structure relationships to maximize its own benefits while providing sufficient inducements to maintain partner cooperation.

Yet even asymmetric DSI contains elements of genuine mutual benefit that distinguish it from pure exploitation. Iran gains infrastructure, technology, and connectivity it could not otherwise acquire. Chinese projects, even when structured to favor Beijing, nonetheless deliver real developmental benefits: faster railways, more efficient ports, improved energy systems, and employment in industrial parks. The asymmetry lies not in whether Iran benefits, but in the distribution of benefits and the terms of engagement. China captures larger shares of economic value, secures preferential resource access, and accumulates strategic influence, while Iran receives necessary but often insufficient developmental gains that leave it dependent on continued Chinese cooperation.

This dynamic sets China's approach apart from older forms of imperial extraction. The BRI does not operate through direct control or territorial dominance. Instead, it achieves influence through systems of connection that generate both functionality and constraint. The developmental gains are real, but so too are the dependencies. Infrastructure becomes a political instrument disguised as a developmental gift, a form of diplomacy that aligns interests by embedding material realities.

The contrast with Saudi Arabia that has threaded throughout this analysis proves essential to understanding DSI's adaptability. In Saudi Arabia, Chinese infrastructure serves an agenda of national transformation and strategic choice. The kingdom pursues Belt and Road engagement not from necessity but from calculated interest, leveraging Chinese investment to accelerate Vision 2030 while maintaining strategic hedging through simultaneous engagement with Western powers. The relationship is characterized by designed ambition: mutual interest in specific projects, clear identification of benefits to both parties, and deliberate calibration to avoid excessive dependence.

In Iran, by contrast, Chinese infrastructure serves an agenda of survival under constraint. Tehran pursues BRI engagement not from confidence but from necessity, accepting terms it might otherwise resist because alternatives have been systematically foreclosed. The relationship is characterized by enforced dependency: structural imbalance favoring the stronger party, limited choices for the weaker, and gradual embedding within frameworks established without meaningful input from the dependent state.

These contrasting cases illustrate DSI's adaptability. The same strategic logic of sequenced, layered infrastructure investment produces fundamentally different political dynamics depending on the structural context within which it operates. In Saudi Arabia, it represents one tool among many, deployed by a confident state to advance ambitious goals. In Iran, it represents the primary tool available to a constrained state seeking to maintain functionality in the face of systematic exclusion.

The Sino-Iranian relationship epitomizes the central argument of this book: that twenty-first-century statecraft is being rewritten through infrastructure. China's BRI is not merely an economic project but a strategic reconfiguration of global order, one that advances influence through construction, connectivity, and code. In the Middle East, a region long defined by military intervention and ideological rivalry, Beijing's approach represents a new mode of engagement: incremental, technical, and profoundly durable. Iran stands at the forefront of this experiment, where every fiber-optic line, industrial park, and smart city sensor contributes to an infrastructural diplomacy designed not only to connect but to reshape.

Yet this very achievement contains embedded paradoxes and limits. Infrastructure, while powerful, remains contingent on continued technical function and ongoing provision of benefits. Should Chinese infrastructure prove unreliable or fail to deliver promised benefits, the political foundation of the relationship weakens. Should Beijing's strategic interests shift dramatically, reducing willingness to maintain support for Iranian projects, the relationship could fracture despite material interdependence. Should Iranian domestic politics produce leadership fundamentally opposed to Chinese engagement, resistance could override structural incentives for cooperation.

The relationship proceeds through continuous negotiation and adjustment rather than following a predetermined script. Iranian bureaucratic politics, local resistance, sanctions complications, and implementation difficulties impose real limits on what infrastructural diplomacy can achieve. Yet the very fact that these projects advance at all within such a hostile international environment testifies to the resilience of infrastructure as a diplomatic instrument.

The cumulative effect is the quiet reordering of regional power through infrastructural means. Railways, data cables, refineries, and industrial parks form the material grammar of a new diplomacy in which influence is exercised through connectivity rather than coercion. For Iran, participation in this architecture promises modernization and resilience but also carries the risk of entrapment within a web of dependencies whose design serves another's long-term vision. For China, it demonstrates that global power can be consolidated not through alliances or bases but through embeddedness, through systems that make alternatives costly and exit unimaginable.

Power in the contemporary international system no longer resides solely in military capability or ideological persuasion, but in the ability to build, connect, and sustain. By designing systems that others depend upon, Beijing redefines influence as architecture, replacing the old logic of alliance with a new logic of alignment. In Iran, this strategy has found its most revealing expression: a relationship forged in necessity, stabilized by infrastructure, and emblematic of how twenty-first-century order is being rebuilt not through conquest or coercion, but through construction itself.

6 Strategic Convergence Under Constraint: Iran's Bounded Agency

The depiction of Iran as a passive recipient of Chinese infrastructural influence, however analytically useful for understanding asymmetric dependencies, risks obscuring the agency Tehran retains even within severe structural constraints. Iranian policymakers have not simply capitulated to Chinese dominance but have pursued deliberate strategies to preserve autonomy, diversify partnerships, and leverage their geographic position to extract concessions. These efforts operate within narrow parameters, but they demonstrate that even deeply constrained states can exercise meaningful agency in shaping the terms of asymmetric relationships.

Iran's hedging strategy manifests most clearly in its simultaneous cultivation of relationships with Russia and India alongside its deepening ties with China. The 2023 entry into the SCO formalized Iran's integration into Eurasian security architectures, but it also provided Tehran with a multilateral forum in which to engage both Beijing and Moscow without exclusive dependence on either (Ramani, 2020). This triangular dynamic allows Iran to play Chinese and Russian interests against each other in specific domains. When negotiating infrastructure financing, Iranian officials can reference Russian alternatives. When discussing defense cooperation, they can invoke Chinese technological capabilities. Neither Russia nor China provides a complete substitute for the other, but together they offer Iran more bargaining space than exclusive reliance on a single patron would permit.

India's involvement in Chabahar Port, despite persistent delays and underinvestment, serves a similar hedging function. By maintaining Indian stakes in a strategic asset that China also courts, Iran creates competitive dynamics that potentially improve terms and prevent Chinese monopolization of critical infrastructure (Pant, 2018). Iranian officials have explicitly framed Chabahar as a counterbalance to Gwadar, signaling to Beijing that Tehran retains options beyond exclusive Chinese partnership. The practical impact of this hedging remains limited given India's reluctance to defy U.S. sanctions comprehensively, but symbolically it reinforces Iran's claim to strategic autonomy.

Domestically, Iranian debates about Chinese engagement reveal considerable elite ambivalence despite the structural imperatives driving cooperation. Reformist politicians and technocrats tend to emphasize the developmental benefits of Chinese investment while downplaying sovereignty concerns, framing BRI participation as a pragmatic response to Western hostility. Conservative factions, particularly those aligned with the IRGC, express greater skepticism about long-term Chinese intentions and the risks of technological dependence. These debates rarely result in policy reversals given the absence of viable alternatives, but they impose constraints on the scope and speed of Chinese engagement. Projects that might proceed rapidly in more autocratic contexts encounter bureaucratic resistance, regulatory delays, and demands for local content requirements that complicate implementation (Garver, 2013).

The 25-Year CSP, signed in 2021, illustrates this tension. While the agreement institutionalizes Sino-Iranian cooperation across multiple domains, its actual implementation has proceeded more slowly than initial projections suggested. Many provisions remain aspirational rather than operational. Iranian officials have insisted on maintaining control over strategic sectors and resisted Chinese demands for exclusive access to certain resources or infrastructure nodes. The agreement itself includes provisions for periodic review and adjustment, suggesting that even within this formalized framework, Iran retains some capacity to renegotiate terms as circumstances evolve (Ullah & Xinlei, 2025).

Subnational dynamics further complicate the picture. Provincial governments in economically marginalized regions like Sistan-Baluchestan, where Chabahar is located, or Yazd and Kerman, where Chinese industrial parks operate, have become vocal advocates for deeper Chinese engagement. These regions benefit disproportionately from Chinese investment and employment generation, creating constituencies that pressure central authorities to maintain favorable relations with Beijing. Yet this very decentralization of interests also means that implementation depends on cooperation from local actors who may have priorities distinct from central government preferences. Corruption, inefficiency, and competing local interests can delay or derail projects, imposing transaction costs that limit Chinese influence.

Iranian strategic culture, characterized by what scholars term pragmatic anti-hegemony, shapes how elites frame Chinese engagement domestically and internationally (Saghafi-Ameri, 2009). Rather than portraying China as a new hegemon replacing the United States, Iranian discourse emphasizes partnership among equals resisting Western domination. This narrative allows Tehran to accept materially asymmetric relationships while maintaining ideological consistency with anti-imperialist principles. Chinese cooperation is framed not as subordination but as solidarity among victims of American coercion. Whether this framing reflects genuine belief or strategic necessity matters less than its political function: it enables elite consensus around Chinese engagement while preserving rhetorical commitment to sovereignty and independence.

Iran has also sought to leverage its position as a critical node in Eurasian connectivity to extract better terms from Chinese partners.

By emphasizing its role in the China-Central Asia-West Asia Economic Corridor and its unique position outside the Persian Gulf, Iranian negotiators have framed their country not as a desperate supplicant but as an indispensable geographic asset. This framing has limited practical effect given the stark power asymmetries, but it shapes the tenor of negotiations and occasionally yields marginal improvements in financing terms or technology transfer provisions.

The extent of Iranian agency should not be overstated. Tehran operates within constraints far tighter than those facing Saudi Arabia, the UAE, or even Pakistan. The absence of Western alternatives, acute economic distress from sanctions, and technological isolation drastically limit Iran's bargaining power. Yet within these constraints, Iranian policymakers have demonstrated persistent efforts to preserve autonomy, diversify dependencies, and leverage geography for marginal advantage. The resulting relationship is not one of complete Iranian subordination but rather what might be termed constrained acquiescence: acceptance of asymmetric terms combined with continuous efforts to mitigate the most extreme forms of dependence.

7 The Limits of Designed Interdependence: Sanctions, Volatility, and Mutual Constraints

For all the sophistication of China's infrastructural strategy and the depth of Iranian dependence, the relationship faces substantial constraints that limit Beijing's ability to translate infrastructure into reliable political influence. These limits stem from three sources: the persistent effects of U.S. sanctions that constrain even Chinese firms, Iran's political and economic volatility that threatens project viability, and China's own vulnerabilities that prevent it from treating Iran as expendable.

U.S. secondary sanctions have proven remarkably effective at complicating Chinese infrastructure projects in Iran despite Beijing's official disregard for American extraterritorial jurisdiction. Chinese state-owned enterprises, particularly those with international operations or dollar-denominated financing needs, face genuine risks when operating in Iran. While smaller Chinese firms less exposed to Western financial systems can proceed with greater freedom, major players like Sinopec and CNPC must carefully calibrate their Iranian engagement to avoid triggering sanctions that could disrupt their global operations (Nephew, 2017). This creates a two-tier system wherein China's most capable firms remain constrained while smaller, less sophisticated companies take on projects for which they may lack adequate technical capacity or financing.

Iran's political volatility and periodic domestic unrest introduce additional risks that Chinese planners cannot ignore. The 2022–2023 protests triggered by Mahsa Amini's death in police custody demonstrated the regime's fragility and the potential for rapid escalation of civil disorder. Chinese investments in Iranian infrastructure, particularly digital surveillance systems that have been deployed to monitor protests, create reputational risks for Beijing in international forums and potentially expose Chinese firms to future accountability demands should the Islamic Republic eventually fall. These concerns have reportedly led to more cautious Chinese engagement in the most politically sensitive domains and greater emphasis on projects with shorter payback periods.

Iran's limited economic capacity also constrains the relationship's depth. Despite its large population and resource wealth, decades of sanctions and mismanagement have left Iran's economy chronically underperforming. Its GDP remains below its pre-revolution levels in real per capita terms, and its consumer market lacks the dynamism of more successful emerging economies. This limits Iran's value to China as a commercial market for goods beyond energy and raw materials. Chinese infrastructure projects in Iran, unlike those in larger emerging markets, cannot rely on growing domestic consumption to ensure profitability. They depend instead on geopolitical logic and connectivity functions, making them more vulnerable to shifts in strategic priorities.

China's own energy security dependence on Iran introduces vulnerabilities that constrain Beijing's ability to exercise leverage coercively. Iranian crude oil, particularly when Western sanctions have reduced global supply or when tensions in the Gulf threaten shipping, provides China with an important hedge against supply disruptions (Calabrese, 2006). Beijing cannot simply abandon Iran without risking energy security, a consideration that gives Tehran residual leverage even within an asymmetric relationship. Iranian officials understand this mutual dependence and occasionally signal willingness to redirect energy exports toward other markets if Chinese terms become too unfavorable, though the credibility of such threats remains limited given the absence of alternative buyers willing to operate under sanctions.

Implementation challenges plague even projects that overcome financing and sanctions obstacles. Iranian regulatory environments, characterized by overlapping jurisdictions, unclear authority, and frequent policy reversals, create transaction costs that frustrate Chinese firms accustomed to more streamlined bureaucratic processes. Corruption, while facilitating some transactions, also introduces unpredictability and diverts resources from productive uses. Technical capacity gaps within Iranian partner institutions require extensive training and hand-holding that slows implementation and increases costs. These challenges mean that Chinese infrastructure projects in Iran tend to proceed more slowly, cost more, and deliver less reliable returns than comparable projects elsewhere.

The digital infrastructure domain faces particular constraints. While Chinese firms have achieved significant market share in Iranian telecommunications and smart city projects, the actual functionality and integration of these systems remains partial. Iran's existing infrastructure, much of it outdated and incompatible with modern standards, creates integration challenges that limit the effectiveness of new Chinese systems (Azad, 2024). Sanctions-driven component shortages mean that even sophisticated Chinese equipment sometimes operates at reduced capacity or requires workarounds that compromise performance. These technical limitations reduce the strategic value of digital infrastructure as an instrument of influence, as systems that function poorly generate resentment rather than dependence.

Moreover, China's broader strategic position constrains how aggressively it can leverage infrastructure for political ends. Beijing's efforts to position itself as a responsible stakeholder in global governance and its cultivation of relationships across the Middle East, including with U.S. allies like Saudi Arabia and the UAE, create tensions with too visible support for Iran. Chinese officials must balance deepening ties with Tehran against risks of alienating Gulf Arab states whose economic importance far exceeds Iran's (Fulton, 2019). This triangular dynamic prevents China from fully committing to Iran in ways that might maximize infrastructural leverage but would compromise relationships elsewhere in the region.

Geopolitical uncertainties further constrain long-term planning. The possibility of U.S.-Iran rapprochement, however remote it currently appears, introduces risks for Chinese investments predicated on Iranian isolation. Should sanctions lift and Western firms return to Iran, Chinese companies would face genuine competition that could erode their current advantageous position. Conversely, military conflict between Iran and the United States or Israel could render infrastructure investments worthless overnight. These tail risks make Chinese firms more cautious about irreversible commitments and more focused on projects with quicker returns or clear strategic value beyond narrow commercial logic.

The relationship proceeds, then, not as the smooth unfolding of a Chinese grand strategy but as a continuous negotiation between mutual needs and mutual constraints. China requires Iranian energy, geographic access, and demonstrations of its capacity to operate in sanctioned environments. Iran requires Chinese capital, technology, and political backing. Yet neither party can fully exploit the other's vulnerabilities without risking the collapse of a relationship that serves important, if asymmetric, interests for both. This mutual constraint produces a relationship that is stable not because of its strength but because alternatives for both parties remain worse. Infrastructure creates binding interdependence, but that interdependence binds both parties, albeit unequally, limiting the extent to which DSI can translate into unconstrained political control.

References

Akram, R. (2024). Sino-US rivalry: Expansion of cyberspace influence on Iran. *Social Sciences Spectrum, 3*(4), 443–458.

Alfayad, F. S. (2019). Huawei and the Gulf region: Market opportunities despite the ongoing US-China trade war. *International Review of Management and Marketing, 9*(4), 47.

Alterman, J. B., & Garver, J. W. (2008). *The Vital Triangle: China, the United States, and the Middle East* (Vol. 30). CSIS.

Amineh, M. P., & Houweling, H. (2005). Central Eurasia in global politics. *Conflict, security and development* (2nd ed.). Brill.

Azad, S. (2024). Cutting both ways: The transfer of Chinese technology to Iran in the post-JCPOA headwind. *East Asia, 41*(1), 91–107.

Baldwin, D. A. (2020). *Economic statecraft* (New edition ed.).

Bashirov, G., Akbarzadeh, S., Yilmaz, I., & Ahmed, Z. S. (2025). Diffusion of digital authoritarian practices in China's neighbourhood: The cases of Iran and Pakistan. *Democratization*, 1–24.

Blanchard, J.-M. F., & Flint, C. (2017). The geopolitics of China's maritime silk road initiative. In (Vol. 22, pp. 223–245): Taylor & Francis.

Brautigam, D. (2020). A critical look at Chinese 'debt-trap diplomacy': The rise of a meme. *Area Development and Policy, 5*(1), 1–14.

Brewster, D. (2014). *India's Ocean: The story of India's bid for regional leadership*. Routledge.

Calabrese, J. (2006). *China and Iran: Partners perfectly mismatched. Manuscript.* Middle East Institute.

Cardoso, F. H. (1982). Dependency and development in Latin America. In *Introduction to the Sociology of "Developing Societies"* (pp. 112–127). Springer.

Caskey, G. W. (2024). The political economy of China's Belt and Road Initiative. *Journal of Institutional Economics, 20*, Article e31.

Cilluffo, F. J. (2013). Cyber threats from China, Russia and Iran: Protecting American Critical Infrastructure. *Testimony before the US House of Representatives, Committee on Homeland Security Subcommittee on Cybersecurity, Infrastructure Protection, and Security Technologies*.

Cooley, A. (2012). *Great games, local rules: The new great power contest in Central Asia*. Oxford University Press.

Cordesman, A. H. (2020). *China in the Gulf: A New Partnership with Iran?* Center for Strategic & International Studies.

Cordesman, A. H., Gold, B., & Coughlin-Schulte, C. (2014). *Iran: Sanctions, energy, arms control, and regime change*. Rowman & Littlefield.

de Seta, G. (2023). China's digital infrastructure: Networks, systems, standards. *Global Media and China, 8*(3), 245–253.

EIA. (2014). *Country analysis brief: Iran*. U.S. Energy Information Administration. https://www.iranwatch.org/sites/default/files/us-doe-irananalysisbrief072114.pdf

Erickson, A. S., & Strange, A. M. (2015). China's Blue Soft Power: Antipiracy, engagement, and image enhancement. *Naval War College Review, 68*(1), 71–92.

Erickson, A. S., & Strange, A. M. (2016). *Six years at sea... and counting: Gulf of aden anti-piracy and China's maritime commons presence*. Brookings Institution Press.

Feldstein, S. (2019). *The global expansion of AI surveillance* (Vol. 17). Carnegie Endowment for International Peace Washington, DC.

Fulton, J. (2019). China's changing role in the Middle East. *The Atlantic Council*.

Garver, J. W. (2015). *China's quest: The history of the Foreign relations of the People's Republic of China*. Oxford University Press.

Hamza, M. A., Ejaz, U., & Kim, H.-c. (2024). Cyber5Gym: An integrated framework for 5G cybersecurity training. *Electronics, 13*(5), 888. https://www.mdpi.com/2079-9292/13/5/888

Hirschman, A. O. (1980). *National power and the structure of foreign trade* (Vol. 105). Univ of California Press.

Ho, S. (2020). Infrastructure and Chinese power. *International Affairs, 96*(6), 1461–1485.

Jinbo, W. (2022). The China–Central Asia–West Asia economic corridor. In *The Routledge handbook of the belt and road* (pp. 225–230). Routledge.

Kashfi, M. (2014). Prospect of sanctions' end highlights woes of Iranian oil and gas industry. *Oil & Gas Journal, 112*(3), 36-+.

Lasker, R. H. (2025). Chabahar port capacity to be expanded, linked to rail network by mid-2026. *Hindustan Times*. https://www.hindustantimes.com/india-news/chabahar-port-capacity-to-be-expanded-linked-to-rail-network-by-mid2026-101748344266703.html

Lin, J. Y., & Wang, Y. (2017). *Going beyond aid: Development cooperation for structural transformation*. Cambridge University Press.

Mackinder, H. J. (2004). The geographical pivot of history (1904). *The Geographical Journal, 170*(4), 298–321.

Marks, S. G. (2020). *Road to power: The Trans-Siberian railroad and the colonization of Asian Russia, 1850–1917*. Cornell University Press.

McMeekin, S. (2010). *The Berlin-Baghdad express: The Ottoman Empire and Germany's bid for world power*. Harvard University Press.

Mohammadi, M., Sohrabi, M. S., & Rabiei, S. (2025). The geoeconomic impacts of China's Belt and Road Initiative on Iran: Benefits and challenges. *Discover Global Society, 3*(1), 56. https://doi.org/10.1007/s44282-025-00206-4

Mueller, M. L. (2010). *Networks and states: The global politics of Internet governance*. MIT Press.

Nephew, R. (2017). *The art of sanctions: A view from the field*. Columbia University Press.

Painter, D. S. (2014). Oil and geopolitics: The oil crises of the 1970s and the Cold War. *Historical Social Research / Historische Sozialforschung, 39*(4 (150)), 186–208. http://www.jstor.org/stable/24145533

Pant, H. V. (2018). India-Iran cooperation at Chabahar port. *CSIS Briefs*, 1–4.

Peyrouse, S. (2016). Discussing China: Sinophilia and sinophobia in Central Asia. *Journal of Eurasian Studies, 7*(1), 14–23.

Ramachandran, S. (2019). The standoff over the Myitsone dam project in Myanmar: advantage China. *China Brief*, *19*(8).

Ramani, S. (2020). Russia and the UAE: An ideational partnership. *Middle East Policy*, *27*(1).

Roberts, D. B. (2025). The Gulf's evolving security mosaic: Balancing the manifest retrenchment and latent influence of the United States. *International Affairs, 101*(6), 2193–2214.

Saghafi-Ameri, N. (2009). Iranian foreign policy: Concurrence of ideology and pragmatism. *Middle East Institute Viewpoints: The Iranian Revolution at*, *30*.

Steil, B. (2018). *The Marshall Plan: Dawn of the cold war*. Simon and Schuster.

Takeyh, R., & Maloney, S. (2011). The self-limiting success of Iran sanctions. *International Affairs, 87*(6), 1297–1312.

Tianyang, L. (2019). Belt & Road Initiative expands China-Iran cooperation. *China Daily*. https://www.chinadaily.com.cn/a/201901/25/WS5c4aa81da3106c65c34e6912.html

Time. (1992). *Egypt: The Russians v. the Nile*. Time. https://time.com/archive/6624026/egypt-the-russians-v-the-nile/

Times, T. (2023). China launches direct shipping line to Iran's Chabahar port. *Tehran Times*. https://www.tehrantimes.com/news/480298/China-launches-direct-shipping-line-to-Iran-s-Chabahar-port

Tunnicliffe, H. (2018). *Sinopec to upgrade Iran's Abadan refinery*. The Chemical Engineer. https://www.thechemicalengineer.com/news/sinopec-to-upgrade-iran-s-abadan-refinery

Ullah, A., & Xinlei, L. (2025). Systemic constraints and state behavior: A neorealist perspective on China's BRI and Iran's strategic calculations. *Iranian Studies, 58*(3), 526–547. https://doi.org/10.1017/irn.2025.28

Waltz, K. (1979). *Theory of international politics*. McGraw.

Womack, B. (2003). Asymmetry and systemic misperception: China, Vietnam and Cambodia during the 1970s. *Journal of Strategic Studies, 26*(2), 92–119.

Zweig, D., & Jianhai, B. (2005). China's global hunt for energy. *Foreign Affairs*, 25–38.

CHAPTER 6

Mediation by Design: China's Infrastructure Diplomacy and the Iran–Saudi Reconciliation

1 From Infrastructure to Influence: China's Mediation by Design

The Middle East has long been a region where external powers sought to mediate rivalries and shape alignments. For much of the twentieth century, Western actors dominated this role, particularly the United States. American military presence, alliance structures, and security guarantees defined the parameters of regional diplomacy. The American-led order in the Gulf rested on a distinctive architecture: bilateral security pacts with monarchies, the containment of revolutionary Iran, the projection of naval power through the Fifth Fleet, and the orchestration of regional balances that prevented any single actor from achieving hegemony. This system, while frequently contested and never entirely stable, provided the scaffolding within which Middle Eastern states navigated their external relations and managed their internal competitions.

Yet the twenty-first century has witnessed a gradual but unique recalibration. The relative retrenchment of the United States, evident in the withdrawal from Iraq, the limited intervention in Syria, and the diplomatic pivot toward Asia, has created perceptible gaps in the regional security architecture. Simultaneously, the persistence of regional fragmentation has intensified demands for external mediation even as traditional mediators have grown more reluctant or incapable. The Saudi–Iranian rivalry, the Syrian civil war, the Yemen conflict, the war in Gaza, and

A. Ullah, *Diplomacy by Design*,
https://doi.org/10.1007/978-981-95-7876-4_6

broader Sunni-Shia sectarian tensions all cry out for diplomatic solutions. Into this vacuum, new external actors have emerged, among them Russia, Turkey, and most consequentially, China. Beijing's growing role represents not merely the addition of another player to an already crowded field, but a qualitative shift in the modalities through which external powers engage the region.

The preceding chapters have demonstrated how China's infrastructural engagements in Saudi Arabia and Iran have embedded Beijing into the region's economic and logistical fabric. Ports, railways, energy grids, and digital networks provide the material foundations of China's presence, connecting Gulf economies to Asian markets and anchoring long-term commercial relationships that transcend political volatility. Infrastructure functions as more than economic facilitation; it constitutes the physical substrate through which China achieves strategic depth without deploying military assets or constructing formal alliances. Yet infrastructure alone cannot explain why regional states increasingly accept China as a mediator, why rivals such as Iran and Saudi Arabia recalibrate their policies in Beijing's presence, or why China can facilitate accommodation without military guarantees or ideological alignment.

The puzzle is both empirical and theoretical. China's mediation of the 2023 Iran–Saudi Arabia reconciliation marked a watershed moment in Middle Eastern diplomacy, yet it occurred without the traditional instruments of great power statecraft. Beijing wielded neither military guarantees nor conditional aid packages; it did not threaten sanctions nor promise territorial adjustments. Existing frameworks struggle to account for this form of influence. Realist paradigms emphasize material capabilities and security guarantees as the foundations of mediation (Mearsheimer, 2001; Walt, 1987), yet China offered neither. Liberal institutionalist perspectives highlight multilateral frameworks and rule-based diplomacy (Keohane & Nye Jr, 1973), yet China's approach was distinctly bilateral and pragmatic rather than institutionalized. Constructivist accounts point to normative alignment and shared identity (Wendt, 1999), yet China shares little ideological common ground with either Tehran or Riyadh.

This chapter addresses a central question: not what China has built, but how it translates embedded presence into diplomatic influence. To address this puzzle, the chapter draws on the concept of DSI introduced in previous chapters. DSI captures how Beijing deliberately structures interdependence to serve diplomatic and strategic objectives, moving beyond passive economic integration toward intentional configurations of mutual reliance (Jones & Zeng, 2020; Norris, 2016). The framework rests on three interlocking dimensions that together constitute a distinctive mode of statecraft.

First, DSI involves the intentional design of economic and infrastructural ties to generate long-term leverage through the creation of shared stakes in stability and continued cooperation. Unlike predatory forms of interdependence that extract resources or impose conditionality, DSI operates through alignment of interests, making disruption costly for all parties. Infrastructure projects yield genuine benefits to host states while simultaneously creating operational dependencies that raise the costs of disengagement and make cooperation increasingly rational.

Second, DSI embeds these material ties within broader diplomatic strategies, ensuring that economic relationships serve larger geopolitical purposes. Infrastructure projects become nodes in a network of influence; trade relationships translate into diplomatic access; energy partnerships generate political goodwill. This integration ensures that economic presence undergirds and enables political leverage in ways that isolated commercial relationships cannot achieve.

Third, DSI cultivates strategic ambiguity that allows China to operate across rival blocs without triggering zero-sum backlash, maintaining productive relationships with adversaries while avoiding the perception of alignment that would undermine its mediator credentials. This ambiguity is not indecision but deliberate design: a way of structuring engagement that maximizes diplomatic options while minimizing political risks.

China's diplomatic posture, rooted in a long tradition of non-interference and pragmatic engagement, provides credibility as a mediator. Where Western mediation often demands political reform, regime change, or alignment with particular normative frameworks, Chinese mediation emphasizes sovereignty, non-interference, and mutual benefit (Brigg, 2003). This approach resonates strongly in a region historically scarred by interventionism and where suspicion of external agendas runs deep. Tehran values China's willingness to defy Western sanctions and provide economic lifelines; Riyadh appreciates China's massive energy purchases and investment commitments. Neither feels that engaging with Beijing requires choosing sides in great power competition, and both recognize that their mutual hostility imposes costs on relationships with their largest Asian partner.

The 2023 reconciliation between Iran and Saudi Arabia, brokered in Beijing, illustrates this transformation. The rapprochement between these longstanding rivals, announced in March after years of proxy conflicts and diplomatic severance, surprised regional observers and Western policymakers alike (Ullah, 2023). It was not infrastructure alone that brought the two rivals to the table, but the convergence of embedded presence, strategic ambiguity, and carefully designed interdependence. China's ability to maintain strong ties with both Tehran and Riyadh, while avoiding entanglement in their rivalries, positioned it uniquely as a trusted broker. This episode exemplifies mediation by design, a form of diplomacy that relies on structured interdependence, shared incentives, and the quiet orchestration of stability rather than dramatic public commitments or formalized security arrangements.

The broader significance lies in its implications for international relations theory and practice. China's mediation in the Middle East reflects a redefinition of diplomatic norms in the twenty-first century. Unlike Western approaches, which often rely on conditionality, alliance politics, or overt pressure, China's strategy emphasizes embedded presence, pragmatic flexibility, and the cultivation of long-term interdependence. This represents neither pure revisionism nor simple status quo maintenance, but rather a reconfiguration of the rules and instruments through which influence operates in regional systems.

2 Conceptual Foundations: From Material Interdependence to Designed Strategic Interdependence

The study of international relations has long grappled with the question of how states exert influence beyond the use of military force. Scholarship has produced a rich taxonomy of influence mechanisms, from coercive diplomacy and alliance formation to normative persuasion and institutional embedding (Baldwin, 1978). Yet in the Middle East, where external powers have historically relied on coercion, alliances, and resource politics, China's approach presents a puzzle that existing frameworks inadequately capture. Beijing's growing role cannot be fully explained by traditional theories that emphasize dependency, complex interdependence, or soft power. Each captures part of the story, revealing particular dimensions of China's engagement, yet none provides a comprehensive account of how

China has positioned itself as a credible mediator in one of the world's most fragmented regions.

Classical dependency theory, rooted in Latin American structuralist thought and developed by scholars such as Fernando Henrique Cardoso and Enzo Faletto, emphasizes how economic asymmetries lock weaker states into subordinate positions within global capitalist hierarchies (Cardoso, 1982; Cardoso & Faletto, 2024). Applied to the Middle East, one might argue that China's investments in energy infrastructure, logistics networks, and digital systems create new forms of dependency, binding regional states to Beijing's economic orbit. Yet this perspective proves insufficient upon closer examination. Dependency theory assumes asymmetric vulnerability and limited agency among dependent states, treating them as objects acted upon rather than strategic actors capable of sophisticated navigation (Caporaso, 1978).

In the contemporary Middle East, this assumption fails to capture empirical reality. Saudi Arabia views Chinese investment not as a trap but as a complement to its Vision 2030 diversification strategy, successfully negotiating technology transfers, joint ventures in renewable energy, and collaboration in advanced manufacturing. Iran, even while operating under severe Western sanctions, has demonstrated remarkable agency in shaping the terms of its engagement with China, resisting demands for exclusive access to energy resources and insisting on technology localization provisions (Ullah & Xinlei, 2025). The United Arab Emirates, despite its close security partnership with the United States, has systematically deepened economic ties with China, becoming a major transhipment hub for Chinese goods (Ulrichsen, 2014). If Chinese engagement truly produced structural dependency, one would expect regional states to exhibit resistance or attempts at diversification. Instead, deepening engagement and increasing acceptance of China as a legitimate stakeholder persist.

The concept of complex interdependence offers a more nuanced framework, highlighting how multiple channels of interaction reduce the salience of military force and create incentives for cooperation (Keohane, 1977, pp. 20–22). Applied to China's role in the Middle East, this framework captures important dynamics. The proliferation of trade relationships, joint ventures, and infrastructural connections between China and various Middle Eastern states has created constituencies for stability and generated incentives against destabilizing behavior. However, complex interdependence assumes that such ties emerge organically from globalization and mutual interest, the unintended consequence of market forces rather than deliberate strategic design (Ibid., pp. 24–27). The framework treats interdependence as something that happens to states, a structural condition that constrains behavior but lacks intentional architecture.

China's approach to the Middle East is not merely about allowing interdependence to evolve through market mechanisms; it is about structuring relationships in ways that create leverage, embed presence, and generate diplomatic options while maintaining sufficient flexibility to avoid entrapment in local conflicts (Jones & Zeng, 2020). This requires careful sequencing of investments, strategic selection of partners and projects, calibrated provision of public goods, and continuous diplomatic cultivation. The distinction is crucial: where Keohane and Nye saw interdependence as an emergent property of international economic integration, China's strategy involves conscious construction of interdependence patterns designed to serve broader strategic objectives. The Iran–Saudi reconciliation provides a particularly revealing instance. The interdependence that facilitated dialogue between these longtime rivals was not the accidental byproduct of globalization but resulted from years of parallel, carefully calibrated engagement with both sides, investments structured to create mutual exposure to Chinese markets, and diplomatic initiatives timed to leverage these economic foundations (Ullah & Xinlei, 2024).

Joseph Nye's concept of soft power, which emphasizes attraction through culture, values, and legitimacy rather than coercion or payment, has become increasingly influential in analyses of Chinese foreign policy (Nye, 2004, pp. 5–6). Some scholars have argued that China's mediation role in the Middle East reflects its growing soft power in the region, derived from its longstanding principle of non-interference and its reputation as a pragmatic partner willing to engage without imposing political conditionality (Edney et al., 2020). This interpretation highlights genuine aspects of China's appeal. Beijing's refusal to lecture regional governments about democracy, human rights, or governance reform contrasts sharply with Western approaches and resonates with Middle Eastern states sensitive about sovereignty after decades of external intervention.

Yet soft power theory suggests that states align their policies with attractive powers voluntarily, drawn by admiration for their values, culture, or model. Middle Eastern states do not engage with China primarily because of cultural affinity or ideological appeal. Opinion polling in the Middle East consistently shows that improved perceptions of China correlate strongly with economic engagement and material benefits rather than with cultural attraction or normative alignment (Sharma, 2023). The attraction operates at an instrumental level. Regional actors value China's approach because it offers a framework of engagement that reduces costs, preserves autonomy, and creates tangible material benefits. Furthermore, soft power alone cannot explain why strategic rivals such as Iran and Saudi Arabia would entrust Beijing with facilitating reconciliation after years of proxy warfare. Attraction might explain why states seek Chinese investment, but it cannot account for the willingness to grant Beijing a mediating role in core security matters (Nye, 2011, pp. 81–95). Mediation requires more than likability; it demands credibility, perceived neutrality, and the capacity to impose costs or provide benefits significant enough to alter calculations.

Designed Strategic Interdependence: Theoretical Integration and Innovation

These limitations in existing frameworks point toward the need for a more precise analytical lens. DSI provides this lens by arguing that China does not simply benefit from interdependence as an ambient condition of the global economy, but actively designs interdependence relationships to serve specific diplomatic and strategic objectives. The concept argues that the manner in which interdependence is structured matters as much as its mere existence. Two states can be equally economically integrated yet experience fundamentally different political outcomes depending on whether that integration was designed strategically or allowed to develop organically.

DSI involves three integrated elements that together constitute a distinctive mode of statecraft. First, it emphasizes the intentional structuring of economic and infrastructural ties to create configurations of mutual exposure that raise the costs of disengagement while preserving flexibility for the stronger party. China prioritizes projects that create long-term operational dependencies, such as ports that require ongoing Chinese management, telecommunications infrastructure that embeds Chinese standards, or industrial zones that integrate regional economies into Chinese supply chains. These choices reflect strategic calculation rather than purely commercial logic, designed to ensure that partner states develop vested interests in maintaining stable relationships with Beijing.

Second, DSI involves the systematic embedding of economic presence within broader diplomatic initiatives and political frameworks. Infrastructure investments are consistently linked to initiatives such as the Belt and Road, which provides both material resources and ideological framing. Energy partnerships become foundations for political dialogue through mechanisms like the China-Arab States Cooperation Forum and bilateral strategic partnerships. This integration ensures that economic relationships translate into diplomatic access, political influence, and mediating potential rather than remaining isolated commercial transactions. The result is a form of presence that operates simultaneously at economic, diplomatic, and strategic registers, multiplying effectiveness through layered engagement across multiple domains.

Third, DSI relies on strategic ambiguity and the cultivation of overlapping spheres of engagement with rival powers. By maintaining productive relationships with competing actors, China creates situations in which multiple parties have incentives for restraint and where Beijing can credibly position itself as a neutral facilitator. This requires careful management of perceptions, avoiding actions that might be interpreted as alignment with one side against another, while ensuring that each partner values its relationship with China sufficiently to consider Chinese preferences in their calculation. Strategic ambiguity is not weakness or indecision but disciplined design: a way of structuring influence that maximizes diplomatic options while minimizing risks of entanglement.

In the Middle Eastern context, DSI explains dynamics that other frameworks struggle to reveal. Regional states recognize China as an actor that has embedded itself in regional structures in ways that make cooperation preferable to confrontation, that has cultivated relationships too valuable to jeopardize through reckless behavior, and that possesses the neutrality and leverage necessary for credible mediation. The framework explains not only why China can mediate between rivals, but why those rivals accept Beijing's mediation even when they might prefer to resolve disputes autonomously. The answer lies not in Chinese charm or soft power, but in the structural reality that disengagement from Chinese partnerships would impose substantial costs while cooperation promises material benefits.

This framework also captures an essential truth often overlooked in international relations scholarship: power in the twenty-first century increasingly derives not from the ability to impose costs through military force or economic punishment, but from the ability to structure relationships in ways that make cooperation the rational choice for all parties. DSI operationalizes this insight by showing how infrastructure, economic ties, and diplomatic embedding can together create conditions where alignment emerges from interest rather than coercion. This represents a fundamental shift in how great power statecraft operates in conditions of multipolarity and economic interdependence, a shift with profound implications for understanding contemporary international relations and the mechanisms through which influence is exercised in contested regions.

3 Historical Precedents: China's Mediation Traditions

China's growing role as a mediator in the Middle East may appear novel to observers accustomed to viewing Beijing primarily through the lens of economic expansion or strategic competition with the United States. Yet this mediating function is rooted in a longer history of diplomatic practices that privilege pragmatism, restraint, and quiet facilitation over the more assertive forms of intervention characteristic of traditional great powers. From the early years of the People's Republic, Beijing has experimented with forms of mediation that differ fundamentally from Western approaches, developing a distinctive repertoire of diplomatic techniques adapted to contexts where overt power projection proves counterproductive or unfeasible. Understanding this genealogy proves essential for contextualizing contemporary developments, revealing that China's current mediation practices in the Middle East represent not rupture but adaptation, the application of longstanding principles through mechanisms scaled to match China's expanded capabilities and global reach.

The Foundational Moment: Bandung and the Five Principles

The foundational moment for China's mediation diplomacy emerged during the 1950s, particularly through the Bandung Conference of 1955, which brought together newly independent Asian and African states seeking to chart a course between Cold War blocs (Ampiah, 2007). Premier Zhou Enlai's diplomatic performance at Bandung proved transformative, establishing China's credentials as a supporter of decolonization and advocate for what would become the Non-Aligned Movement

(Tan & Acharya, 2008). Yet Bandung represented more than rhetorical positioning; it established a set of operational principles that would structure Chinese diplomacy for subsequent decades.

Zhou's articulation of the Five Principles of Peaceful Coexistence, originally formulated in negotiations with India and Burma, provided an ideological framework that resonated powerfully with states emerging from colonial domination. These principles emphasized mutual respect for sovereignty and territorial integrity, non-aggression, non-interference in internal affairs, equality and mutual benefit, and peaceful coexistence regardless of ideological differences (Zhang & Buzan, 2012). While these tenets functioned partly as ideological positioning against both Western imperialism and Soviet hegemonism, they also reflected genuine Chinese experiences with foreign intervention and shaped subsequent diplomatic practice in consequential ways.

What distinguished China's approach was not material power but philosophical coherence. Beijing presented itself not as a patron dispensing conditional assistance but as a fellow traveler sharing struggles against hegemony and committed to respecting sovereignty even where ideological sympathies might suggest otherwise. This positioning proved diplomatically valuable precisely because it appeared principled rather than instrumental. Newly independent states, having experienced colonial extraction and Western conditionality, found Chinese engagement refreshing because it appeared to lack the condescension that characterized much Western development assistance and the heavy-handedness that Soviet engagement occasionally displayed (Alden, 2007).

Mediation efforts in Southeast Asia during the 1950s and 1960s, though often conducted quietly, reflected a clear preference for dialogue over intervention. In the complex Cambodian conflicts of that era, China engaged in behind-the-scenes facilitation aimed at preventing escalation while avoiding the kind of direct involvement that might compromise its non-aligned credentials or trigger superpower confrontation (Buszynski, 1986). These early practices established a template that would prove remarkably durable: China would not impose solutions through military force or economic coercion, but would instead create diplomatic space for local actors to negotiate settlements reflecting their own interests and preserving their autonomy. The approach emphasized process over outcomes, facilitation over dictation, and the creation of conditions enabling dialogue rather than the determination of specific settlements.

This philosophy emerged partly from necessity. China's limited power projection capabilities during the Cold War constrained its ability to impose outcomes even had it wished to do so. Yet over time, constraint transformed into strategic choice. Chinese leaders came to view limited direct involvement as an asset rather than a liability, a way of maintaining credibility with diverse actors and avoiding the kind of entanglement that had compromised other powers' mediating roles. By refusing to demand specific outcomes, Beijing preserved its ability to engage with multiple parties even when their positions diverged sharply.

This approach matured during the 1970s and 1990s as China extended its mediation posture to Africa and additional parts of Asia, operating within the constraints imposed by limited power projection capabilities but leveraging growing diplomatic networks (Shinn & Eisenman, 2012). In conflicts surrounding Zimbabwean independence and the protracted tensions between Ethiopia and Eritrea, Beijing positioned itself as a supportive but non-intrusive partner, offering material assistance and political recognition without demanding exclusive alignment or imposing governance models (Chun, 2014; PRC, 2000). China's role in these conflicts was often overshadowed by more muscular interventions from the United States, the Soviet Union, or former colonial powers. Yet China's approach was distinctive precisely in its restraint and its emphasis on process over outcomes.

Unlike superpowers that frequently tied mediation to strategic objectives within the broader Cold War competition, China avoided deep entanglement in alliance politics, instead offering economic assistance, infrastructure development, and political recognition as tools of quiet influence that generated goodwill without creating formal obligations or triggering nationalist backlash (Brautigam, 2009). This strategy reinforced the principle that credibility in mediation derives not primarily from coercive power but from perceived neutrality, respect for sovereignty, and genuine acceptance of diverse political systems and developmental paths. African leaders, many of whom had experienced heavy-handed interventions from former colonial powers or found themselves trapped in superpower proxy competitions, often responded positively to Chinese engagement precisely because it appeared to lack the conditionality and interference that characterized other external relationships.

The Six-Party Talks: Scaling Up Mediation

The end of the Cold War and China's subsequent economic rise during the 1990s and early 2000s created new opportunities for Beijing to operationalize its mediation practices on a larger scale and in more consequential contexts. The Korean Peninsula emerged as a critical testing ground where China demonstrated its ability to convene rivals and facilitate dialogue on highly sensitive security matters. Beijing's hosting of the Six-Party Talks, initiated in 2003 to address North Korea's nuclear program, represented a significant evolution in China's mediating role (Zhang & Han, 2013).

Unlike earlier mediation efforts conducted quietly and often peripherally to major power diplomacy, the Six-Party Talks positioned China explicitly as the convenor and primary facilitator in negotiations involving not only the two Koreas but also the United States, Russia, and Japan. This role required sophisticated diplomatic management, as China needed to maintain productive relationships with all parties despite their mutual antagonisms and divergent objectives, while also pursuing its own interests in preventing conflict on its borders and forestalling outcomes that might enhance American strategic presence in Northeast Asia (Ross, 2013).

The Six-Party Talks exemplified China's preference for process-oriented diplomacy that emphasized incremental confidence-building rather than demanding comprehensive settlements or imposing predetermined outcomes. Beijing structured the negotiations to focus on technical issues and phased implementation, creating frameworks within which parties could demonstrate commitment without requiring immediate political concessions that domestic audiences might perceive as capitulation. This approach reflected a belief, grounded in both philosophical traditions emphasizing harmony and gradualism and practical experience with reform processes, that stability could be achieved through dialogue structured around shared interests and mutual accommodation rather than through coercive pressure or winner-take-all bargaining.

While the Six-Party Talks ultimately failed to achieve denuclearization and were suspended in 2009, they demonstrated China's capacity to organize complex multilateral processes and maintain engagement even when immediate progress proved elusive. The emphasis throughout remained on designing interdependence rather than enforcing conditionality, creating incentives for cooperation through positive inducements rather than threatening punishment for non-compliance. This recognition would inform subsequent refinements in Chinese mediation practice, leading to greater emphasis on economic embedding and infrastructural integration as foundations for diplomatic leverage. If interdependence created through dialogue could be insufficient to compel outcomes, perhaps interdependence created through material investments could provide more durable foundations for influence.

Transition to Material Embedding: From Process to Structure

When applied to the Middle East in the twenty-first century, these diplomatic traditions take on new significance and operate at substantially different scales. Unlike in Asia or Africa during earlier periods, where China's mediation was often peripheral to dynamics driven by other powers, in the contemporary Middle East Beijing has become indispensable to regional political economy and increasingly central to diplomatic processes. China's transformation into the world's largest energy importer fundamentally altered its relationship with Gulf producers, creating mutual dependencies that extend far beyond commercial transactions (Al Shidhani & Baig, 2024).

Energy security imperatives drive Chinese engagement, but they also provide foundations for broader strategic relationships. Saudi Arabia, the UAE, Iran, Iraq, and other major producers depend on Chinese demand for revenue generation and market access, while China relies on stable Gulf supplies to fuel its economic growth and industrial development. This mutual exposure creates structural incentives for maintaining stable relationships that did not exist during earlier periods when China's energy needs could be met domestically or through limited imports.

Infrastructural investments and growing trade ties have embedded China deeply in the region's material fabric through mechanisms examined in previous chapters. Yet the style of mediation remains consistent with historical precedent. China continues to avoid overt alignment with particular factions or states against others, carefully balancing relationships with rivals and maintaining productive engagement across sectarian, ideological, and political divides. The emphasis on sovereignty and non-interference, articulated at Bandung seven decades earlier, remains central to Chinese diplomatic rhetoric and practice in the Middle East.

What distinguishes the contemporary moment from earlier precedents is fundamentally a matter of scale, capability, and intentional design rather than wholesale departure from established patterns. China now possesses material resources, global reach, and economic centrality that enable it to operationalize mediation principles with far greater effect than was possible during the Cold War era. More critically, China has learned to deliberately design interdependence as a strategic tool rather than simply allowing relationships to develop through organic market forces or episodic diplomatic engagement. The concept of DSI captures this evolution, representing both continuity with longstanding principles and innovation in implementation.

In the Middle East, where rivalries are shaped by sectarian identities, historical grievances, and competing visions of regional order, China's approach stands out as an alternative model. Instead of imposing predetermined solutions, alliance obligations, or ideological agendas, China engages pragmatically, emphasizing material incentives and mutual benefit. It respects sovereignty, accepts diverse political systems, and avoids demanding political reforms. Rather than forcing binary choices between competing powers, China maintains simultaneous engagement with rivals, framing interdependence as a shared asset rather than a zero-sum contest (Ehteshami & Horesh, 2017).

The transformation from historical tradition to contemporary design represents a maturation of Chinese statecraft adapted to the realities of multipolarity and economic globalization. Early mediation efforts operated within severe material constraints and functioned primarily at the margins of major power politics. Contemporary Chinese mediation in the Middle East operates from a position of centrality rather than peripherality, leveraging massive economic flows, critical infrastructure investments, and sustained diplomatic engagement to shape regional dynamics in meaningful ways. Yet this enhanced capability has not produced a fundamentally different diplomatic philosophy or abandoned principles established during earlier periods. Instead, China has found ways to operationalize longstanding commitments to sovereignty, pragmatism, and non-interference through material mechanisms that give these principles practical effect.

4 Contemporary Practices: The Belt and Road as Diplomatic Platform

China's expanding role in the Middle East is frequently described in terms of the BRI, a vast network of infrastructure, trade, and investment projects stretching across Eurasia and linking Asia, Africa, and Europe through multiple terrestrial and maritime corridors. In the Middle East specifically, the BRI has been most visible in ports such as Gwadar in Pakistan and Duqm in Oman, industrial zones in Egypt and the UAE, energy pipelines traversing Central Asia and the Caspian region, and digital networks that embed Chinese telecommunications standards across multiple countries.

Yet to interpret the BRI solely as an economic enterprise driven by commercial logic or developmental imperatives is to miss its deeper significance as a mechanism of statecraft. In practice, the BRI functions as a diplomatic platform, embedding China into the political fabric of the Middle East and enabling the deliberate design of strategic interdependence through mechanisms that transcend purely economic calculations (Ferdinand, 2016). The distinctive characteristic of BRI projects in the regional context lies in their systematic integration within broader diplomatic frameworks rather than their implementation as stand-alone commercial ventures.

The CASCF, established in 2004 and elevated significantly after 2016, provides a multilateral platform linking Beijing with twenty-two Arab League members through ministerial meetings, strategic dialogues, and sectoral cooperation mechanisms spanning energy, infrastructure, technology, and cultural exchange (Hurley et al., 2018). The China-Gulf Cooperation Council Strategic Dialogue, initiated in 2010 and intensified throughout the 2010s, creates a dedicated channel for engagement with the six Gulf monarchies that collectively represent China's largest energy suppliers and most significant Middle Eastern investment destination (He, 2015). Bilateral comprehensive strategic partnerships, the highest tier of Chinese diplomatic relationships, have been extended to Saudi Arabia, the UAE, Iran, Egypt, and Algeria, formalizing cooperation across security, economic, and technological domains while signaling long-term commitment and mutual importance.

These frameworks achieve multiple objectives simultaneously. They legitimize commercial projects by embedding them within state-to-state relationships rather than presenting them as mere corporate ventures.

They create formal channels through which disputes can be managed and new cooperation opportunities identified. They generate diplomatic momentum that sustains engagement even when specific projects encounter difficulties. Most importantly, they ensure that economic interdependence continuously reinforces political dialogue and that political frameworks facilitate economic expansion. This circulation of benefits and responsibilities across registers multiplies the stickiness of relationships.

What distinguishes this approach from traditional development assistance is its deliberate ambiguity about hierarchy. Western aid programs, whether bilateral or multilateral, typically operate through explicit donor-recipient frameworks that establish clear power asymmetries and conditionality mechanisms. China's BRI engagement, by contrast, is rhetorically framed as win–win cooperation among equals, even when material asymmetries clearly favor Beijing. This rhetorical equality, whatever its relationship to actual power dynamics, resonates with states sensitive about sovereignty and suspicious of external interference. It allows regional governments to present Chinese engagement domestically as partnership rather than subordination, facilitating political acceptance and reducing nationalist backlash.

Energy Interdependence as Mediation Foundation

Before examining infrastructure and digital networks, it is essential to recognize that energy interdependence constitutes the material bedrock upon which China's entire Middle Eastern diplomatic architecture rests. China's transformation into the world's largest oil importer by 2017 fundamentally altered the strategic calculus of Gulf producers and created mutual vulnerabilities that provide the foundation for Beijing's mediating role.

Saudi Arabia and the UAE collectively supply approximately 20 percent of China's crude oil imports, making them indispensable to Chinese energy security. Iran, despite sanctions complications, has remained a significant supplier through both official and informal channels, with Chinese purchases providing Tehran with crucial hard currency during periods of maximum pressure. Iraq, Kuwait, and Oman complete a network of Gulf suppliers whose combined exports to China exceed one billion barrels annually. This dependence is mutual: China has become the largest export market for most Gulf producers, absorbing volumes that European markets no longer require and providing price stability through long-term contracts denominated in yuan.

This energy interdependence creates what might be termed strategic mutual exposure. China cannot afford prolonged disruption to Gulf oil flows without severe economic consequences. Gulf producers cannot afford to lose access to Chinese markets without catastrophic revenue losses. Neither Iran nor Saudi Arabia can risk actions that might prompt China to reduce purchases or shift sourcing elsewhere. This mutual vulnerability constrains behavior in ways that formal alliances or security guarantees cannot replicate. When Beijing convenes rivals for dialogue, both parties recognize that their economic relationship with China, anchored in energy flows worth hundreds of billions of dollars annually, provides Beijing with structural leverage independent of military capabilities or diplomatic pressure.

Moreover, energy relationships create regularized interactions that facilitate broader diplomatic engagement. Chinese and Gulf energy officials meet continuously to negotiate contracts, coordinate production levels, discuss infrastructure investments, and manage supply chain logistics. These technical interactions build personal relationships, generate trust, and create communication channels that can be activated for political purposes. When Saudi and Iranian officials arrived in Beijing for reconciliation talks in March 2023, they were not entering unfamiliar terrain but rather leveraging relationships built through years of energy cooperation facilitated by Chinese intermediaries.

The strategic significance extends beyond bilateral relationships to regional dynamics. By maintaining energy partnerships with rival producers simultaneously, China creates situations where both parties have incentives to avoid actions that might jeopardize Chinese demand. A Saudi decision to escalate tensions with Iran risks prompting Chinese calls for restraint and potentially reduced Saudi access to Chinese investment in non-energy sectors. An Iranian decision to disrupt Gulf shipping threatens Chinese energy security and invites Beijing to reconsider technology transfers or infrastructure financing. Energy interdependence thus operates as a form of structural mediation, creating constraints on behavior that operate continuously rather than episodically.

Infrastructure as Embedded Presence and Sequenced Engagement

Beyond energy, physical infrastructure projects embed China into regional space in ways that create enduring operational dependencies. The Chinese-funded port facility in Duqm, Oman, exemplifies this approach. Positioned outside the Persian Gulf to provide alternative access routes that bypass the Strait of Hormuz, it operates simultaneously as a commercial hub, a latent strategic asset, and a diplomatic gesture demonstrating alignment with Omani development priorities while avoiding the militarization associated with foreign bases (Ehteshami & Horesh, 2017). The Chinese-financed rail link connecting Tehran to Central Asian networks reduces Iran's isolation, challenges the logic of Western sanctions, and forges durable operational ties between Chinese state-owned enterprises and Iranian authorities, ensuring that economic cooperation continuously reinforces political dialogue (Ullah & Xinlei, 2025b).

These projects exemplify an embedded mode of statecraft in which regular technical coordination, shared stakes in project outcomes, and mutual dependence create a political environment conducive to stable relations. When Egyptian President Abdel Fattah el-Sisi faced international isolation following the 2013 military coup, China maintained and even expanded economic engagement, providing crucial legitimacy and material support during a period of diplomatic vulnerability (Alterman, 2013). When Saudi Arabia confronted Western criticism over the 2018 killing of journalist Jamal Khashoggi, Chinese investment and diplomatic support continued unaffected, signaling that Beijing evaluated relationships through different criteria than Western capitals. When Iran endured comprehensive sanctions, Chinese cooperation persisted despite risks to Chinese firms and financial institutions.

The sequencing logic central to DSI becomes particularly visible in how China structures BRI engagement across time and sectors. Beijing does not build indiscriminately or respond passively to whatever investment opportunities regional governments present; instead, it layers projects in ways that create cumulative interdependence, each phase establishing foundations for subsequent expansion while deepening mutual exposure (Hurley et al., 2018). Energy cooperation typically precedes industrial investment, establishing long-term commercial relationships and generating revenue streams that demonstrate mutual benefit. Industrial investment then paves the way for digital infrastructure, technology transfer, and financial integration, each layer adding complexity and interconnection that raises switching costs and creates constituencies favoring continued cooperation.

In Saudi Arabia, China's engagement followed this deliberate sequence. Initial energy purchases built trust and signaled long-term commitment. Downstream petrochemical partnerships deepened technical cooperation and aligned interests in price stability. Vision 2030 projects in renewable energy, NEOM smart city development, and advanced manufacturing embedded Chinese technology and standards in priority sectors, with each step reinforcing the next and expanding interdependence (Aoun & Kellner, 2015). In Iran, despite sanctions constraints, a similar pattern emerges: long-term energy agreements denominated in yuan provided the base, transport projects including Chabahar port upgrades and rail corridors into Central Asia reduced Iranian isolation, and digital infrastructure supplied by Huawei and ZTE filled technology gaps the West would not meet (Calabrese, 2006).

This layered approach reflects sophisticated understanding of how interdependence operates: multiple shallow dependencies prove more resilient than single deep dependencies because they distribute risk, create diverse constituencies, and ensure that relationship maintenance serves multiple interests simultaneously. An Iranian decision to exit Chinese energy partnerships would be economically devastating but might be politically survivable if alternatives could be found. An Iranian decision to exit energy, transport, and digital partnerships simultaneously becomes politically impossible because it would require disrupting too many dimensions of national development at once. The layering of interdependence ensures that defection becomes incrementally more costly, each new layer raising the barriers to disengagement.

Digital Infrastructure and Normative Convergence

The DSR adds a distinct dimension that transcends physical infrastructure's material logic. Chinese telecommunications networks, cloud computing platforms, e-commerce systems, and smart city technologies extend across the Middle East, particularly in Gulf states, creating technical dependencies that operate at multiple levels simultaneously. Huawei's 5G networks require ongoing maintenance, software updates, and technical support from Chinese providers. Cloud computing platforms route data through Chinese servers, generating potential access and leverage. E-commerce integration through Alibaba and WeChat Pay creates payment dependencies that bypass Western financial systems (Blanchard & Hooijmaaijers, 2021; Nouwens et al., 2021).

Beyond technical dependencies, digital infrastructure facilitates what might be termed technocratic convergence, wherein governance practices in partner states gradually align with Chinese models not through ideological persuasion but through the adoption of Chinese technologies that embed particular approaches to data collection, population monitoring, and algorithmic governance. When Gulf states deploy Chinese facial recognition systems, adopt Chinese smart city platforms, or implement Chinese e-governance solutions, they do not simply acquire neutral tools but import systems designed around Chinese assumptions about state-society relations, surveillance legitimacy, and the proper balance between security and privacy.

This convergence operates subtly, through the gradual normalization of practices rather than explicit policy coordination. A Saudi official working within a Chinese-designed smart city platform makes decisions shaped by the system's architecture, prioritizing data points the system collects and pursuing objectives the system optimizes. Over time, this shapes institutional culture, bureaucratic practice, and policy preferences in ways that align with Chinese approaches even absent conscious ideological affinity. This represents a form of influence more durable than traditional soft power because it operates through infrastructure rather than persuasion, embedding alignment within the material systems through which governance occurs.

China's consistency across political volatility constitutes perhaps the BRI's most underappreciated diplomatic asset. Western engagement with the Middle East has historically been episodic, surging during crises and receding during periods of stability, responsive to domestic political cycles, media attention, and shifting strategic priorities. Chinese engagement, by contrast, proceeds incrementally and persistently, insulated from electoral cycles, media pressure, and ideological disputes. This reliability operates at both state and subnational levels, creating resilience in relationships because multiple constituencies have stakes in their continuation.

Political leaders can rely on Chinese partnerships persisting regardless of electoral outcomes, leadership transitions, or shifts in domestic political alignments. Business communities can anticipate that Chinese investors will maintain commitments through political volatility rather than withdrawing when circumstances change. Workers and consumers benefit from infrastructure regardless of regime composition. This consistency creates structural rather than contingent relationships, making any single political realignment insufficient to sever ties.

The result is a form of embedded presence that transcends individual projects or transactions. China becomes woven into the fabric of regional political economy in ways that make its role increasingly difficult to disentangle even when specific policies generate controversy or when geopolitical circumstances shift. This is precisely what DSI aims to achieve: influence that derives not from moment-to-moment leverage but from structural positioning that makes cooperation the rational choice across diverse scenarios and changing conditions. The BRI, understood as diplomatic platform rather than mere economic initiative, represents the operationalization of this strategic logic at regional scale.

5 Case Study: The 2023 Iran–Saudi Arabia Reconciliation

The March 2023 agreement between Iran and Saudi Arabia to restore diplomatic relations, brokered in Beijing, marked one of the most consequential diplomatic breakthroughs in the Middle East in decades. For the first time since the Cold War's conclusion, a non-Western power facilitated rapprochement between two of the region's most entrenched rivals, states whose antagonism had shaped regional conflicts, driven arms races, and generated proxy wars across multiple theaters for nearly half a century. The agreement, announced on March 10 following intensive negotiations hosted by the Chinese government, was formally modest in scope, addressing the reopening of embassies, the re-establishment of diplomatic channels, and commitments to respect sovereignty and non-interference. Yet its deeper significance lies far beyond these technical provisions, revealing fundamental shifts in the architecture of Middle Eastern diplomacy and highlighting the logic of DSI that distinguishes contemporary Chinese statecraft from traditional great power approaches.

The Historical Context: Decades of Rivalry and Failed Mediation

Iran and Saudi Arabia have stood at opposite poles of Middle Eastern politics since the 1979 Islamic Revolution transformed Iran from a monarchical U.S. ally into a revolutionary Islamic republic challenging the regional status quo. Their rivalry is rooted in multiple overlapping dimensions: sectarian division between Shia Iran and Sunni Saudi Arabia, competing claims to Islamic leadership and legitimacy, divergent visions of regional order pitting Iranian revisionism against Saudi conservatism, and geopolitical competition for influence across the Arab world. This multidimensional antagonism has proven remarkably resistant to resolution precisely because it operates simultaneously at ideological, strategic, and material registers, making compromise on any single dimension insufficient to resolve the broader conflict (Ullah & Xinlei, 2024).

The rivalry intensified dramatically after 2011 as the Arab uprisings created power vacuums and opportunities for proxy competition across the region. In Syria, Iran deployed military forces, mobilized Shia militias, and provided crucial support that enabled Bashar al-Assad's regime to survive a devastating civil war, while Saudi Arabia armed and financed Sunni opposition groups in a failed attempt to overthrow the government and sever the Tehran-Damascus axis. In Yemen, Saudi Arabia launched a military intervention in 2015 aimed at reversing Houthi gains and restoring the internationally recognized government, viewing the Houthi movement as an Iranian proxy threatening Saudi borders and undermining Saudi influence in the Arabian Peninsula. Iran provided varying degrees of support to the Houthis, though the extent and significance of this assistance remains contested, while using the conflict to impose costs on Saudi Arabia through asymmetric means (Ibid.).

In Lebanon, Hezbollah's dominance, backed by Iranian support, has effectively created a state within a state that constrains Saudi influence and threatens Israeli security. In Iraq, Iranian-backed militias and political factions have achieved predominant influence over state institutions despite Saudi attempts to cultivate Sunni constituencies and balance Iranian power. In Bahrain, Iranian rhetorical support for Shia opposition movements has reinforced Saudi perceptions of Iranian subversion threatening GCC stability. Across this landscape of proxy conflicts, both states invested enormous resources in zero-sum competition that destabilized entire societies, displaced millions, generated humanitarian catastrophes, and produced strategic stalemate rather than decisive advantage for either party.

Diplomatic relations were severed in January 2016 following the execution of prominent Shia cleric Nimr al-Nimr by Saudi authorities and the subsequent storming of the Saudi embassy in Tehran by protesters, triggering a seven-year rupture marked by sustained hostility, military escalation, and proxy conflicts that imposed enormous costs on regional populations (Albarasneh, 2025). The rupture formalized what had been de facto hostility, eliminating even minimal diplomatic channels for communication and crisis management. This complete breakdown in bilateral relations amplified risks of miscalculation, eliminated mechanisms for de-escalation, and enabled proxy conflicts to intensify without diplomatic constraints.

Previous mediation efforts by Iraq, Oman, Pakistan, and Western actors had failed to produce breakthrough despite creating channels for dialogue. Between 2019 and 2022, Baghdad hosted at least five rounds of direct talks between Iranian and Saudi security officials, facilitated by Iraqi Prime Minister Mustafa al-Kadhimi who viewed Saudi–Iranian rapprochement as essential for Iraqi stability and sovereignty (Ali et al., 2024). These talks, conducted secretly to avoid domestic political backlash, achieved modest progress in reducing rhetorical hostility and establishing communication protocols, but failed to produce formal agreements or restore diplomatic relations. Oman, which maintained productive relationships with both Tehran and Riyadh and hosted numerous back-channel negotiations, similarly facilitated dialogue without achieving breakthrough.

These regional mediation efforts, while valuable in maintaining contact and preventing further escalation, lacked the weight and leverage to overcome fundamental obstacles to normalization. Both facilitators were smaller regional powers whose influence, while locally significant, could not compel either Iran or Saudi Arabia to make concessions they deemed contrary to core interests. More critically, neither Iraq nor Oman could offer the kinds of material inducements or impose the kinds of costs that might shift calculations in Tehran or Riyadh. Their mediation was purely diplomatic, operating through persuasion and facilitation rather than through structural leverage or material incentives.

Western involvement proved similarly limited and ultimately counterproductive. The United States was perceived as too closely aligned with Riyadh, having provided unwavering support for Saudi Arabia's Yemen intervention through arms sales, intelligence sharing, and logistical support, while simultaneously pursuing a maximum pressure campaign against Iran that included comprehensive sanctions, military threats, and diplomatic isolation (Ullah & Xinlei, 2025b). This structural alignment made Washington an unacceptable mediator from Tehran's perspective, as Iranian officials viewed American mediation as inherently biased toward

Saudi interests and designed to extract Iranian concessions without reciprocal Saudi compromises.

European actors, while maintaining diplomatic relations with both sides and occasionally floating proposals for dialogue, lacked the material leverage to influence either Tehran or Riyadh significantly. European trade with both countries, while substantial, paled in comparison to Asian economic relationships. European political influence, constrained by transatlantic coordination requirements and limited capacity for independent action, could not compete with powers offering genuine alternatives to Western-dominated systems. European mediation efforts thus remained symbolically important but practically ineffective, generating communiques and working groups but failing to alter fundamental strategic calculations in either capital.

The Convergence of Pressures and Strategic Recalculation

By 2023, however, both states faced mounting pressures that created openings for recalibration and generated incentives for de-escalation that had not existed previously. These pressures operated at multiple levels simultaneously, creating what crisis management theorists term a ripeness for resolution, wherein the costs of continued conflict begin to outweigh the perceived benefits and alternatives to confrontation become increasingly attractive.

For Iran, the strategic environment had deteriorated markedly across multiple dimensions. The Islamic Republic was grappling with severe economic isolation resulting from American sanctions reimposed after the Trump administration's 2018 withdrawal from the JCPOA. These sanctions had devastated Iran's economy, reducing oil exports from 2.5 million barrels per day in 2017 to less than 500,000 barrels per day officially by 2020, triggering currency collapse that saw the rial lose more than 70 percent of its value, and generating inflation exceeding 40 percent annually that eroded living standards and fueled social discontent (Gordon, 2013).

The economic crisis intersected with mounting domestic unrest that challenged the Islamic Republic's legitimacy in unprecedented ways. The September 2022 death of Mahsa Amini in morality police custody triggered nationwide protests that mobilized diverse segments of Iranian society including women, youth, ethnic minorities, and working-class populations in sustained demonstrations against the regime. Unlike previous protest waves that focused on specific economic grievances or political factions, the 2022–2023 protests articulated broader demands for fundamental change in governance, social policy, and the role of religion in public life. The protests persisted for months despite violent state repression, revealed deep societal alienation from the clerical establishment, and demonstrated the regime's vulnerability to popular mobilization.

These domestic pressures occurred against a backdrop of regional isolation and military vulnerability. Israeli strikes against Iranian facilities in Syria, assassinations of nuclear scientists and IRGC commanders, and sabotage operations against nuclear infrastructure demonstrated Iran's inability to deter adversaries or protect critical assets despite rhetorical defiance. The Taliban's return to power in Afghanistan in 2021 eliminated a manageable neighbor and created unpredictable border security challenges. Relations with Azerbaijan deteriorated over Baku's cooperation with Israel and Turkey. Even Russia, Iran's primary military partner, prioritized its own interests in Ukraine over Iranian concerns, reducing arms deliveries and diplomatic support.

Within this context of comprehensive pressure, Iranian leaders calculated that easing regional tensions might reduce international pressure, create space for economic recovery, and allow concentration on domestic challenges rather than costly regional conflicts. The strategic logic was straightforward: maintaining confrontation with Saudi Arabia imposed costs including military expenditures supporting proxies across multiple theaters, diversion of scarce resources from domestic needs, and international isolation that complicated efforts to attract investment or evade sanctions, without yielding commensurate strategic gains. The Yemen war had reached stalemate, neither Iran nor Saudi Arabia could achieve decisive victories in Syria or Iraq, and Lebanon's collapse threatened to destabilize Hezbollah.

De-escalation offered possibilities for reducing these costs while potentially opening space for sanctions relief, economic normalization, or at minimum breathing room to address domestic instability. This was not ideological transformation or strategic defeat but pragmatic reassessment of costs and benefits under changed circumstances. Iranian officials, particularly pragmatists within the foreign ministry and among technocratic elites, argued that confrontation had reached diminishing returns and that selective de-escalation could serve Iranian interests by reducing pressure, complicating Western efforts to isolate Iran, and demonstrating

Iranian rationality to international audiences skeptical of Tehran's intentions.

For Saudi Arabia, parallel pressures generated similar receptivity to recalibration, though operating from a position of relative strength compared to Iran's acute vulnerability. Crown Prince Mohammed bin Salman's ambitious Vision 2030 modernization and diversification program, announced in 2016 as the framework for transforming Saudi Arabia's political economy, prioritized economic development, technological advancement, and social transformation that required stable regional environments, substantial foreign investment, and sustained focus on domestic transformation rather than external conflicts. The Crown Prince recognized that regional instability deterred investment, diverted resources from development priorities, and complicated Saudi Arabia's carefully cultivated image as a modernizing state open for business.

The Yemen war, despite massive Saudi expenditures estimated at over $200 billion and comprehensive military intervention involving coalition forces, extensive bombing campaigns, and naval blockades, had produced military stalemate and humanitarian catastrophe that damaged Saudi Arabia's international reputation without achieving core strategic objectives (Gause, 2016). The Houthi movement, far from being defeated, had demonstrated remarkable resilience, launching drone and missile strikes against Saudi territory, disrupting Saudi oil infrastructure, and imposing ongoing security costs. International criticism of Saudi conduct, including allegations of war crimes, indiscriminate bombing, and complicity in humanitarian disaster, generated reputational damage that undermined Vision 2030's objectives and complicated relationships with Western partners whose technological cooperation and investment were deemed essential.

Moreover, Saudi Arabia faced its own external pressures and constraints. The Biden administration's approach to Saudi Arabia, while more measured than campaign rhetoric suggested, nevertheless signaled reduced American willingness to provide unconditional support and increased emphasis on human rights, particularly following the Khashoggi killing. European partners imposed arms embargoes and reduced diplomatic engagement. The 2019 attacks on Saudi oil facilities at Abqaiq and Khurais, attributed to Iran despite Houthi claims of responsibility, demonstrated Saudi vulnerability to precision strikes and revealed limitations of American security guarantees when Washington declined to respond militarily. This combination of constraints suggested that indefinite confrontation with Iran carried escalating risks without clear pathways to favorable resolution.

Within this context, Saudi strategic calculations shifted toward pragmatic accommodation. If Yemen could not be won militarily, if proxy conflicts elsewhere were stalemated, if international criticism was mounting, and if Vision 2030 required stability and focus, then selective de-escalation with Iran might serve Saudi interests. This did not represent abandonment of core Saudi concerns regarding Iranian regional behavior, nuclear program, or support for non-state actors. Rather, it reflected recognition that managing these concerns required different tools than military confrontation and proxy warfare. Diplomatic normalization could enable direct communication, create mechanisms for managing disputes, and potentially reduce risks of miscalculation while allowing Saudi Arabia to concentrate resources on domestic transformation.

Crucially, both states had reasons to recalibrate their approaches, but neither trusted Western mediation or felt confident that dialogue would succeed without external facilitation capable of providing guarantees, managing the process, and ensuring implementation. Previous rounds of talks had demonstrated that bilateral negotiations alone, even when facilitated by regional actors, were insufficient to overcome decades of accumulated mistrust, domestic political constraints that made concessions politically costly, and the absence of enforcement mechanisms that could ensure commitments were honored. Both capitals required an external mediator with sufficient leverage to make success likely, sufficient neutrality to be acceptable to both sides, and sufficient credibility to serve as guarantor of any agreement reached.

China's Embedded Leverage: Energy, Infrastructure, and Strategic Positioning

China's emergence as the broker was not accidental, opportunistic, or simply a matter of offering neutral facilitation. Rather, it was the product of years of embedded engagement with both states across multiple domains that had created unique conditions enabling effective mediation. Beijing had cultivated deep ties with both Tehran and Riyadh extending across energy, infrastructure, technology, finance, and diplomacy, creating relationships too valuable for either side to jeopardize through confrontation. This embedded presence generated what might be termed structural leverage, wherein influence derives not from explicit threats or promises but from the recognition that disrupting relationships with Beijing would impose substantial costs across multiple dimensions simultaneously.

For Iran, China's role as economic lifeline had become indispensable by 2023. Chinese oil purchases, maintained even during periods of maximum sanctions pressure when virtually all other major buyers withdrew, provided Iran with crucial hard currency flows estimated between $15–30 billion annually depending on volumes and prices. These purchases occurred through various mechanisms including formal contracts with Chinese state-owned enterprises, transactions with independent refiners operating outside Western financial systems, and ship-to-ship transfers in international waters designed to evade monitoring. While official Chinese customs data showed minimal Iranian oil imports during peak sanctions periods, independent tracking and analysis consistently identified substantial flows continuing throughout, demonstrating Beijing's willingness to maintain economic relationships despite American pressure and secondary sanctions risks.

This energy relationship extended beyond crude oil purchases to encompass technology cooperation, infrastructure investment, and financial arrangements that together created comprehensive interdependence. Chinese companies had invested in Iranian oil and gas field development, including the South Pars gas field, despite sanctions risks and project delays. Chinese telecommunications firms, particularly Huawei and ZTE, filled technology gaps created by Western sanctions, providing equipment, technical support, and expertise that enabled Iran to maintain and expand digital infrastructure. Chinese construction firms participated in port development at Chabahar, railway modernization connecting Tehran to Central Asian networks, and industrial park development in provincial regions (Ullah & Xinlei, 2025).

The 25-Year CSP signed in 2021, though more declaratory than immediately operational in many respects, formalized this relationship and signaled long-term Chinese commitment that provided psychological reassurance alongside material benefits. The agreement, negotiated over five years and encompassing cooperation across economic, political, and strategic domains, represented China's most comprehensive bilateral framework with any Middle Eastern state. While implementation proceeded slowly due to sanctions complications, technical challenges, and bureaucratic obstacles, the agreement's existence demonstrated Beijing's willingness to publicly align with Iran at a moment of maximum international isolation, a signal that resonated powerfully with Iranian officials accustomed to conditional engagement from most partners.

Simultaneously, China had become an indispensable partner for Saudi Arabia through mechanisms that created parallel interdependencies of comparable significance. Chinese oil purchases made the Kingdom reliant on Asian demand in ways that reshaped Saudi strategic calculations. By 2023, China imported approximately 1.8 million barrels per day of Saudi crude, representing roughly 17 percent of total Saudi oil exports and constituting the Kingdom's largest single customer. This relationship extended beyond commodity transactions to encompass downstream integration, with Saudi Aramco investing in Chinese refining capacity, establishing joint ventures with Sinopec and other Chinese firms, and developing strategic petroleum reserves in China that created operational interdependencies extending years into the future.

Beyond energy, Chinese participation in Vision 2030 initiatives had embedded Chinese firms, technologies, and standards into sectors central to Saudi diversification objectives. Renewable energy projects including solar farms and wind installations involved Chinese companies providing equipment, financing, and technical expertise. NEOM smart city development, the Crown Prince's signature project envisioning a futuristic urban center in northwestern Saudi Arabia, incorporated Chinese technologies in telecommunications, artificial intelligence, and urban management systems. Advanced manufacturing partnerships brought Chinese firms into Saudi industrial zones, creating joint ventures in electric vehicles, petrochemicals, and technology sectors (Fulton, 2019).

Crucially, China maintained these relationships without aligning exclusively with either side, carefully balancing engagement to preserve neutrality and avoid perceptions of favoritism that would undermine mediating credentials. This strategic ambiguity gave Beijing credibility as a neutral facilitator acceptable to both parties. Unlike Washington, perceived as Riyadh's security guarantor through formal alliances, military presence, and arms sales creating structural alignment despite occasional policy disagreements, or Moscow, whose partnership with Tehran through military cooperation in Syria, arms sales, and diplomatic coordination was overt and strategic, China positioned itself as a partner to both without being perceived as aligned with either against the other.

This positioning was not accidental but carefully cultivated through consistent diplomatic practice. When tensions escalated between Iran and

Saudi Arabia, China avoided taking sides publicly, instead calling for dialogue and restraint equally directed at both parties. When conflicts in Yemen or Syria intensified, China abstained from UN Security Council votes that would have required choosing between competing resolutions favored by different sides, maintaining neutrality even when this frustrated both parties. When Iran faced maximum pressure sanctions, China maintained economic engagement but avoided the kind of comprehensive diplomatic support that would have signaled complete alignment with Tehran against Riyadh. When Saudi Arabia sought support for regional initiatives, China participated selectively without endorsing positions that would antagonize Iran.

This sustained neutrality, maintained across years and multiple crises, generated credibility that proved essential when opportunities for mediation emerged. Both Tehran and Riyadh had observed China maintain balanced relationships despite intense pressure from both sides to align more clearly. This track record of even-handedness, combined with the material reality that both capitals depended substantially on Chinese economic relationships, created conditions wherein both sides could accept Chinese mediation without fearing that Beijing would exploit the process to advance partisan interests at their expense.

The Beijing Talks: Process, Substance, and Symbolic Significance

The actual negotiations that produced the March 2023 agreement unfolded across multiple tracks and timelines, with the Beijing summit representing the culmination of preparatory work rather than a spontaneous breakthrough. While the four days of intensive talks in Beijing between March 6–10 received global attention and generated the formal agreement, this represented only the visible apex of a process that had been developing for months through back-channel communications, preliminary meetings, and carefully orchestrated confidence-building measures.

Chinese officials had been engaging both parties separately throughout 2022, using various mechanisms to explore possibilities for reconciliation. Wang Yi, then China's State Councilor and Foreign Minister, met separately with Iranian Foreign Minister Hossein Amir-Abdollahian and Saudi counterpart Prince Faisal bin Farhan during bilateral visits and multilateral forums, using these encounters to gauge receptivity to dialogue and communicate Beijing's willingness to facilitate. Chinese diplomats conveyed messages between the two capitals, floating trial balloons and testing positions without committing either side to public stances that might prove politically costly if talks failed.

This preparatory work established the parameters within which substantive negotiations could proceed, identifying areas of potential agreement, clarifying red lines that neither side could cross, and developing confidence that serious engagement was possible. By the time senior officials arrived in Beijing in early March 2023, much of the groundwork had been completed, allowing the summit itself to focus on finalizing details, crafting language that both sides could accept, and managing the public announcement in ways that maximized political benefits for all parties.

The Iranian delegation was led by Ali Shamkhani, Secretary of Iran's Supreme National Security Council, a figure of considerable weight in Iran's security establishment with direct access to Supreme Leader Ali Khamenei and authority to negotiate on sensitive matters. The Saudi delegation was headed by Musaad bin Mohammed Al-Aiban, the Kingdom's National Security Adviser, similarly positioned at the apex of Saudi decision-making with direct reporting lines to Crown Prince Mohammed bin Salman. The choice of security officials rather than foreign ministry diplomats signaled that negotiations addressed core security concerns rather than merely diplomatic formalities, and that any agreements reached would have buy-in from the security establishments in both countries (EPRC, 2023).

Chinese facilitation was led by Wang Yi, with support from senior diplomats specializing in Middle Eastern affairs. The Chinese role involved both substantive mediations, helping parties identify areas of agreement and crafting compromise language, and logistical management, structuring meetings, managing timing, and ensuring that talks proceeded in environments conducive to candid exchange. The choice of Beijing as venue itself carried symbolic weight, demonstrating China's centrality to regional diplomacy and reinforcing both parties' recognition that their relationships with China constituted shared interests transcending bilateral disputes.

The agreement itself, announced jointly by all three countries on March 10, included several key provisions that together constituted a framework for gradual normalization rather than immediate comprehensive reconciliation. First, both countries committed to reopening embassies within two months, with Iran re-establishing its embassy in

Riyadh and Saudi Arabia reopening its embassy in Tehran along with consulates in Mashhad. This commitment addressed the most fundamental absence in bilateral relations, restoring official diplomatic presence and creating formal channels for communication, coordination, and crisis management (Parisa Hafezi, 2023).

Second, the agreement included commitments to respect sovereignty and territorial integrity, not interfere in each other's internal affairs, and cooperate in areas of common interest including security, economy, and trade. While formulaic in language, these provisions addressed core concerns that had fueled mutual antagonism. Iranian support for Shia opposition movements in Gulf states and Saudi support for Iranian opposition groups had been persistent sources of tension; commitments to non-interference, if honored, could reduce these flashpoints. Sovereignty commitments similarly addressed concerns about proxy conflicts, with both sides implicitly agreeing to constrain support for non-state actors operating against the other's interests.

Third, the agreement called for revival of security cooperation agreements dating to 2001 and economic cooperation agreements from 1998, creating frameworks for expanded engagement beyond purely diplomatic normalization (Ullah & Xinlei, 2024b). The 2001 security cooperation agreement had established mechanisms for counter-terrorism coordination, intelligence sharing on transnational threats, and cooperation on border security, but had remained largely dormant as bilateral relations deteriorated. Reviving this framework suggested willingness to cooperate on practical security matters despite broader strategic competition. The 1998 economic agreement had established foundations for trade facilitation, investment protection, and commercial cooperation, but had been overtaken by sanctions and political hostility. Its revival signaled intentions to expand economic engagement as relations normalized.

Additional provisions addressed technical matters including aviation agreements enabling direct flights between the two countries, visa facilitation for business and religious travel, and mechanisms for regular consultations at various levels of government. These practical arrangements, while seemingly minor, were essential for operationalizing normalization and ensuring that diplomatic restoration translated into tangible improvements in bilateral relations rather than remaining purely symbolic.

The fact that the agreement was signed in Beijing and announced jointly by representatives of all three countries underscored China's role not only as facilitator but also as potential guarantor of the process, a party with interests in implementation success and capabilities to encourage compliance through its relationships with both signatories (Ullah, 2023). This guarantor function, while not explicitly articulated in the agreement's text, was implicit in the structure of the announcement and the symbolism of Beijing as venue. Both Iran and Saudi Arabia recognized that China would monitor implementation, that Beijing's satisfaction with progress would influence its willingness to expand economic cooperation with each party, and that Chinese diplomatic support might prove valuable in managing implementation challenges.

The symbolic significance of the Beijing agreement extended far beyond its immediate provisions. That the most consequential Middle Eastern diplomatic breakthrough in decades occurred in the Chinese capital rather than Washington, Geneva, or a Gulf state capital represented a powerful statement about shifting hierarchies in global diplomacy. For decades, Middle Eastern peace processes had been synonymous with American mediation, from the Camp David Accords to the Oslo Process to various Iran nuclear negotiations. The image of Iranian and Saudi officials shaking hands in Beijing, with Chinese diplomats facilitating, challenged assumptions embedded in post-Cold War international order about Western centrality to global governance and diplomatic problem-solving.

For China, the agreement provided tangible evidence of its arrival as a global diplomatic power capable of facilitating solutions to intractable conflicts that had eluded traditional mediators. Chinese state media extensively covered the announcement, framing it as validation of Chinese diplomatic principles, demonstration of the BRI's contribution to peace and stability, and proof that Chinese models offered viable alternatives to Western approaches. The agreement enabled Beijing to project an image of responsible stakeholder addressing regional security challenges, countering Western narratives portraying China as revisionist power undermining existing order.

For the Middle East, the agreement signaled that the region's diplomatic future might be increasingly shaped by Asian powers whose approaches differ fundamentally from traditional Western mediation. This shift carried implications for how regional states would navigate future conflicts, whom they would approach for facilitation, and what kinds of diplomatic frameworks might prove effective. The success of Chinese mediation suggested that pragmatic, interest-based approaches emphasizing material incentives and non-interference might prove more effective than ideologically driven mediation emphasizing normative alignment and political transformation.

Implementation, Limitations, and Durability

The period following the March 2023 agreement has revealed both the genuine significance of the rapprochement and its inherent limitations as a transformation of Iran–Saudi relations. Implementation proceeded incrementally rather than comprehensively, with progress on diplomatic restoration occurring more smoothly than substantive cooperation in security or economic domains. By mid-2023, both countries had reopened embassies in each other's capitals and restored formal diplomatic representation, fulfilling the agreement's most visible commitment. Iranian Ambassador Alireza Enayati presented credentials in Riyadh in August 2023, while Saudi Ambassador Abdullah bin Saud Al-Anzi arrived in Tehran shortly thereafter, marking the formal restoration of diplomatic ties.

Direct flights between the two countries resumed, facilitating business travel and religious tourism, particularly for Iranian pilgrims visiting Mecca and Medina during Hajj and Umrah seasons. This practical cooperation, while seemingly minor, carried significant symbolic weight by normalizing bilateral interaction and demonstrating that normalization extended beyond governmental level to include people-to-people exchange. Trade between the two countries began to expand modestly from its near-zero baseline during the rupture period, with Iranian officials expressing interest in exporting agricultural products, petrochemicals, and manufactured goods to Saudi Arabia while importing Saudi dates, construction materials, and food products.

However, substantive cooperation on core security issues has proceeded far more cautiously, constrained by enduring mutual suspicion, conflicting strategic interests, and domestic political sensitivities in both countries. In Yemen, while high-intensity combat operations have decreased and diplomatic initiatives have gained momentum, Iranian support for the Houthis and Saudi backing for the internationally recognized government continue, albeit at reduced levels. The April 2023 Oman-mediated talks between Saudi Arabia and the Houthis, occurring after the Beijing agreement, suggested that Saudi priorities had shifted toward finding face-saving exits from the conflict rather than pursuing military victory, a shift that the Iran rapprochement facilitated by reducing fears of appearing weak toward Iran.

In Syria, Lebanon, and Iraq, proxy competitions continue despite rhetoric about non-interference and cooperation. Iranian-backed militias remain active across all three countries, pursuing objectives that frequently conflict with Saudi interests. Saudi efforts to rebuild relationships with Damascus and engage with Iraqi factions continue despite Iranian predominance in both capitals. Hezbollah's position in Lebanon remains unchanged, with Saudi Arabia maintaining cautious distance from a political system dominated by Iranian allies. These continuities suggest that rapprochement has established frameworks for managing competition rather than eliminating it, creating channels for communication and crisis management while leaving fundamental strategic contests unresolved.

The durability of the rapprochement faces several ongoing challenges that will determine whether March 2023 represents a durable shift in bilateral relations or a temporary tactical adjustment that could be reversed if circumstances change. First, domestic politics in both countries create constraints on how far normalization can proceed. In Iran, hardline factions within the IRGC and conservative clerical establishment view Saudi Arabia with enduring suspicion, interpreting rapprochement as tactical necessity rather than strategic reorientation. Any perception that normalization requires significant Iranian concessions or undermines Iranian regional interests could generate internal opposition that constrains the government's flexibility.

In Saudi Arabia, segments of the ruling family, religious establishment, and security services remain deeply skeptical of Iranian intentions, viewing the Islamic Republic as an existential threat to Saudi and Gulf security. Crown Prince Mohammed bin Salman's personal investment in rapprochement provides political cover for normalization, but this personalization also creates fragility; shifts in leadership, domestic priorities, or regional circumstances could alter Saudi calculations. Public opinion in both countries, shaped by decades of mutual antagonism and proxy conflicts, requires careful management as governments navigate normalization without appearing to betray national interests or security concerns.

Second, external factors beyond either country's control could disrupt rapprochement. A military confrontation between Iran and Israel, increasingly likely given escalating tensions over Iran's nuclear program and Israeli strikes against Iranian facilities, could force Saudi Arabia to choose between its rapprochement with Iran and its developing relations with Israel. American pressure on Saudi Arabia to limit engagement with Iran, particularly if a future U.S. administration adopts more confrontational approaches toward both Tehran and Riyadh's China relationship, could constrain Saudi flexibility. Regional crises in Iraq, Lebanon, or the Gulf could reignite tensions despite diplomatic frameworks intended to manage such contingencies.

Third, the structural drivers that produced rapprochement, while significant, have not eliminated the fundamental conflicts of interest that generated rivalry in the first place. Iran continues to pursue regional influence through non-state actors, support for Shia communities, and alignment with resistance movements challenging U.S.-aligned order. Saudi Arabia continues to view Iranian regional activities as threatening, to maintain security partnerships with the United States, and to pursue leadership in the Arab and Islamic worlds that conflicts with Iranian claims. These structural factors suggest that rapprochement represents management of competition rather than its resolution, establishing guardrails rather than eliminating the contest.

Yet despite these limitations and challenges, the rapprochement has proven more durable than many skeptics anticipated. As of late 2024, nearly two years after the Beijing agreement, diplomatic relations remain intact, high-level exchanges continue, and both governments maintain rhetorical commitment to continued engagement. Neither side has experienced significant domestic backlash that would force reversal. Regional conflicts have not escalated to levels that would rupture the relationship. This durability, even if the relationship remains limited in scope and plagued by mistrust, suggests that the structural incentives created through Chinese-mediated interdependence provide genuine constraints on behavior and reasons for continued engagement that operate independently of sentiment or trust.

The China factor itself constitutes a significant source of durability. Both Iran and Saudi Arabia recognize that their relationships with Beijing, worth hundreds of billions of dollars in trade, investment, and technology cooperation, constitute strategic assets they cannot afford to jeopardize through actions that would force China to reconsider its balanced engagement. The recognition that Beijing facilitated reconciliation and maintains interest in its success creates an additional constraint: reversing course would not only damage bilateral Iran–Saudi relations but would also disappoint a major power whose goodwill both countries value.

This triangular dynamic, wherein bilateral behavior is partially shaped by concerns about third-party reactions, exemplifies how DSI creates structural constraints that operate continuously rather than episodically.

6 Institutionalizing Mediation: Can China Build a Sustainable Middle East Security Architecture?

The March 2023 Iran–Saudi Arabia reconciliation raises a question more consequential than the agreement itself: does China's successful mediation represent an ad-hoc diplomatic achievement capitalizing on a unique convergence of circumstances, or does it mark the beginning of a more systematic Chinese role in Middle Eastern security governance? This question carries profound implications not only for the region's future stability but also for understanding the evolution of Chinese foreign policy, the transformation of global governance institutions, and the emerging architecture of multipolar order. If China's mediation remains episodic and opportunistic, the Iran–Saudi deal may prove historically significant but strategically isolated, a demonstration of capability without sustained commitment. If, however, Beijing leverages this success to construct enduring mechanisms for regional security management, the implications could reshape Middle Eastern order as fundamentally as American involvement did following World War II.

From Episodic Facilitation to Sustained Security Governance

The history of great power engagement in the Middle East suggests that episodic mediation, however successful, rarely produces durable regional stability without institutional frameworks that routinize engagement, establish mechanisms for ongoing dialogue, and create enforcement capacity that transcends individual agreements. The United States demonstrated this lesson following World War II, when it constructed a comprehensive security architecture encompassing bilateral defense treaties, multilateral forums, military basing arrangements, and economic institutions that together sustained American predominance for decades (Elliott & Roberts, 2025). The Camp David Accords succeeded not merely because of Jimmy Carter's diplomatic skill but because they were embedded within broader American security commitments to both Israel and Egypt that made implementation rational and defection costly.

Similarly, the Oslo Process, despite its ultimate failure to resolve the Israeli–Palestinian conflict, demonstrated how institutionalized mediation creates frameworks for sustained engagement even when immediate breakthroughs prove elusive. The process established permanent negotiating structures, created international monitoring mechanisms, generated coordinated donor support, and normalized high-level diplomatic exchanges that persisted through multiple crises. These institutional features, while insufficient to overcome fundamental conflicts of interest, nevertheless represented qualitative differences from one-off mediation attempts that lack follow-through mechanisms or sustained external support (Foot & Walter, 2010).

China's Iran–Saudi mediation, by contrast, occurred through ad-hoc bilateral facilitation lacking formal institutional frameworks, ongoing monitoring mechanisms, or explicit enforcement capacities. The Beijing talks convened specific parties to address particular disputes, produced an agreement with implementation timelines, and concluded with public announcements celebrating success. Yet no permanent secretariat emerged to monitor compliance, no regular consultation mechanisms were established to manage implementation challenges, and no enforcement mechanisms were created to address violations or backsliding. The agreement's durability depends primarily on the parties' continued perception that cooperation serves their interests, reinforced by their respective relationships with China, rather than on institutional structures that would routinize cooperation and create costs for defection independent of Chinese attention.

This institutional deficit reflects deliberate Chinese choices rooted in longstanding foreign policy principles rather than mere oversight or capacity constraints. Beijing's emphasis on sovereignty and non-interference creates profound reluctance to construct institutions that might be perceived as imposing external authority over regional actors or limiting their policy autonomy. Chinese diplomatic culture prioritizes flexibility and ambiguity that preserve options and avoid entrapment, making formalized commitments that require sustained engagement potentially problematic. Moreover, Chinese leaders recognize that institutionalized security roles carry risks of entanglement in regional conflicts, create expectations for intervention during crises, and generate demands for resources that might exceed what Beijing wishes to commit.

Yet the question remains whether successful ad-hoc mediation can transition to sustainable security governance without institutional infrastructure. Historical precedents suggest skepticism. The Iran–Saudi agreement addresses immediate diplomatic rupture and establishes frameworks for dialogue, but it does not resolve underlying conflicts in Yemen, Syria, Iraq, or Lebanon. It does not create mechanisms for managing future crises or preventing escalation during periods of renewed tension. It does not establish enforcement capacity that could deter violations or punish defection. Without institutional follow-through, the agreement's implementation depends entirely on continued Chinese engagement and the parties' sustained calculation that cooperation serves their interests, factors that could shift as circumstances evolve.

Potential Pathways to Institutionalization

Despite these constraints, several pathways exist through which China might gradually institutionalize its mediation role without abandoning core principles or accepting commitments it deems excessive. These pathways reflect adaptive strategies that leverage existing platforms, build on established relationships, and proceed incrementally rather than requiring dramatic departures from current practice.

The CASCF represents the most obvious institutional platform through which expanded security engagement might proceed. Established in 2004 and elevated significantly after 2016, CASCF already encompasses ministerial meetings, strategic dialogues, and sectoral cooperation spanning economic, technological, and cultural domains. Expanding CASCF's mandate to include explicit security coordination, confidence-building measures, and conflict mediation mechanisms would formalize China's regional role while operating through multilateral frameworks that reduce perceptions of bilateral dominance. CASCF could evolve toward a security forum analogous to the ASEAN Regional Forum, creating regular consultations on regional security challenges, establishing working groups on specific conflicts, and generating norms around crisis management and conflict resolution.

Such evolution would require Arab states' acceptance of expanded Chinese engagement in security domains and Chinese willingness to assume greater institutional responsibilities. The former appears increasingly plausible given regional receptivity to Chinese mediation demonstrated through the Iran–Saudi case and growing recognition that American retrenchment creates demand for alternative security frameworks. The latter remains more uncertain, as Chinese leaders must balance desires for influence against risks of entanglement and resource commitments.

A second pathway involves bilateral strategic partnerships that could be upgraded to include explicit security cooperation and mediation mechanisms. China has established comprehensive strategic partnerships with Saudi Arabia, the UAE, Iran, Egypt, and Algeria, relationships that formalize cooperation across multiple domains and signal long-term commitment. These partnerships could incorporate regular security dialogues at ministerial and working levels, establish joint working groups on regional conflicts, and create mechanisms for coordinating positions on multilateral security issues. Such bilateral deepening would avoid the complexities of multilateral institution-building while still routinizing security engagement and establishing frameworks for sustained Chinese involvement in regional stability.

The SCO, which admitted Iran as a full member in 2023, provides another potential platform. While the SCO's primary geographic focus remains Central Asia rather than the Middle East proper, Iran's membership creates linkages between these regions and establishes frameworks through which Chinese security engagement with Iran can be regularized and institutionalized. The SCO's emphasis on counter-terrorism, border security, and regional stability aligns with Chinese principles of non-interference while providing multilateral cover for security cooperation. Expanding SCO mechanisms to address Middle Eastern security challenges, perhaps through observer status for additional regional states or working groups on specific conflicts, could gradually extend Chinese institutional engagement southward from Central Asia into the Gulf and broader Middle East (He & Feng, 2013).

A third, more ambitious pathway involves establishing new multilateral mechanisms specifically designed for Middle Eastern security governance under Chinese leadership. This might take the form of a Gulf Security Dialogue modeled loosely on the Helsinki Process that helped manage Cold War tensions in Europe, bringing together Gulf states, Iran, Iraq, and potentially external powers in regular consultations aimed at confidence-building, arms control, and crisis management. Such an institution would represent a dramatic expansion of Chinese ambition and commitment, requiring sustained diplomatic investment, willingness to chair sensitive negotiations, and acceptance of responsibility for outcomes. While this appears unlikely in the near term given Chinese preferences for minimizing formal commitments, the success of the Iran–Saudi mediation demonstrates Chinese capability to facilitate dialogue among hostile parties, suggesting that more systematic frameworks might become feasible as Chinese confidence and regional demand increase.

Structural Obstacles and Strategic Constraints

Yet multiple structural obstacles constrain China's ability or willingness to institutionalize its mediation role in ways that would constitute genuine security governance rather than episodic facilitation. These obstacles operate at several levels simultaneously, creating interdependent challenges that must be addressed collectively rather than individually.

First, China's limited military presence in the Middle East fundamentally constrains its capacity to provide the security guarantees that typically undergird effective regional security architectures. The United States maintains extensive military infrastructure including major bases in Qatar, Bahrain, Kuwait, and the UAE, forward-deployed naval forces including carrier strike groups, and security assistance relationships involving arms sales, training programs, and intelligence sharing that create dependencies and enable leverage. China, by contrast, maintains only a small naval facility in Djibouti, conducts occasional port calls and joint exercises, and provides limited arms sales compared to American, Russian, or European suppliers. This military asymmetry means that Chinese mediation cannot credibly threaten force to deter violations of agreements or promise protection to incentivize compliance in ways that American mediation historically could.

This limitation proves particularly acute in contexts where security guarantees constitute essential components of diplomatic settlements. The Camp David Accords succeeded partly because the United States could credibly promise military assistance and security cooperation to both Israel and Egypt, making implementation rational for both parties. Chinese mediation of the Iran–Saudi deal occurred without comparable security dimensions; China offered facilitation and economic incentives but not military backing or protection. This works for diplomatic normalization between states that do not face immediate military threats from each other, but it may prove insufficient for conflicts where security dilemmas drive escalation and where parties require external guarantees to accept vulnerability inherent in compromise.

Second, China's emphasis on non-interference and sovereignty creates profound tensions with the sustained engagement and occasional intervention that effective security governance requires. Successful regional security architectures historically involve not only facilitation of agreements but also monitoring of implementation, mediation of disputes over interpretation, and sometimes coercive enforcement when parties defect from commitments. The United Nations peacekeeping missions, NATO interventions in the Balkans, and American security guarantees in East Asia all involve degrees of interference in sovereign affairs that Beijing's principles formally oppose. While China participates in UN peacekeeping and has accepted limited interventions in specific contexts, it remains fundamentally skeptical of doctrines that legitimate external involvement in states' internal affairs.

This creates a dilemma: how can China construct institutional frameworks for security governance without compromising principles that constitute sources of its diplomatic appeal? Regional states value Chinese engagement precisely because it avoids the conditionality and interference associated with Western involvement. Institutionalizing Chinese mediation in ways that require monitoring, enforcement, or intervention risks undermining this distinctive approach and generating the kinds of resentment and resistance that have plagued Western security architectures. Yet without such mechanisms, institutional frameworks may lack the teeth necessary to ensure compliance and manage implementation challenges, rendering them symbolic rather than substantive.

Third, China's strategic priorities lie primarily in East Asia and the Western Pacific rather than the Middle East, creating resource allocation challenges and limiting Beijing's willingness to assume open-ended commitments in a secondary theater. Chinese military modernization focuses on scenarios involving Taiwan, the South China Sea, and potential conflict with the United States in the Indo-Pacific (Buzan & Cox, 2013). Chinese diplomatic attention concentrates on managing relationships with Japan, South Korea, ASEAN states, and India. Chinese economic integration centers on Asian production networks and trade relationships. The Middle East, while important for energy security and as a BRI region, remains peripheral to these core strategic concerns.

This prioritization means that China may lack the willingness to invest resources and political capital necessary for sustained security governance in the Middle East. Ad-hoc mediation like the Iran–Saudi facilitation requires limited commitments and can be presented as consistent with China's global role and peaceful development rhetoric. Institutionalized security governance, by contrast, demands sustained attention, ongoing resource commitments, and potential involvement in crises that could escalate in ways drawing China into conflicts it prefers to avoid. Unless Middle Eastern instability directly threatens Chinese core interests in ways that justify such commitments, Beijing may prefer to maintain its current approach of selective engagement and limited institutionalization.

Fourth, regional resistance to any single external power assuming hegemonic security roles constrains Chinese institutionalization regardless of Beijing's own preferences. Middle Eastern states have long experience with external hegemony, from Ottoman to British to American, and have developed sophisticated strategies for preserving autonomy through hedging, balancing, and playing external powers against each other. Even as regional states welcome Chinese investment and appreciate its mediation, many remain wary of excessive dependence on Beijing that might replicate patterns of subordination experienced with previous external powers.

Gulf states maintain security partnerships with the United States precisely to hedge against potential Chinese dominance. Iran cultivates relationships with Russia to avoid complete dependence on China. Egypt balances Chinese, Russian, and Western engagement to maximize autonomy. This multipolar hedging strategy reflects deliberate choices by regional actors to preserve flexibility and avoid entrapment in exclusive relationships with any single external power. While this creates opportunities for Chinese engagement without triggering zero-sum competition, it also limits how far regional states will accept institutionalized Chinese security governance that might constrain their autonomy or force them to choose sides in great power competition.

Implications for Regional Order and Global Governance

The question of whether China will institutionalize its mediation role carries profound implications for both Middle Eastern regional order and broader patterns of global governance. If China constructs sustained security mechanisms in the Middle East, it would mark the first instance since the Cold War of a non-Western power establishing comprehensive regional security architecture in a strategically vital area, challenging assumptions about Western indispensability to global governance and demonstrating the viability of alternative models based on different principles and practices.

For the Middle East, institutionalized Chinese security engagement could provide alternatives to American-dominated frameworks that have shaped regional order since the mid-twentieth century. This might enable regional states to diversify security partnerships, reduce dependence on any single external power, and pursue interests unconstrained by Western conditionality or ideological expectations. It could also create competitive dynamics wherein multiple external powers offer security goods and mediation services, potentially improving outcomes as regional states leverage competition to secure better terms and more responsive engagement.

Yet institutionalized Chinese security governance might also introduce new forms of hierarchy and dependence that replicate problematic aspects of previous external dominance. Economic interdependence created through BRI projects and energy relationships could translate into political leverage that constrains regional autonomy, particularly for states like Iran that lack alternatives due to sanctions or isolation. Chinese principles of non-interference might prove selective, applied strictly when convenient for Beijing but relaxed when Chinese interests demand intervention or influence. The absence of democratic accountability and human rights considerations in Chinese engagement might enable or even encourage authoritarian practices that Western security frameworks, despite their flaws and hypocrisies, occasionally constrained.

For global governance, Chinese institutionalization of its Middle Eastern mediation role would contribute to a broader pattern wherein rising powers construct alternative governance mechanisms that compete with and potentially replace Western-dominated institutions. This could enhance governance effectiveness by introducing institutional competition and innovation, forcing existing institutions to adapt and improve to retain relevance. It could also generate fragmentation wherein different regions operate according to divergent principles and norms, potentially undermining universal standards and creating incompatibilities that complicate cooperation on transnational challenges (Ikenberry, 2008).

The trajectory of Chinese institutionalization efforts will therefore constitute an important indicator of how twenty-first century global governance evolves. If China proves willing and able to construct sustained security mechanisms in the Middle East, it would validate arguments that global governance is becoming genuinely multipolar, with different powers offering distinct models that coexist and compete. If China instead maintains its current approach of ad-hoc facilitation without institutional follow-through, it would suggest that alternative governance models face significant obstacles and that existing Western-dominated frameworks, despite their limitations, retain advantages in providing sustained security governance that other powers cannot yet replicate.

Beyond the Iran–Saudi Deal: Testing Institutionalization Through Additional Mediation

The ultimate test of whether China can build sustainable security architecture lies not in theoretical potential but in empirical practice. The Iran–Saudi reconciliation provides one data point, demonstrating Chinese capability to facilitate diplomatic breakthroughs between hostile parties. Yet a single success does not constitute a pattern, and institutionalization requires demonstrating capacity across multiple contexts, sustained engagement over time, and ability to manage implementation challenges and subsequent crises.

Several ongoing conflicts provide opportunities for China to demonstrate whether its mediation role will expand and institutionalize or remain limited to favorable circumstances. Yemen presents an immediate test case, as the conflict directly involves parties to the Iran–Saudi reconciliation and offers opportunities for China to facilitate implementation of commitments to reduce proxy conflicts. If Beijing brokers Saudi-Houthi negotiations or facilitates humanitarian access agreements that advance conflict resolution, it would signal serious commitment to operationalizing the Iran–Saudi framework. If Chinese engagement remains rhetorical without substantive facilitation, it would suggest that mediation remains opportunistic rather than systematic.

Syria presents more complicated challenges but greater strategic significance. The conflict involves multiple regional actors including Iran, Turkey, Saudi Arabia, and the UAE, alongside external powers including Russia and residual American presence. Chinese mediation could potentially address specific dimensions such as reconstruction financing, refugee return frameworks, or normalization between Damascus and Arab states. Success in facilitating even partial settlements would demonstrate Chinese capacity to operate in complex multilateral environments and manage relationships with multiple competing interests simultaneously. Failure or non-engagement would reveal limitations of Chinese mediation in contexts where military dimensions dominate and where Chinese interests may conflict across different parties.

The Israeli–Palestinian conflict represents the ultimate test of Chinese mediation ambition and capacity. This protracted conflict has defeated American mediation efforts for decades despite massive resources and sustained engagement. Chinese success where America failed would constitute definitive proof of alternative mediation models' superiority and establish China as preeminent Middle Eastern mediator. Yet the obstacles are formidable: China lacks deep relationships with Israel comparable to those with Arab states, ideological dimensions of the conflict resist pragmatic solutions emphasizing economic incentives, and any Chinese mediation would occur in shadow of extensive American involvement and commitment. Chinese reluctance to engage this conflict meaningfully might reflect realistic assessment of limited prospects rather than lack of commitment to regional mediation.

Beyond specific conflicts, institutionalization would manifest through establishment of permanent mechanisms, regular diplomatic processes, and accumulated precedents that normalize Chinese mediation as expected feature of Middle Eastern security governance. This might include annual security dialogues convened by China, standing working groups on specific regional challenges, Chinese special envoys with permanent mandates for mediation, or formal Chinese commitments to provide good offices for regional disputes. Such developments would transform Chinese mediation from episodic achievement to systemic feature of regional order.

The next several years will prove decisive in determining which trajectory China pursues. If the Iran–Saudi reconciliation generates momentum for expanded Chinese security engagement, if Beijing leverages this success to address additional conflicts, and if institutional frameworks emerge to routinize Chinese mediation, then China's role in Middle Eastern security governance will have fundamentally transformed from peripheral commercial actor to central political facilitator. If, alternatively, Chinese mediation remains limited to favorable circumstances requiring minimal commitments, if institutional development stalls, and if regional conflicts continue without Chinese facilitation, then the Iran–Saudi deal may prove historically significant but strategically isolated.

What appears certain is that the demand for mediation in the Middle East exceeds the supply that traditional Western mediators currently provide, creating opportunities for Chinese engagement regardless of Beijing's preferences. American retrenchment, European preoccupation with other challenges, and regional states' desires for alternatives to Western-dominated frameworks generate structural demand for mediation services that China is uniquely positioned to provide given its economic centrality, established relationships across regional divides, and distinctive diplomatic principles. Whether Beijing responds to this demand by institutionalizing its mediation role or maintains its preference for limited engagement will significantly shape regional order and constitute an important indicator of Chinese foreign policy evolution as it navigates the responsibilities and risks accompanying great power status.

References

Al Shidhani, R., & Baig, S. (2024). Balancing power and prosperity: China's geoeconomic engagement with the Gulf Cooperation Council. *Asian Review of Political Economy, 3*(1), 20. https://doi.org/10.1007/s44216-024-00040-6

Albarasneh, A. (2025). From Arab Spring to regional reset: Saudi-Iranian rivalry and strategic contestation in the Gulf (2011–2023) [Review]. *Frontiers in Political Science, 7–2025*. https://doi.org/10.3389/fpos.2025.1634560

Alden, C. (2007). *China in Africa: Partner, competitor or hegemon?*

Ali, N., Mehdi, A., & Ali, K. (2024). China's quiet diplomacy: Assessing its role in Saudi-Iran reconciliation process. *Annals of Human and Social Sciences, 5*(2), 467–479.

Ampiah, K. (2007). *The political and moral imperatives of the Bandung Conference of 1955*. Global Oriental.

Aoun, E., & Kellner, T. (2015). The crises in the Middle East: A window of opportunity for rising China. *European Journal of East Asian Studies, 14*(2), 189–224.

Baldwin, D. A. (1978). Power and interdependence: World politics in transition. By Robert O. Keohane and Joseph S. Nye. (Boston: Little, Brown, 1977. pp. x+ 268. 5.95, paper.). *American Political Science Review, 72*(3), 1165–1168.

Blanchard, J.-M.F., & Hooijmaaijers, B. (2021). Connecting into the social sustainability effects of infrastructure through China's digital silk road: Issues, indices, and indications. *Sustainability, 13*(22), 12739.

Brautigam, D. (2009). *The dragon's gift: The real story of China in Africa*. Oxford University Press.

Brigg, M. (2003). Mediation, power, and cultural difference. *Conflict Resolution Quarterly, 20*(3), 287–306.

Buszynski, L. (1986). Soviet foreign policy and Southeast Asia: Prospects for the Gorbachev Era. *Asian Survey, 26*(5), 591–609.

Buzan, B., & Cox, M. (2013). China and the US: Comparable cases of 'peaceful rise'? *Chinese Journal of International Politics, 6*(2), 109–132.

Calabrese, J. (2006). *China and Iran: Partners perfectly mismatched*. Manuscript. Middle East Institute.

Caporaso, J. A. (1978). Dependence, dependency, and power in the global system: A structural and behavioral analysis. *International Organization, 32*(1), 13–43.

Cardoso, F. H. (1982). Dependency and development in Latin America. In *Introduction to the sociology of "developing societies"* (pp. 112–127). Springer.

Cardoso, F. H., & Faletto, E. (2024). *Dependency and development in Latin America*. University of California Press.

Chun, Z. (2014). China–Zimbabwe Relations: A Model of China–Africa Relations? *The South African Institute of International Affairs*.

Edney, K., Rosen, S., & Zhu, Y. (2020). *Soft power with Chinese characteristics*. Routledge Milton Park, UK.

Ehteshami, A., & Horesh, N. (2017). *China's presence in the Middle East*. Taylor & Francis.

Elliott, I. C., & Roberts, A. (2025). The concept of the strategic state: An assessment after 30 years. *Australian Journal of Public Administration, 84*(3), 558–569.

EPRC. (2023). *Joint trilateral statement by the People's Republic of China, the Kingdom of Saudi Arabia, and the Islamic Republic of Iran*. Retrieved from https://mm.china-embassy.gov.cn/eng/zgxw/202303/t20230311_11039241.htm

Ferdinand, P. (2016). Westward ho—The China dream and 'one belt, one road': Chinese foreign policy under Xi Jinping. *International Affairs, 92*(4), 941–957.

Foot, R., & Walter, A. (2010). *China, the United States, and global order*. Cambridge University Press.

Gause, F. G. (2016). The future of US-Saudi relations: The kingdom and the power. *Foreign Affairs, 95*(4), 114–126.

Gordon, J. (2013). The human costs of the Iran sanctions. *Foreign Policy, 10*(08).

He, K. (2015). Contested regional orders and institutional balancing in the Asia Pacific. *International Politics, 52*(2), 208–222.

He, K., & Feng, H. (2013). *Prospect theory and foreign policy analysis in the Asia Pacific: Rational leaders and risky behavior*. Routledge.

Hurley, J., Morris, S., & Portelance, G. (2018). *Examining the debt implications of the Belt and Road Initiative from a policy perspective*.

Ikenberry, G. J. (2008). The rise of China and the future of the West-Can the liberal system survive. *Foreign Affairs, 87*, 23.

Jones, L., & Zeng, J. (2020). Understanding China's 'belt and road initiative': Beyond 'grand strategy'to a state transformation analysis. In *Rising powers and state transformation* (pp. 19–43). Routledge.

Keohane, R. O., & Nye, J. S., Jr. (1973). Power and interdependence. *Survival, 15*(4), 158–165.

Keohane, R. O., & Nye, J. S. (1977). *Power and interdependence: World Politics in Transition* Boston, Little and Brown.

Mearsheimer, J. (2001). *The tragedy of great power politics/John J. Mearsheimer*. WW Norton & Company.

Norris, W. J. (2016). *Chinese economic statecraft: Commercial actors, grand strategy, and state control*. Cornell University Press.

Nouwens, M., Lons, C., Shehab, N., Malcomson, S., & Neill, A. (2021). *China's digital silk road: Integration into national IT infrastructure and wider implications for Western defence industries*.

Nye, J. (2004). *Soft power: the means to success in world politics*, ed. Public Affairs.

Nye, J. S. (2011). *The future of power*. Public affairs.

Parisa Hafezi, N. A. a. A. E. Y. (2023). Iran and Saudi Arabia agree to resume ties in talks brokered by China. *Reuters*. https://www.reuters.com/world/middle-east/iran-saudi-arabia-agree-resume-ties-re-open-embassies-iranian-state-media-2023-03-10

PRC, M. (2000). *Border dispute between Ethiopia and Eritrea*. Ministry of Foreign Affairs People's Republic of China. Retrieved 12/10/2024 from.

Ross, R. S. (2013). US grand strategy, the rise of China, and US national security strategy for East Asia. *Strategic Studies Quarterly, 7*(2), 20–40.

Sharma, A. (2023). China's soft power in the Middle East. In Y.-C. Kim (Ed.), *China's engagement with the Islamic Nations: A clash or collaboration of modern civilisation?* (pp. 23–40). Springer Nature Switzerland. https://doi.org/10.1007/978-3-031-31042-3_2

Shinn, D. H., & Eisenman, J. (2012). *China and Africa: A century of engagement*. University of Pennsylvania Press.

Tan, S. S., & Acharya, A. (2008). *Bandung revisited: The legacy of the 1955 Asian-African conference for international order*. Nus Press.

Ullah, A. (2023). The implications of Iran-Saudi Arabia deal for regional stability. *China Daily*. https://www.chinadaily.com.cn/a/202303/13/WS640edcc9a31057c47ebb42d9.html

Ullah, A., & Xinlei, L. (2024). Navigating the Persian Gulf security complex: Saudi-Iran rapprochement in an era of great power competition. *East Asia, 41*(3), 273–300. https://doi.org/10.1007/s12140-024-09430-2

Ullah, A., & Xinlei, L. (2025). Systemic constraints and state behavior: A neorealist perspective on China's BRI and Iran's strategic calculations. *Iranian Studies, 58*(3), 526–547. https://doi.org/10.1017/irn.2025.28

Ulrichsen, K. C. (2014). The uprising in Bahrain: Regional dimensions and international consequences. In *Routledge handbook of the Arab Spring* (pp. 133–144). Routledge.

Walt, S. M. (1987). *The origins of alliances*. Cornell University Press.

Wendt, A. (1999). *Social theory of international politics* (Vol. 67). Cambridge University Press.

Zhang, J., & Han, Y. (2013). Testing the rhetoric of China's soft power campaign: A case analysis of its strategic ambiguity in the Six Party Talks over North Korea's nuclear program. *Asian Journal of Communication, 23*(2), 191–208.

Zhang, Y., & Buzan, B. (2012). The tributary system as international society in theory and practice. *Chinese Journal of International Politics, 5*(1), 3–36.

CHAPTER 7

From Bilateral to Regional: How Designed Strategic Interdependence Scales Up

The March 2023 Iran–Saudi Arabia reconciliation, analyzed in detail in Chapter 6, marked a turning point in Middle Eastern diplomacy. Yet to interpret this breakthrough as merely a bilateral diplomatic achievement facilitated by a capable external mediator is to miss its deeper significance. The reconciliation was not an isolated event made possible by skillful Chinese diplomacy at a fortuitous moment, but rather the visible expression of a comprehensive regional architecture that China has systematically constructed over two decades. This architecture transforms individual bilateral relationships into an integrated system of interdependence that operates at regional scale, creating dynamics and possibilities that no single bilateral partnership could generate independently.

The previous chapters established DSI as a framework for understanding how China structures relationships to serve its diplomatic and strategic objectives. Chapters 4 and 5 examined how infrastructure creates embedded leverage in the Saudi and Iranian cases. Chapter 6 demonstrated how China's mediation role derives from years of cultivated relationships with both Iran and Saudi Arabia, built through energy partnerships, infrastructure investments, and institutional engagement. These bilateral case studies revealed crucial mechanisms: how embedded presence generates credibility, how strategic ambiguity preserves flexibility, and how deliberately designed interdependence enables mediation without coercion. Yet examining bilateral relationships in isolation,

A. Ullah, *Diplomacy by Design*,
https://doi.org/10.1007/978-981-95-7876-4_7

however thoroughly, cannot capture the full scope and systematicity of China's regional influence. To understand why China could mediate between Iran and Saudi Arabia requires understanding not just its relationships with each state individually, but how those relationships exist within a broader regional architecture that makes such mediation possible and effective.

China's presence in the Middle East is best understood not as an accumulation of discrete projects or a collection of isolated bilateral relationships, but as a regional architecture: a deliberately structured system of infrastructure, institutions, principles, and sequenced engagement that together constitute a new mode of influence operating simultaneously across multiple dimensions and scales. This architecture differs fundamentally from hegemonic models that have historically characterized great power engagement with contested regions. Unlike American military alliances anchored in forward bases and security guarantees, or Soviet ideological blocs sustained through revolutionary solidarity, China's design is deliberately non-hegemonic. It relies not on coercion that compels compliance, military presence that projects force, or ideological export that demands internal transformation, but on the careful structuring of interdependence that creates mutual vulnerabilities and shared stakes embedded across multiple layers of regional economic, political, and social life.

This chapter argues that understanding China's regional role requires shifting analytical scales from the bilateral to the regional, from examining specific instances of influence to comprehending the comprehensive architecture that makes such influence systematic and durable. The Iran–Saudi reconciliation becomes comprehensible not as diplomatic artistry but as the logical outcome of an architecture in which both parties had become embedded in overlapping networks of Chinese engagement spanning energy, infrastructure, technology, and diplomacy. Their bilateral tensions imposed costs not only on each other but on their respective relationships with their largest Asian partner, creating structural incentives for accommodation that Chinese mediation could activate but did not create ex nihilo.

The chapter unfolds through a progression that moves from concrete to abstract, from what China has built to what these constructions mean for regional order. Section 1 examines the building blocks of China's regional architecture: the ports, railways, pipelines, digital networks, institutional forums, and strategic partnerships that constitute the material and diplomatic foundations of Chinese presence. These are not random commercial ventures pursued opportunistically but deliberately selected and sequenced investments designed to embed China into the region's economic and political fabric while creating constituencies favoring continued cooperation.

Section 2 analyzes how these building blocks interact to create network effects that transcend individual bilateral relationships. When China invests in ports in Oman, Pakistan, and Iran simultaneously, these are not isolated projects but nodes in an integrated maritime network whose strategic value derives from their relationships to one another. When Beijing establishes forums linking it collectively to Arab states and the Gulf Cooperation Council while maintaining differentiated bilateral partnerships, these institutional mechanisms reinforce each other to create redundancy and flexibility. The section demonstrates how bilateral ties, when systematically structured and layered, generate regional-level dynamics including competitive interdependence among regional actors, structural incentives for stability, and distributed constituencies favoring Chinese engagement.

Section 3 addresses a puzzle that any account of China's regional strategy must explain: how Beijing manages simultaneous engagement with intense rivals including Iran and Saudi Arabia, Israel and Palestinian authorities, competing Gulf monarchies, and diverse regional actors with contradictory interests and opposing regional visions. The section examines differentiated engagement as strategic capability, showing how China calibrates relationships according to each partner's specific circumstances, needs, and constraints while preserving the strategic ambiguity essential to its mediating role. This is not contradiction or incoherence but a deliberate design that maximizes diplomatic options and maintains credibility across rival camps.

Section 4 shifts from description to analysis, examining what this regional architecture means for Middle Eastern order and for understanding contemporary great power influence in multipolar contexts. The section argues that China's approach represents neither traditional hegemony nor benign economic integration but something qualitatively distinct: structured interdependence that shapes regional behavior through embedded presence and aligned incentives rather than through coercion or alliance obligations. This has profound implications for regional states' autonomy, for the sustainability of American predominance, and for how scholars and policymakers conceptualize influence in twenty-first century international politics.

The organizing principle throughout is scalar progression: from bilateral building blocks to regional network effects to differentiated management to systemic implications. This progression reflects the chapter's central argument: DSI, introduced and operationalized in previous chapters through bilateral cases, scales up to regional level in ways that fundamentally transform its operation and significance. What works bilaterally becomes more powerful regionally through network effects, redundancy, and the creation of overlapping dependencies that make the architecture resilient to disruption at any single point. Regional scale also introduces new challenges including managing contradictory commitments, preserving strategic ambiguity amid competing demands for alignment, and preventing overextension that might trigger coordinated balancing.

By examining China's regional architecture comprehensively while maintaining analytical clarity through systematic progression from concrete to abstract, this chapter demonstrates that the Iran–Saudi reconciliation was not an anomaly or lucky break but the predictable product of a deliberately constructed system. China did not stumble into a mediating role through commercial opportunism or reactive diplomacy but built the foundations for such a role systematically over decades through patient accumulation of presence, cultivation of credibility, and structuring of interdependence. Understanding this architecture reveals not only how Chinese influence operates in the Middle East but offers broader insights into how power functions in contemporary international politics, where influence increasingly derives from the ability to structure relationships and embed presence rather than from military dominance or ideological coherence. The result is a form of regional order that operates quietly without the visibility of military deployments or alliance formations, yet shapes regional dynamics profoundly by altering the material foundations and institutional contexts within which states make strategic choices.

1 The Building Blocks: What China Has Constructed

China's regional architecture in the Middle East rests on tangible foundations: physical infrastructure that reshapes connectivity, institutional forums that routinize engagement, and strategic partnerships that formalize long-term commitments. These building blocks, constructed systematically over two decades, constitute the material and diplomatic basis through which China has embedded itself into the region's economic and political fabric. Unlike opportunistic commercial ventures pursued for immediate returns, these investments reflect deliberate strategic design aimed at creating enduring presence, generating constituencies favoring cooperation, and establishing the foundations for diplomatic influence. This section examines three categories of building blocks that together form the infrastructure of Chinese regional influence: physical connectivity through ports, railways, pipelines, and digital networks; institutional mechanisms through multilateral forums and bilateral frameworks; and the principles that legitimate and guide engagement.

Physical Infrastructure: Reshaping Regional Connectivity

Energy infrastructure forms the foundational layer of China's physical presence, reflecting Beijing's status as the world's largest energy importer and corresponding vulnerability to supply disruptions. Yet China's energy relationships with the Middle East are not structured as simple bilateral transactions between the buyer and seller but as a deliberately diversified architecture spanning multiple suppliers simultaneously (Garver, 2015). This diversification serves dual strategic purposes: reducing vulnerability to political shocks or conflicts that might disrupt any single supply relationship, while simultaneously generating leverage by ensuring that multiple producers compete for Chinese market share and recognize that antagonizing Beijing risks losing access to the world's most important growth market.

Chinese state-owned enterprises maintain extensive operational presence in Iraqi oil fields, particularly in the southern supergiant fields of Rumaila, West Qurna, and Majnoon that constitute Iraq's primary revenue sources (Mills, 2016). These represent not merely equity stakes or service contracts but deep operational involvement requiring sustained technical coordination, knowledge transfer, and management integration that create enduring dependencies. Simultaneously, China maintains its position as Iran's largest oil customer despite comprehensive American sanctions explicitly designed to isolate Tehran economically, demonstrating commitment that generates Iranian gratitude and structural dependence. China has also become Saudi Arabia's primary energy customer, importing more crude than any other purchaser globally while participating in downstream petrochemical ventures and refining partnerships that deepen interdependence beyond simple commodity exchanges (Ullah & Xinlei, 2025a).

The strategic genius of this triangulation lies in what it prevents: no single state can monopolize Beijing's energy relationships or leverage exclusive access for political advantage. When Iraq, Iran, and Saudi Arabia recognize that confrontation with one another might reduce their respective shares of Chinese demand or trigger Beijing's diversification toward alternative suppliers, they face material incentives to manage tensions and pursue dialogue rather than escalation. This dynamic does not eliminate underlying competition or resolve fundamental political differences, but it structurally alters cost–benefit calculations by making continued restraint economically rational. Energy infrastructure thus functions as material foundation for mediation even before explicit diplomatic initiatives commence.

Maritime infrastructure anchors China's presence along critical sea routes that carry the bulk of Gulf energy exports and connect the region to global markets. The distribution of Chinese-invested ports and logistics facilities creates networks that enhance redundancy while reducing vulnerability to disruption at any single node (Ehteshami & Horesh, 2017, 2019). Table 1 maps the major Chinese-invested maritime nodes and their strategic functions across Middle Eastern geography, revealing how these constitute not isolated commercial ventures but integrated components of regional connectivity architecture.

Duqm's development reflects carefully calibrated strategic and economic choices. Positioned on Oman's Arabian Sea coast, the port sits outside the politically charged waters of the Persian Gulf and provides direct access to international shipping routes without exposing vessels to vulnerabilities of the Strait of Hormuz. Chinese companies, particularly through the Oman Wanfang consortium, have committed substantial investment to establish a large industrial park spanning heavy and light manufacturing, energy projects, and logistics (Al-Sudairi, 2021).

Table 1 China's maritime nodes in the Middle East (2022–2025)

Node/Port	*Location*	*Strategic function*	*Primary activity*	*Chinese investment*	*Partner state*
Duqm	Oman (southern coast)	Alternative to Hormuz; Indian Ocean access	Logistics hub, industrial zone, container terminal	\$10B (Sino-Oman Industrial Park)	Oman
Gwadar	Pakistan (Arabian Sea)	CPEC anchor; energy gateway	Deep-water port, energy hub	\$62B (CPEC total)	Pakistan
Chabahar	Iran (Gulf of Oman)	Ocean access; Afghanistan trade	Port expansion, railway integration	Primarily Indian-led (\$370M); China indirect via \$400B Iran pact	Iran
Bandar Abbas	Iran (Strait of Hormuz)	Strategic chokepoint presence	Energy transport, refining	No major port investment; Chinese-linked logistics/military supplies	Iran
Jizan	Saudi Arabia (Red Sea)	Vision 2030 industrial hub	Manufacturing, export capacity	\$10-11B (Chinese car plant, industrial projects)	Saudi Arabia

Although Duqm features deep-water berths and advanced ship-repair facilities, its functions remain predominantly commercial rather than military, yet its geography enables China to maintain assured access in the northwestern Indian Ocean without visibility or tension that typically accompany deployments deeper inside the Gulf.

In Saudi Arabia, Jizan's transformation under Vision 2030 underscores how maritime infrastructure serves economic, strategic, and diplomatic functions simultaneously. The Jizan City for Primary and Downstream Industries is being developed as a large industrial and export hub with deep Chinese involvement: China Communications Construction Company helped build key port infrastructure, while other Chinese firms invest in downstream industries like petrochemicals and aluminum (JIC, n.d; Yang et al., 2020). Strategically, this gives China a foothold on the Red Sea, a vital maritime corridor. Diplomatically, participation in Jizan ties Beijing into Saudi Arabia's flagship modernization agenda, creating long-term economic interdependence and shared interest in project success.

Transport corridors extend spatial logic beyond energy into broader economic connectivity. The Gulf-Levant corridor concept, though implementation remains partial due to political obstacles, exemplifies corridor diplomacy's strategic potential. The vision encompasses rail and road links extending from the Arabian Peninsula through Iraq and Syria to Mediterranean ports, potentially connecting to Turkish networks and extending to European markets (Fulton, 2022). For Gulf producers, such connectivity would reduce dependence on maritime routes vulnerable to piracy or blockade at critical chokepoints. For Iraq, participation promises transit revenues and infrastructure development in neglected western provinces. For Syria, eventual incorporation would offer pathways toward economic recovery through functional cooperation that sidesteps immediate resolution of political conflicts.

The strategic ingenuity of corridor diplomacy lies in its ability to generate material incentives for cooperation without necessitating formal political concessions. Technical domains such as railway gauges, customs procedures, and border infrastructure standards serve as conduits for addressing political impediments under ostensibly apolitical frameworks. When Iraqi, Saudi, and Syrian officials cannot convene for direct political negotiations due to diplomatic ruptures, they can engage in Chinese-facilitated technical dialogues that implicitly confront the same underlying challenges through functionalist mechanisms.

Digital infrastructure extends spatial logic into cyberspace, creating interdependencies through telecommunications networks, data flows, and technology standards increasingly central to contemporary economic and social functioning. The DSR encompasses not merely physical infrastructure like fiber optic cables and cell towers, but entire technological ecosystems including cloud computing platforms, e-commerce systems, digital payment mechanisms, and smart city technologies that embed Chinese technical standards and create long-term dependencies on Chinese providers (Shen, 2018).

Huawei's construction of 5G networks across Saudi Arabia, the United Arab Emirates, and Iran creates overlapping technological dependencies that transcend political rivalries and operate relatively independently of broader geopolitical tensions. These networks establish technical standards, create compatibility requirements, and generate switching costs that prove prohibitively expensive to reverse without substantial disruption (Eder et al., 2019). Submarine fiber optic cables linking Gulf states to Asian markets and data centers processing regional information flows create additional layers of digital interdependence less visible than ports or railways but equally consequential, as modern economies rely fundamentally on data transmission and storage capabilities.

The strategic significance of digital corridors extends beyond technical capacity to encompass systemic embedding of Chinese technical norms and standards. Once Iranian telecommunications operators adopt Chinese equipment, Saudi planners integrate Chinese smart city platforms, or Gulf financial institutions depend on Chinese cloud infrastructure, these choices generate path dependencies that make alternative systems progressively more costly. Infrastructure operates as a form of quiet standardization: Chinese protocols become default pathways not through coercive imposition but through technical adoption and accumulated investment.

Institutional Forums: Routinizing Regional Engagement

If physical infrastructure provides the material foundations for Chinese presence, institutional forums constitute the diplomatic mechanisms that transform connectivity into political influence. Infrastructure alone, however precisely positioned or strategically calibrated, does not automatically generate leverage or establish mediating authority. Physical presence must be embedded within durable institutional arrangements through which dialogue becomes routinized, cooperation becomes normalized, and economic interdependence generates political capital extending beyond individual transactions.

The CASCF, established in 2004, provides Beijing's broadest institutional platform for collective Arab engagement while simultaneously complementing bilateral relationships rather than substituting for them (Ullah & Xinlei, 2025a). The forum convenes all twenty-two members of the Arab League with China for regular ministerial meetings and periodic summit-level gatherings spanning energy, trade, infrastructure, culture, education, and technology sectors. CASCF's institutional evolution reflects China's expanding regional ambitions. Early iterations concentrated primarily on economic cooperation and cultural exchange while deliberately circumventing politically sensitive issues. The 2016 Arab Policy Paper marked a consequential shift, elevating engagement from primarily commercial arrangements to explicitly political coordination, bringing regional security, counterterrorism cooperation, and coordinated positioning on international issues into forum discussions (SCPRC, 2016).

CASCF's institutional architecture generates strategic effects that distinguish it from purely transactional commercial arrangements. Ministerial meetings provide sustained high-level interaction, maintaining momentum even when specific initiatives encounter obstacles. Sectoral working groups covering energy, infrastructure, and technology create channels for technical bureaucrats to build personal relationships and institutional linkages extending beyond immediate political negotiations (Murphy, 2021). Joint declarations emerging from CASCF meetings offer policy frameworks guiding subsequent bilateral negotiations. The forum thus functions simultaneously as a diplomatic platform and organizational infrastructure, enabling Beijing to maintain its presence across the Arab world while accumulating institutional capital.

The China-Gulf Cooperation Council Strategic Dialogue, provides more focused institutional engagement with the six GCC monarchies while preserving strategic ambiguity central to China's regional positioning (MoFA-PRC, 2010). By engaging Gulf states collectively rather than exclusively through bilateral channels, Beijing can coordinate Gulf diplomacy without appearing to privilege particular actors. This institutional design proves particularly consequential given fundamental tensions among GCC members: Saudi Arabia's aspiration to regional hegemony, UAE's independent strategic ambitions, and Qatar's distinct interests create an environment where exclusive bilateral relationships would compromise Beijing's capacity to operate across all parties simultaneously.

The dialogue format permits China to address issues of collective concern including energy security, infrastructure connectivity, and technology cooperation, while maintaining bilateral relationships differentiated according to specific national priorities (Cheng, 2016). The 2017–2021 Qatar crisis tested this institutional architecture severely. When Saudi Arabia, UAE, Bahrain, and Egypt severed relations with Doha, China maintained productive relationships with all parties, avoided public criticism, and continued economic engagement without allowing regional crisis to disrupt bilateral partnerships (Yenigun et al., 2021). This capacity to operate across divides, preserved by flexibility inherent in dialogue-based architecture, enhanced Beijing's potential mediating role.

Strategic Partnerships: Formalizing Long-Term Commitments

Comprehensive strategic partnerships constitute China's highest tier of bilateral diplomatic relationship, formalizing cooperation across multiple domains simultaneously and signaling long-term commitment extending beyond immediate commercial transactions (He, 2015). Beijing has extended comprehensive strategic partnership designations to Iran, Saudi Arabia, the United Arab Emirates, Egypt, and Algeria. These agreements establish formal frameworks through which cooperation is systematized, bureaucratic mechanisms are institutionalized for coordination, and political momentum is created favoring continued engagement.

China's 25-year CSP with Iran, signed in March 2021, illustrates how these frameworks function as diplomatic anchors embedding parties into sustained cooperation. The agreement covers oil and gas development, infrastructure construction including port and railway development, telecommunications advancement, industrial partnership, and security cooperation. While many details remain deliberately opaque to preserve operational flexibility and avoid triggering additional Western sanctions, the publicly acknowledged elements signal cooperation spanning Iran's most consequential economic sectors. The 25-year timeframe proves particularly significant as diplomatic signal, communicating Beijing's assessment that the relationship merits strategic depth transcending immediate political circumstances.

Equally consequential is the agreement's embedding of China within Iran's most significant economic relationships. Given Iran's extreme international isolation following American withdrawal from the JCPOA, the Chinese partnership becomes structurally central to Tehran's economic survival. China's position deepens further through integrated oil production agreements, infrastructure projects creating operational interdependencies, and technology partnerships in telecommunications that tie Iranian economy to Chinese supply chains. Once embedded in relationships upon which Iranian economic stability partially depends, China acquires influence extending beyond immediate project-level negotiations.

China's deepening partnership with Saudi Arabia demonstrates parallel dynamics operating in contrasting circumstances. Rather than anchoring relationships through isolation-driven dependence, Beijing's Saudi partnership becomes central to the kingdom's most ambitious domestic modernization initiative. Vision 2030, Saudi Arabia's comprehensive program to diversify away from oil dependence, represents a transformation upon which current regime legitimacy substantially rests. China's involvement extends beyond commercial transactions to encompass knowledge transfer, institutional capacity building, technology localization, and industrial partnership integrated throughout Vision 2030's sectoral initiatives (Vaidya, 2023). This involvement creates operational interdependencies requiring sustained cooperation, as project delays or partnership disruption would jeopardize modernization initiatives central to regime legitimacy.

While physical infrastructure and institutional mechanisms constitute tangible building blocks, principles form the conceptual foundations legitimizing China's regional presence and differentiating its approach from Western engagement. Three principles prove particularly consequential: sovereignty, non-interference, and mutual benefit. These function not as abstract ideals articulated for rhetorical ornament but as operational norms that shape engagement patterns, structure regional expectations, and generate credibility that material capabilities alone could not produce (Sun & Zoubir, 2014).

Sovereignty constitutes the foundational principle, operationalized through consistent insistence on respect for national territorial integrity and domestic policy autonomy across all engagement contexts. Joint communiqués from CASCF explicitly reaffirm respect for diverse national development paths. Strategic dialogues with the GCC emphasize national autonomy. Bilateral comprehensive strategic partnerships consistently foreswear political prescriptions, focusing overwhelmingly on infrastructure, energy, and technology while remaining deliberately silent on governance structures or political systems (Zheng, 2016).

This institutionalization through formal agreements and repeated diplomatic practice generates credibility that rhetoric alone could not achieve. When Egypt faced international isolation following the 2013 military coup, China maintained and expanded economic engagement without demanding democratic restoration or publicly condemning the overthrow of elected government (Sun & Xu, 2023). When Saudi Arabia confronted Western criticism over the Khashoggi assassination and Yemen intervention, Chinese cooperation continued unaffected by human rights advocacy that constrained Western partnerships. This behavioral consistency builds credibility valuable when China seeks to mediate conflicts or facilitate accommodation.

Non-interference signifies embedded material and economic presence without overt political control, sustained engagement across infrastructure and trade networks without attempts to dictate governance arrangements (Johnston, 2019). Chinese state-owned enterprises construct ports, railways, and digital networks that become integral to host country infrastructure, yet these entities refrain from demanding policy changes or conditioning continued operation on governance reforms. Beijing engages productively across the full spectrum of regional political systems: absolute monarchies in the Gulf, theocratic republic in Iran, hybrid systems in Egypt and Algeria. This embedded non-interference creates an apparent paradox: Beijing manifests deep material presence yet remains politically unobtrusive, refraining from overt alignment in domestic contests (Ren, 2021).

Mutual benefit as foundational principle deliberately reframes cooperation as reciprocal exchange serving interests of all parties rather than hierarchical relationship benefiting primarily the dominant partner. Chinese investments are consistently presented to generate tangible outcomes: host countries receive infrastructure addressing development needs, technology building productive capacity, and employment generating political support, while China gains market access, energy security, and strategic presence. By structuring projects to deliver benefits extending beyond immediate commercial transactions and emphasizing mutual advantage, Beijing differentiates its engagement from imperial extraction patterns that regional actors remember negatively (Barton, 2018).

Together, these building blocks constitute the material, institutional, and normative foundations of China's regional architecture. Ports, pipelines, and digital networks provide physical connectivity and embedded presence. Forums and partnerships institutionalize relationships and routinize cooperation. Principles generate legitimacy and differentiate Chinese engagement from alternatives that regional actors view skeptically. None of these elements alone would prove sufficient to establish China as a consequential regional actor, but together they create integrated architecture whose strategic significance derives from their systematic integration and mutual reinforcement. The Iran–Saudi reconciliation becomes comprehensible not as isolated diplomatic achievement but as activation of this pre-existing architecture, demonstrating how building blocks constructed over decades can enable breakthrough when political circumstances become propitious.

2 Network Effects: How Building Blocks Create Regional Dynamics

The building blocks examined in Sect. 1—ports, pipelines, forums, partnerships, and principles—constitute more than a collection of discrete investments or relationships. When systematically structured and layered, they generate network effects that transcend individual bilateral ties and create regional-level dynamics qualitatively different from the sum of their parts. A single port might serve local economic needs; multiple ports connected through coordinated investment create redundant maritime networks that reshape regional logistics. A bilateral partnership establishes one relationship; simultaneous partnerships with rivals create triangular dynamics wherein each party's relationship with China affects calculations about relationships with each other. Forums engaging states individually prove consequential; forums engaging rivals collectively create platforms for indirect dialogue and confidence-building that bilateral channels cannot replicate.

This section examines three types of network effects that distinguish China's regional architecture from simple bilateral engagement: competitive interdependence among regional actors who find themselves simultaneously exposed to Chinese economic relationships; structural incentives for stability wherein multiple parties recognize that regional conflict imposes costs on valuable Chinese partnerships; and distributed constituencies favoring continued engagement that operate at subnational, sectoral, and transnational levels, creating resilience against disruption at any single point. Together, these network effects transform China's presence from bilateral relationships that could be managed or terminated independently into a regional system whose strategic significance derives from interconnection and mutual reinforcement.

Competitive Interdependence: When Rivals Share Dependencies

The most consequential network effect generated by China's regional architecture is competitive interdependence: a condition wherein rival states find themselves simultaneously dependent on economic relationships with Beijing, creating calculations about bilateral tensions that must account for potential Chinese reactions and the possibility that conflict might jeopardize valuable partnerships. This dynamic differs fundamentally from traditional alliance politics wherein states align with one external power against another, or from bilateral dependency wherein a single state becomes a subordinate to an external patron. Instead, multiple regional actors across rival camps find themselves embedded in Chinese economic networks simultaneously, creating structural incentives for restraint and accommodation that operate independently of explicit Chinese demands or diplomatic pressure.

The triangulation of Chinese energy relationships with Iran, Iraq, and Saudi Arabia exemplifies this dynamic. As established in Sect. 1, China has become the largest oil customer for both Iran and Saudi Arabia while maintaining extensive operational presence in Iraqi oil fields. This is not accidental overlap but deliberate strategic design that serves Chinese interests in supply diversification while simultaneously creating competitive dynamics among suppliers (Garver, 2015). Each producer recognizes that confrontation with rivals might prompt Chinese diversification toward alternative suppliers, reducing their respective market shares in the world's most important growth market for hydrocarbon demand. This recognition does not eliminate fundamental conflicts of interest or resolve deep-rooted political antagonisms, but it alters cost–benefit calculations by making continued restraint economically rational and escalatory behavior potentially costly.

The Iran–Saudi reconciliation brokered by China occurred within this context of competitive interdependence. Both states had reasons to pursue accommodation rooted in their domestic circumstances and regional calculations, but the timing and format of reconciliation reflected recognition that their mutual hostility imposed costs on relationships with their largest energy customer. Iranian officials recognized that reducing tensions with Saudi Arabia might improve China's willingness to expand investment and technology cooperation, particularly in sensitive sectors where Iranian isolation created risks for Chinese firms. Saudi officials calculated that accommodation with Iran would demonstrate to Beijing the kingdom's commitment to regional stability, potentially strengthening Saudi Arabia's position as China's preferred Gulf partner and generating goodwill valuable for Vision 2030 cooperation.

This competitive interdependence extends beyond energy to encompass infrastructure and technology sectors. When China invests in port development at both Chabahar in Iran and Duqm in Oman, it creates parallel logistics hubs that compete for transit traffic and regional connectivity roles while simultaneously providing China with redundancy and leverage. Iranian authorities recognize that excessive demands or unreliable cooperation might prompt Chinese emphasis on alternative routes through Oman or Pakistan. Omani planners understand that their value to China depends partly on providing alternatives when Iranian routes prove problematic due to sanctions or political tensions. Neither can monopolize Chinese logistics partnerships, and both face incentives to demonstrate reliability and accommodate Chinese preferences to preserve their positions within Chinese networks.

Similarly, China's simultaneous technological partnerships with Saudi Arabia, UAE, and Iran in telecommunications and smart city development create competitive dynamics wherein each seeks to position itself as China's primary Gulf technology partner. Saudi Arabia's Vision 2030 initiatives in renewable energy and digital infrastructure compete with UAE's ambitions to become the region's technology hub, while both compete with Iran's efforts to leverage Chinese technology to mitigate sanctions effects. This competition generates opportunities for China to extract favorable terms and secure access to multiple markets simultaneously, while creating incentives for regional actors to demonstrate cooperation and reliability that might confer advantages over competitors (Eder et al., 2019).

Competitive interdependence proves particularly consequential because it operates continuously rather than episodically. Unlike diplomatic initiatives that mobilize attention during crises and recede during periods of calm, competitive interdependence structures ongoing calculations about economic relationships, infrastructure cooperation, and technology partnerships. Regional actors must continuously assess whether their bilateral tensions with rivals might jeopardize relationships with China, whether accommodation might generate Chinese goodwill translating into expanded cooperation, and whether competitors are positioning themselves more favorably in Beijing's calculations. These assessments occur not during dramatic negotiations but through routine interactions between officials, business communities, and technical specialists who recognize that their individual sectors depend on Chinese markets, investment, or technology.

Structural Incentives for Regional Stability

A second network effect generated by China's regional architecture is the creation of structural incentives for stability that extend beyond bilateral relationships to encompass regional dynamics more broadly. When multiple states across rival camps find themselves economically integrated with China through overlapping infrastructure networks, institutional forums, and strategic partnerships, regional conflict threatens not only bilateral relationships among combatants but also valuable economic ties with Beijing. This creates constituencies within multiple states who recognize that regional instability imposes costs extending beyond immediate security concerns to encompass economic relationships, development projects, and technological cooperation that governments across the region have come to value highly.

The logic operates through several reinforcing mechanisms. Infrastructure investments create sunk costs and operational dependencies that regional conflicts threaten to disrupt. A railway corridor linking multiple states requires cross-border cooperation for maintenance, operations, and regulatory coordination; military conflict disrupts these operations and jeopardizes investments. Port facilities serving regional trade depend on stable shipping routes and predictable customs procedures; conflict creates risks that reduce port utility and threaten profitability. Digital networks spanning multiple countries require technical cooperation and regulatory harmonization; conflict complicates these coordination mechanisms and reduces network value (Shen, 2018).

The Gulf-Levant corridor concept, though implementation remains partial, illustrates how infrastructure creates structural incentives for stability. The envisioned transport links connecting Saudi Arabia through Iraq and Syria to Mediterranean ports would generate substantial economic benefits for all participants: transit revenues for Iraq, reduced dependence on maritime chokepoints for Gulf states, and economic recovery opportunities for Syria (Fulton, 2020). Yet functionality depends on sustained cooperation across borders and political stability in transit countries. Iraqi officials recognize that hosting such infrastructure creates economic opportunities but requires managing relationships with both Saudi Arabia and Iran to prevent conflict from disrupting operations. Syrian authorities understand that participation requires accommodation with regional actors and political stabilization that reassures investors. This creates distributed incentives wherein multiple parties recognize that regional stability serves their interests by enabling infrastructure functionality and preserving economic benefits.

Forums like CASCF and the China-GCC Strategic Dialogue reinforce these infrastructure-based incentives by creating institutional mechanisms through which states can coordinate responses to regional challenges without requiring formal political agreements or explicit commitments. When Yemen conflict threatens Red Sea shipping lanes used by multiple states, CASCF provides the platform for discussing maritime security cooperation without demanding resolution of political disputes that generated the conflict. When sectarian tensions threaten regional stability, the GCC dialogue creates space for coordination on counterterrorism and border security without requiring states to abandon political alignments or compromise on fundamental principles (Murphy, 2021).

These structural incentives prove particularly valuable because they operate independently of Chinese preferences or explicit demands. Beijing does not need to threaten sanctions against states that generate regional instability or promise rewards for maintaining peace. Instead, the architecture creates situations wherein regional actors themselves recognize that conflict imposes costs on relationships they value and that stability creates opportunities for economic cooperation and development. Chinese officials can remain largely silent on regional conflicts while the architecture itself generates pressures toward restraint and accommodation.

The limits of this dynamic warrant acknowledgment. Structural incentives for stability do not prevent all conflicts or resolve deep-rooted political antagonisms. The Yemen war persisted for years despite its disruption of regional trade and infrastructure. Tensions between Israel and Iran continue despite economic costs. Sectarian conflicts in Iraq and Syria have persisted through massive destruction of infrastructure and economies. Structural incentives shape calculations but do not determine outcomes, particularly when security concerns, ideological commitments, or domestic political imperatives override economic considerations. Yet even in these cases, the existence of structural incentives creates constituencies arguing for restraint, generates opportunities for de-escalation when circumstances become propitious, and establishes frameworks through which accommodation can occur when political conditions allow.

Distributed Constituencies and Resilient Networks

A third network effect generated by China's regional architecture is the creation of distributed constituencies favoring continued engagement that operate at multiple levels simultaneously: national governments invested in strategic partnerships, subnational authorities benefiting from infrastructure projects, business communities dependent on Chinese markets or investment, technical specialists trained in Chinese systems, and populations employed in Chinese-funded facilities. This distribution creates resilience wherein disruption of relationships at any single point encounters resistance from multiple constituencies with material interests in maintaining cooperation.

At the national level, governments across the region have become invested in Chinese partnerships through mechanisms examined in Sect. 1. Iran's economic survival depends substantially on Chinese energy purchases and technology cooperation. Saudi Arabia's Vision 2030 modernization relies significantly on Chinese investment and knowledge transfer. Egypt's infrastructure development depends heavily on Chinese financing. UAE's technology ambitions require Chinese partnerships. These dependencies create governmental constituencies favoring continued engagement even when political tensions arise or when domestic critics question the terms of cooperation.

Subnational dynamics reinforce national-level dependencies by creating distributed interests that operate partially independently of central government preferences. Chinese industrial parks in provincial regions of Iran generate employment and economic activity that create local governmental and business constituencies favoring continued cooperation regardless of national-level political calculations. Port development in Oman's Duqm region creates provincial economic interests in maintaining Chinese investment even if national-level strategic calculations might suggest diversification (Al-Sudairi, 2021). Saudi Arabia's Jizan development ties regional economic prospects to continued Chinese participation, creating subnational pressures for maintaining partnerships.

Business communities constitute particularly consequential constituencies given their organizational capacity, political influence, and material stakes in continued cooperation. Chinese and regional business networks spanning energy, logistics, technology, and manufacturing sectors create transnational constituencies with shared interests in maintaining stable economic relationships regardless of political tensions. Saudi Aramco's downstream partnerships with Chinese firms, UAE logistics companies' integration with Chinese e-commerce platforms, and Iranian technology firms' dependence on Chinese equipment create business coalitions that lobby governments to preserve relationships and manage tensions that might disrupt commercial operations.

Technical communities represent a frequently overlooked but strategically significant constituency. Iranian telecommunications operators trained on Chinese equipment, Saudi smart city planners familiar with Chinese platforms, and Gulf energy specialists experienced with Chinese technical standards develop professional identities and career prospects tied to continued Chinese engagement. These technical communities possess specialized knowledge making them valuable to their governments while simultaneously creating personal and professional interests in maintaining systems and partnerships through which they have developed expertise. When political leaders consider reducing Chinese engagement or diversifying toward alternative partners, technical communities often advocate for maintaining existing systems by emphasizing switching costs, integration challenges, and risks of disrupting operational networks (Eder et al., 2019).

The distributed nature of these constituencies creates network resilience wherein disruption at any single point encounters resistance from multiple directions. A government decision to reduce Chinese infrastructure cooperation faces opposition from subnational authorities whose regions benefit from projects, business communities whose commercial interests depend on partnerships, technical specialists whose expertise becomes less valuable, and populations whose employment depends on Chinese-funded facilities. This distributed resistance does not prevent relationship adjustments or guarantee that all Chinese initiatives succeed, but it raises the political costs of dramatic reversals and creates constituencies arguing for continuity and accommodation rather than disruption.

Network Effects and the Iran–Saudi Reconciliation

The network effects examined in this section clarify why the Iran–Saudi reconciliation proved possible in 2023 and why China rather than alternative mediators could facilitate the breakthrough. Competitive interdependence meant that both states recognized their mutual hostility imposed costs not only on bilateral relations but also on valuable relationships with their largest economic partner. Structural incentives for stability created distributed constituencies within both countries recognizing that continued confrontation threatened economic cooperation and development prospects. The existence of institutional platforms like CASCF and the GCC dialogue provided mechanisms through which indirect communication could occur and confidence-building could proceed even during periods of diplomatic rupture.

Yet network effects alone did not produce reconciliation. They created conditions making accommodation rational and facilitated Chinese mediation, but political decisions by Iranian and Saudi leaders to pursue rapprochement reflected their own assessments of costs, benefits, and strategic circumstances. Network effects structured the environment within which those decisions occurred, altering calculations by creating economic stakes in accommodation and reducing the appeal of continued confrontation. They made Chinese mediation credible by demonstrating Beijing's embedded presence in both countries and its capacity to understand their respective concerns and constraints. They provided mechanisms through which dialogue could proceed and commitments could be institutionalized.

The broader significance lies in revealing how bilateral relationships, when systematically structured through overlapping investments, institutions, and partnerships, generate regional dynamics that transcend individual bilateral ties. China's relationships with Iran and Saudi Arabia were not isolated bilateral partnerships but nodes in an integrated regional architecture whose network effects created possibilities for mediation that bilateral relationships alone could not generate. Understanding this architecture requires moving beyond bilateral analysis to examine how relationships interact, how dependencies overlap, and how constituencies distribute across multiple levels and locations to create regional systems whose behavior reflects emergent properties rather than simple aggregation of bilateral components.

This network-level analysis reveals the sophistication of China's regional strategy and the mechanisms through which DSI operates at scale. DSI succeeds not merely by creating bilateral dependencies but by structuring relationships across multiple actors simultaneously in ways that generate competitive dynamics, create shared stakes in stability, and distribute constituencies favoring cooperation. The result is influence that operates through network position and structural incentives rather than through coercion or bilateral leverage, making it simultaneously more subtle and potentially more durable than traditional forms of great power influence that rely on military capabilities or alliance obligations.

3 Differentiated Engagement: Managing Simultaneous Relationships with Rivals

The network effects examined in Sect. 2 reveal how China's building blocks interact to create regional dynamics transcending bilateral relationships. Yet these dynamics generate a strategic puzzle that any account of China's regional architecture must address: how does Beijing maintain simultaneous productive relationships with intense rivals whose interests often conflict directly and whose regional visions prove mutually incompatible? Iran and Saudi Arabia have engaged in proxy conflicts across multiple theaters for decades. Israel and Palestinian authorities remain locked in intractable confrontation. Gulf monarchies experience periodic crises that sever diplomatic ties and impose economic blockades. Turkey, Syria, and Kurdish authorities pursue contradictory objectives amid ongoing conflict. Yet China maintains working relationships across all these divides, engaging rivals simultaneously without triggering demands for exclusive alignment or accusations of betrayal that typically accompany great power involvement in contested regions.

This capacity for differentiated engagement constitutes a distinctive feature of China's regional strategy and proves essential to its mediating role. Differentiated engagement is not contradiction or incoherence but deliberate strategic design that calibrates relationships according to each partner's specific circumstances, needs, and constraints while preserving the strategic ambiguity essential to mediating credibility. Understanding differentiated engagement reveals how DSI operates in complex multipolar environments where influence requires preserving flexibility across competing camps rather than demanding alignment within exclusive blocs.

Calibrated Bilateralism: Tailoring Relationships to Partner Circumstances

China's approach to regional engagement rests on calibrated bilateralism: the structuring of relationships according to each partner's specific political economy, strategic circumstances, and domestic constraints rather than applying uniform templates or demanding conformity to standardized frameworks. This allows Beijing to engage states with radically different governance systems, competing regional ambitions, and contradictory policy preferences without requiring convergence or forcing binary choices between alignment and opposition.

The contrast between China's partnerships with Iran and Saudi Arabia illustrates calibrated bilateralism's operation. Both relationships encompass energy cooperation, infrastructure investment, and technology partnerships, yet their specific configurations differ fundamentally according to each state's circumstances. For Iran, operating under comprehensive Western sanctions and facing acute international isolation, China represents an economic lifeline providing market access, technology cooperation, and financial mechanisms that enable survival of the Islamic Republic's political economy. The 25-year CSP reflects this reality: cooperation extends across sectors essential to Iranian economic functioning, from oil exports to infrastructure development to telecommunications, creating dependencies wherein Chinese engagement becomes structurally necessary rather than merely beneficial (Ullah & Xinlei, 2025b).

Yet China calibrates this relationship to account for Iranian political sensitivities and regime preferences. Beijing refrains from demanding governance reforms, accepts opacity regarding implementation timelines and project specifications that would prove unacceptable in more transparent partnerships, and maintains engagement despite sanctions risks that deter most international actors. This calibration recognizes that Iran's value to China derives partly from its willingness to defy Western pressure, its geographic position connecting Central Asia to the Gulf, and its role in demonstrating that Chinese partnerships offer alternatives to Western-dominated systems. The relationship is structured to exploit these asymmetries while managing risks through deliberate ambiguity about commitments and flexible implementation that accommodates Iranian unpredictability and sanctions complications.

Saudi Arabia's partnership, by contrast, operates from a position of relative confidence and strategic choice rather than survival necessity. The kingdom possesses vast financial resources, maintains sophisticated relationships with multiple powers simultaneously, and approaches Chinese engagement as complement to rather than substitute for Western partnerships. Vision 2030's modernization agenda creates demand for Chinese investment, technology, and expertise, but Saudi Arabia negotiates from strength, extracting technology transfer provisions, joint venture requirements, and training commitments that reflect bargaining power unavailable to more vulnerable partners (Vaidya, 2023). China calibrates this relationship accordingly, accepting Saudi demands for transparency, providing high-quality technology and management expertise, and tolerating Saudi hedging that maintains strong security ties with the United States even while expanding economic cooperation with Beijing.

The key insight is that these relationships, though addressing similar sectors and employing comparable instruments, operate according to different logics reflecting different power dynamics and strategic circumstances. Iran receives essential support enabling survival; Saudi Arabia receives valued cooperation accelerating modernization. Iran accepts terms reflecting limited alternatives; Saudi Arabia negotiates terms reflecting substantial bargaining power. Yet both relationships serve Chinese interests by embedding Beijing in the region's two most consequential states across rival camps, creating the foundation for mediation that bilateral relationships structured identically could not provide.

Calibrated bilateralism extends beyond these prominent cases to encompass the full range of China's regional partnerships. Egypt receives infrastructure financing addressing acute developmental needs and government legitimacy concerns, calibrated to operate despite political instability and governance challenges that deter many investors. The UAE receives technology partnerships supporting its ambitions to become a regional innovation hub, calibrated to acknowledge Emirati sophistication and integrate with existing Western partnerships rather than demanding exclusive alignment. Iraq receives energy sector investment operating despite severe political instability and governance dysfunction, calibrated to accept risks and delays that would prove unacceptable in more stable environments. Qatar receives infrastructure cooperation expanding post-blockade, calibrated to demonstrate Chinese reliability during crisis while avoiding pressure to choose between GCC relationships and Chinese partnerships (Havlová, 2020).

Strategic Ambiguity: Avoiding Exclusive Alignment

If calibrated bilateralism structures individual relationships according to partner circumstances, strategic ambiguity governs how China positions itself across competing camps and conflicting interests. Strategic ambiguity is not indecision, inconsistency, or diplomatic weakness but deliberate maintenance of flexibility that preserves options, avoids entanglement in conflicts beyond Chinese core interests, and sustains mediating credibility by preventing perception of alignment with particular parties against others.

China's management of Iran–Saudi tensions prior to the 2023 reconciliation exemplifies strategic ambiguity's operation. Throughout years of proxy conflicts, diplomatic rupture, and escalating regional tensions, Beijing maintained productive relationships with both states while carefully avoiding public positioning that would suggest alignment with either party's grievances or regional vision. When conflicts in Yemen or Syria intensified, China abstained from UN Security Council votes requiring choices between competing resolutions favored by different sides, maintaining neutrality that frustrated both parties but preserved flexibility. When Iran faced maximum pressure sanctions, China maintained economic engagement but avoided comprehensive diplomatic support that would signal complete alignment with Tehran against Riyadh. When Saudi Arabia sought support for regional initiatives, China participated selectively without endorsing positions that would antagonize Iran (Christensen, 2011).

This sustained ambiguity generated credibility that proved essential when mediation opportunities emerged. Both Tehran and Riyadh had observed China maintain balanced relationships despite intense pressure from both sides to align more clearly. This track record of ambiguity, combined with material reality that both capitals depended substantially on Chinese economic relationships, created conditions wherein both sides could accept Chinese mediation without fearing that Beijing would exploit the process to advance partisan interests. The 2023 reconciliation reflected not sudden Chinese diplomatic initiative but activation of credibility accumulated through years of strategic ambiguity that established Beijing as the acceptable facilitator to both parties (Ullah & Xinlei, 2024).

Strategic ambiguity operates similarly across other regional divides. China maintains working relationships with both Israel and Palestinian authorities while carefully managing rhetoric and avoiding actions that would force binary choices. Beijing provides rhetorical support for Palestinian rights and two-state solutions, satisfying Arab partners and demonstrating solidarity with the developing world's anti-colonial positioning. Simultaneously, China expands economic and technology cooperation with Israel, importing advanced technology, attracting Israeli investment, and participating in joint research ventures. This apparent contradiction functions as deliberate ambiguity: neither relationship requires abandoning the other, and both parties accept Chinese engagement across the divide because they recognize that demanding exclusivity would likely prompt Chinese disengagement rather than alignment (Olimat, 2012).

During the 2017–2021 Qatar blockade, when Saudi Arabia, UAE, Bahrain, and Egypt severed relations with Doha and imposed comprehensive economic isolation, China maintained relationships with all parties without taking positions on the underlying disputes. Chinese officials avoided public criticism of the blockade that might antagonize the blockading states, while maintaining economic engagement with Qatar that demonstrated Beijing would not abandon partners facing regional pressure. This positioned China uniquely when reconciliation occurred in 2021, as all parties recognized that Beijing had preserved relationships and avoided alignment despite intense pressure to choose sides (Yenigun et al., 2021).

The strategic value of ambiguity derives from several sources. First, it preserves diplomatic flexibility by avoiding commitments that might constrain options during future contingencies or crises. Second, it prevents entanglement in regional conflicts whose outcomes China cannot control and whose escalation might threaten Chinese interests. Third, it maintains credibility across rival camps by demonstrating that Beijing evaluates relationships according to Chinese interests rather than regional alignments. Fourth, it enables mediation by establishing Beijing as the acceptable facilitator precisely because it has not aligned exclusively with any party's position.

Institutional Mechanisms: Engaging Rivals Through Multilateral Platforms

Multilateral forums provide institutional mechanisms through which China can engage rivals simultaneously while managing tensions that bilateral engagement might exacerbate. CASCF and the China-GCC Strategic Dialogue create platforms where states maintaining strained bilateral relationships can interact through collective mechanisms, preserving communication channels even when direct dialogue proves politically difficult. This institutional design transforms rivalry from zero-sum competition for Chinese favor into overlapping engagement wherein multiple parties participate in forums addressing shared interests while maintaining distinct bilateral relationships reflecting national circumstances (Murphy, 2021).

CASCF brings together all Arab League members including states with deeply antagonistic relationships: Saudi Arabia and Iran both participate despite their rivalry, Syria and states that backed opposition forces during the civil war engage collectively despite ongoing tensions, and GCC members who experienced the Qatar blockade maintain forum participation despite periodic bilateral crises. The forum's focus on functional cooperation including energy security, infrastructure development, and technology transfer creates space for interaction on shared interests without requiring resolution of political disputes or demands for bilateral reconciliation as prerequisite for participation (Yao, 2014).

The strategic genius of this institutional design lies in creating overlapping rather than exclusive engagement patterns. States do not face choices between Chinese partnerships and relationships with rivals; instead, they participate in collective forums while maintaining differentiated bilateral relationships. This institutional structure reinforces strategic ambiguity by preventing exclusive alignment while creating regular occasions for interaction that can build confidence and identify areas of potential cooperation even amid ongoing political tensions.

The China-GCC Strategic Dialogue operates similarly, engaging all six Gulf monarchies collectively while acknowledging their diverse interests and periodic tensions. During the Qatar blockade, the dialogue continued despite the crisis, with China engaging both Qatar and the blockading states without suspending collective consultations. This demonstrated that regional conflicts need not disrupt Chinese engagement and that institutional mechanisms could persist through crises that severed other diplomatic channels. The dialogue's continuation signaled to all parties that maintaining relationships with China did not require resolving intra-GCC disputes and that Beijing would preserve engagement across divides (Cheng, 2016).

While differentiated engagement has enabled China to maintain relationships across rival camps and establish mediating credibility, it also generates tensions and encounters limits that constrain its effectiveness and sustainability. Three tensions prove particularly consequential: the challenge of maintaining ambiguity as relationships deepen and partners demand greater commitment; the risk that deepening ties with one party alienate rivals and undermine mediating credibility; and the difficulty of managing contradictory expectations as partners develop incompatible interpretations of Chinese commitments.

The first tension emerges as relationships deepen and partners begin demanding clearer commitments. Strategic ambiguity functions effectively when relationships remain primarily economic and technical, but as engagement extends into security cooperation and political coordination, ambiguity becomes harder to sustain. Iran's 25-year partnership includes security provisions that signal substantial Chinese commitment, potentially concerning Saudi Arabia about Chinese alignment with its primary regional rival. Saudi Arabia's expanding defense cooperation with China, while remaining modest compared to American partnerships, nonetheless generates Iranian concerns about Chinese military ties with the kingdom's adversary (Ullah & Xinlei, 2025b).

These tensions have not yet produced relationship crises or forced China into exclusive alignments, but they illustrate how differentiated engagement becomes progressively more difficult as relationships deepen across multiple dimensions. At some point, partners may demand clarity about Chinese commitments or present situations requiring Beijing to choose sides in ways that ambiguity cannot manage. A major military conflict between Iran and Saudi Arabia, Israeli strikes against Iranian nuclear facilities, or Gulf security crises requiring external involvement might force China into positions that alienate one party despite efforts to maintain balance.

The second tension involves the risk that deepening engagement with one party undermines relationships with rivals. China's extensive cooperation with Iran, particularly in sensitive technology sectors like telecommunications and surveillance systems, generates concerns among Gulf states about Chinese support for their adversary. Conversely, Chinese participation in Saudi Vision 2030 and expanding GCC partnerships create Iranian anxieties about Beijing prioritizing relationships with wealthier Gulf monarchies at Tehran's expense. While China has thus far managed these tensions through calibrated engagement that provides sufficient reassurance to both sides, the potential for alienation increases as commitments deepen and as regional conflicts intensify pressures for alignment.

The third tension emerges from contradictory partner expectations about Chinese commitments. Iran interprets the 25-year partnership as signaling substantial Chinese commitment to Iranian security and economic development, expecting Beijing to resist Western pressure for sanctions enforcement and to expand cooperation despite risks. Saudi Arabia interprets its expanding partnership as signaling Chinese recognition of the kingdom's regional centrality and expects Beijing to maintain balanced relationships that don't empower Iranian adversaries. These interpretations are not fully compatible, and situations could arise wherein satisfying one party's expectations alienates the other.

These tensions suggest that differentiated engagement, while effective under current conditions, operates within constraints that could tighten as relationships deepen, regional conflicts intensify, or partners demand greater clarity about Chinese commitments. The sustainability of China's approach depends on Beijing's ability to continue managing these tensions through calibrated engagement, strategic ambiguity, and institutional mechanisms that distribute relationships across multilateral and bilateral channels. It also depends on regional actors' continued acceptance of ambiguity and their calculation that maintaining relationships with China despite its engagement with rivals serves their interests better than demanding exclusive alignment or abandoning partnerships altogether.

Differentiated engagement is not peripheral to China's regional architecture but constitutes an essential feature enabling its operation and success. The capacity to engage rivals simultaneously allows China to embed itself across competing camps, creating the overlapping dependencies that generate network effects and structural incentives for stability. The maintenance of strategic ambiguity preserves mediating credibility that proves essential when opportunities for facilitation arise. The calibration of relationships according to partner circumstances enables China to address diverse needs and constraints without requiring conformity to uniform templates that would prove unacceptable to states with radically different political economies and strategic circumstances.

Understanding differentiated engagement reveals the sophistication of DSI at regional scale. The framework succeeds not by creating uniform dependencies or imposing standardized relationships but by structuring diverse engagements that together create an integrated architecture whose strategic value derives from its flexibility, redundancy, and capacity to accommodate contradiction. China's regional presence proves durable precisely because it does not require exclusive alignment, does not demand resolution of political disputes, and does not force binary choices that would trigger resistance or balancing behavior.

The Iran–Saudi reconciliation becomes fully comprehensible only when viewed through this lens of differentiated engagement. China could mediate not despite maintaining relationships with both rivals but because it had structured those relationships in ways that created mutual exposure while preserving sufficient ambiguity to remain acceptable to both parties. The reconciliation reflected not diplomatic breakthrough achieved through superior negotiating skills but careful management of differentiated relationships over extended periods that created conditions making mediation feasible when political circumstances became propitious. This is DSI operating at regional scale through mechanisms that embrace rather than resolve contradiction, that leverage rather than eliminate rivalry, and that succeed through ambiguity rather than clarity.

4 Regional Reconfiguration: What China's Architecture Means for Middle Eastern Order

The building blocks, network effects, and differentiated engagement examined in previous sections constitute not merely description of Chinese activities but reveal a fundamental reconfiguration of how power operates in the Middle East. For over seven decades, regional order has been structured primarily through American military predominance, alliance networks, and security guarantees that established hierarchies, constrained options, and shaped strategic calculations. This American-led architecture, while contested and never fully stable, provided the scaffolding within which regional states navigated rivalries, managed conflicts, and pursued their interests. China's expanding presence does not simply add another external actor to an existing system but introduces qualitatively different mechanisms of influence that operate through embedded interdependence rather than military dominance, through structured incentives rather than alliance obligations, and through strategic ambiguity rather than explicit commitments.

Enhanced Autonomy Through Strategic Hedging

Perhaps the most immediate consequence of China's regional architecture is the enhanced capacity for strategic hedging that it provides to regional actors. Historically, Middle Eastern states faced pressures to align with competing external powers, accepting security guarantees and economic partnerships that came bundled with political expectations and constraints on policy autonomy. During the Cold War, alignment with the United States or Soviet Union carried ideological baggage, alliance obligations, and expectations of loyalty that limited flexibility. In the post-Cold War era, American predominance created pressures for alignment with Washington's regional preferences, from support for peace processes to cooperation on counterterrorism to acquiescence in sanctions policies.

China's presence transforms this dynamic by providing alternatives that enable diversification without requiring abandonment of existing relationships or exclusive alignment with new partners. Regional states can now pursue what might be termed portfolio diversification in their external relationships: maintaining security partnerships with the United States while expanding economic cooperation with China, preserving access to Western technology while incorporating Chinese systems, and participating in American-led initiatives while engaging Chinese forums and partnerships. This diversification enhances autonomy by reducing dependence on any single external power and creating competition among external actors that regional states can leverage for better terms and greater flexibility (Guzansky, 2014).

Saudi Arabia's strategic trajectory exemplifies this dynamic. The kingdom maintains its security partnership with the United States including arms purchases, military cooperation, and intelligence sharing that remain foundational to Saudi defense capabilities. Yet it simultaneously expands economic ties with China spanning energy, infrastructure, technology, and financial cooperation that have become essential to Vision 2030's success. This dual engagement enables Saudi Arabia to resist American pressure on issues where interests diverge, from oil production levels to regional diplomacy to human rights practices, while assuring Washington that the security relationship remains viable. It provides Saudi Arabia with alternatives that enhance bargaining power with both partners while avoiding exclusive dependence on either (Ullah & Xinlei, 2025a).

The United Arab Emirates pursues even more sophisticated hedging, maintaining security partnerships with the United States and emerging defense cooperation with France while expanding technology partnerships with China, preserving Western financial ties while exploring yuan-denominated transactions, and participating in American initiatives while engaging Chinese forums. This multi-alignment strategy reflects Emirati recognition that autonomy in the twenty-first century derives not from exclusive alignment with the strongest power but from the capacity to operate across multiple partnerships simultaneously without forcing binary choices that would constrain flexibility (Ulrichsen, 2016).

Even states with closer alignments to particular external powers find that China's presence expands their room for maneuver. Egypt, despite receiving substantial American military assistance and maintaining close security cooperation with Washington, has significantly expanded Chinese infrastructure partnerships and economic cooperation that provide alternatives when American support proves insufficient or comes with unacceptable conditions. When American military assistance faced congressional restrictions following the 2013 coup, Egyptian officials could point to Chinese alternatives as leverage in negotiations with Washington. Qatar, facing the 2017 blockade from neighbors allied with the United States, found that Chinese engagement provided economic alternatives and diplomatic support that reduced vulnerability to regional pressure (Havlová, 2020).

This enhanced hedging capacity generates several consequential effects for regional order. First, it reduces the coercive leverage that any single external power can exert through threats of abandonment or economic pressure. When regional states possess alternatives, threats become less credible and demands become more negotiable. Second, it creates competitive dynamics among external powers wherein each must offer better terms to preserve relationships, potentially benefiting regional actors through improved partnerships. Third, it enables regional states to pursue interests that might diverge from preferences of their primary external partners without risking catastrophic consequences, as alternatives provide insurance against abandonment.

Yet enhanced autonomy through hedging also introduces instability and uncertainty into regional order. When commitments become ambiguous and alignments become fluid, crisis management becomes more complex and miscalculation risks increase. External powers become less certain about regional partners' reliability during crises, potentially leading to either overcommitment to demonstrate credibility or retrenchment to avoid entrapment. Regional actors face temptations to exploit external competition in ways that could trigger backlash or overreach in ways that undermine relationships with multiple partners simultaneously. The system becomes more multipolar but potentially less stable, as established hierarchies erode without clear replacement frameworks emerging.

Challenging Traditional Security Architectures

China's regional architecture challenges traditional security models based on military alliances, forward presence, and explicit security guarantees that have structured Middle Eastern order since World War II. The American-led security system rests on formal alliances with Israel, extensive basing arrangements in Qatar, Bahrain, Kuwait, and UAE, arms sales creating dependencies and interoperability, and explicit security guarantees that deter aggression while constraining partner behavior. This military-centric architecture has provided stability through deterrence while generating resentment through perceived subordination and creating vulnerabilities through dependence on American commitments whose reliability fluctuates with domestic politics and competing global priorities (Campbell & Ratner, 2018).

China offers an alternative model that operates through economic interdependence rather than military alliances, through embedded presence rather than forward bases, and through structural incentives rather than explicit guarantees. This model proves attractive to regional actors for several reasons. It avoids the sovereignty costs associated with hosting foreign military bases or accepting subordinate positions within alliance hierarchies. It reduces vulnerability to shifts in external powers' domestic politics or strategic priorities that might lead to sudden changes in security commitments. It enables engagement with multiple external actors simultaneously without triggering zero-sum competition or demands for exclusive alignment. And it allows regional states to preserve autonomy in decision-making while still benefiting from external engagement.

Yet China's model also possesses significant limitations that prevent it from fully substituting for traditional security architectures. Most fundamentally, economic interdependence cannot provide the deterrence that military alliances offer against immediate security threats. When states face military aggression, invasion threats, or coercive pressure from regional adversaries, infrastructure partnerships and energy relationships provide limited immediate protection. China's limited military presence in the region and explicit reluctance to provide security guarantees mean that its model offers structural incentives for stability but not immediate deterrence against aggression (Ghiasy & Zhou, 2022).

This creates a paradoxical situation wherein China's economic model proves attractive for its flexibility and respect for autonomy, yet regional states still require traditional security relationships to address immediate threats. The result is a hybrid order wherein states pursue economic diversification toward China while maintaining security dependencies on the United States, creating complex balancing acts and potential tensions if American and Chinese interests diverge sharply. Table 2 maps this hybrid engagement pattern across key regional actors, revealing how states calibrate military and economic relationships according to threat perceptions and developmental priorities.

The table reveals several patterns with profound implications for regional order. First, security and economic partnerships increasingly diverge rather than reinforce each other, creating potential tensions if American and Chinese interests conflict sharply. Second, states with greater threat perceptions (Saudi Arabia facing Iran, UAE managing regional instability) maintain stronger American security ties despite Chinese economic expansion, while states with lower immediate threats (Egypt, Qatar) can pursue more balanced engagement. Third, Iran represents an exceptional case wherein sanctions-driven isolation forces alignment with China economically while maintaining security ties with Russia, creating triangular dynamics distinct from other regional patterns.

This hybrid order proves stable under current conditions wherein American and Chinese interests in regional stability largely align and wherein both powers accept divided influence spheres. Yet several scenarios could destabilize this arrangement. Intensifying Sino-American competition could force regional states to choose between partners, undermining hybrid strategies and potentially fracturing the region into competing camps. Major conflicts requiring external intervention could expose the limitations of China's economic model while testing American willingness to honor security commitments. Domestic political changes in the United States could produce retrenchment that forces regional states to seek alternative security arrangements, potentially drawing China into military roles it has historically avoided.

Competitive Coexistence: American and Chinese Models

The most consequential implication of China's regional architecture is the emergence of competitive coexistence between fundamentally different models of external engagement. The American model operates through military alliances, explicit security guarantees, forward presence, and political partnerships that historically came bundled with governance expectations and ideological preferences. The Chinese model operates

Table 2 Hybrid engagement patterns in the Middle East

State	*Primary Security Partner*	*Security Dependencies*	*Primary Economic Partner*	*Economic Focus*	*Hedging Strategy*
Saudi Arabia	United States	Arms sales ($100B+); intelligence sharing; military training; deterrence guarantee	China	Energy exports (18% of oil exports); Vision 2030 investment ($10-20B); technology transfer	Maintain US security umbrella while diversifying economic relationships; leverage Chinese investment to enhance autonomy
UAE	United States / France	F-35 purchases; Al Dhafra air base; naval access; defense industrial cooperation	China	Technology partnerships; logistics hub for Chinese goods; smart city development; AI cooperation	Sophisticated multi-alignment; balance Western security with Chinese technology/ economic ties
Egypt	United States	$1.3B annual military aid; weapons systems; training programs; strategic cooperation	China	Infrastructure financing ($20B +); Suez Canal economic zone; technology imports	Use Chinese investment to offset aid conditionality; maintain US military ties for regime security
Iran	Russia/ China	Russian arms sales; military cooperation in Syria; air defense systems; strategic coordination	China	Oil exports (primary market); infrastructure investment ($400B framework); technology cooperation	Forced alignment due to sanctions; seek to balance Russia-China to preserve autonomy

(continued)

Table 2 (continued)

State	*Primary Security Partner*	*Security Dependencies*	*Primary Economic Partner*	*Economic Focus*	*Hedging Strategy*
Iraq	United States (limited)	Training mission; counterterrorism; limited arms sales; advisory role	China	Oil field development ($3B +); infrastructure reconstruction; energy sector dominance	Maximize Chinese economic engagement while managing US political influence
Qatar	United States	Al Udeid air base (largest US base in region); arms purchases; security cooperation	China	LNG exports; infrastructure investment; post-blockade economic diversification	Use Chinese alternatives to resist regional pressure; maintain US security guarantee

through economic interdependence, infrastructure embedding, institutional forums, and pragmatic partnerships that deliberately avoid governance conditionality and ideological export. These models compete for influence while simultaneously coexisting as regional states engage both powers through hybrid strategies examined above.

This competitive coexistence generates several dynamics that distinguish contemporary regional order from Cold War bipolarity or post-Cold War American unipolarity. Unlike Cold War competition wherein states aligned with one superpower or the other in relatively stable blocs, contemporary competition allows simultaneous engagement with both powers through differentiated relationships. Unlike post-Cold War unipolarity wherein American preferences largely structured regional behavior, contemporary multipolarity enables regional actors to play powers against each other and resist pressures from either side. The result is a more fluid but also more complex order wherein influence derives not from military dominance or alliance hierarchies but from the ability to provide valued services, accommodate diverse interests, and adapt to changing circumstances (Acharya, 2014).

Figure 1 visualizes this transformation from Cold War bipolarity through post-Cold War unipolarity to contemporary multipolar competition, illustrating how regional actors' engagement patterns have evolved from exclusive alignment to hybrid strategies that engage multiple external powers simultaneously.

The figure illustrates three distinct eras. During the Cold War, regional states aligned relatively firmly with either American or Soviet camps, creating stable but rigid blocs. Post-Cold War unipolarity concentrated relationships around American partnerships, creating hierarchical but relatively coherent order. Contemporary multipolarity enables hybrid engagement wherein states maintain differentiated relationships with multiple external powers simultaneously, creating fluid but complex arrangements.

This competitive coexistence produces several observable effects on regional behavior. Regional states increasingly frame relationships with external powers as commercial partnerships rather than alliance commitments, reducing political obligations and enhancing flexibility. States explicitly pursue hedging strategies that distribute relationships across multiple powers, publicly articulating this as prudent risk management rather than disloyalty. Institutional forums multiply as regional states engage different external powers through differentiated platforms, creating overlapping rather than exclusive memberships. And normative discourse shifts toward emphasizing sovereignty and non-interference as principles legitimizing simultaneous engagement with powers whose governance models and international visions differ fundamentally.

These shifts create both opportunities and challenges. Opportunities include enhanced autonomy for regional states, competitive dynamics that potentially improve terms of engagement, and institutional pluralism that creates alternatives when particular partnerships prove problematic. Challenges include reduced reliability of security commitments when alignment becomes ambiguous, increased complexity of crisis management when interests and obligations prove unclear, and risks of miscalculation when states overestimate their capacity to balance competing relationships or when external powers underestimate partners' willingness to shift alignments.

Implications for Theorizing Contemporary Power

The reconfiguration of regional order examined in this section carries profound implications for how scholars and policymakers conceptualize power and influence in twenty-first century international politics. Traditional theories of power emphasize military capabilities, alliance hierarchies, and coercive instruments that compel desired behavior through

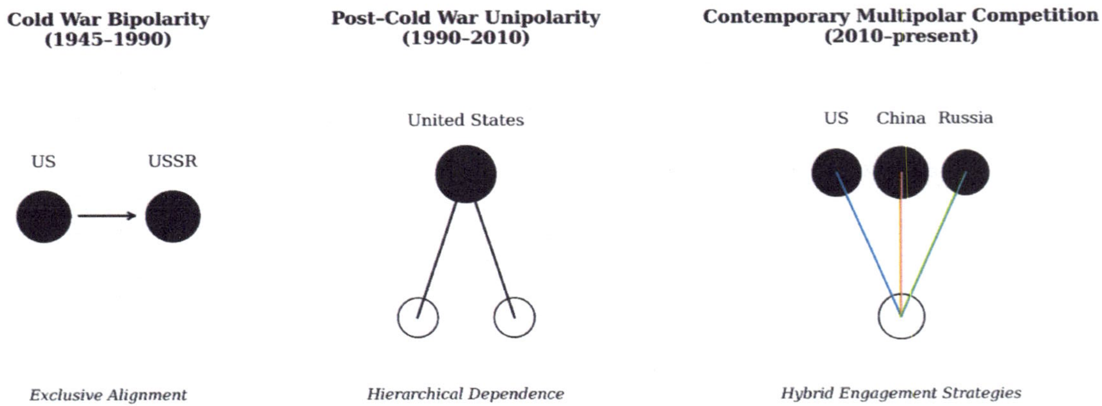

Fig. 1 Evolution of external power engagement patterns in the Middle East

threatened punishment or promised rewards. Yet China's regional architecture demonstrates that influence can operate effectively through alternative mechanisms that eschew coercion in favor of embedded presence, eschew alliances in favor of strategic ambiguity, and eschew conditionality in favor of pragmatic engagement.

The concept of DSI developed throughout this book provides analytical vocabulary for understanding these alternative mechanisms. DSI captures how influence derives not from military dominance or ideological coherence but from the deliberate structuring of relationships that create mutual vulnerabilities, shared stakes in stability, and constituencies favoring cooperation. It explains how power operates through network position rather than hierarchical control, through structural incentives rather than explicit commands, and through accumulated credibility rather than immediate leverage. It reveals how influence compounds over time through patient cultivation of relationships rather than materializing suddenly through decisive interventions.

The Middle Eastern case demonstrates DSI's operation at the regional scale and reveals several insights applicable beyond this specific context. First, influence increasingly derives from the ability to engage rivals simultaneously without triggering zero-sum competition, suggesting that strategic ambiguity and differentiated engagement constitute valuable capabilities in multipolar contexts where exclusive alignment proves counterproductive. Second, infrastructure and economic interdependence can generate political leverage comparable to military capabilities and alliance obligations when deliberately structured to create dependencies and constituencies, suggesting that twenty-first century statecraft requires attention to material embedding alongside traditional instruments of power. Third, mediating capacity derives not primarily from neutral positioning or superior diplomatic skills but from embedded presence that creates credibility and relationships with all parties, suggesting that influence requires long-term cultivation rather than episodic intervention.

These insights challenge assumptions embedded in much contemporary international relations scholarship and policy analysis. Realist theories emphasizing military capabilities and alliance systems as foundations of influence struggle to account for China's success in mediating between Iran and Saudi Arabia without possessing significant military presence or alliance networks in the region. Liberal theories emphasizing normative attraction and institutional frameworks cannot fully explain how China achieves influence despite limited soft power appeal and operating through informal rather than legalized institutions. Constructivist accounts highlighting identity and shared norms face difficulties explaining how China builds relationships across sectarian, ideological, and political divides that define regional identities.

DSI provides an alternative framework that integrates insights from these approaches while addressing their limitations. Like realism, it recognizes that power matters and that states pursue interests strategically. Yet it shows that power derives not only from military capabilities but from structural positioning and embedded presence. Like liberalism, it emphasizes how interdependence constrains conflict and creates incentives for cooperation. Yet it demonstrates that interdependence must be deliberately designed rather than emerging organically to serve strategic objectives effectively. Like constructivism, it acknowledges that norms and principles matter for legitimizing engagement and shaping expectations. Yet it reveals that principles function strategically rather than merely reflecting ideational commitments, serving to differentiate approaches and generate credibility rather than expressing authentic normative consensus.

Table 3 synthesizes these theoretical implications by comparing traditional and DSI-based approaches across key dimensions of power and influence, revealing how China's regional architecture embodies distinctive mechanisms that challenge conventional wisdom while offering frameworks for understanding contemporary international politics.

The table reveals systematic differences between approaches that help explain both China's successes and its limitations. Traditional approaches emphasizing military capabilities and alliance hierarchies correctly identify that China lacks the coercive instruments and formal commitments that have historically defined great power influence. Yet they fail to recognize alternative mechanisms through which influence operates in contemporary contexts. DSI-based approaches illuminate these alternative mechanisms while acknowledging that they cannot fully substitute for traditional instruments in all contexts. The result is a more nuanced understanding that recognizes multiple pathways to influence operating simultaneously in complex regional environments.

The reconfiguration of Middle Eastern order examined in this section represents not peripheral commercial expansion but fundamental transformation in how external powers engage contested regions and how regional actors navigate their external relationships. China's architecture creates possibilities for autonomous action, hedging strategies, and institutional pluralism that did not exist under American-dominated order. Yet

Table 3 Comparative framework for understanding power and influence

Dimension	*Traditional approach*	*DSI Approach*	*Middle East application*
Source of Influence	Military capabilities; alliance networks; coercive threats	Embedded presence; structured interdependence; network position	China influences through economic centrality, infrastructure control, institutional platforms rather than military force
Mechanism of Control	Command and compliance; conditionality; explicit demands	Structural incentives; altered calculations; constituency creation	Regional actors align with China because cooperation serves interests, not because Beijing demands it
Relationship Structure	Hierarchical; exclusive alignment; patron-client dynamics	Network-based; overlapping dependencies; ambiguous commitments	China engages rivals simultaneously; states maintain hybrid relationships with multiple powers
Temporal Logic	Immediate leverage; crisis response; episodic intervention	Long-term cultivation; cumulative effects; sustained presence	China's mediation reflects decades of relationship-building, not sudden diplomatic initiative
Legitimation Strategy	Ideological alignment; normative coherence; shared values	Pragmatic engagement; sovereignty respect; mutual benefit	China appeals through non-interference and respect for autonomy rather than governance models
Strategic Objective	Dominance; exclusive control; subordination of partners	Embedded influence; structural positioning; preservation of options	China seeks indispensability rather than hegemony; ambiguity rather than clarity
Measurement of Success	Alliance reliability; compliance with demands; military presence	Network centrality; mediating capacity; constituency distribution	Success measured by ability to facilitate Iran-Saudi reconciliation, not by forcing alignment

it also introduces ambiguities, complexities, and potential instabilities that differ from but do not necessarily improve upon previous arrangements. Whether this reconfiguration proves durable and whether it generates more stable or more conflictual regional order remains uncertain and will depend on factors including Sino-American relationship trajectory, regional actors' capacity to manage hybrid strategies, and the evolution of conflicts and challenges that test the architecture's resilience.

What appears clear is that understanding contemporary regional order requires attending to mechanisms of influence that operate through embedded presence and structured interdependence alongside traditional instruments of military power and alliance politics. The Middle East is not unique in experiencing these dynamics; similar patterns emerge in Southeast Asia, Central Asia, Africa, and parts of Eastern Europe, where Chinese engagement similarly reshapes regional orders without reproducing the hierarchical dominance characteristic of earlier great powers. In these regions, as in the Middle East, influence increasingly flows through connectivity corridors, financing structures, standards-setting, and institutional embedding rather than through formal alliances or coercive military leverage. The Middle Eastern case therefore should be read not as an outlier driven by regional exceptionalism, but as an advanced manifestation of a broader transformation in how power is exercised under conditions of multipolarity and dense interdependence.

Taken together, the analysis in this section suggests that China's impact on Middle Eastern order cannot be adequately assessed through binary categories of ascent versus constraint or revisionism versus status quo orientation. China neither replaces the United States as the regional security guarantor nor merely free-rides on an American-provided order. Instead, it alters the operating environment within which both regional actors and the United States pursue their interests. By lowering the political costs of engagement, expanding economic and institutional density, and maintaining strategic ambiguity, China enables regional actors to diversify partnerships while avoiding the obligations and vulnerabilities associated with exclusive alignment. This produces an order that is more flexible and pluralistic, yet also more opaque and potentially fragile.

For policymakers, this implies that strategies premised on forcing regional states to choose sides underestimate both the durability of hedging behavior and the structural appeal of China's engagement model. For scholars, it underscores the need to move beyond singular metrics of power—military presence, alliance commitments, or ideological attraction—toward frameworks capable of capturing how influence accumulates through long-term embedding, network centrality, and the shaping of incentives rather than direct control. The Middle East thus offers a critical empirical lens for understanding twenty-first century regional orders: not as arenas of clear hierarchy or decisive dominance, but as layered systems in which multiple forms of power coexist, interact, and compete over time.

References:

Acharya, A. (2014). *The end of American world order* (Vol. 6). Polity Press Cambridge.

Al-Sudairi, M. (2021). Sino-Omani relations. In *Routledge handbook on China–Middle East relations* (pp. 205–223). Routledge.

Barton, B. (2018). China's security policy in Africa: A new or false dawn for the evolution of the application of China's non-interference principle? *South African Journal of International Affairs, 25*(3), 413–434.

Campbell, K. M., & Ratner, E. (2018). The China reckoning: How Beijing defied American expectations. *Foreign Affairs, 97*, 60.

Cheng, J. Y. (2016). China's relations with the Gulf cooperation council states: Multilevel diplomacy in a divided Arab world. *The China Review*, 35–64.

Christensen, T. J. (2011). The advantages of an assertive China: Responding to Beijing's abrasive diplomacy. *Foreign Affairs*, 54–67.

Eder, T. S., Arcesati, R., & Mardell, J. (2019). Networking the 'Belt and Road'–The future is digital. *Mercator Institute for China Studies, 28.*

Ehteshami, A., & Horesh, N. (2017). *China's Presence in the Middle East.* Taylor & Francis.

Ehteshami, A., & Horesh, N. (2019). *How China's rise is changing the Middle East.* Routledge.

Fulton, J. (2022). The China-Iran comprehensive strategic partnership: A tale of two regional security complexes. *Asian Affairs, 53*(1), 145–163.

Garver, J. W. (2015). *China's Quest: The history of the Foreign Relations of the People's Republic of China.* Oxford University Press.

Ghiasy, R., & Zhou, J. (2022). *Silk road economic belt: Considering security implications and EU--China cooperation prospects.* Stockholm International Peace Research Institute.

Guzansky, Y. (2014). *The Arab Gulf states and reform in the Middle East: Between Iran and the "Arab Spring."* Springer.

Havlová, R. (2020). Sino-Qatari relations after the 'Qatar Blockade' in the context of the regional implementation of the belt and road initiative. *Central European Journal of International & Security Studies, 14*(2), 4.

He, K. (2015). Contested regional orders and institutional balancing in the Asia Pacific. *International Politics, 52*(2), 208–222.

JIC. (n.d). *Jazan city for primary and downstream industries*. Royal Commission for Jubail and Yanbu. Retrieved 12/12/2024 from https://www.rcjy.gov.sa/en/jazan

Johnston, A. I. (2019). China in a world of orders: Rethinking compliance and challenge in Beijing's international relations. *International Security, 44*(2), 9–60.

Mills, R. (2016). *Under the mountains–Kurdish oil and regional politics.*

MoFA-PRC. (2010). *Press Communiqué of the First Ministerial Meeting of the Strategic Dialogue Between the People's Republic of China and The Cooperation Council for the Arab States of the Gulf*. Retrieved from https://www.mfa.gov.cn/eng/zy/gb/202405/t20240531_11367249.html

Murphy, D. C. (2021). Chinese diplomatic outreach to MENA: Cooperation Forums and Special Envoys. In *Routledge handbook on China–Middle East relations* (pp. 384–395). Routledge.

Olimat, M. (2012). *China and the Middle East: From silk road to Arab spring.* Routledge.

Ren, M. (2021). Interpreting (non)-intervention and turning to the China's case. In M. Ren (Ed.), *Beyond rigidity: China's non-intervention policy in the Post-Cold War Period* (pp. 27–71). Springer Singapore. https://doi.org/10.1007/978-981-33-4623-9_2

SCPRC. (2016). *Full text of China's Arab Policy Paper*. Retrieved from https://english.www.gov.cn/archive/publications/2016/01/13/content_281475271412746.htm

Shen, H. (2018). Building a digital silk road? Situating the internet in China's belt and road initiative. *International Journal of Communication, 12*, 19.

Sun, D., & Xu, R. (2023). China and Egypt's comprehensive strategic partnership in the Xi-sisi era: A 'role theory'prism. *Mediterranean Politics, 28*(5), 764–784.

Sun, D., & Zoubir, Y. (2014). China's response to the revolts in the Arab world: A case of pragmatic diplomacy. *Mediterranean Politics, 19*(1), 2–20.

Ullah, A., & Xinlei, L. (2025a). Navigating complex interdependence: An in-depth analysis of Iran and Saudi Arabia's strategic engagement with the BRI in the Middle East. *Chinese Political Science Review, 10*(1), 72–100.

Ullah, A., & Xinlei, L. (2025b). Systemic constraints and state behavior: A neorealist perspective on China's BRI and Iran's strategic calculations. *Iranian Studies*, 1–22.

Ulrichsen, K. (2016). *The United Arab Emirates: Power, politics and policy-making*. Routledge.

Vaidya, S. (2023). Analysing China-Saudi comprehensive strategic partnership. *Organisation for Research on China and Asia*.

Yang, Z., Du, L., & Ding, L. (2020). The China-Saudi Arabia (Jizan) industrial park under the belt and road initiative. *Asian Journal of Middle Eastern and Islamic Studies, 14*(4), 528–537.

Yao, K. (2014). China-Arab states cooperation forum in the last decade. *Journal of Middle Eastern and Islamic Studies (in Asia), 8*(4), 26–42.

Yenigun, C., Albasoos, H., & Al-Zadjali, S. (2021). The impact of the Qatar crisis on the Omani relations. *European Journal of Psychology of Education, 58*(5).

Zheng, C. (2016). China debates the non-interference principle. *The Chinese Journal of International Politics, 9*(3), 349–374.

CHAPTER 8

Diplomacy by Design and the Middle East's Strategic Reordering

1 The Transformation of Regional Influence: From Visibility to Embeddedness

The post-Cold War order that Washington constructed across the Middle East rested fundamentally on visibility. American dominance announced itself through unique instruments of power: the continuous deployment of U.S. carrier strike groups to the Persian Gulf from 1991 onward, the establishment and expansion of permanent bases such as Al Udeid in Qatar (opened 1996, later hosting U.S. Central Command's forward headquarters), Camp Arifjan in Kuwait (2000), and the Fifth Fleet's headquarters in Bahrain (reconstituted 1995), and a network of bilateral defense agreements including the 1991 U.S. Kuwait Defense Cooperation Agreement, the 2003 U.S. Bahrain Free Trade Agreement with embedded security clauses, and long-standing commitments to Saudi Arabia dating back to 1945 but formalized through large-scale training, arms sales, and pre-positioned equipment after 1991.

Through these mechanisms, Washington articulated a legible strategic doctrine, codified in the Carter Doctrine (1980) and reaffirmed in subsequent National Security Strategies, that signaled to both adversaries and partners the scope of U.S. interests: freedom of navigation, protection of Gulf energy infrastructures, and deterrence of regional revisionist actors. Regional elites operated within a hierarchy whose contours were stable, predictable, and explicitly communicated through military

A. Ullah, *Diplomacy by Design*,
https://doi.org/10.1007/978-981-95-7876-4_8

posturing, public speeches, and published doctrinal statements (Fawcett, 2016; Gause III, 2009). Visibility generated dissent, but it also generated clarity, and the operating grammar, however contested, remained intelligible.

This model of influence achieved important objectives. It limited interstate conflict among U.S.-aligned states, protected oil flows, and constrained revisionist actors. Military predominance provided structural leverage that compelled regional actors to integrate American capabilities into their strategic calculations. These arrangements were visible, trackable, and highly credible, allowing partners and rivals alike to anticipate Washington's likely responses and align their policies accordingly. Institutionalized alliances extended this influence through joint planning, interoperable missile defense systems, long-term procurement contracts, and integrated operational routines that created deep bureaucratic entanglement.

The U.S.–Israel relationship exemplifies this logic: military and technological support fostered structural dependence, institutional integration ensured continuity, and normative narratives legitimized alignment despite opposition or regional grievances. Saudi Arabia provides a parallel although less symmetrical case, where reliance on U.S. security guarantees and procurement interdependence produced a system in which American preferences carried weight, even as Riyadh maintained significant autonomy (Blanchard, 2018).

Yet this framework also created structural liabilities. Scholars have identified patterns of strategic fatigue, dependency traps, credibility gaps, and partner moral hazard that complicate the sustainability of American leadership (Posen, 2018). Prolonged engagements in Iraq and Afghanistan eroded domestic support for Middle Eastern commitments. Partners learned that crises often produced increased American assistance rather than reduced entanglement. Meanwhile, periodic debates about retrenchment generated uncertainty among allies who increasingly hedged against perceived American decline. The model's reliance on visible military presence and explicit alliance commitments proved both its strength and its constraint.

China's regional epistemology differs fundamentally. Its presence accumulates in ways that elude the traditional indicators to which diplomats and strategists, trained in Cold War paradigms, remain attuned. Chinese influence grows through long-horizon infrastructure finance, multi-decade concession agreements, and commercial joint ventures, forms of engagement that do not trigger the diplomatic alarms normally associated with power projection. For instance, the 25-year Sino-Iranian cooperation framework (first outlined in 2016, formalized in 2021), the long-term industrial partnerships with Saudi Aramco in Fujian and Liaoning (2007 to present), and multi-decade port involvement at Khalifa Port in Abu Dhabi and Duqm in Oman expand Chinese influence, but do so under the guise of economic cooperation rather than military intrusion (Calabrese, 2018).

The BRI's project-finance structures, typically without public conditionality or ideological language, resist the binary classification, ally or rival, aligned or threatening, that Western analysts are trained to impose. Multilateral platforms such as the CASCF (established 2004) issue communiqués almost entirely devoid of hegemonic language, frustrating attempts to map Beijing's intentions through the discursive markers used for Western strategy.

Yet this apparent quietude masks extraordinary strategic consequence. The region is experiencing not the arrival of another external suitor, but a transformation in how external power is exercised, which channels it travels through, and what expectations states hold about external engagement. Influence now operates through the cumulative effect of finance, technology, logistics infrastructure, port access, renewable energy projects, arms co-production, and data systems integration, domains that rarely produce the kind of declarative signaling one associates with traditional hegemony but nonetheless reshape states' strategic horizons.

This transformation reflects the core logic of what this book has termed diplomacy by design: statecraft that constructs material interdependence deliberately, embeds presence across overlapping technical, digital, infrastructural, and financial systems, and employs strategic ambiguity to attain influence without the coercive mechanisms historically associated with hierarchical orders. DSI's logic diverges sharply from alliance-based models. It does not demand ideological alignment, as evidenced by Beijing's simultaneous partnerships with Iran, Saudi Arabia, and the UAE, states that share no coherent ideological project. It avoids zero-sum alignments, allowing partners to maintain U.S. security ties without penalty. And it does not require exclusive loyalty, tolerating and even encouraging states' engagement with multiple external powers.

Rather than replacing existing security architectures, China constructs parallel institutional and material landscapes: technology ecosystems such as Huawei 5G networks across the Gulf since 2018, energy partnerships such as Sino-Saudi green hydrogen ventures announced from 2021 onward, and industrial corridors such as the Jizan refinery complex, partially financed and operated by Chinese firms. These architectures do not contest Washington's military dominance directly; instead, they redirect developmental choices, investment flows, and technological standards into pathways that place Beijing at the center of long-term planning.

What distinguishes this approach is its reliance on strategic quietude, a modality that prioritizes embedded presence over military visibility, long-term entanglement over episodic intervention, and calibrated ambiguity over explicit alignment. Strategic quietude does not signal restraint or an unwillingness to shape regional outcomes. Rather, it reflects deliberate choices grounded in the logic of DSI. It operates through the construction of mutual dependencies that create shared incentives for cooperation, through institutional pathways that normalize routine interaction, and through political signaling that reassures partners that engagement does not require ideological conformity or exclusive commitment. Strategic quietude gives China a presence that is continuous but not confrontational, influential but not domineering, and deeply embedded without displacing regional autonomy.

This model avoids many liabilities of traditional power projection. It does not provoke the nationalist backlash frequently triggered by American military presence or European conditionality. It does not expose China to the quagmires associated with Russian-style security interventions. It preserves flexibility across rival states because China does not demand exclusive loyalty or impose ideological alignment (Alterman & Garver, 2008). This allows Beijing to build relationships simultaneously with Iran, Saudi Arabia, the UAE, Israel, and Turkey without generating perceptions of zero-sum competition. Regional actors find this model appealing because it maximizes their autonomy. They can engage China for development and technology while retaining American security guarantees or European market access.

Empirical evidence illustrates the effectiveness of this approach. Chinese mediation in the 2023 Saudi–Iranian rapprochement relied not on military guarantee or imposed settlement, but on accumulated presence. Years of economic engagement, infrastructural investment, and political dialogue had built credibility with both parties. China's neutrality was not performative but grounded in material reality, since Beijing maintained significant economic interests and cooperative frameworks with both Riyadh and Tehran. Mediation thus operated on the basis of DSI principles. China had embedded interests in stability across the Gulf, deepened channels of communication through project implementation and trade partnerships, and established a reputation for non-interference that made its facilitation acceptable to rivals.

The consequences are increasingly visible in regional behavior patterns that older theoretical frameworks struggle to explain. Saudi Arabia's simultaneous deepening of technology, petrochemical, and renewable energy partnerships with China while expanding its defense cooperation with Washington illustrates a strategic environment in which choice is no longer binary. Iran relies on Chinese investment and oil trade to mitigate U.S. sanctions but maintains strategic cooperation with Russia in Syria and defense procurement, demonstrating autonomy rather than dependence. The United Arab Emirates engages with China on logistics, smart-city technology, and AI ecosystems while preserving military interoperability with the United States, reflecting confidence in managing multiple great-power relationships without subordination.

These behaviors should not be misread as vacillation. They represent strategic sophistication in an emerging multipolar order in which DSI creates the structural space for simultaneous engagement with rival external powers. Because DSI operates through non-exclusionary, non-ideological, and non-coercive mechanisms, states can integrate Chinese economic and technological systems without jeopardizing their security alliances or broader foreign policy autonomy. What emerges is not confusion, but a recalibration of agency, with regional actors navigating new opportunity structures produced by a model of influence fundamentally distinct from the American order it now quietly intersects and, in some domains, gradually supersedes.

Strategic quietude thus represents a fundamental innovation in how influence operates within multipolar systems. Military intervention invites nationalist backlash, ideological export prompts suspicion, and alliance systems force binary choices that provoke balancing. Infrastructure aligned with host-state development priorities appears supportive rather than intrusive, operates continuously rather than episodically, and produces distributed dependencies that cannot be severed without substantial domestic costs. This makes strategic quietude particularly effective in regions where sovereignty concerns run deep and suspicion of external agendas shapes political receptivity. China converts these sensitivities into strategic opportunity by offering cooperation that respects sovereignty formally while generating influence structurally, presenting projects as commercial while serving political purposes, and building relationships that appear transactional while producing long-term strategic effects.

These developments signal a broader transformation in the strategic grammar of Middle Eastern politics. Influence is no longer measured primarily by troop deployments, alliance networks, or coercive instruments. Instead, embedded economic presence, infrastructural connectivity, and technological integration increasingly structure the terms of regional decision-making. Strategic quietude demonstrates that a power can shape regional trajectories without replicating hegemonic blueprints, offering a template for how influence accrues through positional advantage rather than normative appeal, from material constraints rather than ideational convergence, and from routinized embeddedness rather than episodic engagement.

2 Infrastructure as Strategic Architecture

China's infrastructure footprint in the Middle East has shifted from commercially oriented ventures to strategically positioned assets that now shape regional power relations. What appeared in the early 2010s as business-driven projects has evolved into deliberate political positioning that enables Beijing to generate influence without formal alliances. These projects operate simultaneously as commercial transactions, channels of embedded diplomacy, and instruments of political presence that do not rely on coercion or military projection.

China's strategic effect derives less from the scale of individual assets and more from their placement across rival states, their dual commercial and political functions, and their integration into national development priorities. Oman's Duqm port offers a clear example. Originally pursued as a commercial logistics hub, it now provides Beijing a strategic hedge against disruptions inside the Gulf and any closure of the Strait of Hormuz, while offering access situated outside the jurisdiction of U.S. naval dominance. The port's location ensures operational continuity during crisis and grants China a durable presence that operates independently of Western security infrastructures.

A similar logic is visible inland at Saudi Arabia's Jizan industrial complex. By embedding Chinese investment, technology, and expertise into Vision 2030 reforms, Beijing becomes indispensable to domestic transformation central to regime legitimacy. This produces structural dependencies that narrow Riyadh's room for maneuver on issues Beijing considers sensitive. The influence emerges not through overt pressure but through the inherent costs built into withdrawing from long-term infrastructure relationships (Chatzky & McBride, 2020). When critical sectors of national development depend on Chinese technology, capital, or supply chain integration, abrupt rupture becomes costly, reducing incentives for hostile alignment shifts.

Huawei's digital architectures in Iran and the United Arab Emirates extend this pattern into the technological realm. These networks generate deep dependencies through proprietary equipment, data standards, maintenance regimes, and cloud integration (Maxigas & ten Oever, 2023). Replacing such systems would impose high financial, operational, and political costs, anchoring long-term engagement despite fluctuations in bilateral relations. These digital ecosystems also create reciprocal vulnerabilities: host states depend on Chinese technology, while China becomes exposed to local regulatory and political environments. This mutual exposure forms the operational core of influence under the DSR.

These investments do not represent isolated commercial ventures but constitute an emerging architecture that embeds China systematically across competing regimes' domestic agendas. The embeddedness generates multiple channels of influence. First, operational requirements create routine access to government officials, regulatory authorities, and technical specialists, forming communication pathways that function even when formal diplomacy cools. Second, consistent performance and non-interference enhance credibility, enabling China to present itself as a reliable development partner. Third, growing interdependencies make disruption costly for both sides, creating incentives to sustain cooperation even during political tensions.

Beyond generating access and credibility, China's infrastructure portfolio operates as a constraint architecture that modifies regional conflict dynamics. By embedding itself in key economic sectors including energy production, transport, logistics corridors, and telecommunications networks, Beijing elevates the cost of confrontation through mechanisms that function automatically once infrastructure becomes operational. A pipeline linking Iraqi oil or Iranian gas to Gulf export terminals functions not only as energy infrastructure but as material deterrent, since conflict would disrupt revenues for all participants while damaging costly assets. A fiber-optic network connecting Saudi and Emirati smart city systems to Chinese cloud infrastructure creates dependencies that raise the risks associated with aggressive policies by threatening disruption of essential services and commercial activity.

This architecture does not eliminate conflict or resolve entrenched rivalries. Yet it alters the logic of escalation by introducing material disincentives operating alongside traditional security calculations. The continuity of infrastructure becomes a shared interest, generating constituencies within each state, including business elites, technocrats, and consumers, who oppose actions that threaten economic connectivity. China does not enforce restraint through threats or impose settlements through superior capabilities. Instead, it designs configurations of interdependence that make accommodation more rational than confrontation by ensuring that aggression harms the aggressor's own developmental priorities.

Infrastructure also functions as diplomatic infrastructure. Physical presence and operational relationships create the conditions enabling political mediation that would otherwise be infeasible. The 2023 Saudi Iran reconciliation explains this dynamic. The agreement did not result from Chinese military leverage, ideological persuasion, or alliance obligations. Rather, it emerged from embedded economic presence in both states, communication channels built through years of project implementation, and credibility established through consistent performance and non-interference. China's material links to both sides produced a perception of neutrality grounded in concrete realities rather than rhetorical claims.

This form of influence differs fundamentally from soft power as conventionally defined. Soft power relies on attractiveness of values or political systems motivating voluntary alignment (Nye, 2004, pp. 5–7). Chinese infrastructure generates influence not because regional actors admire Chinese governance or culture, but because the interdependencies embedded in physical and digital systems create strategic utility that rational actors cannot ignore (Farrell & Newman, 2019; Kastner & Pearson, 2021). Influence thus arises from positional advantage rather than normative appeal, from material constraints rather than ideational convergence, and from routinized embeddedness rather than episodic engagement.

The transition from infrastructure as developmental assistance to infrastructure as political instrument reflects a broader transformation in how influence operates within a multipolar system. This makes infrastructure particularly effective in regions where sovereignty concerns run deep and suspicion of external agendas shapes political receptivity. China converts these sensitivities into strategic opportunity by offering cooperation that respects sovereignty formally while generating influence structurally, presenting projects as commercial while serving political purposes, and building relationships that appear transactional while producing long-term strategic effects.

Infrastructure also enables a strategic pattern that conventional frameworks struggle to explain: China's ability to engage rival states simultaneously without forcing exclusivity or generating counter-coalitions. This capacity stems from deliberate distribution of infrastructure across competing parties, the absence of monopoly partnerships, and parallel projects serving similar functions in different states. The result is operational flexibility grounded in material redundancy rather than diplomatic ambiguity alone. If relations deteriorated with a single partner, Beijing's influence would remain intact through its embedded presence in others.

Strategic ambiguity regarding China's ultimate objectives thus becomes a cultivated asset. Simultaneous engagement across rivalries permits mediation, prevents the emergence of balancing coalitions, and preserves the ability to adjust policies as circumstances evolve. Infrastructure, rather than rhetorical positioning, provides the foundation that makes such ambiguity effective. This differs markedly from traditional approaches where influence depends on capabilities or conditionalities controlled by the external power, generating asymmetric bargaining. DSI creates environments in which cooperation is rational for partner states because embedded interdependence aligns with domestic development, security, and economic priorities. Influence accrues through structured incentives rather than coercion, producing a subtle but durable form of power that reshapes strategic behavior over time.

These infrastructural entanglements reveal the operational core of diplomacy by design: influence generated not through domination or alliance coercion but through embedded material architectures that structure incentives, shape strategic choices, and recalibrate the costs of confrontation. Infrastructure thus becomes both the mechanism and the medium through which the Middle East's strategic landscape is reordered, as states adapt to a power whose presence is felt through systems they depend on rather than doctrines they must obey.

3 Comparative Statecraft: Alternative Modalities of External Influence

Understanding the significance of DSI requires examining it in comparative perspective. External powers have long shaped the Middle East through distinct, historically rooted modalities of influence. The United States, Russia, and the European Union have each relied on characteristic instruments to structure regional behavior, while DSI presents a fundamentally different logic. By embedding interdependencies across multiple domains, structuring incentives, and preserving strategic ambiguity, DSI creates influence without coercion, alliance hierarchy, or conditionality, reshaping the strategic landscape in ways traditional frameworks struggle to capture.

The American Model: Hierarchical Security Architecture

United States influence in the Middle East since the late Cold War has rested on a triad of military dominance, institutionalized alliances, and normative conditionality. Military primacy provides structural leverage. Carrier strike groups, forward bases, integrated intelligence networks, and prepositioned forces compel regional actors to integrate American capabilities into their strategic calculations. These arrangements are visible, trackable, and highly credible, allowing partners and rivals alike to anticipate Washington's likely responses and align their policies accordingly (Gause III, 2009).

Institutionalized alliances extend the influence generated by military primacy. Joint planning, interoperable missile defense systems, long-term procurement contracts, and integrated operational routines create deep operational and bureaucratic entanglement. These structures generate constituencies within partner states, from military planners to civilian technocrats, who have a vested interest in maintaining alignment. The institutional depth of American engagement produces what scholars term alliance dependencies that extend beyond formal treaty obligations into everyday bureaucratic practice (Massie & Paquin, 2020). Military officers trained in American academies, defense officials accustomed to joint exercises, and intelligence services integrated into U.S. networks develop professional identities and operational habits that reinforce alignment independent of shifting political calculations.

Normative conditionality reinforces these layers by linking assistance to governance, human rights, or political reform (Brownlee, 2012). This creates levers of influence that shape domestic political debates and provide American policymakers with credibility when articulating strategic preferences. The logic operates on two levels: instrumental and ideational. Instrumentally, conditionality provides Washington with explicit bargaining leverage, allowing it to withhold aid, arms transfers, or diplomatic support when partners deviate from preferred policies. Ideationally, it frames the U.S.-regional relationship as one premised on shared values rather than mere strategic convenience, legitimizing American involvement and complicating efforts by regional actors to frame U.S. presence as imperial imposition.

The cumulative effect of these mechanisms is evident in the U.S.–Israel relationship. Military and technological support fosters structural dependence, institutional integration ensures continuity, and normative narratives legitimize alignment despite opposition or regional grievances. The relationship operates across multiple dimensions simultaneously: security guarantees deter adversaries, arms transfers maintain qualitative military edge, intelligence sharing enhances operational capacity, diplomatic backing shields Israel in multilateral forums, and economic assistance reinforces domestic stability. This multi-layered engagement creates redundancy that insulates the relationship from disruption, as deterioration in one domain can be compensated by continuity in others.

Saudi Arabia provides a parallel although less symmetrical case. Reliance on U.S. security guarantees, procurement interdependence, and occasional governance pressure produces a system in which American preferences carry weight, even as Riyadh maintains significant autonomy (Blanchard, 2018). The Saudi–U.S. relationship proves both the strengths and limits of the American model. Washington's inability to compel Saudi compliance on issues such as Yemen, oil production, or relations with China demonstrates that even deeply institutionalized relationships do not guarantee automatic alignment. Yet the persistent Saudi interest in maintaining U.S. security ties, despite periodic friction, reveals the enduring value regional actors place on American military capabilities.

Yet this framework also generates constraints that have become increasingly visible. The model's reliance on visible military commitments and explicit alliance structures creates dependencies that constrain American flexibility while generating expectations among partners that crises will produce increased assistance rather than disengagement. Regional actors have learned to exploit these dynamics, confident that their strategic importance or the sunk costs of prior commitments will prevent Washington from withdrawing support even when their actions diverge from American preferences. This moral hazard problem intensifies as partners recognize that escalating regional tensions or internal instability often trigger expanded U.S. engagement rather than reduced entanglement.

Simultaneously, domestic audiences in the United States have grown skeptical of prolonged Middle Eastern engagements following costly interventions in Iraq and Afghanistan. The political sustainability of American commitments therefore faces dual pressure: regional partners demand sustained or expanded involvement, while domestic constituencies question the value and costs of continued engagement. The result is a system where influence remains substantial but increasingly contested both regionally and domestically. Scholars have identified this tension as a structural feature of hegemonic overextension, where the costs of maintaining influence begin to exceed the benefits derived from it (Posen, 2018).

Moreover, the American model's emphasis on visible military presence generates nationalist resistance that complicates long-term influence. The presence of foreign troops, even when invited by host governments, becomes a domestic political liability that opposition groups exploit to challenge regime legitimacy. This dynamic played out repeatedly across the region: in Saudi Arabia where Osama bin Laden cited U.S. troop presence as justification for violence, in Iraq where American occupation fueled insurgency, and in Bahrain where naval base presence became entangled with sectarian politics. Visibility, which serves as a source of credibility in deterring adversaries, simultaneously becomes a source of vulnerability in sustaining domestic political support within partner states.

The Russian Model: Episodic Intervention and Transactional Leverage

Russian influence operates according to a markedly different logic. Moscow emphasizes arms transfers, security partnerships, and selective intervention rather than enduring institutional entrenchment. The 2015 military intervention in Syria exemplifies this approach. Russian forces stabilized the regime, preserved territorial integrity, and provided geopolitical cover, yet the intervention was episodic and did not produce permanent institutional networks capable of constraining or channeling regional decision-making over the long term (de Haas et al., 2020).

The Russian model relies on demonstration effects rather than institutional integration. By intervening decisively in Syria, Moscow signaled its willingness to support embattled partners and its capacity to project force beyond its immediate periphery. This demonstration enhanced Russian credibility as a security partner among regimes facing internal or external threats, particularly those skeptical of Western intentions or constrained by Western conditionality. Yet the model produces influence that is contingent and domain-specific rather than comprehensive and durable.

Other cases, such as Libya, Sudan, and select Gulf partnerships, reveal the transactional nature of Russian engagement. Influence is powerful but contingent, dependent on alignment of immediate interests. Arms sales to Egypt and Algeria provide Moscow with revenue and political access but do not translate into the kind of deep institutional integration that characterizes U.S. relationships. Energy diplomacy with Turkey operates similarly: cooperation on specific projects generates mutual benefits and creates diplomatic channels, but does not produce the structural dependencies that would compel alignment on broader strategic issues.

When Moscow's strategic attention shifts, as it did with the escalation in Ukraine, engagement recedes, exposing the limited durability of its leverage. Russian influence is therefore highly effective in crisis or niche sectors but rarely produces systemic transformation or cross-domain interdependence. Its reliance on security instruments and opportunistic interventions creates relationships that lack the institutional depth necessary for sustained influence across economic, technological, and developmental domains.

The Russian model also faces resource constraints that limit its applicability. Unlike the United States or China, Russia lacks the economic capacity to offer large-scale development assistance, infrastructure finance, or technology transfer that might deepen engagement beyond security domains. Moscow's GDP remains smaller than Italy's, constraining its ability to compete with Chinese infrastructure investment or American economic assistance. This limitation pushes Russian strategy toward niche opportunities where military capability, arms transfers, or diplomatic obstruction at the United Nations provide leverage disproportionate to economic resources. The model succeeds in specific contexts but cannot sustain the comprehensive regional presence that the United States maintains or the developmental partnerships that China constructs.

The European Model: Market Power and Normative Conditionality

European influence in the Middle East relies primarily on market access, regulatory power, and developmental conditionality (Del Sarto, 2021). Trade agreements, investment programs, and technology transfer initiatives are frequently tied to expectations of political reform, governance improvements, or human rights compliance. These instruments generate structural interdependence and provide incentives for policy convergence in specific domains.

The European approach reflects the EU's institutional character as a regulatory rather than military power. Brussels wields influence through its ability to grant or withhold access to European markets, the world's largest integrated economic zone. For North African states in particular, European market access represents a critical economic interest given the geographic proximity, historical ties, and labor migration patterns. The EU leverages this interest to encourage political and economic reforms through frameworks such as the European Neighborhood Policy and the Euro-Mediterranean Partnership.

Yet this influence is inherently constrained. Regional states frequently seek alternative partners to mitigate the political costs of European conditionality. North African and Levantine states often pursue Gulf, Asian, or transnational partnerships that are unconditioned on governance reform, reflecting a preference for diversified and flexible engagement. European leverage is therefore significant but domain specific, with limited capacity to embed influence across security, infrastructure, and economic sectors simultaneously.

The European approach coheres with European self-identity as a normative power but encounters pronounced resistance in polities that guard sovereignty, view democratization pressure with suspicion, or interpret governance demands as neo-colonial intrusion (Schumacher, 2014). Conditionality often generates backlash rather than compliance, as authoritarian and hybrid regimes find it easier to mobilize nationalist sentiment against European governance agendas than to risk domestic instability associated with political opening. The 2011 Arab uprisings initially appeared to vindicate European emphasis on governance and reform, but the subsequent authoritarian resurgence and regional instability reinforced skepticism among European policymakers about the feasibility of externally driven political transformation.

Moreover, European influence faces coordination challenges stemming from the EU's fragmented foreign policy architecture. Member states retain significant autonomy in bilateral relations, producing inconsistent messaging and undermining collective leverage. France, Italy, and Germany often pursue distinct bilateral relationships with regional partners based on historical ties, economic interests, or domestic political considerations, complicating efforts to present a unified European position. This fragmentation contrasts sharply with the centralized decision-making that characterizes U.S. or Chinese engagement, reducing European effectiveness in contexts requiring rapid response or consistent long-term strategy.

The European model also suffers from credibility gaps in security domains. The EU lacks military capacity for large-scale intervention and depends on NATO, effectively U.S. military power, for hard security guarantees. This dependence limits European influence in contexts where security concerns dominate, as regional actors recognize that Europe cannot provide the protection against external threats or internal instability that American military presence offers. As a result, European engagement remains strongest in economic and regulatory domains but weak in security spheres, producing asymmetric influence that regional actors can exploit by compartmentalizing their external relationships.

The Chinese Model: Embedded Interdependence and Strategic Flexibility

The DSI framework operates through mechanisms fundamentally distinct from those employed by the United States, Russia, or the European Union. Rather than relying on coercive military power, episodic intervention, or normative conditionality, DSI establishes durable influence through systematic embedding in infrastructure, industrial projects, technology systems, and institutional processes.

These interdependencies restructure incentives by increasing the costs of disengagement and embedding partner bureaucracies and technocratic constituencies in cooperative routines. Ports, digital networks, energy systems, and industrial zones create tangible stakes for continuity. Partners face rising opportunity costs if they disrupt engagement, while the external actor maintains flexibility and avoids overt political coercion. Institutional routinization, via joint commissions, sectoral committees, and multi-year project cycles, stabilizes interaction and reproduces influence even when high-level political relations experience tension.

What distinguishes DSI is its capacity to generate influence through structural position rather than explicit control. Unlike American alliances that create formal hierarchies with clear obligations, or Russian interventions that demonstrate capability through force, or European conditionality that links benefits to behavioral change, DSI operates through accumulated presence that reshapes the strategic environment within which partners make decisions. This influence is structural rather than episodic, distributed rather than concentrated, and enabling rather than coercive.

The logic operates across multiple dimensions simultaneously. Economically, Chinese investment and trade provide developmental resources without governance conditionality, making engagement politically attractive for regimes wary of Western pressure. Technologically, Chinese platforms and standards create operational dependencies that produce lock-in effects, as replacing integrated systems imposes high costs. Institutionally, routine cooperation through project implementation and joint mechanisms normalizes Chinese presence and creates bureaucratic constituencies with vested interests in continuity. Strategically, simultaneous engagement with rival states provides mediation capacity and reduces the need for exclusive alignment, maximizing partner autonomy while preserving Chinese access.

Normative reassurance is another critical component. Non-interference, respect for sovereignty, and the absence of governance conditionality enhance credibility among regional actors (Fulton, 2019). This approach contrasts sharply with Western conditionality, which often provokes resistance or hedging behavior. Simultaneously, strategic ambiguity enables engagement with rival states without forcing binary choices. Saudi Arabia, Iran, the UAE, and Qatar can deepen engagement while maintaining security, diplomatic, and economic ties with other powers, preserving autonomy and reducing incentives for zero-sum confrontation.

Unlike traditional models, DSI shifts the locus of control. American, Russian, and European influence typically depends on capabilities or conditionalities controlled by the external power, generating asymmetric bargaining dynamics where the external actor possesses explicit leverage. DSI creates environments in which cooperation is rational for partner states because embedded interdependence aligns with domestic development, security, and economic priorities. Influence accrues through structured incentives rather than coercion, producing a subtle but durable form of power that reshapes strategic behavior over time.

The temporal dimension also distinguishes DSI from alternative models. American influence operates through continuous military presence and alliance management, requiring sustained resource commitments and political attention. Russian influence operates episodically through crisis intervention, generating visibility but limited continuity. European influence operates through long-term institutional frameworks but faces implementation challenges and credibility gaps. Chinese influence accumulates gradually through infrastructure projects with decade-long timelines, creating dependencies that deepen over time without requiring continuous diplomatic management or visible military presence.

Comparative Logic and Strategic Implications

The distinctions become clearer when examining specific mechanisms. American influence operates through security guarantees that create dependencies but also generate expectations of protection and intervention. When Washington appears to waver, as during debates over Middle Eastern retrenchment, partners hedge by diversifying security relationships. The model's strength lies in its credibility and depth; its weakness lies in the political and economic costs of maintaining visible commitments across multiple theaters.

Russian influence operates through crisis intervention that demonstrates capability but lacks the institutional continuity necessary for sustained engagement across multiple domains. The model's strength lies in its flexibility and willingness to act decisively; its weakness lies in resource constraints and the transactional nature of relationships that dissolve when strategic priorities shift.

European influence operates through conditionality that can shape governance in specific cases but alienates regimes prioritizing sovereignty over external approval. The model's strength lies in market access and regulatory power; its weakness lies in fragmented decision-making, limited security capacity, and the political backlash that conditionality often generates.

Chinese influence, by contrast, operates through cumulative embedding that creates distributed dependencies across economic, technological, and infrastructural domains. This embedding does not demand ideological conformity, does not require exclusive alignment, and does not impose governance conditions. The result is influence that regional actors perceive as enabling rather than constraining, as supportive of their developmental priorities rather than threatening to their political autonomy. This perception matters because it reduces resistance and facilitates deeper integration over time. The following figure presents a typology of external influence modalities, mapping different models of international engagement along two dimensions: coercive versus structural influence, and episodic intervention versus cumulative embedding (Fig. 1).

The model's strength lies in its structural character: influence derives from material interdependence rather than explicit leverage, operates continuously through embedded systems rather than episodically through interventions, and accommodates partner autonomy rather than demanding subordination. Its potential weakness lies in sustainability questions: whether accumulated presence will eventually trigger balancing behavior as regional actors perceive Chinese influence as threatening, whether infrastructure dependencies will prove durable during severe political instability, and whether strategic ambiguity will remain viable if great power competition forces binary alignment choices.

Viewed comparatively, DSI represents a distinct mode of statecraft. Its combination of embedded interdependence, institutional continuity, sovereignty respect, and strategic ambiguity allows it to operate alongside traditional Western and Russian approaches while producing systemic reordering. Middle Eastern states recalibrate their partnerships not by abandoning existing alignments but by creating portfolios that maximize autonomy and leverage across multiple external actors. This capacity for simultaneous engagement and cross-sectoral embedding is the central mechanism through which DSI is reshaping the regional strategic order.

These distinctions in external modalities establish the strategic context in which regional actors calibrate engagement with multiple powers, including China. The American model creates security dependencies but faces sustainability challenges; the Russian model provides crisis support but lacks developmental depth; the European model offers economic benefits but imposes political costs; the Chinese model provides developmental resources and technological capacity without demanding exclusive alignment or governance reform. Regional actors navigate this complex landscape by constructing differentiated partnerships that leverage the

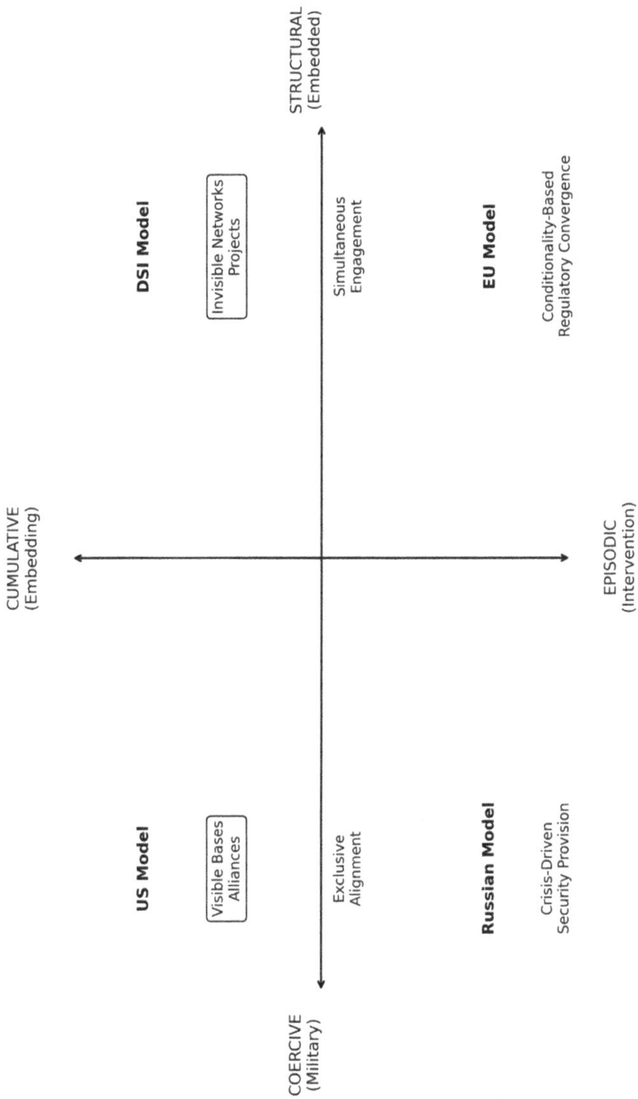

Fig. 1 Typology of external influence modalities

comparative advantages of each external power while minimizing vulnerabilities associated with overdependence on any single patron. This strategic environment, shaped by the coexistence of multiple influence modalities, produces the portfolio strategies and functional compartmentalization patterns explored in the subsequent section.

4 Regional Responses: Strategic Approaches and Functional Compartmentalization

The diffusion of Chinese infrastructure and technological presence across the Middle East has generated a measurable recalibration in how regional actors conceptualize external partnerships. Yet these adjustments cannot be reduced to narratives of a "pivot to China" or continued deference to traditional Western patrons. Instead, states are undertaking a deliberate disaggregation of external relationships: engaging Chinese firms in domains where they offer comparative advantage, retaining American and European partners where they remain indispensable, and constructing redundancy across critical dependencies to avoid excessive vulnerability to any single power (Alterman & Garver, 2008). This emerging pattern reflects neither hedging in the conventional sense nor strategic vacillation, but purposeful design aimed at maximizing autonomy in a structurally multipolar environment.

Regional governments are engaging in what can be conceptualized as strategic recalibration without formal alignment. In this mode, states selectively integrate Chinese capabilities, particularly in infrastructure, advanced manufacturing, and technology, while simultaneously preserving relationships with established powers such as the United States and European countries. This nuanced approach reflects the logic of DSI, a framework in which influence is generated through structured engagement rather than coercion or hierarchical control. The central feature of this recalibration is layered engagement. States do not perceive Chinese engagement as a monolithic substitute for traditional partners; rather, they allocate each external actor to specific domains where it provides comparative advantage.

Saudi Arabia exemplifies this shift more clearly than most cases. Vision 2030, the kingdom's central state-building and diversification blueprint, relies on technologically intensive transformation of infrastructure, energy systems, and industrial capacity. Instead of relying solely on American firms or established Western technology providers, Riyadh has woven

Chinese partners into renewable energy development, smart-city platforms, industrial zones, and 5G. This expansion does not displace U.S. security guarantees, which remain foundational, but supplements them by broadening the technological and developmental toolkit available to the Saudi state.

The kingdom maintains deep security dependence on the United States, including extensive arms procurement, joint exercises, intelligence sharing, and implicit defense commitments against regional threats, while simultaneously expanding economic cooperation with China. Chinese firms are embedded across Saudi Vision 2030 initiatives, encompassing renewable energy, industrial parks, advanced manufacturing, smart mobility, and logistics infrastructure (Schiavi, 2025). Chinese foreign direct investment into Saudi Arabia surged to SAR 31.1 billion (approximately US$8.2 billion) in 2024, reflecting a 28.8% increase over the previous year (Shaeri, 2025). This trend underscores the kingdom's strategic use of Chinese capabilities to advance domestic modernization without compromising its longstanding security relationships with Washington.

Institutionalized investments, such as the Jizan City for Primary and Downstream Industries, embed Chinese industrial expertise into Saudi infrastructure while leaving political and military alignment with the United States intact (Chen & Han, 2019). The pattern illustrates functional compartmentalization: security remains anchored in Washington, technological modernization flows through Beijing, and financial partnerships span European and Asian markets. Chinese firms offer commercially attractive solutions without attaching the governance or human-rights conditionalities increasingly associated with Western engagement (Garlick & Havlová, 2020). The result is not realignment, but functional diversification: security remains anchored in Washington, while development and technological modernization become increasingly distributed across multiple external partners.

This compartmentalization serves multiple strategic purposes. It reduces vulnerability to any single power's leverage by ensuring that no external actor controls all critical domains simultaneously. It allows Riyadh to extract maximum benefits from each relationship by playing partners against one another implicitly, enhancing Saudi bargaining power. It insulates the regime from external pressure by maintaining alternative channels when any single partner attempts to impose conditionality. And it signals strategic autonomy to domestic and regional audiences, demonstrating that Saudi Arabia navigates great power competition rather than subordinating itself to any particular patron.

Iran, operating under significantly more coercive external constraints, has adopted a parallel logic. The 25-year CSP with China provides economic relief and logistical continuity amid U.S. maximum-pressure sanctions, but Tehran has resisted collapsing its external options into a single dependence (Vakil, 2006). The CSP encompasses energy cooperation, infrastructure investment, military coordination, and technological partnerships, offering Iran critical economic lifelines when Western markets remain closed. Yet Iranian policymakers recognize that overreliance on Beijing risks reproducing the very vulnerabilities sanctions have exposed.

Iran continues to cultivate strategic ties with Russia, maintain diplomatic channels with Europe, and expand South-South partnerships across Asia and Latin America. These efforts reflect a recognition that overreliance on Beijing risks reproducing the very vulnerabilities sanctions have exposed. Strategic cooperation with Russia in Syria and defense procurement demonstrates autonomy rather than dependence on China. Diplomatic engagement with Europe, although constrained by sanctions, preserves channels for potential normalization. Expanding ties with India, Venezuela, and other non-aligned states creates alternative trade and investment routes that reduce Chinese leverage.

Diversified connectivity preserves bargaining space and prevents Chinese leverage from becoming structurally determinative. Notably, Beijing has not demanded exclusivity, and Iranian policymakers openly emphasize their intention to prevent any form of substitute dependency (Shirzad, 2022). The relationship thus operates as mutual accommodation rather than hierarchical alignment. China benefits from access to Iranian energy and strategic position, while Iran benefits from Chinese investment and diplomatic backing without surrendering policy autonomy. This arrangement reflects the DSI logic: influence through embedded presence that remains non-coercive and non-exclusive.

The Iranian case shows how even states facing severe external pressure retain agency in managing great power relationships. Despite asymmetric power dynamics, Tehran pursues a strategy designed to prevent any single external actor from acquiring monopolistic influence. This strategy requires continuous diplomatic management and willingness to accept suboptimal outcomes in specific relationships to preserve overall autonomy, but it demonstrates that structural constraints do not eliminate strategic choice.

The United Arab Emirates arguably offers the most refined example of this approach. Abu Dhabi has cultivated expansive partnerships with Chinese firms across logistics, AI, renewable energy, ports, and digital infrastructure, while simultaneously sustaining intimate security relations with the United States, deepening technology partnerships with Israel post-Abraham Accords, and maintaining robust commercial engagement with Europe and India.

Abu Dhabi integrates Chinese technological systems, including smart city platforms, AI-based monitoring, and Huawei 5G infrastructure, while simultaneously maintaining deep security and military relationships with the United States (Ulrichsen, 2020). These relationships are not perceived as competing vectors, but as mutually reinforcing components of a diversified external architecture. Chinese partners generate industrial capacity and digital infrastructure; U.S. protection guarantees deter regional threats; Israeli firms provide technological innovation; European markets offer capital and regulatory cooperation. The UAE thus operationalizes a model of functional alignment, distributing different domains of national strategy across different external partners.

This approach reflects confidence in managing multiple great-power relationships without subordination. Emirati policymakers view external partnerships as tools to be deployed strategically rather than commitments requiring exclusive loyalty. The UAE's small size and lack of natural strategic depth make diversification particularly rational, as overdependence on any single patron creates existential vulnerability. By distributing critical functions across multiple partners, Abu Dhabi ensures that no single external actor can coerce policy changes by threatening withdrawal.

The UAE's approach also reflects a deliberate effort to take advantage of great-power competition. By maintaining partnerships with rivals, Abu Dhabi positions itself as a valuable intermediary and ensures that each external actor has incentives to offer favorable terms to prevent the UAE from tilting toward competitors. This dynamic enhances Emirati bargaining power disproportionate to its material capabilities, demonstrating how smaller states can leverage multipolarity to maximize autonomy.

Smaller Gulf monarchies adopt analogous strategies, although with variations reflecting their distinct vulnerabilities and priorities. Qatar's experience during the 2017–2021 blockade demonstrated the dangers of exclusive reliance on a narrow set of partners. Doha has since constructed a deliberately redundant network of relationships: security ties with the United States, energy cooperation with China and Japan, diplomatic coordination with Turkey and Europe, and selective engagement with Russia (Ulrichsen, 2014).

The blockade experience fundamentally reshaped Qatari strategic thinking. The kingdom learned that regional isolation can occur rapidly and that traditional partnerships may prove insufficient or unwilling to provide decisive support during crises. In response, Qatar systematically expanded its external partnerships to ensure that no combination of regional actors could impose effective isolation again. Chinese infrastructure investment, Turkish military cooperation, and deepened European diplomatic ties all serve as insurance against future coercion.

Similarly, Oman, Bahrain, and Kuwait emphasize diversified connectivity as insurance against coercion. Oman's traditional neutrality in regional conflicts makes diversified partnerships essential to maintaining independence from competing regional blocs. Bahrain's hosting of the U.S. Fifth Fleet headquarters coexists with expanding economic ties to China and diplomatic engagement with Iran, reflecting efforts to preserve autonomy despite deep security dependence on Washington. Kuwait's experience of Iraqi invasion in 1990 generates persistent concern about external threats, pushing it toward maintaining relationships with multiple powers capable of providing protection or diplomatic support.

None of these arrangements indicate a change in geopolitical allegiance; instead, they reflect risk-management strategies shaped by the realities of a multipolar system, where flexibility pays off. The smaller Gulf states lack the material resources to ensure their security or development through autonomous action, making external partnerships essential. Yet they possess sufficient agency to choose how those partnerships are structured and distributed, using diversification to maximize autonomy and minimize vulnerability to coercion by any single external or regional actor.

Iraq demonstrates the extreme case of diversification under acute fragility. Baghdad simultaneously depends on American military support to contain extremist threats, Chinese investment to stabilize electricity and infrastructure networks, Russian diplomatic backing within multilateral forums, and European technological assistance for governance reforms (Mayer, 2018). Rather than a sign of incoherence, this fragmentation reflects an effort to reduce overdependence in a context where no single power can meet Iraq's comprehensive security, economic, and reconstruction needs.

Iraq's profound state weakness following decades of war, sanctions, occupation, and sectarian conflict creates dependencies across multiple domains simultaneously. Security provision requires American and coalition military capabilities that Iraq cannot generate independently. Infrastructure reconstruction requires capital and technical expertise that only Chinese firms offer at scale and speed. Diplomatic protection within international institutions requires backing from Russia and other non-Western powers. Governance reform and institutional development require European technical assistance and legitimacy.

When policymakers rely on Cold War binaries, they risk mistaking flexible multipolar maneuvering for indecision. Iraqi officials understand that their state's fragility prevents exclusive alignment with any single patron, as doing so would alienate others whose support remains necessary. The result is a deliberately fragmented external architecture that distributes dependencies to prevent any single power from acquiring controlling influence. This strategy operates less through sophisticated design than through necessity, but it nonetheless produces the same outcome: preservation of autonomy through diversification.

The Iraqi case also highlights the limits of such strategies in contexts of severe state weakness. Baghdad's inability to coordinate policies across domains or enforce consistent diplomatic positions reduces the strategic value of its diversification. External powers exploit Iraqi fragmentation to advance competing agendas, often undermining Iraqi sovereignty in the process. Yet even under these constrained conditions, diversification provides Iraqi elites with greater maneuverability than exclusive alignment would permit.

Egypt represents a distinct case, influenced by its economic needs and traditional security relationships. In states with acute development needs, Chinese engagement is primarily infrastructural and economically driven. Chinese companies contribute to industrial zones in the Suez Canal Economic Zone, power generation, and digital infrastructure, supplementing but not supplanting European and American financial and technical cooperation (Chen et al., 2023).

Cairo maintains deep military and security ties with Washington, including substantial annual military assistance, joint exercises, and strategic coordination on regional issues. Simultaneously, Egypt expands economic partnerships with China in sectors where Chinese comparative advantage is clear: large-scale infrastructure, industrial development, and renewable energy. European partners remain important for trade, investment, and diplomatic engagement, while Gulf states provide critical financial support that stabilizes Egypt's chronic fiscal vulnerabilities.

These engagements demonstrate that Chinese partnerships are pragmatic and selective, targeting sectors where Chinese comparative advantage aligns with local priorities, rather than imposing political alignment or strategic dependency. Egyptian policymakers view external partnerships through a developmental lens, prioritizing economic growth and infrastructure modernization over ideological considerations. This approach allows Cairo to extract resources from multiple external actors without being captured by any single patron's strategic agenda.

Collectively, these patterns produce what may be termed an embedded equilibrium. Regional states integrate China into specific economic, technological, or infrastructural domains while preserving existing alliances in other spheres. This equilibrium is sustained by three mutually reinforcing dynamics.

First, overlapping dependencies ensure that cooperation with China occurs in sectors critical for economic modernization but does not create total structural dependence. By retaining traditional partners for security, financial, or diplomatic functions, states maintain leverage across multiple domains. No single external actor controls all critical functions simultaneously, preventing monopolistic influence.

Second, calibrated ambiguity allows regional actors to exploit DSI's deliberate lack of exclusivity. States engage with China without triggering defensive coalitions or forcing binary choices between competing powers. Strategic ambiguity preserves flexibility and enables incremental adjustment as geopolitical and economic conditions evolve. Regional actors avoid explicit declarations of alignment that might constrain future options or provoke balancing behavior by rivals.

Third, functional entanglement through infrastructure, technology, and industrial investments embeds China into the operational landscape of host states. These ties generate influence but do not translate into automatic political compliance or strategic subordination. The influence operates through structural incentives rather than coercive leverage, producing subtle but durable effects on partner decision-making without eliminating autonomy.

This recalibration reflects strategic agency, demonstrating that Middle Eastern states are not passive objects of external influence. Instead, they actively manage and sequence their partnerships to maximize developmental and security outcomes while minimizing dependency. This approach preserves flexibility and enables incremental adjustment as geopolitical and economic conditions evolve. Regional actors recognize that multipolarity creates opportunities for maximizing autonomy that did not exist under Cold War bipolarity or post-Cold War American unipolarity.

Across cases, the pattern is consistent: China's embedded presence does not supplant traditional partnerships but alters the strategic environment within which states calibrate external relations. Rather than aligning with Beijing against Washington, regional actors are constructing multivalent partnership portfolios, distributing functions across multiple great powers in ways that enhance autonomy. This strategic elasticity is made possible partly by China's diplomacy by design approach, which, unlike alliance-based models, does not demand exclusivity or conditionality. As a result, states gain new room to maneuver, not because China replaces existing hierarchies, but because its embedded economic and technological presence enables mixed-orientation foreign policy without triggering the balancing pressures associated with traditional power competition.

The rise of these multivalent partnership portfolios underscores how DSI is reshaping the region's strategic grammar. By offering cooperation unconstrained by exclusivity, China enables states to reconfigure external relations along functional rather than ideological lines, facilitating a regional order in which flexibility replaces hierarchy and autonomy replaces alignment. The Middle East's reordering thus emerges not through binary choices between great powers but through the cumulative effects of embedded, domain-specific cooperation that China's model uniquely encourages. This transformation does not eliminate great power competition but changes its character, shifting from zero-sum struggles for exclusive alignment toward parallel engagement strategies where multiple powers maintain simultaneous influence across different domains.

5 Structural Limits and Sustainability Challenges

Despite DSI's demonstrated effectiveness in generating influence and facilitating mediation, the model faces sustainability challenges worth examining directly. These constraints are not theoretical abstractions but correspond to plausible scenarios already visible in the region's political and economic environment. Understanding these limits provides a balanced assessment of DSI's durability and identifies conditions under which the framework might face significant stress or require strategic recalibration.

Political Volatility and Regime Fragility

DSI is most effective when host governments provide consistent policy environments that allow large projects to mature over extended horizons. Chinese engagement is frequently aligned with long-term national development programs such as Saudi Arabia's Vision 2030, Egypt's digital modernization strategies, or Iraq's reconstruction plans. These strategies presuppose governance continuity, elite cohesion, and administrative stability. However, the Middle East remains one of the most politically volatile regions globally. Patterns of authoritarian resilience coexist with persistent risks of upheaval, succession uncertainty, and institutional fragmentation (Lynch, 2016).

Unlike Western states that often employ political conditionality or cultivate deep relationships with local elites, China avoids entrenchment in domestic politics. This non-interference posture enhances Beijing's credibility and protects its access across regime transitions, yet it also limits its capacity to hedge against abrupt political shifts. When regimes collapse or experience contested transitions, Chinese projects can rapidly become stranded assets or contested symbols. Evidence from Libya, Yemen, and Syria shows that foreign infrastructure and commercial projects become highly vulnerable once state authority weakens or rival factions seek to reallocate rents and external partnerships (Hanieh, 2018).

Moreover, nationalist movements frequently politicize foreign investments during periods of upheaval, which risks transforming Chinese presence into a domestic liability. Infrastructure projects that appeared neutral during stable governance can become targets for opposition groups seeking to challenge incumbent regimes or mobilize anti-foreign sentiment. The association of Chinese projects with authoritarian rulers may generate backlash if those rulers face popular opposition, as infrastructure becomes symbolic of regime priorities that neglected public welfare or concentrated benefits among elites.

Even though Beijing has been moderately successful in re-engaging post-crisis governments in Africa and Southeast Asia, the Middle East's higher levels of fragmentation and proxy conflict make comparable resilience less certain. Regional rivalries mean that regime change in one state often triggers intervention by neighbors seeking to install friendly governments or prevent adversarial influence. Chinese infrastructure in such contexts becomes entangled in broader geopolitical struggles, complicating Beijing's efforts to maintain neutrality and preserve assets.

The Syrian case illustrates these dynamics clearly. Chinese engagement in Syria's post-war recovery has been cautious and pragmatic, shaped by both economic opportunity and significant political and security uncertainty. Beijing has pursued limited economic cooperation, such as investment agreements with firms like Fidi Contracting focused on industrial zones, rather than large-scale reconstruction commitments, reflecting concerns about instability and the risks of deep involvement in a fragile environment. Reconstruction in Syria remains extraordinarily challenging. The cost to rebuild infrastructure is estimated in the hundreds of billions of dollars, and progress is constrained by political transition, economic collapse, insecurity, and lingering international sanctions.

Although the former Assad regime fell in late 2024 and a transitional government now seeks to reintegrate Syria into the global economy, foreign investors, including Chinese actors, remain wary. China continues to emphasize sovereignty, stability, and a Syrian-led political process while avoiding large-scale commitments that could be undermined by persistent governance and security risks.

Strategic Overlap Across Rival States

A second stress point arises from China's embedded presence across rival regional actors. DSI's distinctive advantage lies in its ability to maintain concurrent partnerships with Saudi Arabia, Iran, the UAE, Qatar, Egypt, and other states that often mistrust or openly contest one another. This distribution allows Beijing to preserve neutrality, facilitate dialogue, and avoid being subsumed into regional fault lines. Scholarship on networked diplomacy highlights that broad relational portfolio strengthen a mediator's legitimacy and improve access to information and leverage (Kydd, 2005).

However, this same relational spread produces structural exposure when rivalries intensify. The model depends on assumptions that regional actors will tolerate China's parallel partnerships with their adversaries, that Chinese cooperation with rivals does not shift local balances of power in threatening ways, and that Beijing can sustain calibrated ambiguity that reassures all sides. These conditions hold during periods of low to moderate tension. They may not hold if major conflicts escalate.

A direct Saudi–Iranian confrontation, severe Israeli–Iranian escalation, or open UAE-Turkey conflict could force Beijing into choices it wants to avoid. Even if China refrains from taking sides, the perception of imbalance can generate political pressure within partner states to reassess ongoing Chinese projects. Infrastructure investments in one state might be viewed as strengthening an adversary's capabilities, triggering demands that China reduce engagement or risk losing access. Once rivalries intensify beyond a certain threshold, intermediary states lose the space for calibrated ambiguity and experience a rapid erosion of cross-party trust, reducing the viability of simultaneous engagement strategies.

The Iran–Saudi relationship explains both the opportunities and risks of this positioning. China's successful mediation of their 2023 rapprochement demonstrated the value of embedded presence in both states. Yet if tensions re-escalate, perhaps over Yemen, nuclear issues, or regional proxy conflicts, Beijing may face pressure to demonstrate alignment with one side or the other. Saudi Arabia might demand that China curtails certain forms of cooperation with Iran, particularly in advanced technology or military domains, as a condition for continued Saudi partnership. Iran might interpret expanded Chinese–Saudi cooperation as evidence of alignment against Tehran, generating suspicion that undermines the trust necessary for continued engagement.

The risk is not merely hypothetical. Historical patterns suggest that great powers embedded in rival states face difficult choices during acute conflicts. The United States experienced comparable dilemmas during Iran–Iraq War, Arab–Israeli conflicts, and Gulf rivalries, where maintaining relationships with both sides of regional disputes proved increasingly difficult as conflicts intensified. China has thus far avoided these constraints by remaining outside security domains and limiting engagement to economic and technological spheres, but deepening presence may gradually erode this insulation.

Infrastructure Exposure and Economic Risk

A third vulnerability derives from the economic structure of DSI. Chinese investments in ports, industrial zones, telecommunications, logistics corridors, and energy networks involve fixed capital that cannot be easily relocated if political or security conditions deteriorate. Infrastructure-led engagement offers advantages in deepening local entanglement, generating developmental constituencies, and embedding Chinese presence in critical sectors. However, it also exposes China to high sunk costs and long return horizons that depend on the stability and predictability of local governance (Chatzky & McBride, 2020).

These vulnerabilities are acute in several Middle Eastern contexts. In Iraq, logistics corridors linking Basra to regional markets remain threatened by residual extremist cells, militia competition, and administrative fragmentation. Infrastructure projects require secure operating environments, yet Iraq's fragmented security landscape means that different areas fall under control of competing armed groups, each capable of disrupting operations. Even when projects receive nominal government approval, local power brokers may demand additional payments, block operations to extract concessions, or sabotage infrastructure to undermine rivals.

In Lebanon, systemic governance failure, politicized regulatory institutions, and severe fiscal collapse undermine the feasibility of digital infrastructure partnerships. Lebanon's political system, characterized by sectarian power-sharing and clientelistic networks, makes coherent policy implementation extremely difficult. Even when agreements are reached with central government authorities, implementation often falters due to obstruction by sectarian factions, bureaucratic paralysis, or sudden policy reversals triggered by political realignments. The country's financial collapse beginning in 2019 further complicates Chinese engagement, as currency instability, banking sector dysfunction, and capital controls create operational challenges for infrastructure projects requiring sustained financial flows.

In Syria, post-conflict stabilization remains fragile, and reconstruction is constrained by sanctions, territorial fragmentation, and competing security actors. Territorial fragmentation means that large-scale infrastructure projects would need to cross areas controlled by different actors, including Syrian government forces, Kurdish-led authorities, Turkish-backed groups, and residual extremist cells. Competing external powers, including Russia, Iran, Turkey, and residual Western presence, further complicate the operational environment.

As a result, political violence, regulatory opportunism, and persistent state weakness routinely delay or even permanently derail large-scale projects. China's exposure to these risks is heightened by the scale and geographic concentration of its infrastructural footprint. Unlike portfolio investments that can be liquidated or service exports that require minimal fixed assets, infrastructure projects represent multi-year commitments with limited exit options. Once construction begins, abandoning projects generates reputational costs and financial losses, yet continuing projects in deteriorating environments risks escalating costs without corresponding returns.

The broader economic environment also presents challenges. Many Middle Eastern economies remain dependent on hydrocarbons, making them vulnerable to energy price volatility that can rapidly undermine fiscal stability and debt sustainability. States that borrow heavily to finance Chinese infrastructure projects may face debt distress if oil revenues decline, creating political backlash against Chinese creditors and threatening project viability. Although China has generally structured BRI financing to avoid the debt trap dynamics alleged by critics, perception of exploitative lending can generate political opposition that complicates continued engagement regardless of actual contract terms.

Normative Ambiguity and Public Contestation

A fourth potential stress point stem from the normative posture underpinning DSI. China's emphasis on sovereignty, autonomy, and non-interference is widely welcomed by Middle Eastern governments who view external conditionality as a threat to regime security. This approach helps Beijing build trust with regimes that are wary of Western governance agendas. Yet normative ambiguity can become a liability in contexts where Chinese engagement intersects with domestic political contestation.

Civil society actors, opposition groups, and human rights organizations increasingly criticize foreign partnerships that appear to strengthen authoritarian consolidation. The provision of surveillance technologies, digital governance tools, or policing equipment has drawn scrutiny in countries where regimes deploy these tools against domestic dissent (Feldstein, 2019). While such criticism may not determine state policy in authoritarian contexts, it can influence broader social perceptions and erode the political legitimacy of Chinese projects.

Huawei's 5G networks and smart city platforms exemplify these tensions. In the UAE, Egypt, and Saudi Arabia, Chinese firms have provided surveillance infrastructure, facial recognition systems, and data analytics platforms that enhance state capacity for monitoring populations. These technologies serve legitimate governance functions such as traffic management, public safety, and urban planning, but they also enable political control and suppression of dissent. Human rights organizations have documented cases where Chinese-supplied technology facilitated tracking of activists, journalists, and opposition figures.

Western governments and NGOs frequently highlight these issues in attempts to challenge Chinese influence, framing Beijing as complicit in repression. Although China rarely engages directly in ideological contestation, reputational pressures can accumulate, particularly in hybrid regimes where public opinion imposes constraints on foreign policy choices. Even in authoritarian contexts, rulers remain sensitive to nationalist sentiment and popular perceptions of foreign exploitation. If Chinese projects become associated with regime oppression or economic exploitation, they may generate backlash that complicates continued engagement.

Moreover, negative normative framing can erode the neutrality claims that are essential for credible mediation. China's successful mediation of the Iran–Saudi rapprochement rested partly on perceptions of Chinese neutrality and non-interference. If regional actors increasingly perceive Chinese technology partnerships as tools of authoritarian control, or Chinese infrastructure as mechanisms of economic exploitation, Beijing's ability to present itself as an honest broker diminishes. Rivals may question whether Chinese mediation genuinely serves regional stability or primarily advances Chinese interests in preserving access and influence.

The challenge is compounded by the fact that China's own governance model generates suspicion about its long-term intentions. Western narratives portraying China as an authoritarian power seeking to export its governance model, even if exaggerated or instrumentalized for competitive purposes, resonate with populations wary of external domination. These narratives may not determine elite decision-making in the short term, but they shape the broader discursive environment within which Chinese engagement operates, potentially constraining future expansion.

Systemic Shocks and Intensifying Great Power Competition

A final stress point concerns shifts in the global system. DSI operates most effectively within a multipolar environment that allows states to maintain diversified external relations and compartmentalize economic, technological, and security partnerships. If global dynamics shift toward systemic bipolarity or severe fragmentation, the enabling conditions that support DSI may weaken considerably.

The deterioration of United States–China relations, including technological decoupling, financial competition, and the formation of rival strategic blocs, risks constraining Middle Eastern states' room for maneuver. As Washington increases scrutiny of Chinese partnerships in technology, infrastructure, and strategic sectors, regional allies may face pressure to align more closely with American preferences. If technology ecosystems bifurcate, states may be compelled to choose between incompatible digital infrastructures. If financial systems fragment, dual participation in dollar and yuan-based networks may become politically or administratively unviable.

Research on historical great power competitions shows that once rivalry reaches a threshold of system-wide polarization, intermediary strategies become unsustainable, and states are forced into more explicit alignment choices (Kupchan, 2012). The Cold War demonstrated this dynamic: although some states attempted non-alignment, most found that technological, economic, and security interdependencies required choosing between American and Soviet spheres. The contemporary U.S.-China competition has not yet reached comparable levels of systemic polarization, but trends toward technological decoupling, financial fragmentation, and alliance formation suggest movement in that direction.

Under such conditions, Chinese infrastructure could become politicized as indicators of geopolitical alignment rather than neutral developmental assets. American pressure on allies to exclude Huawei from 5G networks previews this dynamic. Washington has explicitly linked technology partnerships with China to broader questions of alliance loyalty and strategic alignment, threatening consequences for states that proceed with Chinese engagement in sensitive sectors. If this logic extends more broadly across infrastructure, energy, and industrial domains, Middle

Eastern states may face increasingly difficult choices between maintaining Chinese partnerships and preserving American security guarantees.

Multilateral institutions sponsored by China could lose convening power if participation is interpreted as a political signal. The CASCF, AIIB, and BRI forums currently operate as platforms for economic cooperation that regional states join without perceiving them as alternatives to Western-dominated institutions. However, if great power competition intensifies, participation in Chinese institutions may be framed as alignment against the West, forcing states to choose between parallel institutional architectures rather than participating in both simultaneously.

Ambiguity, which constitutes one of DSI's core advantages, could become a liability in a world demanding sharper strategic distinctions. Regional states benefit from strategic ambiguity precisely because it allows them to extract resources from multiple powers without committing exclusively to any. This strategy works when great powers tolerate such behavior or lack leverage to compel exclusive alignment. If systemic pressures increase, both the United States and China may demand clearer demonstrations of loyalty, reducing the space for the portfolio strategies that currently characterize regional responses to multipolarity.

The Ukraine conflict and its aftermath provide a relevant case study. Russia's invasion forced many states to take clearer positions than they preferred, as abstention or neutrality became politically untenable under pressure from both sides. Although Middle Eastern states largely avoided explicit alignment during the conflict, maintaining trade with Russia while preserving Western partnerships, the experience demonstrated how systemic shocks can narrow the space for strategic ambiguity. A comparable crisis involving China and the United States could force regional states into alignment choices they have successfully avoided thus far.

Assessment: Resilience and Constraints

These stress points do not invalidate the DSI framework or predict inevitable failure. They highlight the conditions under which DSI functions most effectively, and the structural pressures that could generate constraints or necessitate strategic recalibration. The model's strengths originate from flexibility, embedded economic presence, and the capacity to engage multiple actors concurrently. Its vulnerabilities emerge when political volatility, escalating rivalries, infrastructure exposure, normative contestation, or global polarization undermine the assumptions on which that flexibility depends.

Despite these vulnerabilities, the model proves sufficiently resilient to likely persist across medium-term horizons. The normative foundations remain stronger than Western alternatives given regional historical experiences with conditionality and intervention. The infrastructure interdependencies remain substantial despite vulnerability, creating constituencies within partner states who benefit from continued cooperation. The institutional frameworks possess sufficient depth to continue functioning through localized crises without systemic collapse. And the spatial architecture provides enough redundancy that single-point failures do not cascade through the entire system.

Yet long-term sustainability remains genuinely uncertain, contingent on Beijing's willingness to exercise restraint even as capabilities expand, on regional powers' continued perception that DSI serves their interests, and on the absence of systemic shocks that might render embedded infrastructure networks dysfunctional or force binary alignment choices. A realistic assessment of DSI therefore requires attention not only to its successes but also to the limits that could shape its future trajectory and the conditions under which its advantages might erode or its mechanisms might require fundamental adaptation.

6 The Architecture of Regional Reordering

The Middle East is undergoing a structural transformation in how regional order is constituted, maintained, and contested. This transformation proceeds not through the visible drama of military confrontation or the formal reorganization of alliance structures, but through alterations in the foundational systems that determine economic viability, technological capacity, and developmental trajectory. China's role in this transformation represents neither accidental consequence nor incremental adjustment to existing patterns. It constitutes a deliberate reconfiguration of the material and institutional substrates through which regional politics operate, producing effects that compound over time and resist reversal through conventional policy instruments.

The reordering examined throughout this chapter operates through what can be termed infrastructural layering: the systematic superimposition of new operational networks onto existing regional systems without displacing or directly challenging established structures. This layering creates parallel channels through which resources flow, decisions are coordinated, and dependencies are generated, functioning alongside rather than in opposition to existing security architectures, diplomatic frameworks, and economic relationships. The result is not replacement of one order by another but the production of institutional and material redundancy that fundamentally alters the strategic calculus of regional actors.

Consider the energy sector, historically the domain through which external powers have exercised greatest influence. American strategic dominance rested substantially on its capacity to guarantee Gulf energy exports through naval presence, security commitments, and technological partnerships with national oil companies. This arrangement created asymmetric dependencies: Gulf producers required American protection for export routes and regime security, while American allies and the global economy required stable energy supplies that American power secured. Chinese engagement has not displaced this system but has constructed an alternative energy architecture that operates in parallel. Long-term purchase agreements, joint refining ventures in China itself, investments in upstream production, and participation in downstream petrochemical complexes create interdependencies that function independently of the security frameworks governing export protection (Chen & Han, 2019).

The layering effect becomes visible when analyzing decision-making processes. Saudi Arabia's energy policy now must account for Chinese demand patterns, Chinese investment in domestic capacity, and Chinese participation in Vision 2030 industrial transformation, even as it continues to factor American security guarantees and global market dynamics. The Chinese layer does not eliminate American influence but introduces additional variables that complicate unilateral policy imposition by any external actor. When Washington seeks to mobilize Gulf production to influence global prices or constrain rivals, it encounters constraints imposed by Chinese purchase agreements and joint ventures that create countervailing interests. When Beijing seeks to secure preferential access, it encounters limitations imposed by Saudi commitments to multiple markets and the continued importance of American security provision.

This layering pattern extends across sectors. In telecommunications, Huawei infrastructure operates alongside Western equipment in mixed networks, creating technical interdependencies that resist wholesale substitution in either direction. In port operations, Chinese management and investment at facilities such as Khalifa Port and Duqm function within logistics networks that also serve Western commercial interests and military requirements. In industrial development, Chinese engineering firms participate in complexes that integrate European technology, American management practices, and Gulf capital. The effect is cumulative institutional thickness: each additional layer increases the density of relationships, expands the number of stakeholders with interests in continuity, and raises the costs of disruption.

The reordering process exhibits temporal characteristics that distinguish it from previous efforts to reshape regional order. Historical attempts at regional transformation, whether through revolutionary ideology, military intervention, or rapid institutional construction, operated on compressed timelines that generated intense resistance and often triggered countervailing responses before transformations could consolidate. China's approach inverts this temporal logic, distributing transformation across extended horizons that reduce visibility, minimize resistance, and allow dependencies to mature before their strategic implications become fully apparent.

Infrastructure projects exemplify this temporal asymmetry. A port development requires five to ten years from initial agreement to operational capacity, followed by decades of amortization during which the investment shapes logistics planning, trade patterns, and operational routines. Digital infrastructure exhibits even longer lock-in periods, as proprietary standards, integrated systems, and accumulated data create switching costs that escalate over time. Industrial complexes generate multi-generational effects, as workforce training, supply chain integration, and technological ecosystems produce path dependencies that structure developmental choices for decades beyond initial investment.

This temporal distribution creates strategic advantages that conventional frameworks often overlook. First, it allows transformation to proceed beneath the threshold of acute geopolitical contestation. Projects that appear purely commercial during implementation reveal strategic significance only after operational integration makes disruption costly. Second, it exploits the institutional and political constraints that limit competitor responses. Democratic powers face electoral cycles that complicate long-term strategic patience. Alliance-based systems require consensus among partners with divergent interests. Market-driven actors prioritize short-term returns over multi-decade strategic positioning.

China's state-directed system and ideological emphasis on long-term planning provide comparative advantage in sustaining commitments across timeframes that exceed the planning horizons of alternative models.

Third, temporal distribution allows Chinese engagement to adapt incrementally to changing conditions without abandoning accumulated investments. A port that initially serves commercial functions can gradually assume strategic significance as regional dynamics evolve. Digital infrastructure deployed for civilian purposes creates latent capabilities for surveillance or control that can be activated if circumstances require. Industrial partnerships that begin as technology transfer arrangements can evolve into joint production of sensitive dual-use equipment as relationships deepen and trust accumulates. This evolutionary capacity distinguishes infrastructural engagement from formal alliances or explicit security commitments that lock participants into defined roles and create rigidities that resist adaptation.

Epistemic Transformation and the Reconfiguration of Strategic Cognition

Beyond material and institutional changes, the reordering process operates through epistemic transformation: alterations in how regional actors perceive strategic possibilities, calculate interests, and conceptualize their position within broader systems. This dimension of reordering is less visible than infrastructure construction or diplomatic breakthroughs but may prove more consequential over extended horizons, as cognitive frameworks structure the range of options actors consider viable and determine which strategies appear rational or irrational.

The most significant epistemic shift concerns the relationship between economic interdependence and strategic autonomy. Traditional strategic thought, particularly as codified during the Cold War, treated deep economic integration with external powers as compromising sovereignty and constraining policy autonomy. Dependencies on external technology, capital, or markets were understood as vulnerabilities that adversaries could exploit through economic coercion or withdrawal of critical resources. This cognitive framework generated defensive economic policies, efforts to minimize external dependencies, and preferences for self-reliance even at substantial economic cost.

Chinese engagement has contributed to a fundamental revision of this calculus among Middle Eastern elites. Rather than viewing interdependence as compromising autonomy, sophisticated regional actors increasingly understand interdependence as an instrument for enhancing autonomy when structured appropriately. The key insight is that interdependence need not be hierarchical or unilateral. When dependencies are mutual, distributed across multiple domains, and embedded within systems that serve host-state priorities, they constrain the external power as much as the regional state. China becomes dependent on Gulf energy supplies, on the operational success of infrastructure investments that represent sunk costs, and on regional stability that protects accumulated assets. These reciprocal dependencies create shared interests that limit Chinese capacity for coercion while providing developmental resources that enhance state capacity.

This epistemic reconfiguration manifests in observable policy changes. Saudi Arabia's Vision 2030 explicitly embraces deep technological and economic integration with China while maintaining security dependence on the United States, a strategy that would have appeared irrational under Cold War cognitive frameworks that assumed exclusive alignment. The UAE pursues simultaneous deepening with Chinese digital infrastructure, American security cooperation, and Israeli technology partnerships, treating these not as contradictory choices requiring prioritization but as complementary components of diversified strategy. Iran leverages Chinese economic support to survive sanctions while deliberately cultivating alternative relationships to prevent substitution of American coercion with Chinese dependence.

The cognitive shift extends to how regional actors understand their own agency. Rather than perceiving themselves as objects of great power competition compelled to choose sides, sophisticated regional actors increasingly view themselves as strategic subjects capable of shaping great power behavior through deliberate manipulation of interdependencies. By making themselves valuable to multiple external powers simultaneously, by structuring relationships to prevent monopolistic control, and by exploiting great power competition to extract favorable terms, regional states exercise agency that Cold War frameworks suggested was unavailable to smaller powers in asymmetric relationships.

This transformation in strategic cognition constitutes reordering in its most fundamental sense. It alters not merely the distribution of capabilities or the pattern of alignments but the cognitive structures through which actors interpret their environment and calculate responses. When regional elites perceive interdependence as instrument rather than constraint, when they understand portfolio diversification as enhancing rather than compromising coherent strategy, and when they recognize their own capacity to shape great power behavior rather than simply responding to it, the foundations of regional order have shifted in ways that resist reversal through conventional policy instruments.

Institutional Multiplication and the Fragmentation of Governance Authority

The reordering process has generated institutional multiplication: the proliferation of overlapping forums, mechanisms, and frameworks through which regional governance occurs. This multiplication fragments authority, distributes decision-making across multiple sites, and creates institutional redundancy that insulates regional actors from excessive dependence on any single framework. The effect is not chaos or incoherence but structured pluralism in which different institutional venues serve distinct functions and provide alternative channels when primary mechanisms encounter obstruction.

Chinese initiatives have contributed substantially to this institutional multiplication. The China–Arab States Cooperation Forum, established in 2004, created an alternative venue for regional dialogue operating outside Western-dominated frameworks. Bilateral strategic partnerships with Saudi Arabia (2016), Iran (2021), and the UAE provide institutional mechanisms for high-level coordination independent of multilateral constraints. Sectoral cooperation agreements in energy, technology, infrastructure, and finance create specialized channels through which technical cooperation proceeds regardless of broader political tensions. Investment platforms such as the Silk Road Fund and development finance through Chinese policy banks offer alternatives to Western-dominated financial institutions with their attendant conditionalities.

This institutional multiplication serves multiple strategic functions. First, it provides regional actors with exit options when engagement with established institutions becomes politically costly or operationally constrained. States facing conditionality from the IMF or World Bank can pursue Chinese development finance. Actors blocked in the UN Security Council can seek support through alternative frameworks. Partners frustrated by slow decision-making in consensus-based institutions can pursue bilateral or minilateral channels that accelerate implementation.

Second, institutional multiplication enables compartmentalization that allows contradictory policies to coexist without generating systemic crisis. States can pursue liberal economic reforms within Western-oriented frameworks while maintaining authoritarian governance practices in relationships with China. They can advocate for regional security cooperation in multilateral forums while conducting bilateral security relationships that contradict collective arrangements. They can support multilateral climate initiatives while pursuing bilateral energy partnerships that serve immediate economic interests. The coexistence of multiple institutional venues, each with distinct norms and operational logics, provides the flexibility necessary for managing these contradictions.

Third, multiplication dilutes the normative authority of any single institutional framework. When Western institutions monopolized regional governance, their norms and practices acquired quasi-hegemonic status, structuring expectations about appropriate behavior and legitimate policy. Institutional multiplication challenges this monopoly. Chinese institutions that prioritize sovereignty and non-interference provide alternative normative foundations. Regional institutions that reflect indigenous priorities challenge external prescriptions. The result is normative pluralism in which competing principles coexist, and actors select institutional venues strategically based on which norms align with immediate interests.

The long-term effect of institutional multiplication on regional order remains contested. Some analysts interpret proliferation as evidence of weakening governance and institutional decay. The more persuasive interpretation recognizes multiplication as adaptation to multipolar conditions in which no single power possesses the authority or capacity to impose institutional monopoly. Regional order under these conditions requires mechanisms that accommodate diversity, permit flexibility, and distribute authority across multiple sites. Institutional multiplication, rather than undermining order, may constitute the organizational form through which multipolar regional governance operates effectively.

The Reconfiguration of Competitive Dynamics

China's infrastructural and institutional presence has fundamentally altered the competitive dynamics through which external powers vie for regional influence. Traditional competition operated through zero-sum logic: gains for one power implied losses for others, and influence was measured through relative position within hierarchical rankings. Military bases, alliance partnerships, and exclusive economic relationships served as metrics through which analysts assessed competitive outcomes. The power controlling more bases, commanding more alliance commitments, or capturing larger market shares was understood to be winning the competition.

The contemporary competitive environment exhibits different characteristics. Competition increasingly operates through non-exclusive mechanisms in which multiple powers can simultaneously increase their influence without necessarily diminishing rivals' positions. Chinese infrastructure investment does not prevent American security provision or European commercial engagement. American military presence does not preclude Chinese economic partnerships. European regulatory cooperation coexists with Chinese technological integration. The result is competitive coexistence in which rivalry persists but operates through accumulation rather than displacement.

This shift reflects both the sectoral differentiation of influence and the functional compartmentalization regional actors employ in managing external relationships. When security, economic, and technological domains are managed separately, different external powers can dominate different sectors without generating direct confrontation. The United States maintains military superiority; China accumulates economic and infrastructural advantages; Europe preserves regulatory influence and normative authority. Rather than competing for comprehensive dominance across all domains, powers increasingly specialize in sectors where they possess comparative advantage, accepting limited influence in domains where others prove more effective.

The transformation also reflects changes in what constitutes strategic success. During periods of hegemonic competition, success meant establishing exclusive spheres of influence, compelling alignment, and preventing rival access. Under contemporary conditions, success increasingly means establishing embedded presence, creating dependencies that generate influence, and positioning oneself as indispensable partner even when rivals maintain alternative relationships. China succeeds not by excluding American influence but by making itself necessary for developmental and economic priorities that American military power cannot address. The United States succeeds not by preventing Chinese economic engagement but by maintaining security provision that Chinese capabilities cannot replicate.

This reconfigured competition produces paradoxical outcomes that confound traditional strategic analysis. States deepen partnerships with China while strengthening security ties with the United States. They accept Chinese infrastructure investment while voicing concerns about

Chinese strategic intentions. They participate in Chinese institutional initiatives while maintaining commitments to Western-dominated frameworks. These behaviors appear contradictory when analyzed through zero-sum competitive frameworks but prove rational when understood as portfolio strategies designed to maximize autonomy by preventing any external power from acquiring monopolistic influence.

The regional implications are profound. Competition no longer produces clear winners and losers, exclusive alignments, or stable hierarchies. Instead, it generates complex interdependencies in which all major external powers maintain substantial influence, regional actors preserve significant autonomy, and outcomes remain indeterminate. This competitive environment may prove more stable than zero-sum rivalry that historically generated proxy conflicts and direct confrontation. It may also prove more volatile if escalating great power tensions force regional actors to make exclusive choices that current arrangements allow them to avoid. The trajectory remains contingent on choices made by external powers and regional actors as multipolarity continues to deepen and competitive dynamics continue to evolve.

Synthesis: The Logic of Non-Hegemonic Reordering

The Middle East's transformation under Chinese engagement illuminates a form of reordering that operates without hegemonic ambition or hierarchical imposition. This non-hegemonic reordering proceeds through material embedding rather than political control, through institutional proliferation rather than monopolistic authority, and through cognitive transformation rather than ideological conversion. It generates influence through accumulated dependencies rather than coercive capability, through positioning within networks rather than command over hierarchies, and through constructed indispensability rather than imposed subordination.

This logic of reordering differs fundamentally from historical patterns. It does not seek to establish Chinese dominance replacing American primacy. It does not attempt to organize regional actors into exclusive blocs or formal alliances. It does not demand ideological conformity or political alignment. Instead, it constructs parallel systems that increase regional actors' options while creating dependencies that constrain certain choices, builds institutional redundancy that prevents monopolistic control while embedding Chinese participation across multiple venues, and transforms cognitive frameworks that shape how actors perceive possibilities while avoiding coercive imposition of Chinese preferences.

The sustainability of this reordering model depends on conditions that cannot be guaranteed indefinitely. It requires regional stability sufficient to protect fixed infrastructure investments. It presumes multipolarity permitting diversified external relationships without forced binary choices. It depends on Chinese restraint in exploiting accumulated dependencies for short-term coercive advantage. It assumes continued regional preference for sovereignty and autonomy over the security guarantees that hierarchical alignment provides. Should any of these enabling conditions shift substantially, the mechanisms generating non-hegemonic reordering would face significant stress.

Yet even acknowledging these contingencies, the transformation documented throughout this chapter represents a significant reordering of Middle Eastern strategic dynamics. Regional actors have acquired greater autonomy through portfolio diversification. Competition among external powers operates through more complex mechanisms that resist simple measurement. Institutional governance has fragmented across multiple venues that accommodate normative pluralism. Strategic cognition has evolved to recognize interdependence as instrument rather than constraint. Material infrastructures have created dependencies that function independently of political directives or diplomatic pressure. These changes, individually significant, collectively constitute systemic transformation in how regional order operates, how influence is generated, and how power flows through regional political systems. The Middle East emerging from this transformation exhibits characteristics fundamentally different from the region that existed at the turn of the century, differences that China's infrastructural and institutional engagement has substantially enabled and accelerated.

References

Alterman, J. B., & Garver, J. W. (2008). *The vital triangle: China, the United States, and the Middle East* (Vol. 30). CSIS.

Blanchard, C. M. (2018). Saudi Arabia: Background and US relations (updated). *Current Politics and Economics of the Middle East, 9*(2/3), 431–503.

Brownlee, J. (2012). *Democracy prevention: The politics of the US-Egyptian alliance*. Cambridge University Press.

Calabrese, J. (2018). *Oman's transition to a post-oil economy: Arching toward Asia*. Middle East Institute.

Chatzky, A., & McBride, J. (2020). China's massive belt and road initiative. *Council on Foreign Relations*, *28*(11).

Chen, D., & Han, W. (2019). Deepening cooperation between Saudi Arabia and China. *King Abdullah Petroleum Studies and Research Center*, *24*.

Chen, J., Yang, X., Wang, M., & Su, M. (2023). Evolution of China's interaction with Middle Eastern countries under the Belt and Road Initiative. *PLoS ONE, 18*(11), Article e0293426.

de Haas, M., Gaberščik, E., Jenkins, T., & Kumar, A. (2020). Russia's military action in Syria driven by military reforms. *The Journal of Slavic Military Studies, 33*(2), 292–299.

Del Sarto, R. A. (2021). *Borderlands: Europe and the mediterranean middle east*. Oxford University Press.

Farrell, H., & Newman, A. L. (2019). Weaponized interdependence: How global economic networks shape state coercion. *International Security, 44*(1), 42–79.

Fawcett, L. L. E. (2016). *International relations of the Middle East*. Oxford University Press.

Feldstein, S. (2019). *The global expansion of AI surveillance* (Vol. 17). Carnegie Endowment for International Peace.

Garlick, J., & Havlová, R. (2020). China's "Belt and Road" Economic Diplomacy in the Persian Gulf: Strategic Hedging amidst Saudi-Iranian Regional Rivalry. *Journal of Current Chinese Affairs, 49*(1), 82–105.

Gause, F. G., III. (2009). *The international relations of the Persian Gulf*. Cambridge University Press.

Hanieh, A. (2018). *Money, markets, and monarchies: The Gulf Cooperation Council and the political economy of the contemporary Middle East* (Vol. 4). Cambridge University Press.

Kastner, S. L., & Pearson, M. M. (2021). Exploring the parameters of China's economic influence. *Studies in Comparative International Development, 56*(1), 18–44.

Kupchan, C. (2012). *No one's world: The West, the rising rest, and the coming global turn*. OUP USA.

Kydd, A. H. (2005). *Trust and mistrust in international relations*. Princeton University Press.

Lynch, M. (2016). *The new Arab wars: Uprisings and anarchy in the Middle East*. Public Affairs.

Massie, J., & Paquin, J. (2020). *America's allies and the decline of US hegemony*. Routledge Nueva York.

Maxigas, & ten Oever, N. (2023). Geopolitics in the infrastructural ideology of 5G. *Global Media and China*, *8*(3), 271–288.

Mayer, M. (2018). China's historical statecraft and the return of history. *International Affairs, 94*(6), 1217–1235.

Nye, J. (2004). *Soft power: The means to success in world politics*, ed. Public Affairs.

Posen, B. R. (2018). *Restraint: A new foundation for US grand strategy*. Cornell University Press.

Schiavi, F. (2025). Saudi Arabia deepens China industrial partnership. *Al-Monitor*. https://www.al-monitor.com/newsletter/2025-09-23/saudi-arabia-deepens-china-industrial-partnership

Schumacher, T. (2014). The european union and democracy promotion: Readjusting to the arab spring. In *Routledge handbook of the Arab Spring* (pp. 559–573). Routledge.

Shaeri, N. E.-. (2025). Saudi Arabia sees 28.8% rise in Chinese FDI to reach $8.2bn. *Arab News*. https://www.arabnews.com/node/2612863/business-economy

Shirzad, A. (2022). Looking-East in the Iranian foreign policy: The politico-ideological inclinations and practical imperatives. *Journal of Globalization Studies, 13*(2), 53–75.

Ulrichsen, K. C. (2014). The uprising in Bahrain: Regional dimensions and international consequences. In *Routledge handbook of the Arab Spring* (pp. 133–144). Routledge.

Ulrichsen, K. C. (2020). *Rebalancing regional security in the Persian Gulf* (pp. 14–15). Rice University's Baker Institute for Public Policy.

Vakil, S. (2006). Iran: Balancing east against west. *Washington Quarterly, 29*(4), 51–65.

CHAPTER 9

Conclusion

1 The Anomaly That Demands Explanation

This book begins with an anomaly that the dominant traditions of international relations struggle to explain. A state with no military bases across the Middle East, no regional alliance system resembling NATO or the Cold War blocs, and no ideological message capable of mobilizing publics shaped by Islamic traditions or Arab nationalism nonetheless presided in 2023 over one of the most consequential diplomatic breakthroughs in recent regional history. The long-entrenched rivalry between Iran and Saudi Arabia, an axis around which five decades of Middle Eastern geopolitics have revolved, was not eased by American pressure, European shuttle diplomacy, or regional initiative. Instead, the decisive facilitation occurred in Beijing, under terms that neither side would have accepted from any other external power.

The significance of this outcome extends far beyond the bilateral reconciliation itself. For decades, the Iran-Saudi rivalry has structured regional alignments, fueled proxy conflicts across Yemen, Syria, Iraq, and Lebanon, shaped energy markets through competing production strategies, and constrained diplomatic initiatives that required cooperation between the two powers or their respective allies. Efforts to bridge this divide had foundered repeatedly. American attempts at mediation were compromised by Washington's security alliance with Riyadh and adversarial relationship with Tehran, creating perceptions of bias that undermined

A. Ullah, *Diplomacy by Design*,
https://doi.org/10.1007/978-981-95-7876-4_9

credibility. European initiatives lacked the material leverage necessary to alter cost–benefit calculations in either capital. Regional powers, themselves embedded within the rivalry's sectarian and geopolitical fault lines, could not credibly position themselves as neutral facilitators.

Yet China, despite possessing none of the traditional sources of mediating authority, succeeded where others had failed. This outcome cannot be reconciled with the explanatory models that typically organize strategic analysis. Conventional balancing theory offers little insight, as China possesses no deployable military architecture capable of shaping behavior in the Gulf. The People's Liberation Army maintains no permanent bases in the region, deploys no carrier strike groups to patrol strategic waterways, and has established no formal mutual defense commitments that would compel intervention during crises. Alliance politics frameworks fall short, since Beijing has no binding strategic commitments and no interest in organizing states into exclusive blocs that would force binary alignment choices.

Soft power explanations are equally unpersuasive. Chinese governance norms hold limited appeal for either Iranian or Saudi elites, and Beijing's civilizational discourse inspires neither emulation nor cultural affinity. The Chinese political model, characterized by centralized party control, state-directed development, and tight information management, resonates weakly in contexts shaped by different historical trajectories, distinct religious traditions, and varied institutional configurations. Saudi Arabia's monarchical system draws legitimacy from Wahhabi religious authority and tribal networks, not from Leninist organizational principles. Iran's clerical establishment derives authority from Shia jurisprudence and revolutionary ideology fundamentally different from Chinese Marxist–Leninist adaptation. Neither society looks to Chinese cultural production, educational models, or normative frameworks as sources of inspiration or templates for emulation.

Coercive economic statecraft provides no better footing, for China issued neither threats nor conditionalities that compelled the parties toward reconciliation. Beijing did not threaten to withdraw investment from Saudi Arabia if Riyadh refused to negotiate. It did not condition continued energy purchases from Iran on Tehran's willingness to engage diplomatically with its Gulf rivals. It did not leverage its position in either economy to extract political concessions or force policy changes against the preferences of local leadership. The mediation succeeded not through coercion but through mechanisms that operate according to entirely different logic.

The explanation, developed throughout this book, requires a different conceptual grammar. What unfolded in Beijing cannot be understood through frameworks premised on compulsion, patronage, or ideological conversion. It rests instead on a mode of statecraft in which influence is produced through deliberately structured interdependence, where material embeddedness substitutes for military presence, and where calibrated ambiguity enhances rather than undermines diplomatic capacity. This is DSI, a form of agency exercised not through what a state can coerce or demand, but through the institutional, infrastructural, and economic environments it constructs, environments that enable partners to pursue their own interests while simultaneously generating shared stakes in stability, predictability, and continued engagement.

The Iran-Saudi reconciliation emerged from foundations built over two decades of patient infrastructural and economic engagement. China had cultivated parallel relationships with both states through mechanisms that generated operational dependencies linking Chinese commercial performance to key sectors in both economies. With Saudi Arabia, these mechanisms included long-term oil purchase agreements that provided revenue stability, joint refining ventures that integrated Chinese and Saudi petroleum industries, investments in downstream petrochemical facilities that created production interdependencies, and participation in Vision, 2030 modernization initiatives that embedded Chinese firms in critical development projects. With Iran, they included energy cooperation that sustained Iranian export revenues despite sanctions pressure, infrastructure investments in transportation and telecommunications that modernized Iranian systems, and technology partnerships that provided capabilities unavailable through Western channels due to sanctions restrictions.

These economic relationships generated more than commercial benefit. They created institutional sites of routine interaction through which officials, ministers, and senior technocrats developed durable communication channels independent of high-level political tensions. Joint commission meetings, project implementation coordination, and technical consultations normalized regular contact and built familiarity that reduced political risk associated with diplomatic engagement. They established credibility for Chinese facilitators, as consistent performance on commercial commitments demonstrated reliability and long-term commitment rather than opportunistic intervention. They created material stakes in regional stability, as Chinese investments and commercial relationships would suffer disruption from escalating conflict, aligning Chinese interests with de-escalation in ways that reassured both parties about mediation motives.

Crucially, China had avoided entanglement in the normative contests, ideological narratives, and security rivalries that have historically undermined Western mediation attempts. Beijing issued no judgments about the legitimacy of either political system, imposed no conditions regarding governance practices or human rights standards, and refrained from public criticism that might have generated nationalist backlash or political constraints on engagement. This normative neutrality, combined with material embeddedness and institutional routinization, positioned China uniquely to facilitate dialogue that neither party would have accepted from powers perceived as aligned with opposing sides or committed to normative agendas threatening regime security.

When expressed in abstraction, the concept of DSI appears straightforward. Yet its implications, empirical, theoretical, and normative, reach far beyond the mechanics of the 2023 reconciliation. They touch on foundational questions concerning how influence travels, how order is assembled, and how power operates in a world no longer structured by a singular hegemon. As the preceding chapters have shown, China's approach in the Middle East is not an incremental variation on existing templates; it signals a deeper transformation in the architecture of external engagement. It reveals how authority can be exercised without garrisons, how mediation can be facilitated without alliances, and how strategic relevance can be constructed without ideological conversion or coercive enforcement.

The transformation extends beyond diplomatic breakthroughs to encompass fundamental shifts in regional strategic behavior. Middle Eastern states increasingly pursue portfolio strategies that distribute different functional domains across multiple external powers, extracting developmental resources from China while maintaining security relationships with the United States and commercial ties with Europe. This functional compartmentalization was not viable under Cold War bipolarity or early post-Cold War American primacy but has become characteristic of regional strategic behavior under contemporary multipolar conditions. The emergence of these portfolio strategies signals not confusion or transitional instability but rational adaptation to a transformed strategic environment in which DSI creates structural space for simultaneous engagement with rival powers.

Infrastructure has emerged as a primary medium through which this influence operates, creating material interdependencies that structure incentives and constrain policy options independent of explicit political pressure. Ports, industrial complexes, digital networks, and energy systems function simultaneously as commercial assets and as structural constraints on partner state behavior. The dependencies generated through these investments are neither unilateral nor absolute, but they create opportunity costs for disruption that regional actors find prohibitively expensive absent severe political imperatives. This calculus operates independently of Chinese diplomatic pressure or explicit conditionality, generating influence through the material realities of operational integration rather than through threatened coercion.

Seen from this perspective, the Iran-Saudi reconciliation is not an isolated diplomatic episode but a visible symptom of a wider reordering. It captures the emergence of a logic of power that operates through embedded presence rather than hierarchical command, through infrastructural linkages rather than military preponderance, and through relational design rather than formalized blocs. In this sense, the anomaly that opens this chapter is not merely the puzzle that motivated this book; it is also the clearest window into a changing international system in which influence increasingly rests on the architectures states build, the dependencies they engineer, and the political space their ambiguity makes possible.

The chapters that preceded this conclusion have documented how this transformation operates across multiple dimensions. They have shown how infrastructure functions as political instrument, how regional actors construct sophisticated portfolio strategies in response to DSI, how Chinese engagement differs systematically from American, Russian, and European modalities, and how the model faces structural limits and sustainability challenges that constrain its operation. The task now is to extract broader theoretical and empirical implications from these findings, to assess what the Middle Eastern case reveals about changing dynamics of power and order in international politics, and to identify the scope conditions and limitations that determine where and when DSI proves effective as an instrument of statecraft.

2 How Power Moves Without Moving

China's expanding presence in the Middle East demonstrates a transformation in how external power can shape regional politics without projecting military force, imposing hierarchy, or demanding ideological conformity. This shift is not merely a matter of diplomatic style. It reflects a deeper reconfiguration in the mechanics of influence that DSI seeks to capture. At the core of this transformation is a principle that challenges conventional understandings of how power operates in international politics: influence can accumulate and flow through systems that states construct rather than through capabilities they deploy, through infrastructures they embed rather than through alliances they command, and through incentive structures they design rather than through coercion they threaten.

Traditional great power engagement in the Middle East has been defined by forms of control that required geographic presence and visible assertion of capability. American, European, and Russian strategies in the Middle East and North Africa have relied on controlling resources that regional states need, albeit through different instruments. The U.S. leveraged forward-deployed military bases, carrier strike group rotations, integrated intelligence networks, and security guarantees (Gause III, 2009). Europe exerted influence through market access and regulatory authority over the continent's integrated economic zone, linking developmental assistance to governance and human rights reforms to create conditional dependencies that shaped policy choices (Del Sarto, 2021). Russia, meanwhile, pursued arms transfers, military interventions, and diplomatic support to embed itself in regional conflicts, as seen in Syria in 2015, while arms sales to countries such as Egypt and Algeria generated dependencies on Russian military capabilities, maintenance, and training, giving Moscow leverage over both external defense and internal security (de Haas et al., 2020).

In each case, influence flowed from an external actor's control over assets that regional actors could not easily replace. Military protection, market access, regulatory approval, advanced weaponry, and financial assistance all represented resources that external powers possessed and could grant or withhold based on recipient compliance with preferred policies. The logic was fundamentally hierarchical: the external power occupied a superior position by virtue of controlling critical resources, and the regional actor accepted constraints on autonomy in exchange for access to those resources. Power moved from the external actor to the regional state through explicit channels of dependency and conditionality.

China reverses this logic fundamentally. Instead of seeking control over what Middle Eastern states require, it constructs environments in which states voluntarily align their choices with Chinese-linked infrastructures, technologies, and economic pathways because doing so advances domestic priorities that states define for themselves. A power plant built with Chinese technology and financing becomes integrated into a national electrical grid, its operation essential to industrial production, residential consumption, and commercial activity. Replacing Chinese equipment would require not merely purchasing alternative generators but reconfiguring grid management systems, retraining technical personnel, accepting transitional disruptions to power supply, and absorbing costs that extend far beyond equipment procurement.

A port restructured under Chinese operational management and developed through Chinese investment becomes a logistical artery through which imports and exports flow, employment is generated, and regional connectivity is established (Calabrese, 2018). The port's continued operation depends on Chinese technical expertise, management systems, and integration with global shipping networks in which Chinese firms play central roles. Disrupting the relationship would interrupt trade flows, eliminate jobs, and damage the port's reputation as reliable logistics hub, imposing costs borne primarily by the host state rather than by China.

A digital ecosystem introduced through smart city platforms, telecommunications networks, or cloud infrastructure becomes embedded in governance routines, commercial operations, and daily urban life. Proprietary standards, integrated data systems, and operational dependencies create switching costs that escalate over time as more services, more users, and more government functions rely on the infrastructure (Maxigas & ten Oever, 2023). Moving to alternative systems becomes increasingly costly as dependencies deepen, not because China threatens consequences but because the accumulated investment in training, integration, and operational adaptation makes continuity more rational than disruption.

These systems do not bind states to China through political obligation or explicit conditionality. They bind states through practical necessity and rational calculation. Once embedded, they create patterns of reliance that generate influence without direct enforcement or threatened coercion. The innovation lies in the relational nature of this power. China does not acquire leverage by threatening to withdraw support, as such threats would harm Chinese commercial interests, damage China's reputation as a reliable partner, and provide competitors with opportunities to substitute Chinese presence. Instead, China makes withdrawal undesirable for the host state itself by ensuring that disruption imposes costs that states calculate as prohibitively high relative to benefits that might be gained.

The cost of disruption is borne internally rather than imposed externally. This inversion is crucial. When American military protection is withdrawn or European market access is restricted, the costs are imposed by the external actor as punishment for non-compliance. The mechanism operates through coercion. When Chinese infrastructure becomes inoperative or Chinese technology partnerships are terminated, the costs emerge from internal disruptions to systems that the state itself depends upon for economic performance and political stability. The mechanism operates through self-imposed constraints that arise from rational calculation rather than external punishment.

States maintain cooperation not because Beijing demands compliance but because the infrastructures that sustain their own economic performance and political stability have become integrated with Chinese capabilities. Saudi Arabia continues energy partnerships with China not because Beijing threatens consequences for non-cooperation but because those partnerships contribute to Vision, 2030 objectives, generate employment, transfer technology, and diversify export markets in ways that serve Saudi interests. Iran sustains economic relationships with China not because Beijing coerces cooperation but because those relationships provide critical revenue during sanctions, facilitate infrastructure modernization, and offer technological capabilities unavailable through other channels given Western restrictions (Garlick, 2023).

The result is an incentive structure in which continuity becomes the rational choice even when tensions arise in other areas of the relationship. Political disagreements, diplomatic friction, or competing interests in specific domains do not automatically trigger relationship termination because the material foundations of cooperation serve interests that persist independent of transient political disputes. This generates stability that hierarchical relationships based on explicit conditionality often struggle to replicate, as the latter depend on continuous enforcement of compliance and are vulnerable to challenges when costs of subordination exceed perceived benefits.

This method produces a form of influence particularly suited to the contemporary Middle East, a region characterized by acute sovereignty sensitivities rooted in colonial histories, by suspicion of external intervention generated through decades of foreign military presence, and by developmental imperatives that require external capital and technology but resist political subordination as the price of access. Chinese engagement avoids theatrics and avoids positioning that would present China as an intrusive actor demanding alignment or compliance. It accumulates gradually, often below the threshold of geopolitical spectacle, which reduces the risk of provoking nationalist resistance or triggering balancing coalitions.

It creates domestic constituencies in partner states that view continuity of engagement not as concession to an external power but as alignment with national development. These constituencies exist across ministries responsible for infrastructure and economic planning, municipal governments implementing smart city initiatives, commercial elites whose business models depend on Chinese partnerships, and technological ecosystems integrated with Chinese platforms. The distributed nature of support across multiple sectors and societal groups produces stability that traditional alliance-based influence often struggles to replicate, as the latter typically concentrates support within military establishments or ruling elites whose political fortunes may shift rapidly.

This dynamic explains why China's influence expands even in states that maintain strong security relationships with the United States or deep economic ties with Europe. Chinese engagement offers something that does not demand exclusivity, does not challenge sovereignty, and does not impose political conditions. In doing so, it inserts itself into the operating systems of regional political and economic life while avoiding the liabilities associated with conventional great power projection. Influence becomes less a matter of commanding strategic heights and more a matter of shaping the terrain upon which others operate, less about controlling specific decisions and more about structuring the environments within which decisions are made.

The deeper significance for the region is that this form of power alters how states conceive the landscape of external alignment. Middle Eastern governments have long been accustomed to choosing between patrons who offered security guarantees in exchange for strategic loyalty, who demanded exclusive alignment as the price of protection, and who treated relationships as zero-sum competitions in which partnerships with rivals constituted betrayal. DSI presents a different logic. It allows states to diversify without defecting, to extract benefits without accepting comprehensive constraints, and to pursue autonomy even as interdependence deepens.

It produces a strategic environment where power circulates through networks rather than hierarchies, where alignment occurs through practical embeddedness rather than formal commitment, and where influence derives from positioning within systems rather than from command over capabilities. This represents not merely tactical adjustment but fundamental transformation in how external powers establish presence and how regional actors manage external relationships. The Middle East is being reordered not through the replacement of one hegemon by another but through the proliferation of alternative channels through which influence flows and the construction of material architectures that operate according to different principles than those that structured previous regional orders.

China's ability to move influence without moving forces represents not simply a new strategy but a new grammar of international engagement. In this grammar, relationships are not built through the visible assertion of power but through the quiet accumulation of relevance. Presence is not measured by the number of bases an external actor possesses but by the degree to which its infrastructures, technologies, and institutions shape the rhythms of daily governance and economic activity. Mediation becomes possible not because of military dominance or ideological authority but because the mediator is already structurally present in the political and economic life of opposing actors, possessing material stakes in their stability and maintaining communication channels built through years of routine cooperation.

Influence becomes credible precisely because it is not coercive. States engage willingly because cooperation serves interests, they define autonomously rather than because they fear consequences of noncompliance. The effectiveness of this influence lies in its embedded design, in the deliberate construction of systems that make continued cooperation rational while preserving sufficient autonomy that partners do not perceive themselves as subordinated. This balance, difficult to achieve and requiring strategic patience over extended timeframes, distinguishes DSI from both hegemonic imposition that generates resistance and from purely market-driven engagement that lacks strategic direction.

This is how power moves without moving, and it is central to the reordering underway in the Middle East. It exemplifies how DSI restructures incentives, redefines alignment, and reshapes the very meaning of external presence. China demonstrates that in the contemporary Middle East, power that is woven into the architecture of everyday economic and technological life can be more consequential than power that arrives through warships, military bases, or formal alliances.

3 Theoretical Contributions: Rethinking Power and Influence in Multipolar Systems

The framework developed in this book advances international relations theory by addressing explanatory gaps that established paradigms cannot adequately fill and by introducing conceptual innovations that illuminate dynamics increasingly visible across contested regions where multiple external powers compete for influence without achieving dominance. The contribution operates at multiple levels: it specifies mechanisms through which infrastructure and institutional design generate political influence, integrates bodies of scholarship that international relations often treats separately, and develops middle-range theory contextually grounded rather than artificially universal.

Designed Strategic Interdependence contributes theoretical refinement by demonstrating that interdependence can be structured deliberately to preserve partner autonomy even as it generates influence for the external actor. The empirical chapters reveal states such as Saudi Arabia and Iran preserving meaningful bargaining capacity within deep economic relationships with China. They negotiate conditions restricting Chinese equity stakes in strategic sectors, insist on technology transfer rather than permanent reliance on Chinese expertise, and compartmentalize cooperation to prevent concentration of vulnerability (Chen & Han, 2019; Shirzad, 2022).

The key lies in mutual exposure and distributed dependencies. When Chinese firms invest fixed capital in regional infrastructure, they become exposed to political risk and regulatory change in ways that create reciprocal vulnerabilities. When Chinese energy security depends on stable imports from Gulf producers, disruptions harm Chinese interests as much as producer revenues. This mutual exposure transforms the political economy of interdependence from unilateral dependency enabling coercion into mutual dependency creating shared interests in relationship continuity that constrain both parties.

The influence that accrues to China derives not from the capacity to impose costs through withdrawal but from rational calculation by partners that cooperation serves their interests better than disruption. This is influence through structural positioning rather than hierarchical dominance, through incentive alignment rather than coercive leverage, and through accumulated embeddedness rather than explicit conditionality. DSI therefore demonstrates that economic asymmetry does not automatically translate into political subordination when relationships are structured to preserve autonomy, maintain alternatives, and ensure mutual vulnerabilities.

DSI foregrounds intentional design as an analytical category, challenging persistent assumptions that international politics is shaped primarily by structural forces beyond state control or by unintended consequences of decentralized decisions. China did not wait for market forces to generate interdependence with Middle Eastern states. It pursued deliberate strategies of infrastructure investment prioritizing sectors with high strategic value, energy partnerships structured to create long-term supply relationships, and technology cooperation targeting domains that would generate operational dependencies.

The sequencing of Chinese engagement reveals intentionality. Initial investments in relatively low-risk commercial projects built credibility and established presence. Subsequent expansion into more strategic sectors occurred after trust had accumulated and institutional channels had been established. Technology partnerships followed infrastructure cooperation, as digital dependencies required higher levels of trust and operational integration than physical assets. This progression reflects strategic design rather than random market-driven engagement, with each phase creating foundations for subsequent deepening.

This brings agency, sequence, and strategic choice back into theoretical focus, recognizing that outcomes reflect not merely systemic pressures or market dynamics but deliberate decisions about how to construct relationships, which sectors to prioritize, and how to structure interdependencies to achieve political objectives alongside commercial returns. DSI demonstrates that states can engineer patterns of interdependence that serve strategic purposes while appearing to emerge from economic rationality.

DSI specifies how material position generates influence independent of cultural or normative foundations. Middle Eastern actors engage Chinese partnerships not because they admire Chinese civilization or aspire to replicate Chinese governance but because Chinese firms offer competitive infrastructure pricing, Chinese financing comes without governance conditionalities, and Chinese technology serves developmental objectives (Garlick & Havlová, 2020). Decisions reflect strategic utility grounded in infrastructural, technological, and developmental interdependence rather than cultural attraction or normative appeal.

When critical infrastructure depends on Chinese technology, when energy revenues flow through Chinese purchases, when industrial development relies on Chinese investment, and when technological systems integrate with Chinese platforms, the costs of relationship termination escalate independent of cultural affinity or normative alignment. This represents influence through operational necessity rather than ideational appeal, through structural constraints that make cooperation rational regardless of attraction, and through material embeddedness that is durable and resistant to short-term political fluctuations rather than fragile and vulnerable to cultural shifts.

The theoretical contribution lies in demonstrating that infrastructure, technology, and economic integration can substitute for cultural attraction as foundations for influence, operating through structural mechanisms rather than ideational appeal. This matters because it explains influence patterns that conventional frameworks cannot account for and because it identifies mechanisms through which rising powers lacking cultural appeal can nonetheless establish significant presence in regions where normative frameworks differ fundamentally from their own.

DSI provides mechanism-based explanations that specify how infrastructure investment produces diplomatic capital, how embedded presence enhances credibility, and how strategic ambiguity preserves flexibility without eroding trust. These mechanisms are observable and testable, allowing empirical verification rather than speculative inference.

The infrastructure-to-influence mechanism operates through multiple pathways. Large-scale projects create routine interactions between Chinese firms and host-state bureaucracies, establishing communication channels that function during political tensions when formal diplomatic engagement may be constrained. Infrastructure performance generates credibility through revealed reliability: completing projects on schedule and meeting technical specifications demonstrate commitment and capability in ways that diplomatic statements cannot replicate. Infrastructure creates material stakes in regional stability that align Chinese interests with host-state preferences for conflict avoidance, making Chinese advocacy for de-escalation credible because it reflects genuine interests rather than instrumental positioning.

The embedded presence-to-credibility mechanism operates through temporal accumulation. Extended presence over decades demonstrates sustained commitment that transforms perceptions. When China maintains relationships through political transitions, economic downturns, and regional conflicts, it establishes credibility that episodic engagement cannot replicate. The strategic ambiguity mechanism preserves flexibility that allows simultaneous engagement with rivals without triggering demands for exclusivity, proving crucial for mediation as explicit alignment would compromise neutral positioning necessary for effective facilitation.

DSI integrates economic statecraft, infrastructure politics, and regional order theory in ways that generate effects greater than the sum of individual components. Infrastructure investment constitutes economic statecraft but operates through mechanisms distinct from traditional tools. Rather than leveraging existing economic relationships to extract concessions, it constructs new relationships that reshape strategic environments. Rather than threatening disruption of established patterns, it creates dependencies where none existed previously. Rather than operating through explicit bargaining over specific concessions, it structures long-term incentives that shape broad policy orientations.

This integration reveals that regional order increasingly rests on economic and technological foundations rather than purely security architectures. Military capabilities remain relevant for deterrence and crisis management, but everyday stability derives from economic interdependencies that create distributed stakes in continuity. Regional hierarchies form not only through security dependencies but through technological ecosystems, infrastructure networks, and financial relationships that constrain autonomy while enabling development.

The Iran–Saudi reconciliation demonstrates this integration: the outcome cannot be understood through security analysis alone, as neither party faced military compellence; nor through economic analysis alone, as neither faced economic coercion. It requires understanding how accumulated economic relationships created material foundations for diplomatic initiative, how infrastructure cooperation established communication channels that facilitated negotiation, and how embedded Chinese presence generated credibility that made mediation acceptable to both parties. The outcome emerged from interaction between economic, diplomatic, and institutional dimensions that integrated approaches capture but siloed analyses miss.

DSI develops middle-range theory that specifies conditions under which the framework proves most effective rather than claiming universal applicability (Merton, 1968). It identifies four enabling conditions: strategic multipolarity allowing diversified external relationships; sovereignty sensitivities creating receptivity to engagement that respects formal autonomy; developmental imperatives requiring external capital and technology; and fragmented political orders lacking consolidated hegemonic hierarchy. These conditions characterize the contemporary Middle East and also appear in Southeast Asia, parts of Sub-Saharan Africa, and segments of Central Asia.

The framework proves less applicable in regions with consolidated alliance systems where institutional density restricts alternative engagement modes, or in highly developed regions where states possess capabilities reducing dependence on external infrastructure provision. Specifying scope conditions prevents overextension of theoretical claims and acknowledges that multiple mechanisms of influence coexist in international politics. DSI explains important patterns but does not explain everything, identifying an additional mechanism that operates through different pathways and proves effective under conditions where traditional mechanisms encounter limitations.

These contributions suggest that power is becoming increasingly multidimensional, with economic and technological capabilities assuming greater relative importance alongside military capabilities that remain necessary but not sufficient for comprehensive influence. Influence increasingly operates through structural positioning within networks rather than through hierarchical command over subordinates. International order can emerge from distributed interdependencies rather than requiring hegemonic enforcement, suggesting that stability may prove more durable than theories predicting collapse following hegemonic decline would anticipate. Agency and strategic design matter more than structural theories often acknowledge, as states construct environments deliberately and design interdependencies to achieve political objectives.

DSI advances theory not by claiming universal applicability but by specifying mechanisms, identifying conditions under which they operate effectively, and demonstrating empirical patterns that established theories struggle to explain. It illuminates increasingly important dynamics in contemporary international relations while remaining attentive to limitations, scope conditions, and alternative mechanisms that operate alongside those it emphasizes.

4 Scope Conditions, Replicability, and Structural Limits

Recognition of DSI's effectiveness must be accompanied by clear assessment of the conditions enabling its operation and the structural constraints that limit its reach. The model is neither universally applicable nor immune to disruption. Its success depends on background conditions that cannot be assumed to endure indefinitely, and its mechanisms face vulnerabilities that could erode effectiveness under adverse circumstances.

Enabling Conditions and Regional Variation

DSI proves most effective under specific configurations that characterized the Middle East over the past two decades but may not persist or appear uniformly elsewhere. First, permissive multipolarity allowing states to maintain diversified external relationships without forced binary choices creates the structural space within which portfolio strategies operate. When single powers dominate regions comprehensively, states lack alternatives that would enable simultaneous engagement with rivals. The contemporary Middle East exhibits multipolarity with American military presence, European economic ties, Russian selective engagement, and Chinese infrastructural expansion all coexisting without any actor achieving monopolistic control.

Second, acute sovereignty sensitivities rooted in colonial histories and experiences with external intervention generate receptivity to engagement that respects formal autonomy and avoids explicit conditionality. Regions where states remain confident in their sovereignty prove less receptive to DSI's distinctive characteristics. The Middle East's historical experiences with British and French mandates, American interventions, and persistent external involvement in domestic affairs create political environments where non-interference resonates powerfully with elites and publics alike.

Third, developmental imperatives requiring external capital, technology, and expertise create demand for partnerships that Chinese engagement supplies. States that have achieved advanced development and possess domestic capabilities prove less dependent on external infrastructure provision and less constrained by dependencies that DSI generates. Middle Eastern states pursuing economic diversification, technological modernization, and infrastructure development face resource constraints that Chinese investment and expertise address without the governance conditions that Western engagement often entails.

Fourth, fragmented security architectures without hegemonic consolidation create space for alternative engagement modalities. Regions with entrenched alliances dominated by single external patrons provide fewer opportunities for new models to gain traction. The Middle East's fractured security environment, with overlapping and sometimes contradictory commitments, allows Chinese infrastructural diplomacy to establish presence alongside rather than displacing existing arrangements.

These conditions suggest replicability in Southeast Asia where similar multipolarity, sovereignty concerns, and developmental needs obtain, in parts of Sub-Saharan Africa facing comparable challenges, and in Central Asia where Russian dominance has weakened without alternative hegemony emerging. Conversely, DSI faces constraints in Northeast Asia or Eastern Europe where consolidated American alliances and institutional density restrict alternative engagement modes, or in highly developed regions where infrastructure dependencies generate limited political leverage.

Political Volatility and Regime Fragility

DSI assumes governance continuity allowing large projects to mature over extended horizons. Chinese engagement frequently aligns with long-term national development programs such as Saudi Arabia's Vision, 2030 or Egypt's infrastructure modernization strategies that presuppose elite cohesion and administrative stability. Yet the Middle East remains marked by persistent risks of upheaval, succession uncertainty, and institutional fragmentation.

When regimes collapse or experience contested transitions, Chinese projects can rapidly become stranded assets or contested symbols. Libya, Yemen, and Syria demonstrate how infrastructure becomes vulnerable once state authority weakens or rival factions seek to reallocate rents and external partnerships (Hanieh, 2018). Nationalist movements frequently politicize foreign investments during upheaval, transforming Chinese presence from neutral developmental asset into domestic liability. China's non-interference posture enhances credibility but limits capacity to hedge against abrupt political shifts, as Beijing avoids entrenchment in domestic politics that might protect investments during transitions.

DSI's distinctive advantage lies in maintaining concurrent partnerships with rival regional actors. This distribution allows Beijing to preserve neutrality and facilitate dialogue without being subsumed into regional fault lines. However, this same relational spread produces structural exposure when rivalries intensify. The model depends on assumptions that regional actors tolerate China's parallel partnerships with adversaries and that Chinese cooperation with rivals does not shift local balances of power in threatening ways.

These assumptions hold during periods of moderate tension but may not survive major conflict escalation. Direct Saudi–Iranian confrontation, severe Israeli-Iranian escalation, or open UAE-Turkey conflict could force Beijing into choices it seeks to avoid. Even if China refrains from taking sides, perceptions of imbalance can generate political pressure within partner states to reassess ongoing Chinese projects. Infrastructure investments in one state might be viewed as strengthening an adversary's capabilities, triggering demands that China reduce engagement or risk losing access elsewhere.

Chinese investments in ports, industrial zones, telecommunications, and energy networks involve fixed capital that cannot be easily relocated if conditions deteriorate. Infrastructure-led engagement deepens local entanglement but exposes China to high sunk costs and long return horizons dependent on stability and predictability. In Iraq, logistics corridors remain threatened by militia competition and administrative fragmentation. In Lebanon, systemic governance failure and fiscal collapse undermine digital infrastructure partnerships. In Syria, reconstruction remains constrained by sanctions, territorial fragmentation, and competing security actors.

Political violence, regulatory opportunism, and persistent state weakness routinely delay or derail large-scale projects. China's exposure to these risks is heightened by the scale and geographic concentration of its infrastructural footprint. Unlike set investments that can be liquidated or service exports requiring minimal fixed assets, infrastructure represents multi-year commitments with limited exit options. Once construction begins, abandoning projects generates reputational costs and financial losses, yet continuing in deteriorating environments risks escalating costs without corresponding returns.

DSI operates most effectively within multipolar environments allowing states to maintain diversified external relations and compartmentalize economic, technological, and security partnerships. If global dynamics shift toward systemic bipolarity or severe fragmentation, enabling conditions supporting DSI weaken considerably. Deteriorating U.S.–China relations, including technological decoupling, financial competition, and rival strategic bloc formation, risk constraining Middle Eastern states' room for maneuver.

If technology ecosystems bifurcate, states may be compelled to choose between incompatible digital infrastructures. If financial systems fragment, dual participation in dollar and yuan-based networks may become politically or administratively unviable. Under such circumstances, Chinese infrastructure could become politicized as indicator of geopolitical alignment rather than neutral developmental asset. Ambiguity would shift from advantage to liability as states and external powers demand clarity, loyalty, and exclusivity. Historical patterns suggest that once rivalry reaches system-wide polarization thresholds, intermediary strategies become unsustainable and states face more explicit alignment choices.

These vulnerabilities do not invalidate DSI or predict inevitable failure. The model has demonstrated resilience, and regional actors continue to value Chinese partnerships for developmental, strategic, and political reasons. Infrastructure interdependencies remain substantial despite vulnerabilities, creating constituencies within partner states who benefit from continued cooperation. Institutional frameworks possess sufficient depth to function through localized crises. Spatial architecture provides redundancy preventing single-point failures from cascading systemically.

Yet long-term sustainability remains contingent on Beijing's willingness to exercise restraint as capabilities expand, on regional powers' continued perception that DSI serves their interests, and on absence of systemic shocks rendering embedded infrastructure networks dysfunctional or forcing binary alignment choices. Realistic assessment requires attention not only to successes but also to limits shaping future trajectory and conditions under which advantages might erode or mechanisms require fundamental adaptation. DSI illuminates dynamics specific to China's Middle Eastern engagement while offering insights into rising power strategies in multipolar environments more broadly, but its effectiveness depends on structural conditions that enable operation rather than guaranteeing outcomes independent of context.

5 The Reordering Underway

The transformation currently reshaping the Middle East is not merely a question of shifting actors but of shifting modalities of power itself. The region is experiencing reordering, not replacement: it is not pivoting wholesale from American to Chinese dominance. Rather, the grammar of influence is evolving in ways that have profound implications for how regional politics operate, how external powers compete for presence, and how states navigate increasingly complex strategic environments. Understanding this reordering requires moving beyond accounts of relative power shifts to examine how the very mechanisms through which influence operates are being reconfigured.

Traditional regional order in the Middle East is operated through hierarchical relationships structured by clear alignments with external hegemons. States positioned themselves as junior partners within patron–client arrangements, accepting constraints on autonomy in exchange for security guarantees, economic assistance, or political backing. The Cold War exemplified this pattern, with states aligning with either American or Soviet spheres and accepting the disciplines those alignments entailed. The post-Cold War period maintained hierarchical logic even as American primacy reduced competitive pressures, with Gulf states, Egypt, and Jordan anchoring their security in American commitments while managing relationships with other powers at the margins.

The contemporary order emerging from DSI and regional responses to it exhibits fundamentally different characteristics. Regional states increasingly operate as strategic portfolio managers constructing diversified external architectures that distribute different functional domains across multiple powers. Saudi Arabia maintains deep security dependence on the United States while expanding technological and industrial partnerships with China and pursuing selective cooperation with Russia and Europe. The UAE preserves intimate military coordination with Washington while integrating Chinese digital infrastructure, deepening technology ties with Israel, and maintaining robust commercial engagement across Asia and Europe. Iran leverages Chinese economic support while sustaining strategic cooperation with Russia and diplomatic channels with Europe. This is not hedging in the conventional sense, which assumes temporary balancing between competing patrons until circumstances clarify optimal alignment. It represents permanent portfolio management premised on the recognition that no single external power can or should monopolize all functional domains.

Security provision, technological modernization, economic development, and diplomatic facilitation are disaggregated and allocated to different external actors based on comparative advantage rather than comprehensive alignment. The result is networked order in which influence is distributed, interdependencies are multidirectional, and hierarchy gives way to functional differentiation. This transformation carries profound implications for regional stability. Hierarchical orders generate stability through deterrence and alliance discipline but create rigidity that constrains adaptation. Challenges to hierarchy risk systemic instability as contests over rank threaten entire structures. Networked orders generate stability through distributed interdependencies creating multiple stakeholders in continuity but allow flexibility as states adjust relationships incrementally without threatening systemic stability. Disruption in one relationship can be compensated through others, and gradual shifts in influence distribution occur without triggering catastrophic realignments associated with hegemonic transitions.

The competitive dynamics through which external powers vie for regional influence have fundamentally altered. Traditional competition operated through zero-sum logic where gains for one power implied losses for others, and influence was measured through relative position within hierarchical rankings. Military bases, alliance partnerships, and exclusive economic relationships served as metrics assessing competitive outcomes. Contemporary competition operates through non-exclusive mechanisms in which multiple powers simultaneously increase influence without necessarily diminishing rivals' positions. Chinese infrastructure investment does not prevent American security provision. American military presence does not preclude Chinese economic partnerships. European regulatory cooperation coexists with Chinese technological integration. Competition persists but operates through accumulation rather than displacement, with powers specializing in sectors where they possess comparative advantage rather than competing for comprehensive dominance across all domains.

This reconfigured competition produces outcomes that confound traditional strategic analysis. States deepen partnerships with China while strengthening security ties with the United States. They accept Chinese infrastructure investment while voicing concerns about Chinese strategic intentions. They participate in Chinese institutional initiatives while maintaining commitments to Western-dominated frameworks. These behaviors appear contradictory when analyzed through zero-sum competitive frameworks but prove rational as portfolio strategies designed to maximize autonomy by preventing any external power from acquiring monopolistic influence. Competition no longer produces clear winners and losers, exclusive alignments, or stable hierarchies. Instead, it generates complex interdependencies in which all major external powers maintain substantial influence, regional actors preserve significant autonomy, and outcomes remain indeterminate.

The reordering underway validates a fundamental insight that extends beyond the Middle Eastern case: infrastructure has become strategic currency comparable in significance to military capabilities or alliance commitments. The operational dependencies created through ports, digital networks, energy systems, and industrial complexes shape long-term planning and constrain policy options as effectively as security guarantees. This represents more than tactical adjustment in how powers pursue influence; it signals transformation in what constitutes strategic assets and how those assets generate political effects.

Infrastructure operates across multiple temporal and spatial scales simultaneously. It creates immediate economic benefits through employment, technology transfer, and enhanced connectivity. It generates medium-term dependencies through operational integration and standardization. It produces long-term structural effects through path dependencies that channel developmental choices into particular trajectories. These layered effects make infrastructure particularly powerful as instrument of influence because disruption imposes costs across multiple domains and timeframes, making relationship termination increasingly irrational as dependencies mature.

The changing relationship between credibility and influence reveals deeper transformations in how power operates. Traditional models assumed that military capabilities and alliance commitments generated credibility through demonstrated capacity to protect partners or punish adversaries. Yet the Middle Eastern experience reveals that these instruments, while retaining deterrence value, prove insufficient for generating the trust necessary for sustained influence in contemporary environments. American security guarantees, despite their military credibility, have encountered trust deficits rooted in perceptions of inconsistency, selectivity, and subordination of partner interests to domestic political calculations. Regional actors increasingly question whether American commitments will endure through political transitions and whether alliance relationships serve mutual interests or primarily American preferences. These doubts do not eliminate American influence but constrain it, pushing partners toward diversification strategies that hedge against potential abandonment or coercion.

Chinese engagement generates credibility through different mechanisms. Rather than promising protection through military might, it demonstrates reliability through consistent infrastructure delivery, technology transfer, and sustained commercial relationships across political fluctuations. Rather than demanding alignment as the price of partnership, it accommodates autonomy while deepening economic ties. Rather than conditioning engagement on governance reforms, it respects sovereignty and avoids normative prescriptions. These characteristics build trust that is operational rather than rhetorical, grounded in observable performance rather than declarative commitments. This does not mean China has displaced American influence or that military capabilities have become irrelevant. It means that influence increasingly requires multiple foundations: deterrence capacity remains necessary for crisis management, but sustained peacetime influence requires economic integration, technological cooperation, and demonstrated reliability that operate through different logics than military preponderance.

External powers navigating this transformed environment face distinct challenges that reflect the reordering's systemic character. The United States confronts limitations not in its military capabilities, which remain unmatched, but in translating those capabilities into comprehensive influence when regional actors prioritize developmental imperatives and sovereignty protection over security dependence alone. Sustaining regional presence requires complementing security provision with economic engagement that addresses developmental priorities without imposing conditionalities perceived as infringing sovereignty. European powers encounter resistance to normative conditionality in contexts where sovereignty concerns remain acute, revealing that market access and regulatory power, however significant, prove insufficient when divorced from pragmatic recognition of partner state priorities. China faces challenges of managing success without triggering balancing coalitions, exercising restraint despite growing capabilities, and avoiding the temptation to leverage accumulated influence in ways that would contradict the non-coercive foundations on which DSI rests.

Regional states managing relationships with multiple external powers serving different functions must develop bureaucratic capacity, strategic coherence, and political will to resist pressure for exclusive alignment. The benefits of diversification, enhanced autonomy and leverage across multiple relationships, must be weighed against costs including coordination challenges and risks that escalating great power competition forces choices that current arrangements allow states to defer. Yet the sophistication with which Middle Eastern states have constructed portfolio strategies demonstrates that smaller powers possess agency that structural theories often overlook. They are not passive objects of great power competition but active managers shaping external relationships to serve national interests.

The theoretical and empirical insights developed throughout this book demonstrate that the Middle East is not simply experiencing power transition from one hegemon to another but fundamental reconfiguration of how regional order operates. Influence flows through different channels, competition proceeds according to different logics, and stability emerges from different sources than those that structured previous regional systems. These transformations reflect broader shifts in international politics as capabilities diffuse, traditional hegemonic instruments encounter diminishing returns, and rising powers develop alternative modalities of engagement suited to multipolar environments.

Whether the patterns discussed here prove durable across longer time horizons depends on factors this book has identified but cannot predict: Beijing's willingness to exercise restraint as capabilities expand, regional actors' continued perception that DSI serves their interests, and the absence of systemic shocks that might render current arrangements obsolete or force binary alignment choices that multipolarity currently allows states to avoid. The Iran-Saudi reconciliation that opened this book represents not an endpoint but a milestone in ongoing transformation whose ultimate trajectory remains contingent on choices made by regional and external actors as the strategic environment continues to evolve.

What is certain is that the Middle East entering the third decade of the twenty-first century operates according to fundamentally different principles than the region that emerged from the Cold War or that experienced American primacy in the 1990s. Power no longer moves primarily through military deployments and alliance commitments but through infrastructures that structure daily economic and technological life. Influence derives not only from the capacity to protect or coerce but from embeddedness within systems that partner states depend upon for development and prosperity. Order emerges not from hierarchical discipline imposed by dominant powers but from distributed interdependencies creating multiple stakeholders in stability. Competition proceeds not through displacement and exclusive alignment but through accumulation and functional specialization across domains.

Understanding these transformations matters not only for comprehending Middle Eastern politics but for grasping how international order itself is being reconstituted in an era of multipolarity, diffusing capabilities, and declining efficacy of traditional hegemonic instruments. The Middle East, rather than representing an exceptional case, may preview patterns that will become increasingly visible across contested regions where multiple powers compete without achieving dominance, where states prioritize sovereignty and development over exclusive alignment, and where infrastructure and technology rival military capabilities as foundations of influence. The reordering discussed in this book therefore illuminates not merely one region's transformation but broader dynamics reshaping how power operates, how states interact, and how order emerges in contemporary international politics.

This book has sought to provide both conceptual frameworks and empirical foundations for understanding emerging modalities of influence. It has specified mechanisms through which infrastructure generates political capital, demonstrated how strategic ambiguity enables rather than undermines diplomatic capacity, and shown how rising powers can establish presence without replicating hegemonic models. It has revealed regional actors exercising sophisticated agency in managing external relationships and constructing portfolios that maximize autonomy. It has identified scope conditions determining where these patterns prove most effective and structural limits constraining their operation. Most fundamentally, it has demonstrated that DSI represents not tactical innovation but systemic transformation in how influence operates when power diffuses, when capabilities become multidimensional, and when states possess both incentive and capacity to resist hierarchical subordination while pursuing cooperative engagement.

The transformations highlighted here demand continued intellectual engagement as patterns mature, as other regions exhibit similar dynamics, and as great power competition intensifies or subsides. They demand policy sophistication from external powers recognizing that traditional instruments, while retaining importance, prove insufficient for comprehensive influence in environments where infrastructure rivals military presence and where autonomy-preserving partnerships prove more attractive than hierarchical alignment. They demand strategic sophistication from regional states navigating complexity while avoiding the illusion that diversification eliminates vulnerability or that portfolio management substitutes for coherent national strategy. Above all, they demand recognition that international politics is undergoing fundamental transformation in how influence is established, how order is maintained, and how states position themselves within systems where networks increasingly matter as much as hierarchies, where embeddedness generates leverage comparable to coercion, and where power moves through systems states construct rather than capabilities they deploy. The Middle East's reordering through China's diplomacy by design exemplifies these transformations and illuminates paths along which international order more broadly is evolving.

References:

Calabrese, J. (2018). *Oman's transition to a post-oil economy: Arching Toward Asia*. Middle East Institute.

Chen, D., & Han, W. (2019). Deepening cooperation between Saudi Arabia and China. *King Abdullah Petroleum Studies and Research Center, 24*.

de Haas, M., Gaberščik, E., Jenkins, T., & Kumar, A. (2020). Russia's military action in Syria driven by military reforms. *The Journal of Slavic Military Studies, 33*(2), 292–299.

Del Sarto, R. A. (2021). *Borderlands: Europe and the mediterranean middle east*. Oxford University Press.

Garlick, J. (2023). China's hedged economic diplomacy in Saudi Arabia and Iran: A strategy of risk mitigation. In *China's Engagement with the Islamic Nations: A clash or collaboration of modern civilisation?* (pp. 117–136). Springer.

Garlick, J., & Havlová, R. (2020). China's "belt and road" economic diplomacy in the Persian Gulf: Strategic hedging amidst Saudi-Iranian regional rivalry. *Journal of Current Chinese Affairs, 49*(1), 82–105.

Gause, F. G., III. (2009). *The international relations of the Persian Gulf*. Cambridge University Press.

Hanieh, A. (2018). *Money, markets, and monarchies: The Gulf Cooperation Council and the political economy of the contemporary Middle East* (Vol. 4). Cambridge University Press.

Maxigas, & ten Oever, N. (2023). Geopolitics in the infrastructural ideology of 5G. *Global Media and China*,*8*(3), 271–288.

Shirzad, A. (2022). Looking-East in the Iranian foreign policy: The politico-ideological inclinations and practical imperatives. *Journal of Globalization Studies, 13*(2), 53–75.

Index

A. Ullah, *Diplomacy by Design*,
https://doi.org/10.1007/978-981-95-7876-4

The manufacturer's authorised representative in the EU is Springer Nature Customer Service Centre GmbH, Europaplatz 3, 69115 Heidelberg, Germany. If you have any concerns regarding our products, please contact ProductSafety@springernature.com

Printed and bound by CPI Group (UK) Ltd, Croydon, CR0 4YY

21/09/2026

02219963-0004

List of Figures

List of Tables

Chapter 7

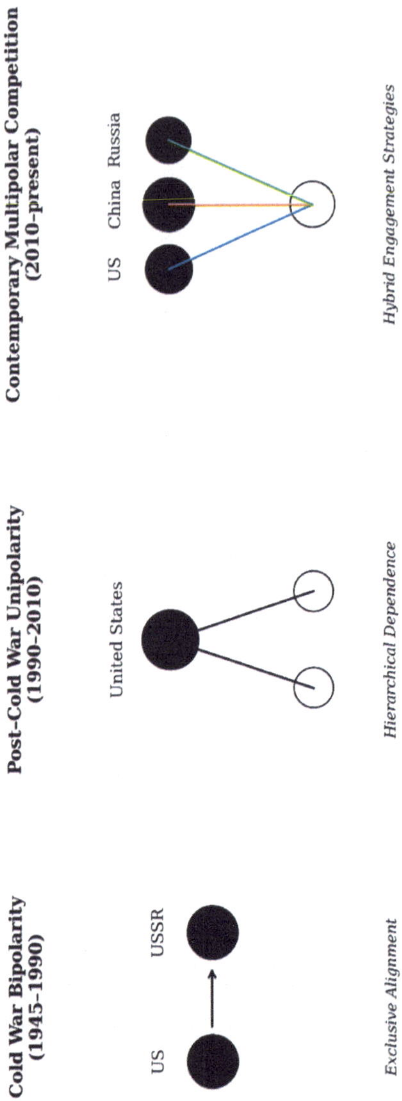

